SERMONS
ON MEN OF THE
⮞ BIBLE ⮜

Other Sermon Collections from Spurgeon

Sermons on Women of the Bible

Sermons on Jesus and the Holy Spirit

Sermons on Prayer

Sermons on the Death and Resurrection of Jesus

SERMONS
ON MEN OF THE
⮞ BIBLE ⮜

CHARLES H. SPURGEON

HENDRICKSON
PUBLISHERS

Sermons on Men of the Bible

Hendrickson Publishers, Inc.
P. O. Box 3473
Peabody, Massachusetts 01961-3473

ISBN 978-1-59856-302-3

Printed in the United States of America

Cover Art: Julius Schnorr von Carolsfeld's (1794-1872) depiction of Gideon and his army attacking the Midianite camp at night. Courtesy of the Pitts Theology Library, Candler School of Theology, Emory University.

Library of Congress Cataloging-in-Publication Data

Spurgeon, C. H. (Charles Haddon), 1834-1892.
  Sermons on men of the Bible / Charles H. Spurgeon.
    p. cm.
  ISBN 978-1-59856-302-3 (alk. paper)
1. Men in the Bible—Biography—Sermons. 2. Sermons, English--19th century. 3. Baptists—Sermons. I. Title.
  BS574.5.S68 2008
  220.9'2081--dc22
                        2008028915

Contents

Men of the Old Testament

Published on Thursday, September 8, 1904; delivered on Thursday evening, July 13, 1876, at the Metropolitan Tabernacle, Newington. No. 2900.

And they heard the voice of the LORD God walking in the garden in the cool of the day: and Adam and his wife hid themselves from the presence of the LORD God amongst the trees of the garden. And the LORD God called unto Adam, and said unto him, "Where art thou?"—GENESIS 3:8–9

Delivered on Lord's Day morning, July 30, 1876, at the Metropolitan Tabernacle, Newington. No. 1307.

And Enoch lived sixty and five years, and begat Methuselah: and Enoch walked with God after he begat Methuselah three hundred years, and begat sons and daughters: and all the days of Enoch were three hundred sixty and five years: and Enoch walked with God: and he was not; for God took him.—GENESIS 5:21–24

By faith Enoch was translated that he should not see death; and was not found, because God had translated him: for before his translation he had this testimony, that he pleased God. But without faith it is impossible to please him: for he that cometh to God must believe that he is, and that he is a rewarder of them that diligently seek him.—HEBREWS 11:5–6

And Enoch also, the seventh from Adam, prophesied of these, saying, "Behold, the Lord cometh with ten thousands of his saints, to execute judgment upon all, and to convince all that are ungodly among them of all their ungodly deeds which they have ungodly committed, and of all their hard speeches which ungodly sinners have spoken against him."—JUDE 14–15

fellow answered and said, "This is nothing else save the sword of Gideon the son of Joash, a man of Israel: for into his hand hath God delivered Midian, and all the host."—JUDGES 7:13–14

Men of the New Testament

Publisher's Preface

Charles Haddon Spurgeon
1834–1892

Ask most people today who Charles Haddon Spurgeon was, and you might be surprised at the answers. Most know he was a preacher, others remember that he was Baptist, and others go so far as to remember that he lived in England during the nineteenth century. All of this is true. Yet Charles Haddon Spurgeon was so much more.

Spurgeon was born into a family of Congregationalists in 1834, his father and grandfather both Independent preachers. This designation seems benign today, but in the mid-nineteenth century, it describes a family committed to a Nonconformist path—meaning they did not conform to the established Church of England. Spurgeon grew up in a rural village, a village virtually cut off from the Industrial Revolution rolling over most of England.

Spurgeon was born again at a Primitive Methodist meeting in 1850, at age sixteen. He soon became a Baptist (to the sorrow of his mother) and almost immediately began to preach. Considered a preaching prodigy—"a boy wonder of the fens"—Spurgeon attracted huge audiences and garnered a reputation that reached throughout the countryside and into London. As a result of his great success, Spurgeon was invited to preach at the New Park Street Chapel in London in 1854, when he was just nineteen. When he first preached at the church, they were unable to fill even two hundred seats. Within the year, Spurgeon filled the twelve-hundred-seat church to overflowing; he soon began preaching in larger and larger venues, outgrowing each, until finally in 1861, the Metropolitan Tabernacle was completed, which seated six thousand persons. This would be Spurgeon's home base for the rest of his career, until his death in 1892, at age fifty-seven.

Spurgeon married Susannah Thompson in 1856 and soon they had twin sons, Charles and Thomas, who would later follow him in his work. Spurgeon opened Pastors' College, a training school for preachers, that trained over nine hundred preachers during his lifetime. He also opened orphanages for underprivileged boys and girls, providing educations to each of the orphans. And with Susannah, he developed a program to publish and distribute Christian literature. He is said to have preached to over ten million people in his forty years of ministry. His sermons sold over twenty-five thousand copies each week, and were translated into twenty languages. He was utterly committed to spreading the gospel, through preaching and through the written word.

During Spurgeon's lifetime, the Industrial Revolution transformed England from a rural, agricultural society, to an urban, industrial society, with all the attendant difficulties and horrors of a society in major transition. The people displaced by these sweeping changes, the factory workers, the shopkeepers, these became Spurgeon's congregation. From a small village himself and transplanted to a large and inhospitable city, he was a common man, and he understood innately the spiritual needs of the common people. He was a communicator who made the gospel so relevant, who spoke so brilliantly to people's deepest needs, that listeners welcomed his message.

Keep in mind that Spurgeon preached in the days before microphones or speakers; in other words, he preached without benefit of amplifier systems. Once he preached to a crowd of over twenty-three thousand people without mechanical amplification of any sort. He himself was the electrifying presence on the platform: he did not stand and simply read a stilted sermon. Spurgeon used an outline, developing his themes extemporaneously, and speaking "in common language to common people." His sermons were filled with stories and poetry, drama and emotion. He was larger than life, always in motion, striding back and forth across the stage. He gestured broadly, acted out stories, used humor, and painted word pictures. For Spurgeon, preaching was about communicating the truth of God, and he would use any gift at his disposal to accomplish this.

Spurgeon's preaching was anchored in his spiritual life, a life rich in prayer and the study of Scripture. He was not tempted by fashion, be it theological, social, or political. Scripture was the cornerstone of Spurgeon's life and his preaching. He was an expositional preacher mostly, exploring a passage of Scripture for its meanings both within the text as well as in the lives of each member of his congregation. To Spurgeon, Scripture is alive and specifically relevant to people's lives, whatever their social status, economic situation, or time in which they live.

One has a sense that Spurgeon embraced God's revelation completely: God's revelation through Jesus Christ, through Scripture, and through his own prayer and study. For him, revelation was not a finished act: God still reveals Himself, if one made oneself available. Some recognize Spurgeon for the mystic he was, one who was willing and eager to explore the mysteries of God, able to live with those bits of truth that do not conform to a particular system of theology, perfectly comfortable with saying "This I know, and this I don't know—yet will I trust."

This collection of sermons includes Spurgeon's thoughts on a broad variety of men whose character and relationship with God made them heroes of a sort, men who responded to God's invitation, and thus experienced a profound intimacy with the Eternal One. These sermons are not a series: they were not created or intended to be sequential. Rather, they are stand-alone sermons, meant to explore specific men whose lives are part of the record of God's dealings with humankind.

Each of these sermons was preached at different times of Spurgeon's career, and each has distinct characteristics. They have not been homogenized or edited to sound as though they are all of a kind. Instead, they reflect the preacher himself, allowing the voice of this remarkable man to ring clearly as he guides the reader into a particular account, a particular event—to experience, with Spurgeon, God's particular revelation.

As you read, *listen*. These words are meant to be heard, not merely read. Listen carefully and you will hear the cadences of this remarkable preaching, the echoes of God's timeless truth traveling across the years. And above all, enjoy Spurgeon's enthusiasm, his fire, his devotion, his zeal to recognize and respond to God's timeless invitation to engage the Creator himself.

Men of the Old Testament

Adam: How God Comes to Man

Published on Thursday, September 8, 1904; delivered on Thursday evening, July 13, 1876, at the Metropolitan Tabernacle, Newington. No. 2900.

*And they heard the voice of the LORD God walking in the garden in the cool of the day: and Adam and his wife hid themselves from the presence of the LORD God amongst the trees of the garden. And the LORD God called unto Adam, and said unto him, "Where art thou?"—*GENESIS 3:8–9

"How will God come to us now that we have rebelled against him?" That is a question which must have greatly perplexed our first parents, and they may have said to one another, "Perhaps God will not come to us at all, and then we shall be orphans indeed. If spared to live on, we must continue to live without God and without hope in the world." It would have been the worst thing that could have happened to our race if God had left this planet to take its own course, and had said, concerning the people upon it, "I will leave them to their own way, for they are given over to idols."

But if he came to our first parents, in what way would he come? Surely Adam and Eve must have feared that he would be accompanied by the angels of vengeance, to destroy them straightaway, or, at any rate, to bind them in chains and fetters forever. So they questioned among themselves, "Will he come; and if he does, will his coming involve the total destruction of the human race?" Their hearts must have been sorely perplexed within them while they were waiting to see what God would do to them as a punishment for the great sin they had committed.

I believe they thought that he would come to them. They knew so much of his graciousness, from their past experience, that they felt sure that he would come; yet they also understood so much of his holy anger against sin that they must have been afraid of his coming; so they went and hid themselves among the trees of the garden, although every tree must have upbraided them for their disobedience, for every one of the trees would seem to say, "Why come you here? You have eaten of the fruit of the tree whereof you were forbidden to partake. You have broken your Maker's command, and his sentence of death has already gone out against you. When he comes, he will certainly come to deal with you in judgment according to his faithful word; and when he does, what will become of you?" Every leaf, as it rustled, must have star-tled and alarmed them. The breath of the evening breeze, as it passed through the garden, must have filled them with fear and dread as to the doom await-ing them.

Now "in the cool of the day" or, as the Hebrew has it, "in the wind of the evening," when the evening breeze was blowing through the garden, God came. It is difficult for us even to imagine how he revealed himself to our first parents. I suppose he condescended to take upon himself some visible form. It was "the voice of the LORD God" they heard in the garden, and you know that it is the Word of God who has been pleased to make himself visible to us in human flesh. He may have assumed some form in which they could see him; otherwise, as a pure Spirit, God could not have been recognized either by their ears or their eyes.

They heard his voice speaking as he walked in the garden in the cool of the day; and when he called unto Adam, albeit that there was righteous anger in the tone of his voice, yet his words were very calm and dignified, and, as far as they should be, even tender; for, while you may read the words thus, "Adam, where art thou?" you may also read them thus, "Where art thou, poor Adam, where art thou?" You may put a tone of pity into the words, and yet not misread them. So the Lord comes thus in gentleness in the cool of the day, and calls them to account; patiently listens to their wicked excuses, and then pronounces upon them a sentence, which, heavy though it be toward the ser-pent, and heavy though it be toward all who are not saved by the woman's wondrous seed, yet has much mercy mingled with it in the promise that the seed of the woman shall bruise the head of the serpent—a promise which must have shone in their sad and sinful souls as some bright particular star shines in the darkness of the night. I learn, from this incident, that God will come to sinful men, sooner or later, and we may also learn, from the way in which he came to our first parents, how he is likely to come to us. His com-ing will be different to different men; but we gather, from this incident, that God will certainly come to guilty men, even if he waits till the cool of the day; and we also understand a little about the way in which he will ultimately come to all men.

Remember this, sinner, however far you may get away from God, you will have to come close to him one of these days. You may go and pluck the fruit that he forbids you to touch, and then you may go and hide yourself among the thick boughs of the trees in the garden, and think that you have concealed yourself; but you will have to come face to face with your Maker at some time or other. It may not be today or tomorrow; it may not be until "the cool of the day" of time; no, it may not be till time itself shall be no more; but, at last, you will have to confront your Maker. Like the comet, that flies far off from the sun, wandering into space for an altogether inconceivable distance, and yet has to come back again, however long the time its circuit takes, so you will have to come back to God, either willingly, repentingly, believingly, or else unwillingly, and in chains, to receive your sentence of doom from the lips of the Almighty, whom you have provoked to anger by your sin. But God and you have to meet, as surely as you are now living here; at some time or other, each one of you must hear the voice of the Lord God saying to you, as he said to Adam, "Where art thou?"

Now, from this meeting between God and fallen man, I learn a few lessons, which I will pass on to you as the Holy Spirit shall enable me.

I. The first is this. When God did meet with fallen man, it was not until the cool of the day. This suggests to me *God's great patience with the guilty.*

Whether Adam and Eve sinned in the early morning, or in the middle of the day, or toward evening, we do not know. It is not necessary that we should know this; but it is probable that the Lord God allowed an interval to intervene between the sin and the sentence. He was not in a hurry to come, because he could not come except in anger, to bring their sins home to them. You know how quick the tempers of some men are. If they are provoked, it is a word and a blow with them, for they have no patience. It is our littleness that makes us impatient. God is so great that he can endure far more than we can; and though our first parents' sin greatly provoked him—and it is his glory that he is so holy that he cannot look upon iniquity without indignation—yet he seemed to say to himself, "I must go and call these two creatures of mine to account for their sin; yet judgment is my strange work, it is mercy in which I delight. This morning, I drew back the curtains that had shielded them during the night, and poured the sunlight in upon them, not a second beyond the appointed time, and I was glad to do it; and, all day long, I have been showering mercies upon them, and the refreshing night dews are already beginning to fall upon them. I will not go down to them till the latest possible moment. I will put it off till the cool of the day." God will do nothing in the heat of passion; everything shall be deliberate and calm, majestic and divine.

The fact that God did not come to question his sinful creatures till the cool of the day ought to teach us the greatness of his patience, and it should also teach us to be ourselves patient with others. How wondrously patient God has been with some of you who are here! You have lived many years and enjoyed his mercies, yet you have scarcely thought about him. Certainly you have not yielded your hearts to him; but he has not come to deal with you in judgment yet. He has waited twenty years for you young people; thirty years, forty years, for you middle-aged folk; fifty years, sixty years, for you who are getting past that period; seventy years, perhaps, or even eighty years he has been known to tarry, for "he delighteth in mercy," but he does not delight in judgment. Seventy years form a long life-day, yet many persons spend all that time in perpetrating fresh sin. Called to repentance over and over again, they only become the more impenitent through resisting the call of mercy. Favored with blessings as many as the sands of the seashore, they only prove themselves the more ungrateful by failing to appreciate all those blessings. It is wonderful that God is willing to wait till the cool of such a long, long day of life as seventy or eighty years make up.

How patient, then, we ought to be with one another! Yet are you, parents, always patient with your children, your young children who may not have willingly or consciously offended you? What patience you ought always to exercise toward them! And have you a like patience toward a friend or a brother who may use rough speech, and provoke you? Yet such your patience ought to be. Never should we take our brother by the throat, and say to him, "Pay me what you owe," so long as we find God deliberately waiting till the cool of the day before he comes to those who have offended him, and even then uttering no more words of anger than should be uttered, and mingling even those words with mercy that has no bound.

II. The second thing that I gather from the Lord's coming to Adam and Eve in the cool of the day is *his divine care for the guilty.*

Though he did not come till the cool of the day, thus manifesting his patience, he did come then, thus manifesting his care for those who had sinned against him. He might have left them all night long—all night long without their God, all night long without him after they had done just what he had forbidden them to do; all night long—a sleepless night, a fearful night, a night that would have been haunted with a thousand fears; all night long with this great battle trembling in the balance, with the great question of their punishment unsolved, and an indefinable dread of the future hanging over them. Many of you know that the trial of being kept in suspense is almost worse than any other trouble in the world. If a man knew that he had to be beheaded, it would be easier for him to die at once than to have to kneel with his neck on the block, and the gleaming axe uplifted above him, and not knowing when it might fall. Suspense is worse than death; we seem to feel a thousand deaths while we are kept in suspense of one. So God would not leave Adam and Eve in suspense through the whole night after they had sinned against him, but he came to them in the cool of the day.

There was this further reason why he came to them, notwithstanding the fact that they had disobeyed him, and that he would have to punish them; he remembered that they were still his creatures. He seemed to be saying within himself, "What shall I do unto them? I must not utterly destroy them, but how can I save them? I must carry out my threatening, for my word is true; yet I must also see how I can spare them, for I am gracious, and my glory is to be increased by the display of my grace toward them." The Lord looked upon them as the appointed progenitors of his elect, and regarded Adam and Eve themselves also, let us hope, as his elect, whom he loved notwithstanding their sin, so he seemed to say, "I will not leave them all night without the promise which will brighten their gloom." It was only one promise; and, perhaps, it was not clearly understood by them; still, it was a promise of God, even though it was spoken to the serpent, "I will put enmity between thee and the woman, and between thy seed and her seed; it shall bruise thy head, and thou shalt bruise his heel." So not one night were God's poor fallen creatures left without at least one star to gleam in the darkness for them, and thus he showed his care for them. And still, dear friends, though God is slow to anger, yet is he always ready to pardon, and very tender and compassionate even when he has to pass sentence upon the guilty. "He will not always chide; neither will he keep his anger forever." You can see his care and consideration even for the most unworthy of us, because he has not cut us off in our sins. We are—

> *Not in torment, not in hell.*

We can see the marks of his goodness in the very garments on our backs and the food of which we partake by his bounty. Many of his gifts come, not merely to those who do not deserve them, but to those who deserve to be filled with the gall and wormwood of almighty wrath forever.

III. Now, third, I want to show you that, *when the Lord did come, he afforded us a pattern of how the Spirit of God comes to arouse the consciences of men.*

I have already said that, sooner or later, God will come to confront each one of us. I pray that, if he has never come to you, dear friend, in the way of awakening your conscience, and making you feel yourself a sinner, he may come to you very speedily. And when he does come, to arouse and awaken you, it is somewhat in this way.

First, *he comes seasonably:* "in the cool of the day." Adam's work was done, and Eve had no more to do until the next day. At that hour, they had been accustomed, in happier times, to sit down and rest. Now God comes to them, and the Spirit of God, when he comes to arouse men, generally visits them when they have a little time for quiet thought. You dropped in, and heard a sermon; the most of it slipped from your memory, but there were some few words that struck you so that you could not get rid of them. Perhaps, though, you thought no more about the message to which you had listened. Something else came in and took off your attention. But, a little while after, you had to watch all night by the bedside of a sick friend; and then God came to you, and brought to your remembrance the words that you had forgotten. Or it may be that some texts of Scripture, which you learned when you were a child, began to speak to you throughout the watches of the night. Or perhaps you were going along a lone country road, or, it may be, that you were out at sea on a dark night, and the billows rolled heavily so that you could not sleep, and you even feared that you would be swallowed up by the raging sea. Then, then came the voice of the Lord God speaking personally to you. When other voices were silenced, there was an opportunity for his voice to be heard.

Not only did the Lord come to Adam and Eve seasonably, but *he spoke to Adam personally*, and said, "Where art *thou?*" One of the great mistakes in connection with all preaching is that so many hearers will persist in lending other people their ears. They hear a faithful gospel sermon, and then say, "That message would fit Neighbor So-and-So admirably. What a pity Mrs. So-and-So did not hear it! That would have been the very word for her." Yes; but when God comes to you, as he came to Adam and Eve—and if you are not converted, I pray that he may—the sermon he will deliver to you will be every word of it for yourself. He will say, "Adam," or, "John," or, "Mary," or whatever your name be, "where art *thou?*" The question will be addressed to yourself alone; it will have no relation to any of your neighbors, but to yourself alone. The question may take some such form as this: "Where are you? What have you been doing? What is your condition now? Will you now repent, or will you still go on in your sins?" Have not you, young man, had some such experience as this? You went to the theater; but when you came home, you said that you had not enjoyed it, and that you wished you had not gone. You went to bed, but you could not sleep. It seemed as if God had come to wrestle with you, and to reason with you about your past life, bringing up one thing after another in which you have sinned against him. At all events, this is the way he deals with many; and if he deals thus with you, be thankful for it, and yield yourself up to him, and do not struggle against him. I am always glad when men cannot be happy in the world; for, as long as they can be, they will be. It is always a great mercy when they begin to be sick of the dainties of Egypt, for then we may lead them, by God's guidance, to seek after the milk and honey of the land of Canaan; but not till then. It is a great blessing when the Lord puts before you, personally, a true view of your own condition in his sight, and makes you look at it so earnestly, concentrating your whole thought upon it, so that you cannot even begin to think about others because you are compelled to examine your own selves, to see what your real condition is in relation to God.

When the Lord thus comes to men, and speaks personally with them, *he makes them realize their lost condition.* Do you not see that this is implied in the question, "Where art thou?" Adam was lost—lost to God, lost to holiness, lost to happiness. God himself says, "Where art thou?" That was to let Adam know this: "I have lost you, Adam; at one time, I could speak with you as with a friend, but I cannot do so any longer. You were my obedient child once, but you are not so now; I have lost you. Where art thou?" May God the Holy Spirit convince every unconverted person here that he or she is lost, not only lost to themselves and to heaven and to holiness and to happiness, but lost to God. It was God's lost ones of whom Christ so often spoke. He was himself the good Shepherd, who called together his friends and neighbors, saying unto them, "Rejoice with me; for I have found my sheep which was lost"; and he represents his Father saying of his son when he has come back to him, "This my son was dead"—dead to me—"and is alive again; he was lost"—lost to me—"and is found." The value of a soul to God, and God's sense of loss in the case of each individual soul, is something worth thinking over, and worth calculating, if it can be calculated. God makes man realize that he is lost by his own moanings and pleadings, even as he said to Adam, "Where art thou?"

You will observe, too, that the Lord not only came to Adam, and questioned him personally, but *he also made Adam answer him;* and if the Lord has, in this way, laid hold of any of you, talking with you in the cool of the day, and questioning you about your lost condition, he will make you confess your sin, and bring you to acknowledge that it was really your own. He will not leave you as Adam wanted to be left, namely, laying the blame for the disobedience upon Eve; and he will not leave you as Eve tried to be left, namely, passing the blame on to the devil. Before the Lord has done with you, he will bring you to this point, that you shall feel and confess and acknowledge that you are really guilty of your own sin, and that you must be punished for it. When he brings you down to that point, and you have nothing at all to say for yourself, then he will pardon you.

I recollect well when the Lord brought me to my knees in this way and emptied out all my self-righteousness and self-trust, until I felt that the hottest place in hell was my due desert, and that, if he saved everybody else, but did not save me, yet still he would be just and righteous, for I had no right to be saved. Then, when I was obliged to feel that it must be all of grace, or else there could be no salvation for me, then he spoke tenderly and kindly unto me; but, at the first, there did not seem to be any tenderness or pity to my soul. There was the Lord coming to me, laying bare my sin, revealing to me my lost condition, and making me shiver and tremble, while I feared that the next thing he would say to me would be, "Depart from me, accursed one, into everlasting fire in hell"; instead of which, he said to me, in tones of wondrous love and graciousness, "I have put thee among my children"; "I have loved thee with an everlasting love, therefore with lovingkindness have I drawn thee." Blessed be the name of the Lord, forever and ever, for such amazing treatment as this meted out to the guilty and the lost.

IV. Now, fourth, and very solemnly, I want to show you that *this coming of the Lord to Adam and Eve is also prophetical of the way in which he will come as a judging Spirit to those who reject him as an arousing Spirit.*

I have already reminded you unconverted ones that, as surely as you live, you will have to come to close terms with God, like the rest of us. Sooner or later, you will have to know him, and to know that he knows you. There will be no way of escaping from an interview which will be most serious and most terrible for you. It will happen "in the cool of the day." I do not know when that may be. On my way to this service, I was called to see a young lady, to whom "the cool of the day" has come at five and twenty, or thirty years of age. Consumption has made her life-day a comparatively short one; but, blessed be God, his grace has made it a very happy one; and she is not afraid, "in the cool of the day," to hear the voice of the Lord God calling her home. It is well that she is not afraid, but you, who have not believed in Jesus, will have to hear that same divine voice in the cool of your life's day. You may be spared to grow old; the strength of youth and of manhood will have gone, and you will begin to lean on your staff, and to feel that you have not the vigor you used to have, and that you cannot do such a hard day's work as you used to do, and you must not attempt to run up the hills as you once did. That will be "the cool of the day" to you, and then the Lord God will come in to you, and say, "Set thine house in order, for thou shalt die, and not live."

Sometimes that cool of the day comes to a man just when he would have liked it to be the heat of the day. He is making money, and his children are multiplying around him, so he wants to stop in this world a little longer. But that cannot be; he must go up to his bed, and he must lie there for so many days and nights, and then he must hear the voice of the Lord God as he begins to question him, and say, "Where art thou in relation to me? Have you loved me with all your heart and mind and soul and strength? Have you served me? Are you reconciled to me through the death of my Son?" Such questions as these will come to us as surely as God made us, and we shall have to give an account of the deeds done in the body, whether they have been good or whether they have been evil. I pray you to think of these things, and not to say, "Ah! that will not happen just yet." That is more than any of us can tell; and let me remind you that life is very short even at the longest. I am especially appealing to those who are of my own age. Do not you, dear friends, find that, when you are between forty and fifty years of age, the weeks seem to be much shorter than they used to be when you were young? I therefore gather that, when our friends are seventy or eighty years of age, time must seem far shorter to them than it ever was before. I think that one reason why Jacob, when he was a hundred and thirty years old, said to Pharaoh, "Few and evil have the days of the years of my life been," was simply this: that he was really such an old man, though not so old as his ancestors, that time seemed even shorter to him than it did to younger men. If that was so, then I suppose that the longer a man lives, the shorter would time appear to be. But, short or long, your share of it will soon be over, and you will be called upon to gather up your feet in the bed, and meet your fathers' God.

When that solemn and decisive hour comes, your interview with God will have to be a personal one. Sponsors will be of no use to anyone upon a dying bed. It will be of no avail, then, to call upon Christian friends to take a share of your burden. They will not be able to give you of their oil, for they have not enough grace for themselves and you. If you live and die without accepting the aid of the one Mediator between God and man, all these questions will have to be settled between your soul and God without anyone else coming between yourself and your Maker; and all this may happen at any moment. This personal talk between God and your soul, at the end of your life, may be ordained to take place this very night; and I am sent, as a forerunner, just to give you this warning, so that you may not meet your God altogether by surprise, but may, at any rate, be invited and exhorted to be prepared for that great interview.

Whenever that interview takes place, God will deal with you in solemn earnestness, personally bringing home your sin to you. You will be unable to deny it, for there will be One present, at that interview, who has seen it all, and the inquiries which he will make about the state of your soul will be very searching ones. He will not merely ask about one sin, but about all your sins. He will not only ask about your public life, but also about your private life; nor yet merely inquire about your doings, but about your sayings, and your willings and your thinkings and about your whole position in relation to himself, even as he asked Adam, "Where art thou?"

In imagination—I pray that it may be only in imagination—I see some of you die unsaved; and I see you as you pass into the next world unpardoned, and your soul realizes, for the first time, what was the experience of the rich man, of whom our Savior said, "In hell he lifted up his eyes"—as though he had been asleep before, and had only just awakened to his true condition. "He lifted up his eyes" and gazed all around, but he could see nothing except that which caused him dismay and horror; there was no trace of joy or hope, no trace of ease or peace. Then, through the awful gloom, there came the sound of such questions as these, "Where are you, sinner? You were in a house of prayer a few weeks ago, and the preacher urged you to seek the Lord; but you procrastinated. Where are you now? You said that there was no such place as hell; but what do you say about it now? Where are you? You despised heaven and refused Christ; where are you now?" What horror will seize the disembodied spirit as it rejects that it has brought itself into the condition of which it was warned, and from which it was invited to escape, but which it willfully chose for itself, thus committing eternal suicide! The Lord in mercy preserve all of you from doing that! But if you will do it, then shall come forth from the lips of the justly offended God the irrevocable sentence, "Depart from me, ye cursed."

One of the most dreadful things in connection with this meeting of God with Adam was that Adam had to answer the Lord's questions. The Lord said to him, "Hast thou eaten of the tree, whereof I commanded thee that thou shouldest not eat?" In our courts of law, we do not require men to answer questions which would incriminate them, but God does; and, at the last great day, the ungodly will be condemned on their own confession of guilt. While they are in this world, they put on a brazen face, and declare that they have done no wrong to anybody, not even to God; they pay their way, and they are as good as their neighbors, and better than the most of them; but all their brag and bravado will be gone at the day of judgment, and they will either stand speechless before God—and by their speechlessness acknowledge their guiltiness in his sight; or if they do speak, their vain excuses and apologies will but convict themselves. They will, out of their own mouths, condemn themselves, like that wicked and slothful servant, who was cast into the outer dark-ness where there was weeping and gnashing of teeth. God grant that we may never know, from sad personal experience, what that expression means!

V. Now, last, this meeting of God with Adam should lead us, who believe in Christ, to *expect to meet him on the most loving terms.*

For if, even when he came to question guilty Adam, and to pass sentence upon him, he did it so gently, and mingled with the thunder of his wrath the soft shower of his grace, when he gave the promise that the seed of the woman should bruise the serpent's head, may we not expect him to meet us, by-and-by, on the most loving terms, if we are in that woman's seed, and have been saved by Jesus Christ his Son?

He will come in the evening, brother and sister, when the day's work is done; so do not fret about the burden and heat of the day. The longest and hottest day will come to an end; you will not live here forever. You will not always have to wear your fingers to the bone in trying to earn a scanty liveli-hood. You will not always have to look around upon your children, and won-der where the bread will be found with which to feed them. No; the days on earth cannot last forever; and, with many of you, the sun has already climbed the hill, and begun to go down the other side, and "the cool of the day" will soon come. I can look upon a good many of you who have already reached that period. You have retired from active service, you have shaken off a good deal of business care, and now you are waiting for your Master to come to you. Rest assured that he will not forget you, for he has promised to come to you. You will hear his voice, before long, telling you that he is walking in the garden, and coming to you. Good old Rowland Hill, when he found himself getting very feeble, said, "I hope they have not forgotten poor old Rowley up there." But he knew that he was not forgotten, nor will you be, beloved.

You will hear your Lord's voice before long; and the mercy is, that you will know it when you do hear it. Have you not often heard it before now? Many a time, in this house, you have heard his voice, and you have been glad. In the cool of many an evening, you have sat still, and communed with God. I like to see an old Christian woman, with her big Bible open, sitting by the hour together, and tracing with her finger the precious words of the Lord; eat-ing them, digesting them, living on them, and finding them sweeter to her soul than honey or the droppings of the honeycomb to her taste. Well, then, as you have heard your Lord's voice, and know its tones so well, as you have been so long accustomed to hear it, you will not be astonished when you hear it in those last moments of your life's day. You will not run to hide yourself, as

Adam and Eve did. You are covered with the robe of Christ's righteousness, so you have no nakedness to fear; and you may respond, "Did you ask, my Lord, 'Where art thou?' I answer, 'Here am I, for you did call me.' Didst you ask where I am? I am hidden in your Son; I am 'accepted in the Beloved.' Did you say, 'Where art thou?' Here I stand, ready and waiting to be taken up by him, according to his promise that, where he is, there I shall be also, that I may behold his glory." Why, surely, beloved, as this is the case, you may even long for the evening to come when you shall hear his voice, and shall go up and away from this land of shadows and chilly night dews, into that blessed place where the glory burns on forever and ever, and the Lamb is the light thereof, and the days of your mourning shall be ended forever.

God grant that you may all have a part and a lot in that glory, for his dear Son's sake! Amen.

Enoch: Walking with God

Delivered on Lord's Day morning, July 30, 1876, at the Metropolitan Tabernacle, Newington. No. 1307.

> *And Enoch lived sixty and five years, and begat Methuselah: and Enoch walked with God after he begat Methuselah three hundred years, and begat sons and daughters: and all the days of Enoch were three hundred sixty and five years: and Enoch walked with God: and he was not; for God took him.*
> —GENESIS 5:21–24

> *By faith Enoch was translated that he should not see death; and was not found, because God had translated him: for before his translation he had this testimony, that he pleased God. But without faith it is impossible to please him: for he that cometh to God must believe that he is, and that he is a rewarder of them that diligently seek him.*—HEBREWS 11:5–6

> *And Enoch also, the seventh from Adam, prophesied of these, saying, "Behold, the Lord cometh with ten thousands of his saints, to execute judgment upon all, and to convince all that are ungodly among them of all their ungodly deeds which they have ungodly committed, and of all their hard speeches which ungodly sinners have spoken against him."*—JUDE 14–15

The three passages of Scripture which I have read are all the authentic information we have concerning Enoch, and it would be idle to supplement it with the fictions of ancient commentators. Enoch is called the seventh from Adam, to distinguish him from the other Enoch of the line of Cain, who was the third from Adam. In the first patriarchs God was pleased to manifest to men portions of the truth in reference to true religion. These men of the olden times were not only themselves taught of God, but they were also teachers of their age, and types in whom great truths were exhibited. Abel taught the need of approaching the Lord with sacrifice, the need of atonement by blood: he laid the lamb upon the altar, and sealed his testimony with his own blood. Atonement is so precious a truth that to die for its defense is a worthy deed, and from the very first it is a doctrine which has secured its martyrs, who being dead yet speak.

Then Seth and Enos taught men the necessity of a distinct avowal of their faith in the Lord, and the need of assembling for his worship, for we read concerning the days of Enos and Seth, "Then began men to call upon the name of the LORD." Those who worshiped through the atoning sacrifice separated themselves from the rest of men, assembled a church in the name of the Lord, and worshiped, calling upon the name of Jehovah. The heart must first believe in the great sacrifice with Abel, and then the mouth must confess the same with Seth. Then came Enoch, whose life went beyond the reception and confession of the atonement, for he set before men the great truth of communion with God; he displayed in his life the relation of the believer to the most High, and showed how near the living God condescends to be to his own children. May our progress in knowledge be similar to the growth of the patriarchal teaching. Brethren, you do know as Abel did the sacrificial lamb, your confidence is in the precious blood, and so by faith you bring to God the most acceptable of all offerings. Having advanced so far the most of us have proceeded a step further, and we have called upon the name, and are the avowed followers of Jesus. We have given ourselves up to the Lord in the solemn burial of baptism, when we were baptized into the name of the Father, and of the Son, and of the Holy Ghost, because we reckoned ourselves dead in Christ to all the world, and risen with him into newness of life. Henceforth the divine name is named on us, and we are no more our own. And now we gather together in our church capacity, we assemble around the table of fellowship, we unite in our meetings for prayer and worship, and the center for us all is the name of the Lord. We are separated from the world, and set apart to be a people who declare his name. Thus far, well; we have seen the sacrifice of Jesus as the way with Abel; and we have avowed the truth with Seth; now let us take the next step and know the life with Enoch. Let us endeavor to walk with God as Enoch did.

Perhaps a meditation upon the holy patriarch's life may help us to imitate it; while considering what he was, and under what circumstances he came to be so, he may by the Holy Spirit be helped to reach the point to which he attained. This is the desire of every godly man, all the saints desire communion with the Father, and with his Son Jesus Christ. The constant cry of our soul is to our Lord, "Abide with me." I buried yesterday one of the excellent of the earth, who loved and feared and served his God far better than most of us; he was an eminently devout brother, and one of the last wishes of his heart he had committed to writing in a letter to a friend, when he little thought of dying. It was this "I have longed to realize the life of Enoch, and to walk with God"—

Oh, for a closer walk with God!

He did but write what you and I also feel. If such be your desires, and such I feel sure they are, so surely as you are the Lord's people, then I hope a consideration of the life of Enoch may help you toward the realization of your wish.

First, then, *what does Enoch's walking with God imply?* It is a short description of a man's life, but there is a mint of meaning in it; second, *what circumstances were connected with his remarkable life?* for these are highly instructive: and third, *what was the close of it?* It was as remarkable as the life itself.

I. First, then, *what is meant by Enoch's walking with God?*

Paul helps us to our first observation upon this by his note in the Hebrews. His walk with God was a testimony that *Enoch was well pleasing to God.* "Before his translation he had this testimony, that he pleased God." This is evidently the apostle's interpretation of his walking with God, and it is a most correct one, for the Lord will not walk with a man in whom he has no pleasure. Can two walk together, except they be agreed? If men walk contrary to God, he will not walk *with* them, but contrary to them. Walking together implies amity, friendship, intimacy, love, and these cannot exist between God and the soul unless the man is acceptable unto the Lord. Doubtless Enoch, like Elijah, was a man of like passions with ourselves. He had fallen with the rest of mankind in the sin of Adam; there was sin about him as there is sin about us by nature, and he had gone astray in act and deed as all we, like sheep, have done: and therefore he needed pardon and cleansing, even as we do. Then to be pleasing with God, it was needful that he should be forgiven and justified, even as we are; for no man can be pleasing to God till sin is pardoned and righteousness is imputed. To this end there must be faith, for there can be no justification except by faith, and as we have said already, there is no pleasing God except our persons are justified. Right well, then, does the apostle say, "Without faith it is impossible to please God," and by faith Enoch was made pleasing to God, even as we are at this day. This is worthy of earnest notice, brethren, because this way of faith is open to us. If Enoch had been pleasing to God by virtue of some extraordinary gifts and talents, or by reason of marvelous achievements and miraculous works, we might have been in despair; but if he was pleasing to God through faith, that same faith which saved the dying thief, that same faith which has been worked in you and in me, then the wicket gate at the head of the way in which men walk with God is open to us also.

If we have faith we may enter into fellowship with the Lord. How this ought to endear faith to us! The highest grades of spiritual life depend upon the lower ones, and rise out of them. If you want to walk with God as a man of God, you must begin by believing in the Lord Jesus Christ, simply, as a babe in grace. The highest saintship must commence by the confession of our sinnership, and our laying hold upon Christ crucified. Not otherwise does the strongest believer live than the weakest believer; and if you are to grow to be among the strongest of the Lord's warriors, it must be by faith which lays hold upon divine strength. Beginning in the Spirit you are not to be made perfect in the flesh; you are not to proceed a certain distance by faith in Christ, and then to commence living by your own works; your walk is to continue as it began. "As ye have received Christ Jesus the Lord, so walk ye in him."

Enoch was always pleasing to God, but it was because he always believed, and lived in the power of his faith. This is worth knowing and remembering, for we may yet be tempted to strive for some imaginary higher style of religious life by looking to our feelings instead of looking alone to the Lord. We must not remove our eye from looking alone to Jesus himself even to admire his image within ourselves; for if we do so we shall go backward rather than forward. No, beloved, by faith Enoch became pleasing to God, and by faith he walked with God: let us follow in his track.

Next, when we read that Enoch walked with God we are to understand that *he realized the divine presence.* You cannot consciously walk with a person whose existence is not known to you. When we walk with a man, we know that he is there; we hear his footfall if we cannot see his face; we have some very clear perception that there is such a person at our side. Now if we look to the Hebrews again, Paul tells us, "He that cometh to God must believe that he is, and that he is the rewarder of them that diligently seek him." Enoch's faith, then, was a realizing faith. He did not believe things as a matter of creed, and then put them up on the shelf out of the way, as too many do: he was not merely orthodox in head, but the truth had entered into his heart, and what he believed was true to him, practically true, true as a matter of fact in his daily life. He walked with God: it was not that he thought of God merely, that he speculated about God, that he argued about God, that he read about God, that he talked about God, but he walked with God, which is the practical and experimental part of true godliness. In his daily life he realized that God was with him, and he regarded him as a living friend, in whom he confided and by whom he was loved. O beloved, do you not see that if you are to reach to the highest style of Christian life, you must do it through the realization of those very things which by faith you have received? Grasp them, let them be to you substance and evidence. Make them sure, look upon them, handle them, taste them in your inmost soul, and so know them beyond all question. You must see him who is invisible, and possess that which cannot be as yet enjoyed. Believe not only that God is, but that he is the rewarder of them that diligently seek him, for this according to Paul is the Enoch faith. God realized as existing, observing, judging, and rewarding human deeds: a real God, really with us—this we must know, or there is no walking with God.

Then, as we read that Enoch walked with God, we have no doubt it signifies that *he had very familiar intercourse* with the most High. I scarcely know an intercourse that is more free, pleasant, and cordial than that which arises out of constant walking with a friend. If I wished to find a man's most familiar friend, it would surely be one with whom he daily walked. If you were to say, "I sometimes go into his house and sit a little while with him," it would not amount to so much as when you can say, "I have from day to day walked the fields and climbed the hills with him." In walking, friends become communicative: one tells his trouble, and the other strives to console him under it, and then imparts to him his own secret in return. When persons are constantly in the habit of walking together from choice, you may be quite sure there are many communications between them with which no stranger may intermeddle. If I wanted to know a man through and through, I should want to walk with him for a time, for walking communion brings out parts of the man which even in domestic life may be concealed. Walking for a continuance implies and engenders close fellowship and great familiarity between friends. But will God in very deed thus walk with men? Yes, he did so with Enoch, and he has done so with many of his people since. He tells us his secret, the secret of the Lord, which he reveals only to them that fear him, and we tell to him alike our joys in praise, our sorrows in prayer, and our sins in confession. The heart unloads itself of all its cares into the heart of him that careth for us; and the Lord pours forth his floods of goodness as he imparts to the beloved ones a sense of his own everlasting love to them. This is the very flower and sweetness of Christian experience, its lily and its rose, its calamus and myrrh. If you would taste the cream of Christian life, it is found in having a realizing faith, and entering into intimate intercourse with the heavenly Father. So Enoch walked with God.

Next it is implied in the term *walked* that *his intercourse with God was continuous*. As an old divine has well remarked, he did not take a turn or two with God and then leave his company, but he walked with God for hundreds of years. It is implied in the text that this was the tenor of his life throughout the whole of its 365 years. Enoch walked with God after Methuselah had been born, three hundred years, and doubtless he had walked with him before. What a splendid walk! A walk of three hundred years! One might desire a change of company if he walked with anybody else, but to walk with God for three centuries was so sweet that the patriarch kept on with his walk until he walked beyond time and space, and walked into paradise, where he is still marching on in the same divine society. He had heaven on earth, and it was therefore not so wonderful that he glided away from earth to heaven so easily. He did not commune with God by fits and starts, but he abode in the conscious love of God. He did not now and then climb to the heights of elevated piety and then descend into the marshy valley of lukewarmness, but he continued in the calm, happy, equable enjoyment of fellowship with God from day to day. Night with its sleep did not suspend it; day with its cares did not endanger it. It was not a run, a rush, a leap, a spurt, but a steady flow.. On, on, through three happy centuries and more did Enoch continue to walk with God.

It is implied also in this phrase that *his life was progressive*: for if a man walks either by himself or with anybody else, he makes progress, he goes forward. Enoch walked with God. At the end of two hundred years he was not where he began; he was in the same company, but he had gone forward in the right way. At the end of the third hundred years Enoch enjoyed more, understood more, loved more, had received more, and could give out more, for he had gone forward in all respects. A man who walks with God will necessarily grow in grace, and in the knowledge of God and in likeness to Christ. You cannot suppose a perpetual walk with God year after year, without the favored person being strengthened, sanctified, instructed, and rendered more able to glorify God. So I gather that Enoch's life was a life of spiritual progress; he went from strength to strength, and made headway in the gracious pilgrimage. May God grant us to be pressing onward ourselves.

Suffer a few more observations upon Enoch's walk. In Kitto's *Daily Bible Readings,* there is an exceedingly pleasing piece, illustrating what it must be to walk with God by the figure of a father's taking his little son by the hand and walking forth with him upon the breezy hills. He says, "As that child walks with thee, so do thou walk with God. That child loves thee now. The world—the cold and cruel world—has not yet come between his heart and thine. His love now is the purest and most beautiful he will ever feel, or thou wilt ever receive. Cherish it well, and as that child walks *lovingly* with thee, so do thou walk *lovingly* with God." It is a delight to such children to be with their father. The roughness of the way or of the weather is nothing to them: it is joy enough to go for a walk with father. There is a warm, tender, affectionate grip of the hand and a beaming smile of the eye as they look up to father while he conducts them over hill and dale. Such a walk is *humble* too, for the child looks upon its father as the greatest and wisest man that ever lived. He considers him to be the incarnation of everything that is strong and wise, and all that his father says or does he admires. As he walks along he feels for his father the utmost affection, but his reverence is equally strong: he is very near his father, but yet he is only a child, and looks up to his father as his king. Moreover such a walk is one of *perfect confidence*. The boy is not afraid of missing his way; he trusts implicitly his father's guidance. His father's arm will screen him from all danger, and therefore he does not so much as give it a thought—why should he? If care is needed as to the road, it is his father's business to see to it, and the child, therefore, never dreams of anxiety; why should he? If any difficult place is to be passed, the father will have to lift the boy over it, or help him through it—the child meanwhile is merry as a bird—why should he not be? Thus should the believer walk with God, resting on eternal tenderness and rejoicing in undoubted love. A believer should be unconscious of dread either as to the present or to the future. Beloved friend in Christ, your Father may be trusted, he will supply all your need.

> *Thou art as much his care as if beside*
> *No man or angel lived in heaven or earth.*

What an *instructive* walk a child has with a wise, communicative parent! How many of his little puzzles are explained to him, how everything about him is illuminated by the father's wisdom. The boy every step he takes becomes the wiser for such companionship. O happy children of God, who have been taught of their Father while they have walked with him! Enoch must have been a man of profound knowledge and great wisdom as to divine things. He must have dived into the deep things of God beyond most men.

His life must also have been a *holy* life, because he walked with God, and God never walks out of the way of holiness. If we walk with God, we must walk according to truth, justice, and love. The Lord has no company with the unjust and rebellious, and therefore we know that he who walked with God must have been an upright and holy man.

Enoch's life must, moreover, have been a *happy* one. Who could be unhappy with such a companion? With God himself to be with us the way can never be dreary. "Yea, though I walk through the valley of the shadow of death, I will fear no evil; for thou art with me." Granted that God is your companion, and your road must be a way of pleasantness and a path of peace.

Did Enoch walk with God, then his pilgrimage must have been safe. What a guard is the great Jehovah! He is Sun and Shield; he giveth grace and glory. He that dwelleth in the secret place of the most High, shall abide under the shadow of the Almighty. Nothing can harm the man who is walking with the Lord God at his right hand.

And oh, what an *honorable* thing it is to walk with the Eternal! Many a man would give thousands to walk with a king. Numbers of people are such worshipers of dignities that if a king did but smile at them they would be intoxicated with delight. What, then, is the honor of walking with the King of kings! What a patent of nobility it is to be permitted to walk with the blessed and only Potentate all one's life long! Who is he that is thus favored to be the King's companion, to walk alone with him, and to become his familiar friend? Jehovah rules earth and heaven, and hell, and is Lord of all who shall walk with him! If it were only for the honor of it, O Christians, how you ought to pant to walk with God. Enoch found it safe, happy, holy, honorable, and I know not how much more that is excellent, but certainly this was a golden life: where shall we find anything to equal it?

II. Second, let us consider *what circumstances were connected with Enoch's walking with God.*

The first remark is that *the details of his life are very few.* We do not know much about Enoch, and this is to his advantage. Happy is the nation which has no history, for a nation which has a history has been vexed with wars and revolutions, and bloodshed; but a nation that is always happy, peaceful, and prosperous has no chronicle to attract the lover of sensations. Happy is Enoch that we cannot write a long biography of him; the few words, "Enoch walked with God," suffice to depict his whole career, until "he was not, for God took him." If you go and look at a farmer's field, and you can say of it when you come back, "I saw yellow flowers covering it till it seemed a cloth of gold, and then I spied out here and there white flowers like silver buttons set on the golden vesture, and blue cornflowers also looked up with their lovely eyes and begemmed the whole," you will think that it is a very pretty field if you are a child; but the farmer shakes his head, for he knows that it is in bad condition and overrun with weeds; but if you come back and simply say, "It is as fine a piece of wheat as ever grew, and that is all," then your description, though brief, is very satisfactory. Many of those dazzling events and striking incidents and sensational adventures which go to make up an interesting biography may attract attention, but they do not minister to the real excellence of the life. No life can surpass that of a man who quietly continues to serve God in the place where providence has placed him. I believe that in the judgment of angels and all pure-minded beings that woman's life is most to be admired which consists simply of this: "She did what she could"; and that man's life shall be the most noteworthy of whom it can be said: "He followed the Lord fully." Enoch's life has no adventures; is it not adventure enough for a man to walk with God? What ambition can crave a nobler existence than abiding in fellowship with the Eternal?

But some will say, "Well, but Enoch must have been very peculiarly situated: he was no doubt placed in very advantageous circumstances for piety." Now, observe that this was not so, for first, *he was a public man*. He is called the "seventh from Adam." He was a notable man, and looked up to as one of the fathers of his age. A patriarch in those days must have been a man of mark, loaded with responsibility as well as with honor. The ancient custom was that the head of the family was prophet, priest, and king in his household, and abroad if he was a man of station and substance he was counselor, magistrate, and ruler. Enoch was a great man in his day, one of the most important of the period; hence we may be sure he had his trials, and bore the brunt of opposition from the powerful ungodly party which opposed the ways of godliness. He is mentioned among a noble list of men. Some have unwisely thought, "I could walk with God if I had a little cottage, if I lived in a quiet village, but, you see, I am a public man; I occupy a position of trust, and I have to mix with my fellowmen. I do not see how I am to walk with God." Ah, my dear friend, but Enoch did; though he was undoubtedly a man distinguished in his time, and full of public cares, yet he lost not the thread of sacred converse with heaven, but held on in his holy course through a life of centuries.

Note again that *Enoch was a family man*. "Enoch walked with God and begat sons and daughters." Some have said, "Ah, you cannot live as you like if you have a lot of children about you. Do not tell me about keeping up your hours of prayer and quiet reading of the Scriptures if you have a large family of little ones; you will be disturbed, and there will be many domestic incidents which will be sure to try your temper and upset your equanimity. Get away into the woods, and find a hermit's cell; there with your brown jug of water and your loaf of bread, you may be able to walk with God, but with a wife, not always amiable, and a troop of children who are never quiet, neither by day nor night, how can a man be expected to walk with God?" The wife on the other hand exclaims, "I believe that had I remained a single woman I might have walked with God. When I was a young woman I was full of devotion, but now with my husband, who is not always in the best of tempers, and with my children, who seem to have an unlimited number of wants, and never to have them satisfied, how is it possible that I can walk with God?" We turn to Enoch again, and we are confident that it can be done. "Enoch walked with God after he begat Methuselah three hundred years, and begat sons and daughters, and all the days of Enoch were three hundred and sixty-five years." Thus, you see, he was a public man, and he was a family man, and yet he walked with God for more than three hundred years. There is no need to be a hermit, or to renounce the married life, in order to live near to God.

In addition to this, *Enoch lived in a very evil age.* He was prominent at a time when sin was beginning to cover the earth, not very long before the earth was corrupt and God saw fit to sweep the whole population from off its surface on account of sin. Enoch lived in a day of mockers and despisers. You know that from his prophecy, as recorded by Jude. He prophesied, saying, "The Lord cometh with ten thousands of his saints, to execute judgment upon all, and to convince all that are ungodly among them of all their ungodly deeds which they have ungodly committed, and of all their hard speeches which ungodly sinners have spoken against him." He lived when few loved God and when those who professed to do so were being drawn aside by the blandishments of the daughters of men. Church and state were proposing an alliance, fashion and pleasure ruled the hour, and unhallowed compromise was the order of the day. He lived toward the close of those primitive times wherein long lives had produced great sinners, and great sinners had invented great provocations of God. Do not complain, therefore, of your times and of your neighbors and other surroundings, for amid them all you may still walk with God.

Enoch walked with God, and in consequence thereof *he bore his witness for God.* "Enoch the seventh from Adam prophesied." He could not be silent; the fire burned within his soul, and could not be restrained. When he had delivered his testimony it is clear that he encountered opposition. I am certain that he did so from the context in Jude, because the passage in Jude has to do with murmurers and "complainers, walking after their own lusts; and their mouth speaketh great swelling words," and Enoch is brought in as having had to do with such persons. His sermon shows that he was a man who stood firm amid a torrent of blasphemy and rebuke, carrying on the great controversy for the truth of God against the wicked lives and licentious tongues of the scoffers of his age; for he says, "Behold, the Lord cometh with myriads of his saints, to execute judgment upon all, and to convince all that are ungodly among them of all their ungodly deeds which they have ungodly committed." It is clear that they spoke against Enoch, they rejected his testimony, they grieved his spirit, and he mourned that in this they were speaking against God; for he speaks "of all their hard speeches which ungodly sinners have spoken against him." He saw their ungodly lives and bore witness against them. It is remarkable that his great subject should have been the second advent, and it is still more noteworthy that the two other men whom one would select as living nearest to

God, namely, Daniel and John, were both men who spoke much concerning the coming of the Lord and the great judgment day. I need not quote the words of Daniel, who tells us of the judgment which is to be set, and of the Ancient of Days who shall come upon his throne; nor need I repeat the constant witness of John concerning the Lord's second coming; I will only mention his fervent exclamation, "Even so, come quickly, Lord Jesus."

Thus you see that Enoch was a preacher of the word of God, and therefore he had a care over and above that which falls to the lot of most of you: and yet with that and all the rest put together he could please God until his life's end, if I may speak of an end to a life which ran into an endless state of joy: he continued as long as he was here to walk in faith, to walk in a manner in which God was pleased, and so his communion with the Lord was never broken.

III. This brings us to conclude with the third head: *what was the close of Enoch's walk?*

We would first remark that *he finished his work early.* Enoch walked with God, and that was such a good, sure, progressive walk that he traveled faster, and reached his house sooner, than those of us who walk with God sometimes and with the world at other times. Three hundred and sixty-five years would have been a long life to us, but it was a short life for that period when several patriarchs attained to nearly a thousand years of age. Enoch's life as compared to the usual life of the period was like a life of thirty or thirty-five years in these short-lived ages; in fact, the best parallel to it is the life of our Lord. As with the extended ages of men of his period, Enoch's life was of about the same length as that of the Lord Jesus in comparison with such lives as ours. He passed away comparatively a young man, as our dear brother and elder Verdon, just departed, has done: and we do not wonder that he did. They say, "whom the gods love die young": and both Enoch and Verdon were men greatly beloved. Perhaps these holy men ended their career so soon because they had done their lifework so diligently that they finished in good time. Some workmen if they have a job to do in your house are about it all day long, or rather all the week long, and make no end of chips and confusion. No wonder that some people live a long while, for they had need to do so to do anything at all! But this man did his work so well, and kept so close to God that his day's work was done at noon, and the Lord said, "Come home, Enoch, there is no need for you to be out of heaven any longer; you have borne your testimony, you have lived your life; through all the ages men will look upon you as a model man, and therefore you may come home." God never keeps his wheat out in the fields longer than is necessary; when it is ripe he reaps it at once: when his people are ready to go home, he will take them home. Do not regret the death of a good man while he is young; on the contrary, bless God that still there is some early ripening wheat in the world, and that some of his saints are sanctified so speedily.

But what did happen to Enoch? I am afraid I have said he died, or that I shall say so, it is so natural to speak of men as dying, but he alone and one other of all the human race are all that have entered the heavenly Canaan without fording the river of death. We are told concerning him that "he was not." Those gentlemen who believe that the word to *die* signifies to be annihilated, would have been still more confirmed in their views if the words in my text, "he was not," had been applied to all departed men, for if any expression might signify annihilation on their mode of translation, this is the one. "He was not" does not, however, mean that he was annihilated, and neither does the far feebler term of *dying* signify anything of the kind. "He was not"; that is to say, he was not *here*, that is all. He was gone from earth, but he was *there*, there where God had translated him. He was, he is with God, and that without having tasted death. Do not grudge him his avoidance of death. It was a favor, but not by any means so great as some would think, for those who do not die must undergo a change, and Enoch was changed. "We shall not all sleep," says the apostle, "but we shall all be changed." The flesh and blood of Enoch could not inherit the kingdom of God: in a moment he underwent a transformation which you and I will have to undergo in the day of the resurrection; and so, though he was not on earth, he was translated or transplanted from the gardens of earth to the paradise above. Now if there is any man in the world that shall never die, it is he who walks with God. If there is any man to whom death will be as nothing, it is the man who has looked to the second advent of Christ and gloried in it; if there is any man who, though he pass through the iron gates of death shall never feel the terror of the grim foe, it is the man whose life below has been perpetual communion with God. Go not about by any other way to escape the pangs of death, but walk with God, and you will be able to say, "O death, where is thy sting? O grave, where is thy victory?"

It is said of him that *"God took him."* A very remarkable expression. Perhaps he did it in some visible manner. I should not wonder. Perhaps the whole of the patriarchs saw him depart even as the apostles were present when our Lord was taken up. However that may be, there was some special rapture, some distinct taking up of this choice one to the throne of the most High. "He was not, for God took him."

Note that *he was missed*. This is one thing which I could not overlook. *He was missed*, for the apostle says he "was not found." Now if a man is not found, it shows that somebody looked after him. When Elijah went to heaven, you remember fifty men of the sons of the prophets went and searched for him. I do not wonder that they did; they would not meet with an Elijah every day, and when he was gone away, body and all, they might well look for him. Enoch was not found, but they looked after him. A good man is missed. A true child of God in a church like this, working and serving his Master, is only one among five thousand; but if he has walked with God his decease is lamented. The dear brother whom we have just buried we shall miss; his brother elders will miss him; the many who have been converted to God and helped by his means will miss him, and assuredly I shall miss him. I look toward the spot where he used to sit—I trust that someone else will sit there who will be half as useful as he was; it will be almost more than I can expect. We do not want so to live and die that nobody will care whether we are on earth or not. Enoch was missed when he was gone, and so will they be who walk with God.

Last of all, *Enoch's departure was a testimony*. What did he say by the fact that "he was not, for God took him," but this: there is a future state. Men had begun to doubt it, but when they said, "Where is Enoch?" and those who had witnessed his departure said, "God took him," it was to them an evidence that there was a God, and that there was another world. And when they said, "But where is his body?" there was another lesson. Two men had died before him, I mean two whose deaths are recorded in Scripture: Abel was killed, and his witness was that the seed of the serpent hates the woman's seed; Adam, too, had died about fifty years before Enoch's translation, whose witness was that, however late the penalty may come, yet the soul that sins it shall die. Now comes Enoch, and his testimony is that the body is capable of immortality. He could not bear testimony to resurrection, for he did not die: for that we have testimony in Christ, who is the firstfruits from among the dead; but the testimony of Enoch went a good way toward it, for it bore evidence that the body was capable of being immortal, and of living in a heavenly condition. "He was not, for God took him."

His departure also was a testimony to mankind that there is a reward for the righteous, that God does not sit with stony eyes regardless of the sins of the wicked, or of the virtues of his saints, but that he sees and is pleased with his people who walk with him, and that he can give them even now present rewards by delivering them from the pangs of death, and therefore he will certainly give rewards to all his people in some way or other. Thus you see, living and dying—no, not dying, again I do mistake—living and being translated,

Enoch was still a witness to his generation, and I do pray that all of us, whether we live or whether we sleep, may be witnesses for God. Oh, that we could live as my good brother Verdon, whom we have lately buried, lived, whose soul was on fire with love to Christ. He had a very passion for souls. I scarcely think there is one among us who did as much as he, for though he had to earn his daily bread, his evenings were spent with us in the service of the Lord, or in preaching the gospel, and then all night long he frequently paced the weary streets, looking after the fallen, that he might bring them in, and often went to his morning's work unrested, except by the rest which he found in the service of Christ. He would sometimes meet a brother with eyes full of joy, and say, "Five souls won for Christ last night." At other times after a sermon here he was a great soul hunter and would fetch inquirers downstairs into the prayer meeting, and when he had squeezed my hand he would say in his Swiss tones, which I cannot imitate, "Jesus saved some more last night: more souls were brought to Jesus." For him to live was to win souls. He was the youngest in our eldership, but the gray-heads do him honor. As we stood weeping about his tomb, there was not one among us but what felt that we had lost a true brother and a valiant fellow soldier. The Lord raise up others among you to do what Elder Verdon did! The Lord quicken the older brethren to be more active than they are, and make the young ones more devoted. Our ranks are broken, who shall fill up the gap? We are getting fewer and fewer as the Lord takes one and another home of the best instructed and of the bravest hearted; but recruits are daily coming in. May others come forward; yes, Lord, bring them forward by thy Holy Spirit to be leaders in the front rank, that as the vanguard melts into the church triumphant, the rear may continually find additions. Translated to the skies are some; may others be translated out of darkness into marvelous light, for Christ's sake. Amen.

Abraham: Prompt Obedience to the Call of God

Delivered on Lord's Day morning, June 27, 1875, at the Metropolitan Tabernacle, Newington. No. 1242.

> *By faith Abraham, when he was called to go out into a place which he should after receive for an inheritance, obeyed; and he went out, not knowing whither he went.*— HEBREWS 11:8

One is struck with the practical character of this verse. Abraham was called, and he obeyed. There is no hint of hesitation, parleying, or delay; when he was called to go out, he went out. Would to God that such conduct were usual, yes, universal; for with many of our fellowmen, and I fear with some now present, the call alone is not enough to produce obedience. "Many are called, but few are chosen." The Lord's complaint is, "I called and ye refused." Such calls come again and again to many, but they turn a deaf ear to them; they are hearers only, and not doers of the word; and, worse still, some are of the same generation as that which Zechariah spoke of when he said, "They pulled away the shoulder, and stopped their ears that they should not hear."

Even among the most attentive hearers how many there are to whom the word comes with small practical result in actual obedience. Here we are in midsummer again, and yet Felix has not found his convenient season. It was about midwinter when he said he should find one, but the chosen day has not arrived. The mother of Sisera thought him long in coming, but what shall we say of this laggard season? We can see that the procrastinator halts, but it were hard to guess how long he will do so. Like the countryman who waited to cross the river when all the water had gone by, he waits till all difficulties are removed, and he is not one whit nearer that imaginary period than he was years ago. Meanwhile, the delayer's case waxes worse and worse, and, if there were difficulties before, they are now far more numerous and severe. The man who waits until he shall find it more easy to bear the yoke of obedience, is like the woodman who found his bundle of wood too heavy for his idle shoulder, and, placing it upon the ground, gathered more wood and added to the bundle, then tried it, but finding it still an unpleasant load, repeated the experiment of heaping on more, in the vain hope that by-and-by it might be of a shape more suitable for his shoulder. How foolish to go on adding sin to sin, increasing the hardness of the heart, increasing the distance between the soul and Christ, and all the while fondly dreaming of some enchanted hour in which it will be more easy to yield to the divine call and part with sin. Is it always going to be so? There are a few weeks and then cometh harvest; will another harvest leave you where you are, and will you again have to say, "The harvest is passed, the summer is ended, and we are not saved"? Shall God's longsuffering mercy only afford you opportunities for multiplying transgressions? Will you always resist his Spirit? Always put him off with promises to be redeemed tomorrow? Forever and forever shall the tenderness and mercy of God be thus despised? Our prayer is that God of his grace may give you to imitate the example of Abraham, who, when he was called, obeyed at once.

The sad point about the refusals to obey the call of the gospel is that men are losing a golden opportunity, an opportunity for being numbered among the choice spirits of the world, among those who shall be blessed among men and women. Abraham had an opportunity, and he had grace to grasp it, and at this day there is not on the beadroll of our race a nobler name than that of "the father of the faithful." He obtained a supreme grandeur of rank among the truly great and good: far higher is he in the esteem of the right minded than the conqueror blood-red from battle, or the emperor robed in purple. He was an imperial man, head and shoulders above his fellows. His heart was in heaven, the light of God bathed his forehead, and his soul was filled with divine influences, so that he saw the day of the Lord Jesus and was glad. He was blessed of the Lord that made heaven and earth, and was made a blessing to all nations. Some of you will never gain such honor; you will live and die ignoble, because you trifle with supreme calls, and yet, did you believe in God, did you but live by faith, there would be before you also a course of immortal honor, which would lead you to eternal glory. Instead thereof, however, choosing the way of unbelief and neglect and delay, you will, I fear, one day awake to shame and to everlasting contempt, and know, to your eternal confusion, how bright a crown you have lost. I am in hopes that there are some among you who would not be losers of the crown of life; who desire, in fact, above all things, to obtain the prize of the high calling of God in Christ Jesus, and to them I shall speak, and while I speak, may the Holy Spirit cause every word to fall with power.

To help them, we shall consider, first, *what was Abraham's special experience which led to his being what he became?* and, second, *what was there peculiar in Abraham's conduct?* and then, third, *what was the result of that conduct?*

I. *What was Abraham's special experience*, which led to his becoming so remarkable a saint?

The secret lies in three things: he had a call, he obeyed it, and he obeyed it because he had faith.

First, then, *he had a call*. How that call came we are not told; whether it reached him through a dream, or by an audible voice from heaven, or by some unmentioned prophet, we cannot tell. Most probably he heard a voice from heaven speaking audibly to him and saying, "Get thee out from thy kindred and from thy father's house." We, too, have had many calls, but perhaps we have said, "If I heard a voice speaking from the sky I would obey it," but the form in which your call has come has been better than that, for Peter in his second epistle tells us that he himself heard a voice out of the excellent glory when he was with our Lord in the holy mount, but he adds, "We have also a more sure word of prophecy," as if the testimony which is written, the light that shines in a dark place, which beams forth from the Word of God, was more sure than even the voice which he heard from heaven. I will show you that it is so; for, if I should hear a voice, how am I to know that it is divine? Might it not, even if it were divine, be suggested to me for many reasons that I was mistaken, that it was most unlikely that God should speak to a man at all, and more unlikely still that he should speak to me? Might not a hundred difficulties and doubts be suggested to lead me to question whether God had spoken to me at all? But the most of you believe the Bible to be inspired by the Spirit of God, and to be the voice of God. Now in this Book you have the call—"Come ye out from among them, be ye separate, touch not the unclean thing; and I will be a Father unto you, and ye shall be my sons and daughters." Do not say that you would accept that call if it were spoken with a voice rather than written; you know that it is not so in daily life. If a man receives a written letter from his father or a friend, does he attach less importance to it than he would have done to a spoken communication? By no means. I reckon that many of you in business are quite content to get written orders for goods, and when you get them you do not require a purchaser to ask you in person, you would just as soon that he should not; in fact, you commonly say that you like to have it in black and white. Is it not so? Well, then, you have your wish, here is the call in black and white; and I do but speak according to common sense when I say that if the Lord's call to you be written in the Bible, and it certainly is, you do not speak truth when you say, "I would listen to it if it were spoken, but I cannot listen to it because it is written." The call as given by the Book of inspiration ought to have over your minds a masterly power, and if your hearts were right before God the word spoken in the Scriptures by the Holy Ghost would be at once obeyed.

Moreover, my undecided hearers, you have had other calls besides those from the Book. There have been calls through the living ministry, when the minister has spoken as pointedly to you as if he were a prophet, and you have known that the Lord spoke by him, for he has depicted your circumstances, described your condition, and the word has come to you, and you have with astonishment owned that it found you out. The message has also been spoken to you by a mother's tender love and by a father's earnest advice. You have had the call, too, in the form of sickness and sore trouble. In the silence of the night, when you could not sleep, your conscience has demanded to be heard, the inward strivings of the Holy Ghost have been with you, and loud have been the knocks at your door. Who among us has not known the like? But, alas, the Lord has called and has been refused, he has stretched out his hands and has not been regarded. Is it not so with many of you? You have not been like Samuel, who said, "Here am I, for thou didst call me," but like the adder which shuts her ear to the voice of the charmer. This is not to be done without incurring great guilt and involving the offender in heavy punishment.

Abraham had a call. So have we, but here was the difference: *Abraham obeyed*. Well does Paul say, "They have not all obeyed the gospel": for to many the call comes as a common call, and the common call falls on a sealed ear, but to Abraham and to those who by grace have become the children of faithful Abraham, to whom are the blessings of grace, and with whom God has entered into league and covenant, to touch it comes as a special call, a call attended with a sacred power which subdues their wills and secures their obedience. Abraham was prepared for instant obedience to any command from God; his journey was appointed, and he went. He was bidden to leave his country, and he left it; to leave his friends, and he left them all. Gathering together such substance as he had, he exiled himself that he might be a sojourner with his God, and took a journey in an age when traveling was infinitely more laborious than now. He knew not the road that he had to take, nor the place to which his journey would conduct him: it was enough for him that the Lord had given him the summons. Like a good soldier, he obeyed his marching orders, asking no questions. Toward God a blind obedience is the truest wisdom, and Abraham felt so, and therefore followed the path that God marked out for him from day to day, feeling that sufficient for the day would be the guidance thereof. Thus Abraham obeyed! Alas, there are some here present, some, too, to whom we have preached now for years, who have not obeyed. Oh, sirs, some of you do not require more knowledge; you need far more to put in practice what you know. Would you wonder if I should grow weary of telling some of you the way of salvation any longer? Do you not yourselves weary of persuading those who will not yield? So far as I have reason to fear that my task is hopeless it becomes a heavy one. Again and again and again have I explained the demands of the gospel and described the blessings of it, and yet I see its demands neglected and its blessings refused. Ah sirs, there will be an end to this before long, one way or the other. Which shall it be? O that you were wise and would yield obedience to the truth! The gospel has about it a divine authority, and is not to be trifled with. Notwithstanding that grace is its main characteristic, it has all the authority of a command. Do we not read of those who "stumbled at the word, being disobedient"? Surely there must be a command and a duty, or else there could not be disobedience. It is awful work when through disobedience to the command of the gospel it becomes a savor of death unto death instead of life unto life, and instead of a cornerstone it becomes a stone of stumbling and a rock of offense. Remember, upon whomsoever it shall fall it will grind him to powder. Christ himself has said it, and so it must be. May he of his infinite mercy give us the willing and the obedient mind that we may not pervert the gospel to our own destruction.

But I reminded you that the main point concerning Abraham was this, *he obeyed the call because he believed God.* Faith was the secret reason of his conflict. We read of certain persons that "the word preached did not profit them, not being mixed with faith in them that heard it," and again we read that "some when they had heard did provoke." But in Abraham's case there was neither unbelief nor provocation. He believed God with a childlike faith. His faith, I suppose, lay in the following items: when the Lord spoke he believed that it was the living God who addressed him. Believing that God spoke, he judged him worthy of his earnest heed; and he felt that it was imperative upon him to do as he was bidden. This settled, he desired nothing more to influence his course: he felt that the will of God must be right, and that his highest wisdom was to yield to it. Though he did not know where he was to go, he was certain that his God knew, and though he could hardly comprehend the reward promised to him, he was sure that the bounteous God never mocked his servants with deceitful gifts. He did not know the land of Canaan, but he was sure if it was a country chosen by God as a peculiar gift to his called servant, it must be no ordinary land. He left all such matters with his heavenly Friend, being fully persuaded that what he had promised he was able also to perform.

What a mighty sway faith has over a man, and how greatly it strengthens him. Faith was to the patriarch his authority for starting upon his strange journey, an authority which enabled him to defy alike the worldly wisdom which advises, and the worldly folly which scoffs. Perhaps they said to him, "Why will you leave your kinsfolk, Abraham?" but he replied, "God bids me." That was for him a sufficient warrant; he wanted no further argument. This also became to him the guide of his steps. If any said, "But, strange old man, how can you journey when you know not the way?" He replied, "I go where the Lord bids me." Faith found in God, chart, compass, and polestar, all in one. The word of the Lord also became the nourishment for his journey. If any said, "How will you be supplied, Abraham, in those wild lands, where will you find your daily bread?" he replied, "God bids me go: it is not possible that he should desert me. He can spread a table in the wilderness, or make me live upon the word which comes out of his mouth, if bread should fail." Probably these suggestions of trial may never have occurred to Abraham, but if they did, his faith swept them aside from his path as so many cobwebs. Perhaps some even dared to say, "But where go you? There is no such country, it is an enthusiast's dream, a land which flows with milk and honey. Where will you find it? O gray-beard, you are in your dotage, seventy years and five have bewildered you." But he replied, "I shall find it, for the Lord has given it to me and leads me to it." He believed God, and took firm hold, and therefore he endured as seeing him that is invisible.

See, then, dear friends, what we must have if we are to be numbered with the seed of Abraham—we must have faith in God and a consequent obedience to his commands. Have we obtained these gifts of the Spirit? I hope that many of us have the living faith which walks by love, and if so we shall rejoice in the will of the Lord, let it be what it may; if we know anything to be right we shall delight to do it, but as for doubtful or sinful deeds we renounce them. For us henceforth our leader is the Lord alone. But is it so with all of you? Let the personal question go around and cause great searching of heart, for I fear that in many instances precious faith is absent. Many have heard, but they have not believed; the sound of the gospel has entered into their ears, but its inner sense and sacred power have not been felt in their hearts. Remember that "without faith it is impossible to please God," so that you are displeasing to the Lord. How long shall it be so? How long shall unbelief lodge within you and grieve the Holy Spirit? May the Lord convince you, yes, at this moment, may he lead you to decision, and enable you henceforth to live by faith. It may be now or never with you. God grant it may be now!

II. This brings me to the second part of our subject: *what was there peculiar in Abraham's conduct?*

For whatever there was essential in his conduct there must be the same in us, if we are to be true children of the father of the faithful. The points of peculiarity in Abraham's case seem to me to have been five.

The first was this, *that he was willing to be separated from his kindred.* It is a hard task to a man of loving soul to put long leagues of distance between himself and those he loves, and to become a banished man. Yet in order to have salvation, brethren, we must be separated from this untoward generation. Not that we have to take our journey into a far country, or to forsake our kindred—perhaps it would be an easier task to walk with God if we could do so—but our calling is to be separate from sinners, and yet to live among them: to be a stranger and a pilgrim in their cities and homes. We must be separate in character from those with whom we may be called to grind at the same mill or sleep in the same bed; and this I warrant you is by no means an easier task than that which fell to the patriarch's lot. If believers could form a secluded settlement where no tempters could intrude, they would perhaps find the separated life far more easy, though I am not very sure about it, for all experiments in that direction have broken down.

There is, however, for us no "garden walled around," no "island of saints," no utopia; we sojourn among those whose ungodly lives cause us frequent grief, and the Lord Jesus meant it to be so, for he said, "Behold I send you forth as sheep among wolves." Come, now, my hearer, are you willing to be one of the separated? I mean this—dare you begin to think for yourself? You have let your grandmother's religion come to you with the old armchair and the antique china, as heirlooms of the family, and you go to a certain place of worship because your family have always attended there. You have a sort of hereditary religion in the same way as you have a display of family plate; pretty battered it is, no doubt, and rather light in weight by this time, but still you cling to it. Now, young man, dare you think for yourself? Or do you put out your thinking to be done for you, like your washing? I believe it to be one of the essentials of a Christian man, that he should have the courage to use his own mental faculties, and search the Bible for himself; for God has not committed our religious life to the guidance of the brain in our neighbor's head, but he has bestowed on each of us a conscience, and an understanding which he expects us to use. Do your own thinking, my friend, on such a business as this. Now if the grace of God helps you rightly to think for yourself, you will

judge very differently from your ungodly friends; your views and theirs will
differ, your motives will differ, the objects of your pursuit will differ. There are
some things which are quite customary with them which you will not endure.
You will soon become a speckled bird among them. The Jews in all time have
been very different from all other nations, and although other races have
become permanently united, the Jewish people have always been a family by
themselves. Though now residing in the midst of all nations, it is still true "the
people shall dwell alone, they shall not be reckoned among the nations." In all
the cities of Europe there are remains of the "Jews' quarter," and we in London had our "Old Jewry," the Jews being evermore a peculiar people. We
Christians are to be equally distinct, not in meats, and drinks, and garments,
and holy days, but as to spirituality of mind and holiness of life. We are to be
strangers and foreigners in the land wherein we sojourn. For we are not resi-
dent traders in this Vanity Fair; we pass through it because it lies in our way
home, but we are ill at ease in it. In no tent of all the fair can we rest.

O traders in this hubbub of trifles, we have small esteem for your great
bargains and tempting cheats; we are not buyers in the Roman row nor in the
French row; we would give all that we have to leave your polluted streets, and
be no more annoyed by Beelzebub, the lord of the fair. Our journey is toward
the celestial city, and when the sons of earth cry to us, "What do you buy?"
we answer, "We buy the truth." O young man, can you take up in the ware-
house the position of being a Christian though there is no other believer in the
house? Come, good woman, dare you serve the Lord, though husband and
children ridicule you? Man of business, dare you do the right thing in business
and play the Christian, though around you the various methods of trading
render it hard for you to be unflinchingly honest? This singularity is demanded
of every believer in Jesus. You cannot be blessed with Abraham unless like him
you come out and stand forth as true men.

> Dare to be a Daniel
> Dare to stand alone;
> Dare to have a purpose true,
> Dare to make it known.

May God grant to us grace to be Daniels, even if the lions' den should
threaten us.

A second peculiarity of Abraham's conduct is seen in the fact that *he was
ready for all the losses and risks that might be involved in obedience to the call of God.*
He was to leave his native country, as we have already said: to some of us that

would be a hard task, and I doubt not it was such to him. The smoke out of my own chimney is better than the fire on another man's hearth. There is no place like home wherever we may wander. The home feeling was probably as strong in Abraham as in us, but he was never to have a home on earth any more, except that he was to realize what Moses afterward sang, "Lord, thou hast been our dwelling place in all generations." For him there was no rooftree [ridgepole] and paternal estate, he owned no portion of the land in which he sojourned, and his sole alcove was a frail tent, which he removed from day to day as his flocks required fresh pasturage. He could say to his God, "I am a stranger and a sojourner with thee." He had to leave those whom he loved, for, though they accompanied him part of the way, they would not go farther; if he followed the Lord fully he must go alone. The patriarch knew nothing of half measures; he went through with his obedience, and left all his kindred to go to Canaan, to which he had been summoned. Those who wished to stop at Haran might stop there. Canaan was his destination, and he could not stop short of it.

No doubt he had many risks to encounter on his journey and when be entered the country. The Canaanite was still in the land, and the Canaanites were a fierce and cruel set of heathen who would have utterly destroyed the wanderer if the Lord had not put a spell upon them, and said, "Touch not mine anointed, and do my prophets no harm." It was a country swarming with little tribes, who were at war continually. Abraham himself was, for Lot's sake, to gird on his sword, and go forth to fight, peace-lover as he was. Of all discomforts and dangers, loss of property, and parting with friends, Abraham made small account. God commanded, and Abraham went.

Now, brethren, can you and I do the same? O you who desire to be saved, I say, can you do this? Have you counted the cost and determined to pay it? You must not expect that you will wear silver slippers and walk on green rolled turf all the way to heaven: the road was rough which your Lord traversed, and if you walk with him yours will be rough too. Can you bear for Jesus' sake all earthly loss? Can you bear the scoff, the cold shoulder, the cutting jest, the innuendo, the sarcasm, the sneer? Could you go further and bear loss of property and suffering in purse? Do not say that it may not occur, for many believers lose all by having to leave the ill pursuits by which they once earned their bread. You must in your intention give all up for Jesus, and in act you must give up all to Jesus. If he be yours, you must henceforth have all things in common with him; you must be joint heirs together, his yours and yours his; you may be well content to make joint stock, when you have so little and he has so much. Oh, can you stand to it, and give up all for him? Well, if you cannot, do not pretend to do it. Yet, except ye take up your cross, ye cannot be his disciples. Except you can give up everything for him, do not pretend to follow him. Listen to this. If you think heaven worth nothing, and Christ worth nothing, if you consider worldly gain to be everything, and comfort everything, and honor everything, if you could not die a martyr's death for Christ, your love to him is not worth much, and the Abraham spirit is not in you. May God enable us to take our places in the battle in the front of the foe, where the fight is most furious. May grace make us sing—

> Jesus, I my cross have taken,
> All to leave and follow thee,
> Destitute, despised, forsaken,
> Thou, from hence, my all shalt be.

If that be said in truth, it is well, my brother; you bid fair to be in all things a partaker with faithful Abraham: you also shall find much blessing in the separated life.

Third, one great peculiarity in Abraham was that *he waived the present for the future*. He went out to go into a place which he should after receive for an inheritance. He left the inheritance he then had to receive one which was yet to come. This is not the way of the world. The proverb says, "A bird in the hand is worth two in the bush," and especially in such a bush as Abraham saw before him. It did not seem very likely he would ever obtain that land; but still he let his bird in the hand go and took to the bird in the bush, being fully persuaded that he should have it in God's good time. Mr. Bunyan sets this forth in his picture of two children, Passion and Patience. Passion would have all his good things now, and he sat among his toys and joys, and laughed and rejoiced. Patience had to bear to see his brother Passion full of mirth, and to hear his scoffing; but then, as Master Bunyan beautifully says, Patience came in last for his portion, and it lasted forever, for there is nothing after the last. So, then, if we are to have our heaven last it will last, and no cloud shall mar it, no calamity bring it to an end. He is the wise man who lets go the shadow to grasp the substance, even though he should have to wait twenty, thirty, or forty years for it. He is blessed who leaves earth's wind and rubble and feeds on more substantial meat. God grant us grace to live more for the future than we have been accustomed to do.

O you ungodly ones, you do not care about the future, for you have never realized death and judgment. You are afraid to look over the edge of this narrow life. As to death, nothing frightens you so much. As for hell, if you are warned to escape from it, instead of thanking the preacher for being honest enough to warn you of it, you straightaway call him a "hell-fire" preacher, or give him some other ugly name. Alas, you little know how pained he is to speak to you on so terrible a subject! You little dream how true a lover of your soul he is, or he would not warn you of the wrath to come. Do you want to have flatterers about you? Such are to be had in plenty if you desire them. As for heaven, you seem to have no regard for it; at any rate you are not making your title to it sure or clear by caring about divine things. If you would have the birthright you must let the present mess of pottage go. The eternal future must come far before the fleeting trifles of today; you must let the things which are seen sink, and bid the "things not seen as yet" rise in all their matchless grandeur and reality before your eyes. You must give up chasing butterflies and shadows and pursue things eternal. My soul immortal pines only for immortal joys. I leave my present lot to be appointed of the Lord as he wills, so long as he will shed his love abroad in my heart. We must be prepared for eternity, and for that purpose we should concentrate our faculties upon divine truth and personal religion, that we may be ready to meet our God. This, then, was the third excellence in Abraham's walk, that he waived present comfort for the sake of the future blessing.

Fourth, and this is the main point, *Abraham committed himself to God by faith*.

From that day forward Abraham had nothing but his God for a portion, nothing but his God for a protector. No squadron of soldiers accompanied the good man's march; his safeguard lay in him who had said, "Fear not, Abraham, I am thy shield and thy exceeding great reward." He had to trust the Lord for his daily bread and daily guidance, for he was to march on and not know half a mile before him. He was ignorant when to stop and when to journey on, except as the Lord God guided him hour by hour. I must not say that Abraham became a poor pensioner upon the daily provision of God, but I will use a better term and describe him as "a gentleman commoner upon the royal bounty of his heavenly King." His lot was to have nothing but to be heir of heaven and earth. Can you thus walk by faith? Has the grace of God brought you who have been hesitating to resolve henceforth to believe God and trust him? If you do you are saved, for faith is the deciding matter. To realize the existence of God and to trust in him, especially to trust in his mercy, through Jesus Christ, is the essential matter. As for the life and walk of faith, they are the most singular things in the world. I seem myself to have been climbing a series of mysterious staircases, light as air and yet as solid as granite. I cannot see a single step before me, and often there seems to the eye to be nothing whatsoever to form a foothold for the next step. I look down and wonder how I came where I am, but still I climb on, and he who has brought me so far supplies me with confidence for that which lies before me. High into things invisible the ethereal ladder has borne me, and onward and forward to glory its rounds will yet conduct me. What I have seen has often failed me, but what I have not seen, and yet have believed, has always held me stably. Have not you found it so, all you children of God? Let us pray that the Lord may lead others to tread the same mystic ascent by beginning today the life of faith.

The last specialty in Abraham's procedure was *what he did was done at once*. There were no "ifs" and "ands" debatings, considerings, and delays. He needed no forcing and driving—

> *God drew him and he followed on,*
> *Charmed to confess the voice divine.*

At once, I say, he went. Promptness is one of the brightest excellencies in faith's actings. Delay spoils all. Someone asked Alexander to what he owed his conquests, and he said, "I have conquered because I never delayed." While the enemy were preparing, he had begun the battle, and they were routed before they knew where they were. After that fashion faith overcomes temptation. She runs in the way of obedience, or rather she mounts on the wings of eagles, and so speeds on her way. With regard to the things of God our first thoughts are best: considerations of difficulty entangle us. Whenever you feel a prompting to do a good thing, do not ask anybody whether you should do it or not; no one ever repents of doing good. Ask your friends afterward rather than beforehand, for it is ill consulting with flesh and blood when duty is plain. If the Lord has given you substance, and you are prompted to be generous to the cause of God, do not count every sixpence over, and calculate what others would give; count it after you have given it, if it must be counted at all, but it would be better still not to let your left hand know what your right hand does. It cannot be wrong to do the right thing at once; no, in matters of duty, every moment of delay is a sin. Thus we have Abraham before us; may the Holy Spirit make us like him.

Now this morning, who will listen to the call of God? Who, like Abraham, will quit the world, with all its folly, and resolve henceforth to be upon the Lord's side? O Spirit of the living God, constrain many a hidden Abraham to come forth!

III. We have to close with two or three words about what was *the result of Abraham's action.*

The question of many will be, *did it pay?* That is the inquiry of most people, and within proper bounds it is not a wrong question. Did it answer Abraham's purpose? Our reply is, it did so gloriously. True, it brought him into a world of trouble, and no wonder: such a noble course as his was not likely to be an easy one. What grand life ever was easy? Who wants to be a child and do easy things? Yet we read in Abraham's life, after a whole host of troubles, "And Abraham was old and well stricken in years, and the Lord had blessed Abraham in all things." That is a splendid conclusion—God had blessed Abraham in all things. Whatever happened, he had always been under the divine smile, and all things had worked for his good. He was parted from his friends, but then he had the sweet society of his God, and was treated as the friend of the most High, and allowed to intercede for others, and clothed with great power on their behalf. I almost envy Abraham. I should do so altogether if I did not know that all the saints are permitted to enjoy the same privileges. What a glorious degree Abraham took when he was called "the friend of God"; was not his loss of earthly friendships abundantly made up to him? What honor, also, the patriarch had among his contemporaries; he was a great man, and held in high esteem. How splendidly he bore himself; no king ever behaved more royally. That pettifogging king of Sodom wanted to make a bargain with him, but the grand old man replied, "I will not take from a thread even to a shoe-latchet, lest thou shouldest say, I have made Abraham rich." Those sons of Heth also were willing to make him a present of a piece of land around the cave of Machpelah; but he did not want a present from Canaanites, and so he said, "No, I will pay you every penny. I will weigh out the price to you, whatever you may demand." In noble independence no man could excel the father of the faithful; his contemporaries look small before him, and no man seems to be his equal, save Melchizedek. His image passes across the page of history rather like that of a spirit from the supernal realms than that of a mere man; he is so thorough, so childlike, and therefore so heroic. He lived in God, and on God, and with God. Such a sublime life recompensed a thousandfold all the sacrifice he was led to make.

Was not his life a happy one? One might wisely say, "Let my life be like that of Abraham." As to temporal things, the Lord enriched him, and in spirituals he was richer still. He was wealthier in heart than in substance, though great ever, in that respect. And now Abraham is the father of the faithful, patriarch of the whole family of believers, and to him alone of all mortal men God said, "In thee shall all the families of the earth be blessed." This very day, through his matchless seed, to whom be glory forever and ever, even Jesus Christ of the seed of Abraham, all tribes of men are blessed. His life was both for time and for eternity, a great success; both for temporals and for spirituals the path of faith was the best that he could have followed.

And now may we all be led to imitate his example. If we never have done so, may we this morning be led to give God his due by trusting him, to give the blood of Christ its due by relying upon it, to give the Spirit of God his due by yielding ourselves to him. Will you do so, or not? I pause for your reply. The call is given again, will you obey it or not? Nobody here will actually declare that he will not, but many will reply that *they hope they shall.* Alas! my sermon is a failure to those who so speak: if that be your answer, I am foiled again. When Napoleon was attacking the Egyptians he had powerful artillery, but he could not reach the enemy, for they were ensconced in a mud fort, and it made Napoleon very angry, because, if they had been behind granite walls, he could have battered them down, but their earthworks could not be blown to pieces; every ball stuck in the mud, and made the wall stronger. Your hopes and delays are just such a mud wall. I had a good deal sooner people would say, "There, now, we do not believe in God nor in his Christ," and speak out straightforwardly, than go on forever behind this mud wall of "we will by-and-by," and "we hope it will be so one day." The fact is, you do not mean to obey the Lord at all. You are deceiving yourselves if you think so. If God be God tomorrow he is God today; if Christ be worth having next week he is worth having today. If there is anything in religion at all, it demands a present surrender to its claims and a present obedience to its laws; but if you judge it to be a lie, say so, and we shall know where you are. If Baal be God, serve him; but if God be God, I charge you by Jesus Christ, fly to him as he is revealed and come forth from the sin of the world and be separate, and walk by faith in God. To this end may the Spirit of God enable you. Amen and amen.

Jacob: Worshiping on His Staff

Delivered at the Metropolitan Tabernacle, Newington. Published in 1878. No. 1401

By faith Jacob, when he was a dying, blessed both the sons of Joseph; and worshiped, leaning upon the top of his staff.— HEBREWS 11:21

"When he was dying." Death is a thorough test of faith. Beneath the touch of the skeleton finger shams dissolve into thin air, and only truth remains; unless indeed a strong delusion has been given, and then the spectacle of a presumptuous sinner passing away in his iniquities is one which might make angels weep. It is hard, very hard, to maintain a lie in the presence of the last solemnities; the end of life is usually the close of self-deception. There is a mimic faith, a false assurance, which lasts under all ordinary heats of trial, but this evaporates when the fires of death surround it. Certain men are at peace and quiet in their conscience, they stifle convictions, they refuse to allow such a thing as self-examination, they count an honest self-suspicion to be a temptation of the devil, and boast of their unbroken tranquility of mind, and go on from day to day with perfect confidence; but we would not be of their order. Their eyes are closed, their ears are dull of hearing, and their heart has waxed gross. A siren song forever enchants them with delight, but also entices them to destruction. Terrible will be their awakening when they lie dying: as a dream their false peace will vanish, and real terrors will come upon them.

That expression, "when he was a dying," reminds me of many deathbeds; but I shall not speak of them now, for I desire each one of you to rehearse the scene of his own departure, for soon of every one a tale will be told commencing—"when he was a dying." I want each one to project his mind a little forward to the time when he must gather up his feet in the bed, pronounce his last farewell, and yield up the ghost. Before your actual departure, probably, there may be allotted to you, unless you are carried away with a sudden stroke, a little time in which it shall be said, "He was a dying." Perhaps it is a desirable thing to occupy some weeks in departure, till the mind seems to have passed through the gate and to be already in the glory, while yet the body lingers here; but as we have had no experience, we are scarcely able to form a judgment.

The text tells us that the patriarch's faith was firm while he was a dying, so that he poured forth no murmurs, but plentiful benedictions, as he blessed both the sons of Joseph. May your faith and mine also be such that whenever we shall be dying, our faith will perform some illustrious exploit that the grace of God may be admired in us. Paul does not say anything about Jacob's life but selects the death scene. There were many instances of faith in Jacob's life story, but you recollect that in the epistle to the Hebrews, Paul is walking through the histories and plucking a flower here and a flower there, and he complains that time fails him even in doing that, so fertile is the garden of faith. I do not doubt, however, that he gathered the best out of each biography; and, perhaps, the finest thing in Jacob's life was the close of it. He was more royal between the curtains of his bed than at the door of his tent: greater in the hour of his weakness than in the day of his power.

The old man of 147 might have been willing to depart through infirmities of age, but yet he had much to keep him below, and make him wish to live as long as possible. After a very troublous life he had enjoyed seventeen years of remarkable comfort, so much so that, had it been ourselves, we should probably have begun to strike our roots into the soil of Goshen, and dread the bare thought of removal; yet there sits the venerable patriarch, with his hand on his staff, ready to go, seeking no delay, but rather waiting for the salvation of God. After all his tossings to and fro, when he had been so long a pilgrim, it must have been a pleasant thing for him to have settled down in a fat land with his sons, and his grandsons, and great-grandsons all around him, all comfortably provided for, with Joseph at the head of the whole country—prime minister of Egypt—reflecting honor upon his old father, and taking care that none of the family wanted anything. The last course of Jacob's feast of life was by far the sweetest, and the old man might have been loathe to retire from so dainty a table. The children of Israel were a sort of foreign aristocracy in the land, and against them would not a dog dare to move its tongue, lest the renowned Joseph should put forth his hand. That seventeen years must have been bright, and full of rest to the old man. But sense has not killed his faith, luxury has not destroyed his spirituality; his heart is still in the tents where he had dwelled as a sojourner with God. You can see that he has not even with one single rootlet of his soul taken hold upon Egypt. His first anxiety is to take care that not even his bones shall lie in Goshen, but that his body shall be taken out of the country as a protest to his family that they are not Egyptians, and cannot be made into subjects of Pharaoh, and that Canaan is their possession to which they must come. By his dying charge to bury him in Machpelah, he practically teaches his descendants that they must set loose by all the good land which they possessed in Goshen, for their inheritance did not lie on the banks of the Nile, but on the other side of the desert in Canaan, and they must be on tiptoe to journey there. The blessing which he gave to the sons of Joseph was but an utterance of his firm faith in the covenant which gave the land to him and to his seed. It was suggested by that faith of his which let go the present and grasped the future, renounced the temporal and seized the eternal, refusing the treasures of Egypt and clinging to the covenant of God.

I. First, then, *his blessing.*

He blessed the two sons of Joseph. Will you have patience with me while I try to show that his blessing the sons of Joseph was an act of faith? Because, first, *only by faith could the old man really give a blessing to anyone.* Look at him. He is too feeble to leave his bed. When he sits up supported by pillows, at what is called the bed's head, he calls for his trusty staff that he may lean upon it while he raises himself up a little, to be in a position to stretch out his hands and to use his voice. He has no strength, and his eyes are dim, so that he cannot see which is Ephraim and which is Manasseh. He is failing in most of his faculties: every way you can see that he is a worn-out old man, who can do nothing for the children whom he loves. If he is able to bestow a blessing, it cannot be by the power of nature; and yet he can and does bless them, and therefore we feel sure that there must be an inner man within that feeble old Jacob; there must be a spiritual Israel hidden away in him, an Israel who by prevailing with God as a prince has obtained a blessing, and is able to dispense it to others. And so there is; and at half a glance we see it. He rises to the dignity of a king, a prophet, and a priest when he begins to pronounce a blessing upon his two grandchildren. He believed that God spoke by him; and he believed that God would justify every word that he was uttering. He believed in the God that hears prayer; his benediction was a prayer; and as he pronounced blessings upon his grandsons he felt that every word he was speaking was a petition which the Lord was answering. They were blessed, and they should be blessed, and he discerned it by faith. Thus, we see, he was manifesting his faith in offering believing prayer and in uttering a confident benediction.

Whether we live or whether we die, let us have faith in God: whenever we preach or teach the gospel, let us have faith; for without faith we shall labor in vain. Whenever you distribute religious books or visit the sick, do so in faith, for faith is the lifeblood of all our service. If only by faith can a dying Jacob bless his descendants, so only by faith can we bless the sons of men. Have faith in God, and the instruction which you give shall really edify, the prayers you offer shall bring down showers of mercy, and your endeavors for your sons and daughters shall be prospered. God will bless what is done in faith; but if we believe not, our work will not be established. Faith is the backbone and marrow of the Christian's power to do good: we are weak as water till we enter into union with God by faith, and then we are omnipotent. We can do nothing for our fellowmen by way of promoting their spiritual and eternal interests if we walk according to the sight of our eyes; but when we get into the power of God, and grasp his promise by a daring confidence, then it is that we obtain the power to bless.

You will notice, also, that *not only the power to bless came to him by faith, but the blessings which he allotted to his grandsons were his upon the same tenure.* His legacies were all blessings which he possessed by faith only. He gave to Ephraim and Manasseh a portion each: but where and what? Did he fetch out a bag from an iron safe and say, "Here, young men, I give you the same portion of ready money as I give my sons"? No, there does not seem to have been a solitary shekel in the case. Did he call for the map of the family estates and say, "I give over to you, my boys, my freehold lands in such a parish, and my copyhold farms under such a manor"? No, no, he gave them no portion in Goshen, but each had a lot in Canaan.

Did that belong to him? Yes, in one sense, but not in another. God had promised it to him, but he had not yet a foot of land in it. The Canaanites were swarming in the land; they were dwelling in cities walled up to heaven and held the country by the right of possession, which is nine points of the law. But the good old man talks about Canaan as if it was all his own, and he foresees the tribes growing into nations as much as if they were already in actual possession of the country. He had, as a matter of fact, neither house nor ground in Palestine, and yet he counts it all his own, since a faithful God had promised it to his fathers. God had said to Abraham, "Lift up now thine eyes and behold to the east and to the west, to the north and to the south. All this will I give thee." And Jacob realizes that gift of God as being a charter and title deed of possession, and he acts upon it while he says, "This is for Ephraim: this is for Manasseh," though the sneering infidel standing by would have said, "Hear how the old man dotes and maunders, giving away what he has not got!" Faith is the substance of things hoped for, and she deals seriously and in a business manner with that which she makes real to herself: blind reason may ridicule, but faith is justified of all her children.

Beloved, in this manner believers bless the sons of men, namely, by faith. We pray for them, and we tell them of good things yet to come, not to be seen of the eye, or to be perceived by the senses, but inconceivably good things laid up by God for them that love him, which shall be the portion of our children and our friends if they believe in the living God. By faith we believe in things not seen as yet. We confess that, like Abraham, Isaac, and Jacob, we are strangers here, and we are journeying toward a place of which God has spoken to us: "A city which hath foundations, whose builder and maker is God." We have learned to talk about the crown which the Lord has laid up for us, and not for us only but for all them that love his appearing; and we delight to tell others how to win this crown. We point them to the narrow gate and to the narrow way, neither of which they can see, and to the end of that narrow road, even to the hilltops crowned with the celestial city where the pilgrims of the Lord shall dwell forever, and enjoy an eternal reward. Faith is wanted to enable us to point men to the invisible and eternal, and if we cannot do this how can we bless them? We must believe for those we love and have hope for them; thus shall we have power with God for them and shall bless them. O you worldly fathers, you may give your sons what heritage you can, and divide among your daughters what wealth you please, but as for us, our longing is to see our children and our children's children dowried with the riches which come from above. If they win a share in the land on the other side of Jordan, as yet unseen, and have a portion now in Christ Jesus, we shall be glad—infinitely more glad than if they were the richest among mankind. Our legacies to our sons are the blessings of grace, and our dowries to our daughters are the promises of the Lord.

It is well worthy of our notice that *the venerable patriarch Jacob in his benediction particularly mentioned the covenant.* His faith, like the faith of most of God's people, made the covenant its pavilion of delightful abode, its tower of defense, and its armory for war. No sweeter word was on his tongue than the covenant, and no richer consolation sustained his heart. He said to Joseph, "God almighty appeared unto me at Luz in the land of Canaan, and blessed me, and said unto me, 'Behold I will make thee fruitful, and multiply thee.'" His confidence rested in the promise of the Lord, and in the divine fidelity: that was the fountain truth from which he drew the inspiration which led him to bless his grandchildren. And, also, you notice, how he dwells upon the name of his father Abraham, and of his father Isaac, with whom the covenant had aforetime been established: the memories of covenant love are precious, and every confirmatory token is treasured up and dwelled upon. Dying men do not talk nonsense. They get to something solid, and the everlasting covenant made with their fathers, and confirmed in their own persons, has been one of the grand things about which dying saints have been wont to deliver their souls. Recollect how David said, "Although my house be not so with God, yet hath he made with me an everlasting covenant, ordered in all things and sure."

While we are sitting here, we can talk about the matter coolly, but when the death dew lies cold upon the brow, and the pulse is failing, and the throat is gradually choking up, it will be blessed to fix the eye upon the faithful Promiser and to feel a calm within the soul which even death pangs cannot disturb, because we can then exclaim, "I know whom I have believed, and I am persuaded that he is able to keep that which I have committed to him until that day."

I want to call your attention to one point which I think extraordinarily illustrates the faith of Jacob. In distributing to these two grandchildren his blessings as to the future, he takes them right away from Joseph, and says, "As Simeon and Reuben shall they be mine." Do you know who those two young gentlemen were? Think a while, and you will see that they were very different in rank, station, parentage, and prospects from any of the sons of Jacob. Jacob's sons had been brought up as laboring men, without knowledge of polite society or learned arts. They were countrymen, mere Bedouins, wandering shepherds, and nothing else; but these two young gentlemen were descended from a princess, and had, no doubt, been liberally educated. Pharaoh had given to Joseph a daughter of Potipherah, priest of On, and the priests of Egypt were the highest class of all—the nobility of the land. Joseph himself was prime minister, and these were partakers of his lofty rank. The sons of Reuben and Simeon were nobodies in the polite circles of Egypt—very good, decent people, farmers and graziers, but not at all of the high class of the Right Honorable Lord Manasseh and the Honorable Ephraim. Indeed, every shepherd was an abomination to the Egyptians, and therefore inadmissible to Egypt's nobility; but Manasseh and Ephraim were of a superior caste, and gentlemen of position and fortune. But *Jacob showed his faith by ignoring worldly advantages for his grandsons.* He says to Joseph, "They are not to be yours. I do not know them as Egyptians, I forget all about their mother's rank and family. The boys have attractive prospects before them; they can be made priests of the idol temple, and rise to high dignities among the Egyptians; but all that glitter we reject for them, and in token thereof I adopt them as my own sons; they are mine; as Simeon and Reuben they shall be mine. For all the gold of Egypt you would not have one of them serve an idol, for I know that you are true to your father's God and your father's faith." And so he takes the boys right away, you see, from all their brilliant opportunities, and bestows upon them that which, to the carnal mind, appears to be an estate in dreamland, a chateau in Spain, something intangible and unmarketable. This was a deed of faith, and blessed are they who can imitate it, choosing rather the reproach of Christ for their sons than all the treasures of Egypt. The joy of it is that these lads accepted the exchange, and let the golden possessions of Egypt go like Moses after them. May our heirs and successors be of like mind, and may the Lord say of them, "Out of Egypt have I called my son"; and again, "When Ephraim was a child then I loved him, and called my son out of Egypt."

We are not done yet, for we notice that Jacob *showed his faith by blessing Joseph's sons in God's order.* He placed Ephraim before Manasseh. It was not according to the rule of nature, but he felt the impulse upon him, and his faith would not resist the divine guidance: blind as he was he would not yield to the dictation of his son, but crossed his hands to obey the divine monition. Faith resolves to do the right thing in the right way. Some persons' faith leads them to do the right thing the wrong way upward, but matured faith follows the order which God prescribes. If God will have Ephraim first, faith does not quarrel with his decree. We may wish to see a favorite child blessed more than another, but nature must forgo her choice, for the Lord must do what seems him good. Faith prefers grace to talent, and piety to cleverness; she lays her right hand where God lays it, and not where beauty of person or quickness of intellect would suggest. Our best child is that which God calls best; faith corrects reason and accepts the divine verdict.

Notice that *he manifested his faith by his distinct reference to redemption.* He alone who has faith will pray for the redemption of his children, especially when they exhibit no signs of being in bondage, but are hopeful and amiable. The good old man prayed, "The angel which redeemed me from all evil, bless the lads." Let your faith bring down upon your children a share in redemption's blessings, for they need to be redeemed even as others. If they are washed in the blood of Jesus, if they are reconciled to God by the blood of his Son, if they have access to God by the blood of atonement, you may die well satisfied; for what is to harm them when once the angel that redeemed you has also redeemed them? From sin, from Satan, from death, from hell, from self—"from all evil" does our Redeemer set us free; and this is the greatest of all benedictions which we can pronounce upon our dearest children.

Jacob showed his faith by his assurance that God would be present with his seed. How cheering is the old man's dying expression, made not only to his boys, but concerning all his family. He said, "Now I die, but God will be with you." It is very different from the complaints of certain good old ministers when they are dying. They seem to say, "When I die, the light of Israel will be quenched. I shall die, and the people will desert the truth. When I am gone the standard-bearer will have fallen, and the watchman on the walls will be dead." Many in dying are afraid for the chariot of Israel and the horsemen thereof; and, sometimes, we who are in good health talk very much in the same fashion as though we were wonderfully essential to the progress of God's cause. I have known some of our church members speak in that manner, and inquire: "What should we do if Mr. So-and-So were dead? If our pastor were gone, what would the church do?" I will tell you what you will do without us: I will put the case as though I were myself to die: "Now I die, but God will be with you." Whoever passes away, the Lord will abide with his people, and the church will be secure. The grand old cause does not depend on one or two of us. God forbid! The truth was mighty in the land before the best man living was born, and the truth will not be buried with him, but in its own immortal youth will still be powerful; yes, and fresh advocates will arise more full of life and vigor than we are, and greater victories will be won. It is grand to say with Jacob, "Now I die, but God will be with you." Such language honors God and bespeaks a mind greatly trustful and completely delivered from the self-conceit which dreams itself important, if not necessary, to the cause of God.

II. We are told, next, that the old man "worshiped"—*worshiped by faith.*

Very briefly let me tell you what worship I think he rendered.

First, while he was dying he offered the worship of *gratitude.* How pleasing is the incident recorded in the tenth and eleventh verses, "Now the eyes of Israel were dim for age, so that he could not see. And Joseph brought his two sons near unto him; and he kissed them and embraced them. And Israel said unto Joseph, 'I had not thought to see thy face: and, lo, God hath showed me also thy seed.'" Ah, yes, we shall often have to say, "O Lord, I had not thought that thou wouldst do as much as this, but thou hast gone far beyond what I asked or even thought." I hope that this will be among our dying speeches and confessions, that the half was never told us, that our good Lord kept the best wine till the last, and that the end of the feast on earth, being but the beginning of the feast eternal in heaven, was the crown of all. Let us declare concerning our Lord that we found him better and better and better and better, even till we entered into his rest. He has been at first better than our fears, then better than our hopes, and finally better than our desires.

Did he not also offer the worship of *testimony,* when he acknowledged God's goodness to him all his life? He says, "The God that fed me all my life long," thus owning that he had been always dependent but always supplied. He had been a shepherd, and he uses a word here which means "the God that shepherdized me—who was a Shepherd to me all my life long." It was a testimony to the care and tenderness of Jehovah. Yes, and I hope we also shall finish life by magnifying the goodness of the Lord. Be this our witness, "He fed me all my life long. I was in straits sometimes, and I wondered where the next bit of bread would come from; but if he did not send a raven, or if he did not find a widow woman to provide for me, yet somehow or other he did feed me all my life long. He worked in his own wise way, so that I never lacked, for the Lord was my Shepherd all my life long."

Notice, too, how reverently he worships the covenant Messenger with the adoration of *reverent love*. He speaks of "the Angel who redeemed me from all evil." He thinks of the Angel that wrestled with him, and the Angel that appeared to him when he fell asleep at Bethel. This is the Angel, not an ordinary angel, but the true archangel—Jesus Christ—the Messenger of the covenant whom we delight in. It is he that has delivered us from all evil by his redeeming blood, for no other being could have accomplished a redemption so complete. Do you remember when he came to you personally, and wrestled with you and tore away your self-righteousness, and made you limp upon your thigh? This it may be was your first introduction to him. You saw him by night, and thought him at the first to be rather your enemy than your friend. Do you recollect when he took your strength away from you, and then at last saved you, because in utter weakness, you were about to fall to the ground, you laid hold of him and said, "I will not let thee go except thou bless me," and so you won a blessing from him? You had thought beforehand that you had strength in yourself, but now you learned that you were weakness itself, and that only as you became consciously weak would you become actually strong. You learned to look out of self to him, and do you not bless him for having taught you such a lesson? Will you not when you come to die bless him for what he did for you then, and all your life long? O my brethren, we owe all things to the redeeming Angel of the covenant. The evils which he has warded off from us are terrible beyond conception, and the blessings he has brought us are rich beyond imagination.

Thus you have had a picture of the old man blessing by faith, and worshiping by faith: faith was the mainspring of the two actions, their essence, their spirit, and their crown.

III. The last matter for us to speak upon is *his attitude*.

He "worshiped leaning upon the top of his staff." The Romanists have made fine mischief out of this text, for they have read it, "He worshiped the top of his staff," and their notion has been, I suppose, that there was a pretty little god carved on the top—an image of a saint or a cross, or some other symbol, and that he held up that emblem, and so worshiped the top of his staff. We know that he did no such thing, for there is no trace in Abraham, Isaac, or Jacob of anything like the worship of images; though teraph worship lingered in their families, it was not with their consent. They were not perfect men, but they were perfectly clear from idolatry, and never worshiped an image. No, no, no; they worshiped God alone. He worshiped on the top of his staff—leaning on it, supporting himself upon it. In Genesis you read that he "bowed himself upon the bed's head." It is a very curious thing that the word for *bed* and the word for *staff* in the Hebrew are so exceedingly like each other that unless the little points had been used, which I suppose were not used at all in the olden time, it would be difficult to tell whether the word is "bed" or "staff." I do not, however, think either Moses or Paul can be wrong. Jacob strengthened himself and sat upon the bed, and he leaned upon his staff too. It is very easy to realize a position in which both descriptions would be equally true. He could sit upon the bed, and lean on the top of his staff at the same time.

But why did he lean on his staff? What was that for? I think besides the natural need which he had of it, because of his being old, he did it emblematically. Do you not remember his saying, "With my staff I cross this Jordan"? I believe he kept that staff throughout life as a memorial. It was a favorite staff of his which he took with him on his first journey, and he leaned upon it as he took his last remove. "With my staff I crossed this Jordan," he had said before, and now with that staff in hand he crosses the spiritual Jordan. That staff was his life companion, the witness with himself of the goodness of the Lord, even as some of us may have an old Bible or a knife or a chair which are connected with memorable events of our lives.

But what did that staff indicate? Let us hear what Jacob said at another time. When he stood before Pharaoh he exclaimed, "Few and evil have been the days of my pilgrimage." What made him use that word *pilgrimage*? Why, because upon his mind there was always the idea of his being a pilgrim. He had been literally so during the early part of his life, wandering hither and thither; and now, though he has been seventeen years in Goshen, he keeps the old staff, and he leans on it to show that he had always been a pilgrim and a sojourner like his fathers, and that he was so still. While he leans on that staff he talks to Joseph, and he says, "Do not let my bones lie here. I have come hither in the providence of God, but I do not belong here. This staff indicates that I am only a sojourner here, and want to be gone. I am in Egypt, but I am not of it. Take my bones away. Do not let them lie here, for if they do, my sons and daughters will mingle with the Egyptians, and that must not be, for we are a distinct nation. God has chosen us for himself, and we must keep separate. To make my children see this, lo, here I die with my pilgrim staff in my hand."

Now, Christian brother, I want you to live in the same spirit, feeling that this is not your rest nor your native country. There is nothing here that is worthy of you. Your home is yonder, on the other side of the desert, where God has mapped out your portion. Christ has gone to prepare your place, and it would ill become you to have no desires for it. The longer you live, the more let this thought grow upon you: "Give me my staff. I must be gone. Poor world, thou art no rest for me; I am not of thy children, I am an alien and a stranger. My citizenship is in heaven, I take my share in Egypt's politics and Egypt's labor, yes, and in Egypt's griefs, but I am no Egyptian; I am a stranger bound for another land." Worship on the top of your staff, and sing—

> A scrip on my back, and a staff in my hand,
> I march on in haste through an enemy's land;
> There is nothing on earth which can tempt me to stay,
> My staff is the emblem of "up and away."

Singular enough is it that each descendant of Jacob came to worship on the top of his staff at last, for on the paschal supper night, when the blood was sprinkled on the lintel and the side posts, they each one ate the lamb with their loins girt and with a staff in his hand. The supper was a festival of worship, and they ate it each one leaning on his staff, as those that were in haste to leave home for a pilgrimage through the wilderness.

My dear hearers, this advice does not apply to all of you, for you are not all Jacobs, nor do you belong to the believing seed. I cannot bid you take your staff, for if you were to take your staff and start off, where would you go? You have no portion in the next world, no promised land, no Canaan flowing with milk and honey. Whither will you go? You must be banished from the presence of the Lord, and from the glory of his power. Alas for you! You cannot worship, for you know not God; you cannot bless others, for you have not been blessed yourselves. May the Lord bring you to his dear Son Jesus Christ, and lead you to put your trust in him, and then I shall hope that being saved you will by faith imitate Jacob, and both bless men, worship God, and wait with your staff in your hand, ready to journey to the eternal rest.

Joseph: A Miniature Portrait

Delivered on Lord's Day morning, July 24, 1881, at the Metropolitan Tabernacle, Newington. No. 1610.

The LORD was with Joseph.—GENESIS 39:2

Scripture frequently sums up a man's life in a single sentence. Here is the biography of Joseph sketched by inspiration—"God was with him," so Stephen testified in his famous speech recorded in Acts 7:9. Here is the life story of Abraham: "Abraham believed God." Of Moses we read, "The man Moses was very meek." Take a New Testament life, such as that of John the Baptist, and you have it in a line: "John did no miracle: but all things that he spoke concerning Jesus were true." The mere name of John—"that disciple whom Jesus loved"—would serve for all an epitaph of him: it pictures both the man and his history. Holy Scripture excels in this kind of full-length miniature painting. As Michaelangelo is said to have drawn a portrait with a single stroke of his crayon, so the Spirit of God sketches a man to the life in a single sentence. "The LORD was with Joseph."

Observe, however, that the portraits of Scripture give us not only the outer, but the inner life of the man. Man looks at the outward appearance, but the Lord looks upon the heart; and so the scriptural descriptions of men are not of their visible life alone, but of their spiritual life. Here we have Joseph as God saw him, the real Joseph. Externally it did not always appear that God was with him, for he did not always seem to be a prosperous man; but when you come to look into the inmost soul of this servant of God, you see his true likeness—he lived in communion with the Most High, and God blessed him: "The LORD was with Joseph, and he was a prosperous man." Dear friends, how would you like to have your inner biography sketched? How would your soul appear if set out in detail before all the world as to its desires, affections, and thoughts? Many lives have looked well on paper, but beneath their surface the biographer never dared to dive, or, perhaps, could not have dived had he been anxious to do so. It is often thought wise in writing a man's life to suppress certain matters: this may be prudent if the design be to guard a reputation, but it is scarcely truthful. The Spirit of God does not suppress the faults even of those whom we most admire, but writes them fully, like the Spirit of truth, as he is. The man who above others was "a man after God's own heart" was yet in some points exceedingly faulty, and he committed one foul deed which will remain through all time as a blemish upon his character. There was in David so firm and undeviating an attachment to the Lord God, and so sincere a desire to do right, and so deep a repentance when he had erred, that the Lord still regarded him as after his own heart, although he smote him heavily for his transgressions. David was a truly sincere man despite the faults into which he fell, and it is the heart of David which is sketched. So here, the Spirit is not looking so much at Joseph as a favorite child or an Egyptian prime minister, as at the innermost and truest Joseph, and therefore he thus describes him: "The LORD was with Joseph."

This striking likeness of Joseph strongly reminds us of our Master and Lord, that greater Joseph, who is Lord over all the world for the sake of Israel. Peter, in his sermon to the household of Cornelius, said of our Lord that he "went about doing good, and healing all that were oppressed of the devil; for God was with him." Exactly what had been said of Joseph. It is wonderful that the same words should describe both Jesus and Joseph, the perfect Savior and the imperfect patriarch. When you and I are perfected in grace, we shall wear the image of Christ, and that which will describe Christ will also describe us. Those who live with Jesus will be transformed by his fellowship till they become like him. To my mind, it is very beautiful to see the resemblance between the firstborn and the rest of the family, between the great typical man, the Second Adam, and all those men who are quickened into his life, and are one with him.

This having the Lord with us is the inheritance of all the saints; for what is the apostolic benediction in the epistles but a desire that the triune God may be with us? To the church in Rome Paul says, "Now the God of peace be with you all." To the church in Corinth he writes, "The grace of the Lord Jesus Christ, and the love of God, and the communion of the Holy Ghost, be with you all. Amen." To the Thessalonians he says, "The Lord be with you all." Did not our glorious Lord say, "Lo, I am with you always, even unto the end of the world"? How better could I salute you this morning than in the words of Boaz to the reapers, "The LORD be with you"? What kinder answer could you give me than "The LORD bless thee"? High up upon the mountains which form the back wall of Mentone I happened one day to meet a Quaker, in the usual costume, a warm-hearted lover of all who love Jesus. He saluted me, and we found great unity of spirit. On parting, I said, "Friend, the Lord be with thee"; and he answered, "And with thy spirit," adding, "It is the first bit of the liturgy that I have ever used." Truly, the more often we can use it with our hearts the better, for none can object to it. Thus do I say to all of you this day, "The Lord be with you," and I know that you are responding, "And with thy spirit." May you find that your desire is granted, by the Holy Spirit's being with my Spirit that I may speak words which shall refresh your hearts.

Now let us think of Joseph and see what we can learn from him. "The LORD was with Joseph": let us consider, first, the fact; second, the evidence of that fact; and third, the result of that fact.

I. First, we will run over Joseph's life, and note *the fact*: "The LORD was with Joseph."

God was gracious to Joseph as *a child*. His father loved him because he was the son of his old age, and also because of the gracious qualities which he saw in him. Before he was seventeen years of age, God had spoken with him in dreams and visions of the night, of which we read that "his brethren envied him; but his father observed the saying." Dear young people, it may be that God will not appear to you in dreams, but he has other ways of speaking to his young Samuels. You remember he said, "Samuel, Samuel," and the beloved child answered, "Speak, LORD, for thy servant heareth." May you answer in the same manner to the call of God by his word. It was the happy privilege of some of us before we had left boyhood and girlhood to have received gracious communications from God: he led us to repentance, he led us to faith in Christ, and he revealed his love in our hearts before we had left the school-room and the playground. They begin well who begin early with Christ: he will be with us to the end if we are with him at the beginning. If Joseph had not been a godly boy, he might never have been a gracious man: grace made him to differ from his brothers in youth, and he remained their superior all his days. If we are gracious while we are yet children, we may be sure that the Lord will be gracious to us even should we live to old age, and see our children's children. Early piety is likely to be eminent piety. Happy are those who have Christ with them in the morning, for they shall walk with him all day, and sweetly rest with him at eventide.

"The LORD was with Joseph" when Joseph was at home, and he did not desert him when he was sent away from his dear father and his beloved home and was sold for *a slave*. Bitter is the lot of a slave in any country, and it was worst of all in those early days. We are told by Stephen that the patriarchs, moved with envy, sold Joseph into Egypt, but the Lord was with him; even when he was being sold the Lord was with Joseph. It must have been a very dreadful journey for him across the desert, urged onward by those rough Ish-maelites, probably traveling in a gang, as slaves do to this day in the center of

Africa. May God put an end to the abominable system! This delicate child of an indulgent father, who had been clothed with a princely garment of many colors, must now wear the garb of a slave, and march in the hot sun across the burning sand; but never was captive more submissive under cruel treatment; he endured as seeing him who is invisible; his heart was sustained by a deep confidence in the God of his father Jacob, for "Jehovah was with him." I think I see him in the slave market exposed for sale. We have heard with what trembling anxiety the slave peers into the faces of those who are about to buy. Will he get a good master? Will one purchase him who will treat him like a man, or one who will use him worse than a brute? "The LORD was with Joseph" as he stood there to be sold, and he fell into good hands. When he was taken away to his master's house, and the various duties of his service were allotted to him, the Lord was with Joseph.

The house of the Egyptian had never been so pure, so honest, so honored before. Beneath Joseph's charge it was secretly the temple of his devotions, and manifestly the abode of comfort and confidence. That Hebrew slave had a glory of character about him which all perceived, and especially his master, for we read, "His master saw that the LORD was with him, and that the LORD made all that he did to prosper in his hand. And Joseph found grace in his sight, and he served him: and he made him overseer over his house, and all that he had he put into his hand. And it came to pass from the time that he had made him overseer in his house, and over all that he had, that the LORD blessed the Egyptian's house for Joseph's sake; and the blessing of the LORD was upon all that he had in the house and in the field." Joseph's diligence, integrity, and gentleness won upon his master, as well they might. O that all of you who are Christian servants would imitate Joseph in this, and so behave yourselves that all around you may see that the Lord is with you.

Then came a crisis in his history, the time of testing. We see Joseph *tried by a temptation* in which, alas, so many perish. He was attacked in a point at which youth is peculiarly vulnerable. His comely person made him the object of unholy solicitations from one upon whose goodwill his comfort greatly depended, and had it not been that the Lord was with him he must have fallen. The mass of mankind would scarcely have blamed him had he sinned: they would have cast the crime upon the tempter, and excused the frailty of youth. I say not so; God forbid I should; for in acts of uncleanness neither of the transgressors may be excused; but God was with Joseph, and he did not slide when set in slippery places. Thus he escaped that deep pit into which the abhorred of the Lord do fall. He was rescued from the snare of the strange woman, of whom Solomon has said, "She hath cast down many wounded;

yes, many strong men have been slain by her. Her house is the way to hell, going down to the chambers of death." Slavery itself was a small calamity compared with that which would have happened to young Joseph had he been enslaved by wicked passions. Happily, the Lord was with him, and enabled him to overcome the tempter with the question, "How can I do this great wickedness, and sin against God?" He fled. That flight was the truest display of courage. It is the only way of victory in sins of the flesh. The apostle says, "Flee youthful lusts which war against the soul." When Telemachus was in the isle of Calypso his mentor cried, "Fly, Telemachus, fly; there remains no hope of a victory but by flight." Wisely Joseph left his garment and fled, for God was with him.

The scene shifts again, and he who had been first a favored child at home, and then a slave, and then a tempted one, now becomes *a prisoner*. The prisons of Egypt were, doubtless, as horrible as all such places were in the olden times, and here is Joseph in the noisome dungeon. He evidently felt his imprisonment very much, for we are told in the Psalms that "the iron entered into his soul." He felt it a cruel thing, to be under such a slander, and to suffer for his innocence. A young man so pure, so chaste, must have felt it to be sharper than a whip of scorpions to be accused as he was; yet as he sat down in the gloom of his cell, the Lord was with him. The degradation of a prison had not deprived him of his divine companion. Blessed be the name of the Lord, he does not forsake his people when they are in disgrace: no, he is more pleasant with them when they are falsely accused than at any other time, and he cheers them in their low estate. God was with him, and very soon the kindly manners, the gentleness, the activity, the truthfulness, the industry of Joseph had won upon the keeper of the prison, so that Joseph rose again to the top, and was the overseer of the prison. Like a cork, which you may push down, but it is sure to come up again, so was Joseph: he must swim, he could not drown, the Lord was with him. The Lord's presence made him a king and a priest wherever he went, and men tacitly owned his influence. In the little kingdom of the prison Joseph reigned, for "God was with him."

He will rise higher than that, however, when opportunity arises for a display of *prophetic power*. Two of those under his charge appeared to be despondent one morning, and with his usual gentleness he asked, "Wherefore look ye so sadly today?" He was always kindly and sympathetic, and so they told him their dreams, and he interpreted them as the events actually fell out. But why did he interpret dreams? It was because God was with him. He tells them there and then that "interpretations belong unto God." It was not that he had knowledge of an occult art, or was clever at guessing, but the Spirit of God rested upon him, and so he understood the secrets veiled beneath the dreams.

This led to further steps, for after having been tried from seventeen to thirty, after having served thirteen years' apprenticeship to sorrow he came to stand *before Pharaoh,* and God is with him there. You can see that he is inwardly upheld, for the Hebrew youth stands boldly forth and talks of God in an idolatrous court. Pharaoh believed in multitudes of gods: he worshiped the crocodile, the ibis, the bull, and all manner of things, even down to leeks and onions, so that one said of the Egyptians, "Happy people, whose gods grow in their own gardens"; but Joseph was not ashamed to speak of his God as the only living and true God. He said, "What God is about to do he showeth unto Pharaoh." Calmly, and in a dignified manner, he unravels the dream, and explains it all to Pharaoh, disclaiming, however, all credit for wisdom. He says, "It is not in me: God shall give Pharaoh an answer of peace." God was with him indeed.

Joseph was made *ruler* over all Egypt, and God was with him. Well did the king say, "Can we find such a man as this is in whom the Spirit of God is?" His policy in storing up corn in the plenteous years succeeded admirably, for God was evidently working by him to preserve the human race from extinction by famine. His whole system, if looked at as executed in the interest of Pharaoh, his master, was beyond measure sensible and successful. He was not the servant of the Egyptians: Pharaoh had promoted him, and Pharaoh he enriched, and at the same time saved a nation from hunger.

God was with him in bringing down his father and the family into Egypt, and locating them in Goshen, and with him till he himself came to die, when he "took an oath of the children of Israel, saying God will surely visit you, and ye shall carry up my bones from hence." The Lord was with him, and kept him faithful to the covenant, and the covenanted race, even to the close of a long life of 110 years. He died faithful to the close to the God of his fathers, for he would not be numbered with Egypt, with all its learning and all its wealth; he chose to be accounted an Israelite and to share with the chosen race, whatever their fortunes might be. He, like the rest of the patriarchs, died in faith, looking for the promised inheritance, and for its sake renouncing the riches and glories of the world, for the Lord was with him.

II. We shall next review *the evidence of the fact* that God was with him.

What is the evidence that the Lord was with Joseph? The first evidence of it is this: *he was always under the influence of the divine presence,* and lived in the enjoyment of it. I shall not need to quote the instances—all of them, at any rate—for everywhere, whenever Joseph's heart speaks, he lets you know that he is conscious that God is with him. Take him under temptation especially. Oh, what a mercy it was for him that he was a God-fearing man! "How can I do this great wickedness, and sin against Potiphar?" No. Yet he would have sinned against Potiphar, who had been a kindly master to him. Does he say, "How shall I do this great wickedness, and sin against this woman?" for it would have been a sin against her. No; but just as David said, "Against thee, thee only, have I sinned, and done this evil in thy sight," making the main point and consideration to be sin against God, so did Joseph, as he fled from the seducer, argue thus, "How can I do this great wickedness, and sin against God?" Oh, if you and I always felt that God was near, looking steadily upon us, we should not dare to sin. The presence of a superior often checks a man from doing what else he might have ventured on, and the presence of God, if it were realized, would be a perpetual barrier against temptation, and would keep us steadfast in holiness. When Joseph afterward at any time spoke of God, when God helped him not only to stand against temptation but to do any service, you will notice how he always ascribes it to God. He will not interpret Pharaoh's dream without first telling him, "It is not in me: God hath showed Pharaoh what he is about to do." He was as conscious of the presence of God when he stood before the great monarch as when he refused that sinful woman. It was the same in his domestic life.

Let me read out of his family register. "And unto Joseph were born two sons before the years of famine came, which Asenath the daughter of Potipherah priest of On bare unto him. And Joseph called the name of the firstborn Manasseh: For God, said he, hath made me forget all my toil, and all my father's house. And the name of the second called he Ephraim: For God hath caused me to be fruitful in the land of my affliction." When his aged father said to him, "Who are these?" he replied very beautifully, "They are my sons, whom God hath given me in this place." I am afraid that we do not habitually talk in this fashion, but Joseph did. Without the slightest affectation he spoke out of his heart, under a sense of the divine presence and working. How like he is in this to our divine Lord! I cannot help speaking of it. If there is any good thing more marked about our Lord Jesus than another it is his sense of the divine presence. You see it when he is a child: "Knew ye not that I must be about my Father's business?" You hear it in the words, "I am not alone, because the Father is with me"; and again, "I know that thou hearest me always."

You perceive it forcibly in the last moment of his earthly life, when the sharpest pang that tortures him is that which makes him cry, "My God, my God, why hast thou forsaken me?" The presence of God was everything to

Christ as it was to Joseph. Now, if you and I set the Lord always before us, if our soul dwells in God, depend upon it, God is with us. There is no mistake about it. If you are under the influence of that text, "Thou God seest me," you may be sure that his presence will go with you, and he will give you rest. No man ever perceived God to be present and therefore walked before him in holiness, and afterward discovered that he had been under a delusion. Grace in the life proves that the God of grace is with us.

The next evidence is this: God was certainly with Joseph because *he was pure in heart*. "Blessed are the pure in heart, for they shall see God"; no other can do so. God will not manifest himself to those whose hearts are unclean. He that hath clean hands and a pure heart, he shall dwell on high. Our Lord Jesus said, "If a man love me, he will keep my words: and my Father will love him, and we will come unto him, and make our abode with him." When the heart is shocked at sin, and enamored of holiness, then it can enter into communion with God, and not till then. "Can two walk together unless they be agreed?" When I hear some professors admit that they have little communion with God, can I wonder at it? How can God have fellowship with us unless we walk obediently in his ways? What fellowship hath light with darkness? Or "what concord hath Christ with Belial?" The intense purity of Joseph was a proof that the thrice holy God was ever with him. He will keep the feet of his saints. When they are tempted he will deliver them from evil, for his presence sheds an atmosphere of holiness around the heart in which he dwells.

The next evidence in Joseph's case was *the diligence with which he exercised himself wherever he was*. God was with Joseph, and therefore the man of God hardly cared as to the outward circumstances of his position, but began at once to work that which is good. He was in the pit: yes, but the Lord was with Joseph, and the pit was not horrible to him: he pleaded with his brothers, and although they would not hear, he did his duty in warning them of their crime. He was carried captive of the Ishmaelites; but in the caravan he was safe, for God was with him. When he came to be a slave in Potiphar's house, the Lord was with him, and he was a prosperous man; the change of scene was not a change of his dearest company. He did not strike an attitude and make a display of his grand intentions, but he went to work where he was, and performed ordinary duties with great heartiness, for the Lord was with him. Many would have said, "I have been unrighteously sold for a slave. I ought not to be here, and I am not bound to perform any duties to Potiphar: rightfully I am a free man, as free as Potiphar, and I shall not work for him for nothing." No, the Lord was with him, and therefore he applied himself to that which lay next to hand, and went to work with a will. No doubt he performed menial service in the house at first, and then, by degrees, he rose to be the manager of the establishment. The truly godly man is ready for anything: he does not vie for place, but accepts the state in which he is found, and does good in it, for the Lord's sake.

The Lord was with Joseph nonetheless when he was cast into the prison. He knew God was with him in prison, and therefore he did not sit down sullenly in his sorrow, but he bestirred himself to make the best of his afflicted condition. Since the Lord was with him there, he was comforted; it would be infinitely better to be there with God than on the throne of Pharaoh without God. He did not mourn and moan, and spend his time in writing petitions to Potiphar, or making appeals to Potiphar. He set himself to be of service to his fellow prisoners and the warders, and very soon he was to the front again, for "The Lord was with him." When he came to be exalted, and Pharaoh made him to be ruler over Egypt, notice what he did. He did not strut about, or take his case at court; he did not stop to enjoy his honors in peace, and leave others to do the business, but he set to his work personally and at once. Read Genesis 41:45: "And Joseph went out over all the land of Egypt." Then read the next verse: "And Joseph went out from the presence of Pharaoh, and went throughout all the land of Egypt." No sooner did he get the office than he gave himself to the execution of it, personally inspecting the whole country. Many are so worn out by their toils in getting a place that they have no strength left for performing its duties. When they get a new situation, their first consideration is how they shall spend the profits of it. Place hunters seldom try to make themselves fit for the situation, but crave the position whether they are fit for it or not. Many when they get an office are exceedingly skillful in showing how not to do it; they get into the circumlocution office, and pass on everything to the next clerk, and, he to the next, so that nothing is done with them: procrastination is the very hinge of business, and punctuality the thief of time. They do as little as they can for the money, upon the theory that if you are too energetic your labors will be too cheap. Joseph, however, was not of that sort, for no sooner was he made commissioner-general of Egypt, than he was up to his eyes in the task of building storehouses, and gathering up grain to fill them. By his wonderful economic policy he supplied the people in the time of famine, and in the process the power of Pharaoh was greatly strengthened. The Lord was with him, therefore he did not think of the honor to which he had been promoted, but of the responsibility which had been laid upon him, and he gave himself wholly to his great work. That is what you and I must do if we are to give practical proof that God is with us.

But notice again, God was with Joseph, and *that made him tender and sympathetic.* Some men who are prompt enough in business are rough, coarse, hard; but not so Joseph. His tenderness distinguishes him; he is full of loving consideration. When he had prisoners in his charge, he did not treat them roughly, but with much consideration. He watched their countenances, inquired into their troubles, and was willing to do all in his power for them. This was one secret of his success in life; he was everybody's friend. He who is willing to be the servant of all, the same shall be the chief of all. God was with Joseph, and taught him compassion, for God himself is very pitiful, and full of sympathy for the suffering.

Perhaps you will object to this, that Joseph seemed for a while to afflict and tantalize his brothers. By no means. He was seeking their good. The love he bore to them was wise and prudent. God, who is far more loving than Joseph, frequently afflicts us to bring us to repentance and to heal us of many evils. Joseph wished to bring his brethren into a right state of heart, and he succeeded in it, though the process was more painful to him than to them. At last he could not restrain himself, but burst into weeping before them all, for there was a big loving heart under the Egyptian garb of Joseph. He loved with all his soul, and so will every man who has God with him, for "God is love." If you do not love, God is not with you. If you go through the world selfish and morose, bitter, suspicious, bigoted, hard, the devil is with you, God is not; for where God is he expands the spirit, he causes us to love all mankind with the love of benevolence, and he makes us take a sweet complacency in the chosen brotherhood of Israel, so that we specially delight to do good to all those who are of the household of faith. This was a mark that God was with him.

Another mark of God's presence with Joseph is *his great wisdom.* He did everything as it ought to be done. You can scarcely alter anything in Joseph's life to improve it, and I think if I admire his wisdom in one thing more than another it is in his wonderful silence. It is easy to talk, comparatively, easy to talk well, but to be quiet is the difficulty. He never said a word, that I can learn, about Potiphar's wife. It seemed necessary to his own defense, but he would not accuse the woman; he let judgment go by default, and left her to her own conscience and her husband's cooler consideration. This showed great power; it is hard for a man to compress his lips, saying nothing when his character is at stake. So eloquent was Joseph in his silence that there is not a word of complaint throughout the whole record of his life. We cannot say that of all the Bible saints, for many of them complained bitterly, indeed we have whole books of lamentations. We do not condemn those who did complain, but we greatly admire those who, like sheep before the shearers, were dumb. The iron entered into his soul, but he does not tell us so; we look to the Psalms for that information; he bore in calm resignation all the great Father's will. When his brothers stood before him, the cruel men who sold him, he did not upbraid them, but he comforted them, saying, "Now therefore be not grieved, nor angry with yourselves, that ye sold me hither: for God did send me before you to preserve life." Making sweet excuse for them, he said, "And God sent me before you to preserve you a posterity in the earth, and to save yourselves by a great deliverance. So now it was not you that sent me hither, but God."

How different from the spirit of those people who pry about, seeking to discover faults, and when an imperfection is marked, they cry, "Look! Do you see that? I told you so. These good men are no better than they should be." Yes, it may be true that there are spots in the sun, but there are greater spots in your eyes or you would see more of the light. Those who see faults so read-ily have plenty of their own. Like the man who stole the goods and ran away, they try to turn the scent by calling, "thief, thief," after others. May God make us blind to the faults of his people, sooner than allow us to have a lynx eye for their flaws and an inventive faculty to ascribe ill motives to them. I wish we were as wisely silent as Joseph was. We may often repent of speech, but I think very seldom of silence. You may complain and be justified in the complaint, but you will have far more glory if you do not complain. For what was there, after all, for Joseph to complain of, since the Lord was with him? He was in prison: that is something to complain of. Yes, but if the Lord was with him the prison was no longer dreary. I would gladly go to prison any day if the Lord would be with me. Who would not? But Joseph was away from his beloved father, and the trotting of those little feet that be loved so much to hear—the feet of little brother Benjamin. I am sure Joseph always missed his mother's only other son, his only full brother. It was a great grief to him to be away from home, but still he was quiet, calm, and happy. God is with him if Ben-jamin is not; if father Jacob is away, God is present; thus he finds no cause for bitter lament, but much reason for accepting his lot and doing his best in each condition.

"God was with him," and this is the last evidence I give of it, that *he was kept faithful to the covenant*, faithful to Israel and to Israel's God right through. Pharaoh gave him in marriage the daughter of a priest; and the priests were the highest class throughout Egypt, and Joseph was thus promoted to be of the nobility by marriage, as well as to be at the head of all the nobility by office. They cried before him, "Bow the knee," and everyone honored him throughout all the land of Egypt. Yet he would not be an Egyptian: he was an Israelite still, and his good old father, when he came down into Egypt, found him one of the family in heart and soul. His father's blessing was greatly prized by him, and he obtained it for himself and for his sons. I notice with much pain that many professors who prosper in this world have not God with them, for they turn into Egyptians: they do not now care for the simple worship of God's people, but they sigh for something more showy and more respectable. They want society, and so they seek out a fashionable church, and swallow their principles. They lay it all upon their children, for who can expect young ladies and gentlemen to attend an ordinary meetinghouse, where such low people go? For the sake of the young people they are bound to mix with society, and so they leave their principles, their people, and their God. They become Egyptians; indeed, some of them would become devil worshipers to gain rank and status. Off they go to Egypt, shoals of them, I have seen it, and shall see it again. If some of you get rich I dare say you will do the same; it seems to be the way of men. As soon as a professor prospers in the world he is ashamed of the truth he once loved. Such apostates will find it heavy work to die. Verily, I say unto you, instead of their being ashamed of us, we have good reason to be ashamed of them, for it is to their disgrace that they cannot be content to associate with God's chosen because they happen to be poor and perhaps illiterate.

Joseph stuck to his people and to their God: though he must live in Egypt, he will not be an Egyptian; he will not even leave his dead body to lie in an Egyptian pyramid. The Egyptians built a very costly tomb for Joseph: it stands to this day, but his body is not there. "I charge you," says he, "take my bones with you; for I do not belong to Egypt, my place is in the land of promise." "He gave commandment concerning his bones." Let others do as they will; as for me, my lot is cast with those who follow the Lord fully. Yes, my Lord, where you dwell, I will dwell; your people shall be my people, and your God my God, and may my children be your children to the last generation. If the Lord is with you, that is what you will say, but if he is not with you, and you prosper in the world, and increase in riches, you will turn your back on Christ and his people, and we shall have to say, as Paul did, "Demas hath forsaken me, having loved this present world."

III. Third, let us observe, *the result of God's being with Joseph.*

The result was that "he was a prosperous man"; but notice that, although the Lord was with Joseph, *it did not screen him from hatred.* The Lord was with him, but his brethren hated him. Yes, and if the Lord loves a man, the world will spite him. We know that we are God's children, because the adversaries of God are our adversaries. Furthermore, "The LORD was with Joseph," but it did not screen him from *temptation* of the worst kind: it did not prevent his mistress casting her wicked eyes upon him. The best of men may be tempted to the worst of crimes. The presence of God did not screen him from *slander*: the base woman accused him of outrageous wickedness, and God permitted Potiphar to believe her. You and I would have said, "If the Lord be with us, how can this evil happen to us?" Ah, but the Lord was with him, and yet he was a slandered man. No, the divine presence did not screen him from *pain*: he sat in prison wearing fetters till the iron entered into his soul, and yet the Lord was with him. That presence did not save him from *disappointment*. He said to the butler, "Think of me when it is well with thee"; but the butler altogether forgot him. Everything may seem to go against you, and yet God may be with you. The Lord does not promise you that you shall have what looks like prosperity, but you shall have what is real prosperity in the best sense.

Now, what did God's being with Joseph do for him? First, *it saved him from gross sin*. He flees, he shuts his ears: he flees and conquers; for God is with him. O young friend, if God is with you in the hour of temptation, you will want no better, no grander result than to remain perfectly pure, with garments unspotted by the flesh.

God was with him, and the next result was it *enabled him to act grandly*. Wherever he is he does the right thing, does it splendidly. If he is a slave his master finds that he never had such a servant before; if he is in prison, those dungeons were never charmed by the presence of such a ministering angel before; if he is exalted to be with Pharaoh, Pharaoh never had such a chancellor of the exchequer in Egypt before, never was Egyptian finance so prosperous.

In such a manner did God help Joseph that he was enabled to *fulfill a glorious destiny*, for if Noah be the world's second father, what shall we say of Joseph, but that he was its foster nurse? The human race had died of famine if Joseph's foresight had not laid by in store the produce of the seven plenteous years, for there was a famine over all lands. The breasts of Joseph nourished all mankind. It was no mean position for the young Hebrew to occupy, to be manager of the commissariat of the whole known world. If God be with us we shall fulfill a noble destiny too. It may not be so widely known, so visible to human eye, but life is always ennobled by the presence of God.

Also *it gave him a very happy life*, for taking the life of Joseph all through, it is an enviable one. Nobody would think of putting him down among the miserable. If we had to make a selection of unhappy men, we certainly should not think of Joseph. No, it was a great life and a happy life; and such will yours be if God be with you.

And, to finish, God gave Joseph and his family *a double portion in Israel,* which never happened to any other of the twelve sons of Jacob. Jacob said, "And now thy two sons, Ephraim and Manasseh, which were born unto thee in the land of Egypt before I came unto thee into Egypt are mine; as Reuben and Simeon they shall be mine," thus making them into a tribe each. Ephraim and Manasseh each stood at the head of a tribe as if they had been actually sons of Jacob. Levi is taken out of the twelve, and provision is made for the Levites as servants of God, and then Ephraim and Manasseh are put in, so that Joseph's house figures twice among the twelve. There are two Josephs in Israel but only one Judah. Joseph has a double portion of the kingdom. Those who begin early with God, and stand fast to the end, and hold to God both in trouble and prosperity, shall see their children brought to the Lord, and in their children they shall possess the double, yes, the Lord shall render unto them double for all they may lose in honor for his name's sake. It may be they shall live to see the hand of the Lord upon their children and their children's children, and to them shall be fulfilled the word, "In thee shall Israel bless, saying, God make thee as Ephraim and as Manasseh." Let us seek after a double part with God's people by keeping heartily with them. Who is willing to suffer with them that he may reign with them? Who is willing to cast the riches of Egypt behind his back that he may have a double portion in the Promised Land, the land flowing with milk and honey? I think I hear some of you say, "Here I am, sir. I shall be glad enough to share with God's people, be it what it may." Carry Christ's cross and you shall wear Christ's crown. Go with him through the mire and through the slough, and you shall be with him in the palaces of glory; you shall share a double portion with him in the day of his appearing. This can only be because the Lord is with you: that must be the beginning and end of it. "The LORD was with Joseph"; O Lord, be with us. O thou, whose name is Emmanuel, God with us, be with us, henceforth and forever. Amen and amen.

Moses: Moses' Decision

⤙ꙮ⤚

Delivered on Lord's Day morning, July 28, 1872, at the Metropolitan Tabernacle, Newington. No. 1063.

> *By faith Moses, when he was come to years, refused to be called the son of*
> *Pharaoh's daughter; choosing rather to suffer affliction with the people of*
> *God, than to enjoy the pleasures of sin for a season; esteeming the reproach*
> *of Christ greater riches than the treasures in Egypt: for he had respect unto*
> *the recompense of the reward.*—HEBREWS 11:24–26

Last Sabbath day we spoke upon the faith of Rahab. We had then to mention her former unsavory character, and to show that, notwithstanding, her faith triumphed, and both saved her and produced good works. Now it has occurred to me that some persons would say, "This faith is, no doubt, a very suitable thing for Rahab and persons of that class; a people destitute of sweetness and light may follow after the gospel, and it may be a very proper and useful thing for them, but the better sort of people will never take to it." I thought it possible that, with a sneer of contempt, some might reject all faith in God, as being unworthy of persons of a higher condition of life and another manner of education. We have, therefore, taken the case of Moses, which stands as a direct contrast to that of Rahab, and we trust it may help to remove the sneer; though, indeed, that may be of small consequence, for if a man is given to sneering it is hardly worthwhile to waste five minutes in reasoning with him. The scorner is usually a person so inconsiderable that his scoffing deserves to be unconsidered. He who is great at sneering is good for nothing else, and he may as well be left to fulfill his vocation.

It occurred to me also that, peradventure, some might, in all seriousness, say, "I have, through the providence of God, and the circumstances which surround me, been kept from outward sin; moreover, I am not a member of the lowest ranks, and do not belong to the class of persons of whom Rahab would be a suitable representative. In fact, I have, by the providence of God, been placed in a choice position, and can, without egotism, claim a superior character." It is possible that such persons may feel as if they were placed under a disadvantage by this very superiority. The thought has passed over their mind, "The gospel is for sinners; it evidently comes to the chief of sinners and blesses them. We are free to admit that we are sinners, but peradventure, because we have not sinned so openly, we may not be so conscious of the sin, and consequently our mind may not be so well prepared to receive the abounding grace of God which comes to the vilest of the vile." I have known some who have almost wished that they were literally like the prodigal son in his wanderings, that they might be more readily like him in his return. It is altogether a mistake under which they labor, but it is by no means an uncommon one. Peradventure, as we introduce to their notice one of the heroes of faith, who was a man of noble rank, high education, and pure character, they may be led to correct their thoughts. Moses belonged to the noblest order of men, but he was saved by faith alone, even by the same faith which saved Rahab. This faith moved him to the faithful service of God and to a self-denial unparalleled. My earnest prayer is that you who are moral, amiable, and educated, may see in the action of Moses an example for yourselves. No longer despise a life of faith in God. It is the one thing which you lack, the one thing above all others needful. Are you young men of high position? Such was Moses. Are you men of spotless character? Such also was he. Are you now in a position where to follow out conscience will cost you dear? Moses endured as seeing him who is invisible, and though for a while a loser he is now an eternal gainer by the loss. May the Spirit of God incline you to follow in the path of faith, virtue, and honor, where you see such a man as Moses leading the way.

We shall first consider the decided action of Moses; and, second, the source of his decision of character—it was "by faith." Third, we shall look into those arguments by which his faith directed his action; after which we shall briefly reflect upon those practical lessons which the subject suggests.

I. And first let us observe *the decided action of Moses.*

"When he was come to years, he refused to be called the son of Pharaoh's daughter." We need not narrate the stories which are told by Josephus and other ancient writers with regard to the early days of Moses, such as, for instance, his taking the crown of Pharaoh and trampling upon it. These things may be true; it is equally possible that they are pure fiction. The Spirit of God has certainly taken no notice of them in holy Scripture, and what he does not think worth recording we need not think worth considering. Nor shall I more than hint at answers to the question why it was that Moses remained no less than forty years in the court of Pharaoh, and doubtless during that time was called "the son of Pharaoh's daughter," and, if he did not enjoy the pleasures of sin, at any rate, had his share in the treasures of Egypt. It is just possible that he was not a converted man up to the age of forty. Probably during his early days he was to all intents and purposes an Egyptian, an eager student, a great proficient in Egyptian wisdom, and also, as Stephen tells us in the Acts, "a man mighty in words and in deeds." During those early days he was familiar with philosophers and warriors, and perhaps in his engrossing pursuits he forgot his nationality.

We see the hand of God in his being forty years in the court of Pharaoh; whatever of evil or indecision in him may have kept him there we see the good result which God brought out of it, for he became by his experience and observation the better able to rule a nation, and a fitter instrument in the hand of God for fashioning the Israelitish state into its appointed form. Perhaps during the forty years he had been trying to do what a great many are aiming at just now; he was trying whether he could not serve God and remain the son of Pharaoh's daughter too. Perhaps he was of the mind of our brethren in a certain church who protest against but still remain in that church which gives to ritualism the fullest liberty. Perhaps he thought he could share the treasures of Egypt and yet bear testimony with Israel. He would be known as a companion of the priests of Isis and Osiris, and yet at the same time would bear honest witness for Jehovah. If he did not attempt this impossibility others in all ages have done so. It may be he quieted himself by saying that he had such remarkable opportunities for usefulness that he did not like to throw them up by becoming identified with the Israelitish dissenters of the period. An open avowal of his private sentiments would shut him out from good society, and especially from the court, where it was very evident that his influence was great and beneficial. It is just possible that the very feeling which still keeps so many good people in a wrong place may have operated upon Moses till he was forty years of age; but then, having reached the prime of his manhood, and having come under the influence of faith, he broke away from the ensnaring temptation, as I trust many of our worthy brethren will before long be able to do. Surely they will not always maintain a confederacy with the allies of Rome, but will be men enough to be free. If when Moses was a child he spoke as a child, and thought as a child, when he became a man he put away his childish ideas of compromise; if, when he was a young man, he thought he might conceal a part of the truth, and so might hold his position, when he came to ripe years enough to know what the truth fully was he scorned all compromise and came out boldly as the servant of the living God.

The Spirit of God directs our eye to the time when Moses came to years, that is to say, when his first forty years of life were over; then, without any hesitation he refused to be called the son of Pharaoh's daughter, and took his part with the despised people of God.

I beg you to consider first, *who he was that did this*. He was a man of education, for he was learned in all the wisdom of the Egyptians. Somebody says he does not suppose the wisdom of the Egyptians was anything very great. No, and the wisdom of the English is not much greater. Future ages will laugh as much at the wisdom of the English as we now laugh at the wisdom of the Egyptians. The human wisdom of one age is the folly of the next. Philosophy, so called, what is it but the concealment of ignorance under hard names, and the arrangement of mere guesses into elaborate theories? In comparison with the eternal light of God's Word, all the knowledge of men is "not light but darkness visible." Men of education, as a rule, are not ready to acknowledge the living God. Philosophy in its self-conceit despises the infallible revelation of the Infinite, and will not come to the light lest it be reproved. In all ages, when a man has considered himself to be wise, he has almost invariably condemned the infinite wisdom. Had he been truly wise, he would have humbly bowed before the Lord of all, but being only nominally so, he said, "Who is the Lord?" Not many great men after the flesh, not many mighty are chosen. Did not our Lord himself say it, and his word is for all time, "I thank thee, O Father, Lord of heaven and earth, that thou hast hid these things from the wise and prudent, and hast revealed them unto babes"? But yet, sometimes a man of education like Moses is led by the blessing of heaven to take the side of truth, and of the right, and when it is so, let the Lord be magnified!

Besides being a man of education, he was *a person of high rank*. He had been adopted by Thermuthis, the daughter of Pharaoh, and it is possible, though we cannot be sure of it, that he was the next heir by adoption to the Egyptian crown. It is said that the king of Egypt had no other child, and that his daughter had no son, and that Moses would, therefore, have become the king of Egypt. Yet, great as he was and mighty at court, he joined with the oppressed people of God. May God grant that we may see many eminent men bravely standing up for God and for his truth, and repudiating the religion of men, but if they do, it will be a miracle of mercy indeed, for few of the great ones have ever done so. Here and there in heaven may be found a king, and here and there in the church may be found one who wears a coronet and prays; but how hardly shall they that have riches enter into the kingdom of heaven. When they do so God be thanked for it.

In addition to this, remember that Moses was *a man of great ability*. We have evidence of that in the administrative skill with which he managed the affairs of Israel in the wilderness; for though he was inspired of God, yet his own natural ability was not superseded but directed. He was a poet: "Then sung Moses and the children of Israel this song unto the Lord." That memorable poem at the Red Sea is a very masterly ode, and proves the incomparable ability of the writer. The Ninetieth Psalm also shows the range of his poetic powers. He was both prophet, priest, and king in the midst of Israel, and a man second to no man save that Man who was more than man. No other man I know of comes so near in the glory of his character to Christ as Moses does, so that we find the two names linked together in the praise of heaven—"they sing the song of Moses the servant of God, and of the Lamb." Thus you see he was a truly eminent man, yet he cast in his lot with God's people. It is not many that will do this, for the Lord has usually chosen the weak things to confound the mighty, and the things that are not to bring to naught the things that are, that no flesh should glory in his presence. Yet here he, who will have mercy on whom he will have mercy, took this great man, this wise man, and gave him grace to be decided in the service of his God. Should I address such a one this morning I would anxiously pray that a voice from the excellent glory may call him forth to the same clear line of action.

Next, consider *what sort of society Moses felt compelled to leave*. In coming forth from Pharaoh's court he must separate from all the courtiers and men of high degree, some of whom may have been very estimable people. There is always a charm about the society of the great, but every bond was severed by the resolute spirit of Moses. I do not doubt that being learned in all the wisdom of Egypt, such a man as Moses would be always welcome in the various circles of science; but he relinquished all his honors among the elite of learning to bear the reproach of Christ. Neither great men nor learned men could hold him when his conscience had once pointed out the path. Be sure, also, that he had to tear himself away from many a friend. In the course of forty years one would suppose he had formed associations that were very dear and tender, but to the regret of many he associated himself with the unpopular party, whom the king sought to crush, and therefore no courtier could henceforth acknowledge him. For forty years he lived in the solitude of the desert, and he only returned to smite the land of Egypt with plague, so that his separation from all his former friendships must have been complete. But, O truehearted spirit, should it break every fond connection, should it tear your soul away from all you love, if your God requires it, let the sacrifice be made at once. If your faith has shown you that to occupy your present position involves complicity with error or sin, then break away, by God's help, without further parley. Let not the nets of the fowler hold you, but as God gives you freedom, mount untrammeled and praise your God for liberty. Jesus left the angels of heaven for your sake; can you not leave the best of company for his sake?

But I marvel most at Moses when I consider not only who he was and the company he had to forgo, but *the persons with whom he must associate,* for in truth the followers of the true God were not, in their own persons, a lovable people at that time. Moses was willing to take upon himself the reproach of Christ, and to bear the affliction of God's people when, I venture to observe again, there was nothing very attractive in the people themselves. They were wretchedly poor; they were scattered throughout all the land as mere drudges, engaged in brick making, and this brick making, which was imposed upon them for the very purpose of breaking down their spirit, had done its work all too well. They were utterly spiritless, they possessed no leaders, and were not prepared to have followed them if they had arisen. When Moses, having espoused their cause, informed them that God had sent him, they received him at first, but when the prophet's first action prompted Pharaoh to double their toil by an enactment that they should not be supplied with straw, they upbraided Moses at once; even as forty years before, when he interfered in their quarrels, one of them said, "Wilt thou slay me as thou didst the Egyptian yesterday?" They were literally a herd of slaves, broken down, crushed and depressed. It is one of the worst things about slavery that it unmans men and unfits them even for generations for the full enjoyment of liberty. Even when slaves receive liberty we cannot expect them to act as those would do who were free born, for in slavery the iron enters into the very soul and binds the spirit.

Thus it is clear that the Israelites were not very select company for the highly educated Moses to unite with: though a prince he must make common cause with the poor; though a free man he must mingle with slaves; though a man of education he must mix with ignorant people; though a man of spirit he must associate with spiritless serfs. How many would have said, "No, I cannot do that; I know what church I ought to unite with if I follow Scriptures fully, and obey in all things my Lord's will; but then they are so poor, so illiterate, and their place of worship is so far from being architecturally beautiful. Their preacher is a plain, blunt man, and they themselves are not refined. Scarce a dozen of the whole sect can keep a carriage; I should be shut out of society if I joined with them." Have we not heard this base reasoning till we are sick of it, and yet it operates widely upon this brainless, heartless generation. Are there none left who love truth even when she wears no trappings? Are there none who love the gospel better than pomp and show? Where God raises up a Moses, what cares he how poor his brethren may be? "They are God's people," says he, "and if they are very poor, I must help them the more liberally. If they be oppressed and depressed, so much the more reason why I should come to their aid. If they love God and his truth, I am their fellow soldier, and will be at their side in the battle." I have no doubt Moses thought all this over, but his mind was made up, and he took his place promptly.

In addition to other matters, one mournful thing must be said of Israel, which must have cost Moses much pain. He found that among God's people there were some who brought no glory to God, and were very weak in their principles. He did not judge the whole body by the faults of some, but by their standards and their institutions: and he saw that the Israelites, with all their faults, were the people of God, while the Egyptians, with all their virtues, were not so. Now it is for each one of us to try the spirits by the Word of God, and then fearlessly to follow out our convictions. Where is Christ recognized as the head of the church? Where are the Scriptures really received as the rule of faith? Where are the doctrines of grace clearly believed? Where are the ordinances practiced as the Lord delivered them? For with that people will I go, their cause shall be my cause, their God shall be my God. We look not for a perfect church this side of heaven, but we do look for a church free from popery and sacramentalism and false doctrine; and if we cannot find one, we will wait until we can, but with falsehood and priestcraft we will never enter into fellowship. If there be faults with the brethren, it is our duty to bear with them patiently, and pray for grace to overcome the evil; but with papists and rationalists we must not join in affinity, or God will require it at our hands.

Consider now *what Moses left by siding with Israel*. He left honor—he "refused to be called the son of Pharaoh's daughter"; he left pleasure—for he refused to "enjoy the pleasures of sin for a season"; and, according to our apostle, he left wealth as well, for in taking up the reproach of Christ, he renounced "the treasures of Egypt." Very well, then, if it comes to this, if to follow God and to be obedient to him I have to lose my position in society and become a pariah; if I must abjure a thousand pleasures, and if I am deprived of emoluments and income, yet the demands of duty must be complied with. Martyrs gave their lives of old, are there none left who will give their livings? If there be true faith in a man's heart, he will not deliberate which of the two to choose, beggary or compromise with error. He will esteem the reproach of Christ to be greater riches than the treasures of Egypt.

Consider yet once more *what Moses espoused* when he left the court. He espoused abounding trial, "choosing rather to suffer affliction with the people of God"; and he espoused reproach, for he "esteemed the reproach of Christ greater riches than the treasures of Egypt." O Moses, if you must needs join with Israel there is no present reward for you; you have nothing to gain but all to lose; you must do it out of pure principle, out of love to God, out of a full persuasion of the truth, for the tribes have no honors or wealth to bestow. You will receive affliction, and that is all. You will be called a fool, and people will think they have good reason for so doing. It is just the same today. If any man today will go without the camp to seek the Lord, if he go forth unto Christ without the gate, he must do it out of love to God and to his Christ, and for no other motive. The people of God have no benefices or bishoprics to offer; they therefore beseech men to count the cost. When a fervent convert said to our Lord, "Lord, I will follow thee whithersoever thou goest," he received for answer, "Foxes have holes and the birds of the air have nests, but I, the Son of man, have not where to lay my head." To this hour truth offers no dowry but herself to those who will espouse her. Abuse, contempt, hard fare, ridicule, misrepresentation—these are the wages of consistency; and if better comes it is not to be reckoned on. If any man be of a noble enough spirit to love the truth for truth's sake, and God for God's sake, and Christ for Christ's sake, let him enlist with those of like mind; but if he seek anything over and above that, if he desire to be made famous or to gain power or to be well beneficed, he had better keep his place among the cowardly dirt eaters who swarm around us. The church of God bribes no man. She has no mercenary rewards to proffer, and would scorn to use them if she had. If to serve the Lord be not enough reward, let those who look for more go their selfish way: if heaven be not enough, let those who can despise it seek their heaven below. Moses, in taking up with the people of God, decidedly, and once for all, acted most disinterestedly, without any promise from the right side, or any friend to aid him in the change; for the truth's sake, for the Lord's sake, he renounced everything; content to be numbered with the downtrodden people of God.

II. Now, second, what was *the source of Moses' decision?*

Scripture says it was faith, otherwise some would insist upon it that it was the force of blood. "He was by birth an Israelite, and therefore," say they, "the instincts of nature prevailed." Our text assigns a very different reason. We know right well that the sons of godly parents are not led to adore the true God by reason of their birth. Grace does not run in the blood; sin may, but righteousness does not. Who does not remember sons of renowned lovers of the gospel, who are now far gone in ritualism? It was faith, not blood, which impelled Moses in the way of truth. Neither was it eccentricity which led him to espouse the side which was oppressed. We have sometimes found a man of pedigree and position who has associated with persons of quite another rank and condition, simply because he never could act like anybody else, and must live after his own odd fashion. It was not so with Moses. All his life through you cannot discover a trace of eccentricity in him: he was sober, steady, law abiding; what if I say he was a concentric man, for his center was in the right place, and he moved according to the dictates of prudence. Not thus can his decision be accounted for. Neither was he hurried on by some sudden excitement when there burned within his soul fierce patriotic fires which made him more fervent than prudent. No, there may have been some haste in his slaying the Egyptian on the first occasion, but then he had forty more years to think it over, and yet he never repented his choice, but held on to the oppressed people of God, and still refused to think of himself as the son of Pharaoh's daughter. It was faith then, faith alone, that enabled the prophet of Sinai to arrive at his decision, and to carry it out.

What faith had he? First, he had *faith in Jehovah*. It is possible that Moses had seen the various gods of Egypt, even as we see them now in the drawings which have been copied from their temples and pyramids. We find there the sacred cat, the sacred ibis, the sacred crocodile, and all kinds of creatures which were reverenced as deities; and in addition there were hosts of strange idols, compounded of man, and beast, and bird, which stand in our museums to this day, and were once the objects of the idolatrous reverence of the Egyptians. Moses was weary of all this symbolism. He knew in his own heart that there was one God, one only God, and he would have nothing to do with Amun, Pithah, or Maut. Truly, my very soul cries to God, that noble spirits may in these days grow weary of the gods of ivory and ebony and silver, which are adored under the name of crosses and crucifixes, and may come to abominate that most degrading and sickening of all idolatries in which a man makes a god with flour and water, bows down before it, and then swallows it, thus sending his god into his belly, and, I might say worse. The satirist said of the Egyptians, "O happy people, whose gods grow in their own gardens"; we may say with equal force, O happy people, whose gods are baked in their own ovens! Is not this the lowest form of superstition that ever debased the intellect of man. Oh, that brave and true hearts may be led to turn away from such idolatry, and abjure all association with it, and say, "No, I cannot, and dare not. There is one God that made heaven and earth, there is a pure Spirit who upholdeth all things by the power of his might, I will worship him alone; and I will worship him after his own law, without images or other symbols, for has he not forbidden them." Has he not said, "Thou shalt not make unto thee any graven image, or any likeness of anything that is in heaven above, or that is in the earth beneath, or that is in the water under the earth: thou shalt not bow down thyself to them, nor serve them: for I the LORD thy God am a jealous God"? Oh, that God would give to men faith to know there is but one God, and that the one God is not to be worshiped with man-ordained rites and ceremonies, for he is "a Spirit; and they that worship him must worship him in spirit and in truth"! That one truth, if it were to come with power from heaven into men's minds, would shiver St. Peter's and St. Paul's from their topmost cross to their lowest crypt; for what do these two churches teach us now but sheer clear idolatry, the one of rule and the other by permission, for now men who boldly worship what they call the "sacred elements" have leave and license to exercise their craft within the Church of England. Every man who loves his God should shake his skirts clear of these abominations, and I pray God that we may find many a Moses who shall do so.

The faith of Moses also *rested in Christ*. "Christ had not come," says one. No, but he was to come, and Moses looked to that coming One. He cast his eye through the ages that were to intervene, and he saw before him the Shiloh of whom dying Jacob sang. He knew the ancient promise which had been given to the fathers, that in the seed of Abraham should all the nations of the earth be blessed; and he was willing, in order to share in the blessing, to take his part in the reproach. Dear friends, we shall never have a thorough faith in God unless we have also faith in Jesus Christ. Men have tried long, and tried hard, to worship the Father apart from the Son; but there stands it, and it always will be so: "No man cometh unto the Father but by me." You get away from the worship of the Father if you do not come through the mediation and atonement of the Son of God. Now, though Moses did not know concerning Christ all that is now revealed to us, yet he had faith in the coming Messiah, and that faith gave strength to his mind. Those are the men to suffer who have received Christ Jesus the Lord. If any man should ask me what made the Covenanters such heroes as they were; what made our Puritan forefathers fearless before their foes; what led the Reformers to protest and the martyrs to die; I would reply, it was faith in the invisible God, coupled with faith in that dear Son of God who is God incarnate. Believing in him they felt such love within their bosoms, that for love of him they could have died a thousand deaths.

But then, in addition to this, Moses had faith *in reference to God's people*. Upon that I have already touched. He knew that the Israelites were God's chosen, that Jehovah had made a covenant with them, that despite all their faults, God would not break his covenant with his own people, and he knew, therefore, that their cause was God's cause, and being God's cause it was the cause of right, the cause of truth. Oh, it is a grand thing when a man has such faith that he says, "It is nothing to me what other people do or think or believe; I shall act as God would have me. It is nothing to me what I am commanded to do by my fellow creatures, nothing to me what fashion says, nothing to me what my parents say, as far as religion is concerned; the truth is God's star, and I will follow wherever it may lead me. If it should make me a solitary man, if I should espouse opinions which no one else ever believed in, if I should have to go altogether outside the camp, and break away from every connection, all this shall be as immaterial to me as the small dust of the balance; but if a matter be true, I will believe it, and I will propound it, and I will suffer for its promulgation; and if another doctrine be a lie, I will not be friends with it, no, not for a solitary moment; I will not enter into fellowship with falsehood, no, not for an hour. If a course be right and true, through floods and flames if Jesus leads me, I will pursue it." That seems to me to be the right spirit, but where do you find it nowadays? The modern spirit mutters, "We are all right, every one of us." He who says yes is right, and he who says no is also right. You hear a man talk with mawkish sentimentality which he calls Christian charity. "Well, I am of opinion that if a man is a Muslim or a Catholic or a Mormon, or a Dissenter, if he is sincere, he is all right." They do not quite include devil worshipers, thugs, and cannibals yet, but if things go on they will accept them into the happy family of the Broad Church. Such is the talk and cant of this present age, but I bear my witness that there is no truth in it, and I call upon every child of God to protest against it, and, like Moses, to declare that he can have no complicity with such a confederacy. There is truth somewhere, let us find it; the lie is not of the truth, let us abhor it. There is a God, let us follow him, and it cannot be that false gods are gods too. Surely truth is of some value to the sons of men, surely there must be something worth holding, something worth contending for, and something worth dying for; but it does not appear nowadays as if men thought so. May we have a respect for God's true church in the world which abides by the apostolic word and doctrine. Let us find it out, and join with it, and at its side fight for God and for his truth!

Once again, Moses had faith in the "recompense of the reward." He said thus within himself, "I must renounce much, and reckon to lose rank, position, and treasure; but I expect to be a gainer notwithstanding, for there will be a day when God shall judge the sons of men; I expect a judgment throne with its impartial balances, and I expect that those who serve God faithfully shall then turn out to have been the wise men and the right men, while those who truckled and bowed down to gain a present ease, shall find that they missed eternity while they were snatching after time, and that they bartered heaven for a paltry mess of pottage." With this upon his mind, you could not persuade Moses that he ought to compromise, and must not be uncharitable, and ought not to judge other good people, but should be large minded, and remember Pharaoh's daughter, and how kindly she had nurtured him, and consider what opportunities he had of doing good where he was; how he might befriend his poor brethren, what influence he might have over Pharaoh, how he might be the means of leading the princes and the people of Egypt in the right way, and perhaps God had raised him up on purpose to be there, who could tell, and so on, and so on, and so on—you know the Babylonian talk, for in these days you have all read or heard the plausible arguments of the deceivableness of unrighteousness, which in these last days teaches men to do evil that good may come. Moses cared for none of these things. He knew his duty, and did it, whatever might be the consequences. Every Christian man's duty is to believe the truth, and follow the truth, and leave results with God. Who dares do that? He is a king's son. But again I say it, who dares do that in these days?

III. Third, we are going to run over in our minds some of the *arguments which supported Moses* in his decided course of following God.

The first argument would be, he saw clearly that God was God and therefore must keep his word, must bring his people up out of Egypt and give them a heritage. Now he said within himself, "I desire to be on the right side. God is almighty, God is all truthful, God is altogether just. I am on God's side, and being on God's side I will prove my truthfulness by leaving the other side altogether."

Then, second, we have it in the text that he perceived the pleasures of sin to be but for a season. He said to himself, "I may have but a short time to live, and even if I live to a good old age, life at the longest is still short; and when I come to the close of life what a miserable reflection it will be that I have had all my pleasure, it is all over, and now I have to appear before God as a traitorous Israelite who threw up his birthright for the sake of enjoying the pleasures of Egypt." Oh, that men would measure everything in the scales of eternity! We shall be before the bar of God all of us in a few months or years, and then think you, how shall we feel? One will say, "I never thought about religion at all," and another, "I thought about it, but I did not think enough to come to any decision upon it. I went the way the current went." Another will say, "I knew the truth well enough, but I could not bear the shame of it; they would have thought me fanatical if I had gone through with it." Another will say, "I halted between two opinions. I hardly thought I was justified in sacrificing my children's position for the sake of being out and out a follower of truth." What wretched reflections will come over men who have sold the Savior as Judas did! What wretched deathbeds must they have who have been unfaithful to their consciences and untrue to their God! But oh! with what composure will the believer look forward to another world! He will say, "By grace I am saved, and I bless God I could afford to be ridiculed, I could bear to be laughed at. I could lose that situation; I could be turned out of that farm, and could be called a fool, and yet it did not hurt me. I found solace in the society of Christ; I went to him about it all, and I found that to be reproached for Christ was a sweeter thing than to possess all the treasures of Egypt. Blessed be his name! I missed the pleasures of the world, but they were no miss to me. I was glad to miss them, for I found sweeter pleasure in the company of my Lord, and now there are pleasures to come which shall never end." O brethren, to be out and out for Christ, to go to the end with him, even though it involve the loss of all things, this will pay in the long run. It may bring upon you much disgrace for the present, but that will soon be over, and then comes the eternal reward.

And, then, again, he thought within himself that even the pleasures, which did last for a season, while they lasted were not equal to the pleasure of being reproached for Christ's sake. This ought also to strengthen us, that the worst of Christ is better than the best of the world, that even now we have more joy as Christians, if we are sincere, than we could possibly derive from the sins of the wicked.

I have only this to say in closing. First, we ought all of us to be ready to part with everything for Christ, and if we are not we are not his disciples. "Master, you say a hard thing," says one. I say it yet again, for a greater Master has said it: "He that loveth son or daughter more than me is not worthy of me." "Unless a man forsake all that he has he cannot be my disciple." Jesus may not require you actually to leave anything, but you must be ready to leave everything if required.

The second observation is this: We ought to abhor the very thought of obtaining honor in this world by concealing our sentiments or by making compromises. If there be a chance of your being highly esteemed by holding your tongue, speak at once and do not run the risk of winning such dishonorable honor. If there be a hope of people praising you because you are so ready to yield your convictions, pray God to make you like a flint never to yield again; for what more damning glory could a man have than to be applauded for disowning his principles to please his fellowmen! From this may the Lord save us!

The third teaching is that we ought to take our place with those who truly follow God and the Scriptures, even if they are not altogether what we should like them to be. The place for an Israelite is with the Israelites, the place for a

Christian man is with Christian men. The place for a thorough-going disciple of the Bible and of Christ is with others who are such, and even if they should happen to be the lowest in the land, and the poorest of the poor, and the most illiterate and uneducated persons of the period, what is all this if their God loves them and if they love God? Weighed in the scales of truth the least one among them is worth ten thousand of the greatest ungodly men.

Lastly, we must all of us look to our faith. Faith is the main thing. You cannot make a thorough character without sincere faith. Begin there, dear hearer. If you are not a believer in Christ, if you believe not in the one God, may the Lord convert you, and give you now that precious gift! To try and raise a character which shall be good without a foundation of faith is to build upon the sand, and to pile up wood and hay and stubble; wood, hay, and stubble are very good things as wood, hay, and stubble, but they will not bear the fire; and as every Christian character will have to bear fire, it is well to build on the rock, and to build with such graces and fruits as will endure trial. You will have to be tried, and if you have, by sneaking through life as a coward, avoided all opposition and all ridicule, ask yourself whether you really are a disciple of that master of the house whom they called Beelzebub, whether you are truly a follower of that crucified Savior who said, "except a man take up his cross daily and follow me, he cannot be my disciple." Suspect the smooth places; be afraid of that perpetual peace which Christ declares he came to break. He says, "I came not to send peace on the earth, but a sword." He came to being fire upon the earth; and "what will I," said he, "if it be already kindled."

> Must I be carried to the skies
> On flowery beds of ease,
> While others fought to win the prize,
> And sailed through bloody seas.
>
> Sure I must fight if I would reign,
> Increase my courage, Lord,
> I'd bear the toil, endure the pain,
> Supported by thy Word. Amen.

Joshua: Strengthening Medicine for God's Servants

⤙※⤚

Delivered at the Metropolitan Tabernacle, Newington. Published in 1875. No. 1214.

I will not fail thee, nor forsake thee.—JOSHUA 1:5

No doubt God had spoken to Joshua before. He had been a man of faith for many years, and his faith enabled him to distinguish himself by such simple truthfulness of character and thoroughly faithful obedience to the Lord's will, that he and another were the only two left of the whole generation that came up out of Egypt. "Faithful among the faithless found," he survived where all else died; standing erect in full vigor, he might have been compared to a lone tree which spreads its verdant branches untouched by the axe which has leveled its fellows with the ground. But now Joshua was about to enter upon a new work: he had become king in Jeshurun instead of Moses, from a servant he had risen to be a ruler, and it now fell to his lot to lead the people across the Jordan, and marshal their forces for the conquest of the Promised Land. On the threshold of this high enterprise the Lord appears to his servant and says, "As I was with Moses, so I will be with thee: I will not fail thee, nor forsake thee." When God's people come into fresh positions, they shall have fresh revelations of his love. New dangers will bring new protections; new difficulties, new helps; new discouragements, new comforts; so that we may rejoice in tribulations also, because they are so many newly opened doors of God's mercy to us. We will be glad of our extremities, because they are divine opportunities. What the Lord said to Joshua was particularly encouraging, and it came precisely when he needed it. Great was his peril, and great was the consolation of that word from the Lord of hosts, "Have not I commanded thee? Be strong and of a good courage; be not afraid, neither be thou dismayed: for the Lord thy God is with thee whithersoever thou goest."

We will waste no time in preface, but at once consider the divine promise. "I will not fail thee, nor forsake thee."

I. Observe here, first, *the suitability of the consolation which these words gave to Joshua.* "I will not fail thee, nor forsake thee."

This must have been very cheering to him *in reference to himself.* He knew Moses, and he must have had a very high esteem for him. He was a great man, one of a thousand; scarcely among all that have been born of woman has there arisen a greater than Moses. Joshua had been his servant, and no doubt considered himself to be very far inferior to that great lawgiver. A sense of his own weakness comes over a man all the more from being associated with a grander mind. If you mingle with your inferiors you are apt to grow vain; but closely associated with superior minds there is a far greater probability that you will become depressed, and may think even less of yourself than humility might require; for humility is, after all, only a right estimate of our own powers. Joshua, therefore, may possibly have been somewhat despondent under a very pressing sense of his own deficiencies; and this cheering assurance would meet his case, "*I* will not fail thee: though thou be less wise, or meek, or courageous than Moses, *I* will not fail thee, nor forsake thee." If God be with our weakness it waxes strong; if he be with our folly it rises into wisdom; if he be with our timidity it gathers courage. It matters not how conscious a man may be of being nothing at all in himself, when he is conscious of the divine presence he even rejoices in his infirmity because the power of God doth rest upon him. If the Lord say unto the weakest man or woman here, "I will not fail thee, nor forsake thee," no craven thought will cross that ennobled Spirit; that word will nerve the trembler with a lionlike courage which no adversary will be able to daunt.

The consolation given to Joshua would be exceedingly suitable *in the presence of his enemies.* He had spied out the land, and he knew it to be inhabited by giant races, men famous both for stature and strength. The sons of Anak were there, and other tribes, described as "great, and many, and tall." He knew that they were a warlike people, and expert in the use of destructive implements of war, such as brought terror upon men, for they had chariots of iron. He knew, too, that their cities were of colossal dimensions—fortresses whose stones at this very day surprise the traveler, so that he asks what wondrous skill could have lifted those masses of rock into their places. The other spies had said that these Canaanites dwelled in cities that were walled up to heaven; and, though Joshua did not endorse that exaggeration, he was very well aware that the cities to be captured were fortresses of great strength, and the people to be exterminated were men of ferocious courage and great physical energy.

Therefore the Lord said, "I will not fail thee, nor forsake thee." What more was needed? Surely, in the presence of God, Anakim become dwarfs, strongholds become as a lodge in a garden of cucumbers, and chariots of iron are as thistledown upon the hillside driven before the blast. What is strong against the most High? What is formidable in opposition to Jehovah? "If God be for us, who can be against us?" They that be with us are more than they that be against us, when once the Lord of hosts is seen in our ranks. "Therefore will we not fear, though the earth be removed, the mountains be carried into the midst of the sea." Though a host should encamp against us, our heart shall not fear: though war should rise against us, in this will we be confident.

This consolation, too, was *sufficient for all supplies*. Perhaps Joshua knew that the manna was no longer to fall. In the wilderness the supply of heavenly bread was continuous, but when they crossed the Jordan they must quarter on the enemy; and with the myriads of people that were under Joshua's command, the matter of providing for them must have been no trifle. According to some computations, nearly three millions of people came up out of Egypt: I scarcely credit the computation and am inclined to believe that the whole matter of the numbers of the Old Testament is not yet understood, and that a better knowledge of the Hebrew tongue will lead to the discovery that the figures have been frequently misunderstood; but still a very large number of people came with Joshua to the edge of the wilderness, and crossed the Jordan into the land of Canaan. Who was to provide for all these hungry bands? Joshua might have said, "Shall all the flocks and the herds be slain for this great multitude, and will the sea yield up her fish, when the manna ceases? How shall these people be fed?" "I will not fail thee, nor forsake thee" was a supply which would meet all the demands of the commissariat. They might eat to the full, for God would find them food; their clothes might wax old upon them now that the miracle of the wilderness would cease, for new garments would be found for them in the wardrobes of their enemies. When the Lord opens all his granaries none shall lack for bread, and when he unlocks his wardrobes none shall go bare. So that there was no room for anxiety in Joshua's mind. As for himself, if weak, this made him strong; as for his enemies, if they were powerful, this promise made him stronger than they; and as for the needs of Israel, if they were great, this promise supplied them all.

Surely this word must often have brought charming consolation to the heart of the son of Nun *when he saw the people failing him*. There was only the venerable Caleb left of all his comrades with whom he had shared the forty years' march through the great and terrible wilderness; Caleb and he were the last two sheaves of the great harvest, and they were both like shocks of corn fully ripe for the garner. Old men grow lonely, and small wonder is it if they do. I have heard them say that they live in a world where they are not known, now that, one by one, all their old friends are gone home, and they are left alone—like the last swallow of autumn when all its fellows have sought a sunnier clime. Yet the Lord says, "I will not forsake thee: I shall not die: I am ever with thee. Thy Friend in heaven will live on as long as thou dost." As for the generation which had sprung up around Joshua, they were very little better than their fathers; they turned back in the day of battle, even the children of Ephraim, when they were armed and carried bows. They were very apt to go aside into the most provoking sin. Joshua had as hard a task with them as Moses had, and it was enough to break the heart of Moses to have to do with them. The Lord seems to bid him put no confidence in them, neither to be discomfited if they should be false and treacherous: "I will not fail thee: *they* may, but *I* will not. I will not forsake thee. They may prove cowards and traitors, but I will not desert thee." Oh, what a blessed thing it is in a false and fickle world, where he that eats bread with us lifts up his heel against us, where the favorite counselor becomes an Ahithophel, and turns his wisdom into crafty hate, to know that "there is a friend that sticketh closer than a brother," One who is faithful and gives us sure tokens of a love which many waters cannot quench.

I might thus dwell upon this point, and show that the consolatory promise has as many facets as a well-cut diamond, each one reflecting the light of divine consolation upon the eye of Joshua's faith. But we will come to other matters.

II. Second, *at what times may we consider this promise to be spoken to ourselves?*

It is all very well to listen to it, as spoken to Joshua, but, O God, if you would speak thus to us how consoled would we be! Do you ever do so? May *we* be so bold as to believe that thus you comfort *us*? Beloved, the whole run of Scripture speaks to the same effect to men of like mind with Joshua. No Scripture is of private interpretation: no text has spent itself upon the person who first received it. God's comforts are like wells, which no one man or set of men can drain dry, however mighty may be their thirst. A well may be opened for Hagar, but that well is never closed, and any other wanderer may drink at it. The fountain of our text first gushed forth to refresh Joshua, but if we are in Joshua's position, and are of his character, we may bring our water pots and fill them to the brim.

Let me mention when I think we may safely feel that God says to us, "I will not fail thee, nor forsake thee." Surely it is when we are *called to do God's work*. Joshua's work was the Lord's work. It was God who had given the country to the people, and who had said, "I will drive out the Canaanite from before thee," and Joshua was God's executioner, the sword in the hand of the Lord for the driving out of the condemned races. He was not entering upon a quixotic engagement of his own choosing and devising; he had not elected himself, and selected his own work, but God had called him to it, put him in the office and bidden him do it, and therefore he said to him, "I will not fail thee, nor forsake thee." Brother, are you serving God? Do you live to win souls? Is it your grand object to be the instrument in God's hand of accomplishing his purposes of grace to the fallen sons of men? Do you know that God has put you where you are and called you to do the work to which your life is dedicated? Then go on in God's name, for, as surely as he called you to his work, you may be sure that to you also he says, as indeed to all his servants, "I will not fail thee, nor forsake thee."

But I hear some of you say, "We are not engaged in work of such a kind that we could precisely call it 'work for God.'" Well, brethren, but are you *engaged in a work which you endeavor to perform to God's glory?* Is your ordinary and common trade one which is lawful—one concerning which you have no doubt as to its honest propriety, and in carrying it on do you follow right principles only? Do you endeavor to glorify God in the shop? Do you make the bells on the horses holiness to the Lord? It would not be possible for all of us to be preachers, for where would be the hearers? Many would be very much out of place if he were to leave his ordinary calling, and devote himself to what is so unscripturally called "the ministry." The fact is, the truest religious life is that in which a man follows the ordinary calling of life in the spirit of a Christian. Now, are you so doing? If so, you are as much ministering before God in measuring out yards of calico or weighing pounds of tea, as Joshua was in slaying Hivites and Jebusites and Hittites. You are as much serving God in looking after your own children and training them up in God's fear, and minding the house, and making your household a church for God, as you would be if you had been called to lead an army to battle for the Lord of hosts. And you may take this promise for yourself, for the path of duty is the path where this promise is to be enjoyed. "I will not fail thee, nor forsake thee."

Now, mark you, if you are living for yourself, if you are living for gain, if selfishness be the object of life, or if you are pursuing an unhallowed calling, if there is anything about your mode of business which is contrary to the mind and will of God and sound doctrine, you cannot expect God to aid you in sin, nor will he do it. Neither can you ask him to pander to your lusts and to assist you in the gratification of your own selfishness. But if you can truly say, "I live to the glory of God, and the ordinary life that I lead I desire to consecrate to his glory entirely," then may you take this promise home to yourself, "I will not fail thee, nor forsake thee."

But, mark you, there is another matter. We must, if we are to have this promise, *take God into our calculations*. A great many persons go about their supposed life-work without thinking about God. I have heard of one who said everybody had left him, and someone said, "But surely, as a Christian, God has not failed you?" "Oh," said he, "I forgot God." I am afraid there are many who call themselves Christians, and yet forget God in common life. Among all the forces that a man calculates upon when he engages in an enterprise, he should never omit the chief force: but often it is so with us. We inquire, "Am I competent for such a work? I ought to undertake it, but am I competent?" And straightaway there is a calculation made of competences. And in these competences there is no item put down—"Item, the promise of a living God. Item, the guidance of the Spirit." These are left out of the calculation. Remember that if you willfully omit them you cannot expect to enjoy them. You must walk by faith if you are to enjoy the privileges of the faithful. "The just shall live by faith," and if you begin to live by sense, you shall join the weeping and the wailing of those who have gone to broken cisterns and have found them empty; and your lips shall be parched with thirst, because you have forgotten the Fountain of living waters to which you should have gone. Do you, brethren and sisters, habitually take God into your calculations? Do you calculate upon omniscient direction and omnipotent aid?

I have heard of a certain captain who had led his troops into a very difficult position, and he knew that on the morrow he should want them all to be full of courage; and so, disguising himself, at nightfall he went around their tents, and listened to their conversations, until he heard one of them say, "Our captain is a very great warrior, and has won many victories, but he has this time made a mistake; for see, there are so many thousands of the enemy, and he has only so many infantry, so many cavalry, and so many guns." The soldier made out the account, and was about to sum up the scanty total when the captain, unable to bear it any longer, threw aside the curtain of the tent, and said, "And how many do you count me for, sir?"—as much as to say, "I have won so many battles that you ought to know that my skill can multiply battalions by handling them." And so the Lord hears his servants estimating how feeble they are, and how little they can do, and how few are their helpers; and I think I hear him rebukingly say, "But how many do you count your God for? Is he never to come into your estimate? You talk of providing, and forget the God of providence; you talk of working, but forget the God who works in you to will and to do of his own good pleasure."

How often in our enterprises have prudent people plucked us by the sleeve, and said we have gone too far? Could we reckon upon being able to carry out what we had undertaken? No, we could not reckon upon it, except that we believed in God, and with God all things are possible. If it be his work, we may venture far beyond the shallowness of prudence into the great deeps of divine confidence, for God who warrants our faith, will honor it before long. O Christian, if you can venture, and feel it to be no venture, then may you grasp the promise, "I will not fail thee, nor forsake thee." When you are on your own feet, you may dash against a stone; when you are running in your own strength, you may faint; but "they that wait upon the Lord shall renew their strength; they shall mount up with wings as eagles; they shall run, and not be weary; and they shall walk, and not faint."

Now, remember, that we may take this promise when we are engaged in God's work, or when we turn our ordinary business into God's work, and when we do really by faith take God into our calculations; but *we must also be careful that we walk in God's ways.* Observe that the next verse to the text runs thus, "Be strong, and of a good courage," and then the seventh verse is a singular one, "Only be thou strong and very courageous, that thou mayest observe to do according to all the law, which Moses my servant commanded thee: turn not from it to the right hand or to the left, that thou mayest prosper whithersoever thou goest."

"Be strong and very courageous." What for? To obey! Does it want courage and strength to obey? Why, nowadays, that man is thought to be courageous who will have no laws of God to bind him; and he is thought to be strong minded who ridicules revelation. But let us rest assured that he is truly strong of mind and heart who is content to be thought a fool, and sticks to the good old truth, and keeps the good old way. There are enough nowadays of "intellectual" preachers; some of us may be excused from this vaunted intellectualism that we may preach the simple gospel. There are enough who can becloud theology with the chill fogs of "modern thought"; we are satisfied to let the Word speak for itself without misting it with our thinkings. I believe it wants more courage and strength of mind to keep to the old things, than to follow after novel and airy speculations. We must not expect the God of truth to be with us if we go away from God and his truth.

Be careful how you dive. To watch every putting down of your foot is a good thing. Be exact and precise as to the divine rule, careless about man's opinion, and even defying it wherein it is error; but dutiful to God's law, bow-ing before it, yielding your whole nature in cheerful subservience to every command of the most High. He that walketh uprightly, walketh surely, and to him the promise is "I will not fail thee, nor forsake thee." Begin your life-course with a policy of your own, and you may get through it how you can; be wise in your own conceit, and trust to your own judgment, and the pro-motion of fools will be your reward; but be simple enough to do God's will only, to leave consequences and to follow truth, and integrity and uprightness will preserve you. Go on doing right at all costs, and the right will repay you all it costs you, and the righteous Lord will be true to his word: "I will not fail thee, nor forsake thee." These, then, I think, are the conditions under which any believing man may take to himself the words of our text.

III. But now, third, let us consider *what this promise does not preclude.*

"I will not fail thee, nor forsake thee." We must not misunderstand this gracious word, lest we be disappointed when things happen contrary to our expectations.

This promise does not exclude effort. A great many mistakes are made about the promises of God. Some think that if God is to be with them they will have nothing to do. Joshua did not find it so. He and his troops had to slay every Amorite and Hittite and Hivite that fell in battle. He had to fight and use his sword arm just as much as if there had been no God at all. The best and the wisest thing in the world is to work as if it all depended upon you, and then trust in God, knowing that it all depends upon him. He will not fail us, but we are not therefore to fold our arms and sit still. He will not forsake us; we are not therefore to go upstairs to bed and expect that our daily bread will drop into our mouths. I have known idle people who have said "Jehovah-Jireh," and sat with their feet over the fender, and their arms folded, and been lazy and self-indulgent; and generally their presumption has ended in this: God has pro-vided them rags and jags, and a place in the county jail before long; the very best provision, I think, that can be made for idle people, and the sooner they get it the better for society. Oh, no, no, no, no, God does not pander to our laziness, and any man who expects to get on in this world with anything that is good, without work, is a fool. Throw your whole soul into the service of God, and then you will get God's blessing if you are resting upon him. Even Muhammad could appreciate this. When one of his followers said, "I will turn my camel loose, and trust in Providence," "No, no," said Muhammad, "tie him up as tightly as you can, and then trust in Providence." Oliver Cromwell had a commonsense view of this truth too. "Trust in God," said he, as they went to battle, "but keep your powder dry." And so must we. I do not believe that God would have his servants act like fools. The best judgment a man has should be employed in the service of God. Common sense is, perhaps, as rare a thing among Christian people as salmon in the Thames. The devil's servants have more wisdom in their generation than the children of light have, but it ought not so to be. If you want to succeed, use every faculty you have, and put forth all your strength; and if it is a right cause, you may then fall back on the promise, "I will not fail thee, nor forsake thee."

Neither does this promise preclude occasional disaster. After Joshua had received this promise he went up to Ai, and suffered a terrible defeat there, because the regulations of the war had been violated. They had defrauded the Lord of a part of the spoil of Jericho, which was hidden in Achan's tent, and this troubled Israel. Yes, and without the violation of any law, the best man in the world must expect in the most successful enterprise that there will be some discouragements. Look at the sea: it is rolling in, it will rise to full tide before long, but every wave that comes up dies upon the shore, and after two or three great waves which seem to capture the shingle there comes a feebler one which sucks back. Very well, but the sea will win, and reach its fullness. So in every good work for God there is a back-drawing wave every now and then. In fact, God often makes his servants go back that they may have all the more room to run and take a huger leap than they could have taken from the place where they stood before. Defeats in the hand of faith are only preparations for victory. If we are beaten for a little, we grind our swords the sharper, and the next time we take more care that our enemies shall know how keen they are. Do not, therefore, let any temporary disappointments dismay you; they are incidental to humanity, and needful parts of our education. Go on. God will certainly test you, but he will not fail you, nor forsake you.

Nor, again, does this promise preclude frequent tribulations and testings of faith. In the autobiography of the famous Francke of Halle, who built and, in the hand of God, provided for the orphan house of Halle, he says, "I thought when I committed myself and my work to God by faith, that I had only to pray when I had need, and that the supplies would come; but I found, that I had sometimes to wait and pray for a long time." The supplies did come, but not at once. The pinch never went so far as absolute want; but there were intervals of severe pressure. There was nothing to spare. Every spoonful of meal had to be scraped from the bottom of the barrel, and every drop of oil that oozed out seemed as if it must be the last; but still it never did come to the last drop, and there was always just a little meal left. Bread shall be given us, but not always in quarter loaves; our water shall be sure, but not always a brook full; it may only come in small cups. God has not promised to take any of you to heaven without trying your faith. He will not fail you, but he will bring you very low. He will not forsake you, but he will test you and prove you. You will frequently need all your faith to keep your spirits up; and unless God enables you to trust without staggering, you will find yourself sorely disquieted at times. Now are any of you brought to the verge of famine in God's work? It is a state in which I have often been—thank God, very often—and I have always been delivered, and, therefore, I can from experience say the Lord is to be trusted, and he will not allow the faithful to be confounded. He has said it, and he will perform it: "I will not fail thee, nor forsake thee."

Dear friends, I would like to say, once more, about this, that *this promise does not preclude our suffering very greatly*, and our dying, and perhaps dying a very sad and terrible death, as men judge. God never left Paul, but I have seen the spot where Paul's head was smitten off by the headsman. The Lord never left Peter, but Peter, like his Master, had to die by crucifixion. The Lord never left the martyrs, but they had to ride to heaven in chariots of fire. The Lord has never left his church, but oftentimes his church has been trodden as straw is trodden for the dunghill; her blood has been scattered over the whole earth, and she has seemed to be utterly destroyed. Still, you know, the story of the church is only another illustration of my text; God has not failed her, nor forsaken her; in the deaths of her saints we read not defeat, but victory; as they passed away one by one, stars ceasing to shine below, they shone with tenfold brilliance in the upper sky because of the clouds through which they passed before they reached their celestial spheres. Beloved, we may have to groan in a Gethsemane, but God will not fail us: we may have to die on a Golgotha, but he will not forsake us. We shall rise again, and, as our Master was triumphant through death, even so shall we through the greatest suffering and the most terrible defeats rise to his throne.

IV. **I must pass on again, and occupy you for a few moments over a fourth point, which is this:** *what, then, does the text mean, if we may have all this trial happening to us?*

It means to those to whom it belongs, first, *no failure for your work*; second, *no desertion for yourself*.

"I will not fail thee." *Your labor shall not be in vain in the Lord*. What is it? Is it the great work of preaching the gospel to thousands? God will not fail you in that. I remember how twenty years ago I was preaching the gospel in the simplicity of my heart, and some little stir was made, but the wise men made light of it and said it was all to end in six months' time. We went on, did we not? And by and by, when we had still greater crowds listening to us, it was "a temporary excitement, a sort of religious spasm"; it would all end like a mere flash in the pan. I wonder where those prophets are now. If there are any of them here, I hope they feel comfortable in the unfulfilled prophecy, which they can now study with some degree of satisfaction. Thousands on earth and hundreds in heaven can tell what God hath wrought. Is it another kind of work, dear brother, that you are engaged in? A very quiet, unobtrusive, unobserved effort? Well, I should not wonder that, little as it is, somebody or other sneers at it. There is scarcely a David in the world without an Eliab to sneer at him. Press on, brother! Stick to it, plod away, work hard, trust in your God, and your work will not fail. We have heard of a minister who added only one to his church through a long year of very earnest ministry—only one, a sad thing for him; but that one happened to be Robert Moffatt, and he was worth a thousand of most of us. Go on. If you bring but *one* to Christ, who shall estimate the value of the one? Your class is very small just now; God does not seem to be working. Pray about it, get more scholars into the class, and teach better, and even if you should not see immediate success do not believe that it is all a failure. Never was a true gospel sermon preached yet, with faith and prayer, that was a failure. Since the day when Christ our Master first preached the gospel, unto this day—I dare to say it—there was never a true prayer that failed, nor a true declaration of the gospel made in a right spirit that fell to the ground without prospering according to the pleasure of the Lord. Fire away, brother. Every shot tells somewhere, for in heavenly as well as earthly warfare, "every bullet has its billet."

And then there shall be *no desertion as to yourself*, for your heavenly Friend has said, "I will not *forsake* thee." You will not be left alone or without a helper. You are thinking of what you will do in old age. Do not think of that: think of what God will do for you in old age. Oh, but your great need and long illness will wear out your friends, you say. Perhaps you may wear out your friends, but you will not wear out your God, and he can raise up new helpers if the old ones fail. Oh, but your infirmities are many and will soon crush you down: you cannot live long in such circumstances. Very well, then you will be in heaven; and that is far better. But you dread pining sickness. It may never come; and, suppose it should come, remember what will come with it: "I will make all thy bed in thy sickness." "I will never leave thee, nor forsake thee"— so runs the promise. "Fear thou not, for I am with thee; be not dismayed, for I am thy God." "'The mountains may depart, and the hills be removed; but the covenant of my love shall not depart from thee,' saith the Lord, that hath mercy on thee." You shall not be a lone one. You shall not wring your hands in despair, and say, "I am utterly wretched, like the pelican of the wilderness—utterly forsaken like the owl of the desert." The mighty God of Jacob forsaketh not his own.

V. And so this brings me to the last point, which is this: *why may we be quite sure that this promise will be fulfilled to us?*

I answer, first, we may be quite sure because it is God's promise. Did ever any promise of God fall to the ground yet? There be those in the world who are challenging us continually, and saying, "Where is your God?" They deny the efficacy of prayer; they deny the interpositions of Providence. Well, I do not wonder that they do so deny, because the bulk of Christians do not realize either the answer of prayer or the interposition of Providence, for this reason, that they do not live in the light of God's countenance, or live by faith. But the man who walks by faith will tell you that he notices Providence, and never is deficient of a Providence to notice; that he notices answers to his prayer, and never is without an answer to his prayer. What is a wonder to others becomes a common fact of everyday life to the believer in Christ. Where God has given his word, "I will not fail thee, nor forsake thee," let us believe it; for

> *His very word of grace is strong*
> *As that which built the skies;*
> *The voice that rolls the stars along*
> *Speaks all the promises.*

Rest ye well assured that if a man be called to do God's work, God will not fail him, because *it is not after the manner of the Lord to desert his servants.* David in the dark day of his sin bid Joab place Uriah, the Hittite, in the forefront of the battle, and leave him there to die by the hand of the children of Ammon. Was it not cruel? It was base and treacherous to the last degree. Can you suspect the Lord of anything so unworthy? God forbid. My soul has known what it is to plead with the Lord my God after this fashion: "Lord, thou hast placed me in a difficult position, and given me service to perform far beyond my capacity. I never coveted this prominent place, and if thou dost not help me now why hast thou placed me in it?" I have always found such argument to be prevalent with God. He will not push his servants into severe conflicts, and then fail them.

Besides, remember that *should God's servants fail,* if they are really God's servants, *the enemy would exult and boast against the Lord himself.* This was a great point with Joshua in after days. He said, "The Canaanites and all the inhabitants of the land shall hear of it, and shall environ us round, and cut off our name from the earth: and what wilt thou do unto thy great name?" If the Lord raises up Luther, and does not help Luther, then it is not Luther that fails; it is God that fails, in the estimation of the world. If the Lord sends a man to bear witness to a truth, and that man's testimony utterly breaks down, then in the estimation of men it is the truth that breaks down, and consequently dishonor is cast upon God and his truth; and he will not have it so. If he uses the weakest instrumentality, he will laugh to scorn his adversaries by it, and they shall never say that the Lord was overcome.

Besides, if God has raised you up, my brother or sister, to accomplish a purpose by you, *do you think he will be defeated?* Were ever any of his designs frustrated? I have heard preachers talk about God being defeated by the free will of man and disappointed by man's depravity, and I do not know what. But such a God is no God of mine. My God is one who has his will and will have it; who, when he designs a thing, accomplishes it; he is a God whose omnipotence none can resist, concerning whom it may be said, "Who shall stay his hand, or say unto him, What doest thou?" The mighty God of Jacob puts his hand to a design and carries it through as surely as he begins; the weakness of the instrument in his hand does not hinder him, nor the opposition of his enemies deter him. Only believe in him, and weak as you are, you shall perform wonders, and in your feebleness the strength of God shall be glorified.

Besides, my brethren, if we trust God, and live for God, *he loves us much too well to leave us.* It is not as though we were aliens and strangers and foreigners— mercenary troops whom the prince who hires them leaves to be cut in pieces: no, we are his own dear children. God sees his own self in all his servants. He sees in them the members of the body of his dear Son. The very least among them is dear to him as the apple of his eye, and beloved as his own soul. It is not to be imagined that he will ever put a load upon his own children's shoulders without giving them strength to bear the burden, or send them to labors for which he will not give them adequate resources. Oh, rest in the Lord, you faithful. "Rest in the Lord, and wait patiently for him," for he will appear unto your rescue. Has he not said, "I will not fail thee, nor forsake thee "?

As I have thus been bringing forth marrow and fatness from the Word, I have been thinking of some of you, poor souls, who cannot eat thereof, and have no share in it. I am glad to see you here, especially on Thursday night, for it is not every unconverted person that will come to these weeknight services. You must have a hungering after these good things, or you would not be here in such numbers. I hope your mouths are watering after the good things of the covenant. I hope, as you see the promises of God on the table, and see how rich they are, you will say to yourself, "Would God I had a share in them!" Well, poor soul, if God gives you an appetite, I can only say, the food is free to you. If you would have God to be your Helper—if you would indeed be saved by Christ—come and welcome, for you are the soul that he desires to bless. If you have half a wish toward God, he has a longing toward you. If you desire him, you have not the start of him; depend upon it, he has long before desired you. Come you to him, rest in him, accept the atonement which his Son has presented, begin the life of faith in real earnest, and you shall find that what I have said is all true, only it falls short of the full truth, for you will say, like the queen of Sheba when she had seen Solomon's glory, "The half hath not been told me." Blessed be the Lord forever, who has taught my poor heart to believe in himself, and to live upon unseen realities, and rest in a faithful God! There is no peace or joy like it, or worthy to be mentioned in the same day. God grant it to each one of you, beloved, for his name's sake. Amen.

Gideon: The Dream
of the Bakery Cake

⚘

Delivered on Lord's Day morning, at the Metropolitan Tabernacle, Newington, November 22, 1885. No. 1873.

> *And when Gideon was come, behold, there was a man that told a dream unto his fellow, and said, "Behold, I dreamed a dream, and, lo, a cake of barley bread tumbled into the host of Midian, and came unto a tent, and smote it that it fell, and overturned it, that the tent lay along." And his fellow answered and said, "This is nothing else save the sword of Gideon the son of Joash, a man of Israel: for into his hand hath God delivered Midian, and all the host."*—JUDGES 7:13–14

The Midianites were devastating the land of Israel. These wandering tribes purposely kept away during the times of plowing and sowing, and allowed the helpless inhabitants to dream that they would be able to gather in a harvest; but no sooner did there come to be anything eatable by man or beast, than these Bedouin hordes came up like locusts, and devoured everything. Imagine a country like Israel, which had at one time been powerful, so greatly reduced as to be unable to keep off these desert rangers; brought so low that the cities and villages were empty, and the inhabitants were hidden in the hillsides, in the watercourses, and in the huge caverns of the rocks. God had forsaken them for their sins, and therefore their own manhood had forsaken them, and they hid themselves from enemies, whom, in better days, they had despised.

In her extremity, the guilty nation began to cry to Jehovah her God; and the answer was not long delayed. An angel came to Gideon and announced to him that the Lord had delivered Midian into his hand, and that he should smite them as one man. Gideon was a man of great faith: his name shines among the heroes of great faith in the eleventh chapter of the epistle to the Hebrews; and you and I will do well if we attain to the same rank in the peerage of faith as he did. But for all that, the best of men are men at the best; and men of strong faith are often men of strong conflicts; and so it was with Gideon. This man's great faith and great weakness of faith both showed themselves in a desire for signs. Once assure him that God is with him, and Gideon has no fear, but hastens to the battle, bravest of the brave. With a handful of men, he is quite prepared to go against a host of adversaries; but he pines for a sign. Again and again he asks it. The anxious question seems to be constantly recurring to him, "Is the LORD with us? If the LORD is with us, where are all his miracles which our fathers told us of, saying, 'Did not the LORD bring us up from Egypt?'" Hence his frequent prayer is, "If now I have found grace in thy sight, show me a sign." He began with this, and this ill beginning colored his whole after career. I have known many persons like this son of Joash; they say, "Let me but know that God is with me, and my fear is gone"; but their repeated question is, "Is the LORD with me? Is Jesus mine, and am I his? Let me but know that I am a true believer, and I am sure that I shall not perish, for God will not forsake his own; but then, am I a believer? Have I the marks and evidences of a child of God?" Hence the practice of severe self-examination, and hence also the weakening habit of craving for tokens and feelings. How many are crying "we see not our signs," when they ought to say, "but we see Jesus!" How many are praying "show me a token for good," when the Lord Jesus has given himself for them, and has thereby given the best token of his grace?

So it happened unto Gideon, that the Lord, knowing his hunger for signs and yet knowing the sincerity of his faith, bade him, on the night of the great battle which was to rout Midian, go down as a spy into the camp with his servant, and there he should receive a token for good, which would effectually quiet all his fears.

I picture Gideon and his attendant creeping down the hill in the stillness of the night, when the camp was steeped in slumber. It was about the end of the first watch, when they were soon to change sentinels. The two brave men, with stealthy footsteps, drew near the pickets, and even passed them. From long habit they had learned to make no more sound with their footfalls than if they had been cats. As they move along, they come near to a couple of men who are talking together, and they listen to their conversation. Whether they were inside the tent, lying on their beds, or whether they were sitting by the campfire whiling away the last half hour of their weary watch, we do not know: but there they were, and Gideon remained breathless to hear their talk. One of them told his fellow that he had dreamed a dream, and he began the telling of it. Then the other ventured an interpretation, and Gideon must have been awestricken when he heard his own name mentioned, and his own success foretold. Do you not see him with streaming eyes and clasped hands silently worshiping God? His assurance overflows, and motioning to his servant, they steal away through the shadows and quietly ascend the hill to the place where the little band of three hundred lay in hiding. They look down upon the sleeping camp, and Gideon cries, "The LORD hath delivered into your hands the hosts of Midian." Obedient to their leader they descend with their trumpets, and with torches covered over with pitchers. At a signal they break the pitchers, display the lights, sound the trumpets, and shout, "The sword of the LORD and of Gideon." Imagining that a vast army is upon them, the tribes of the desert run for their lives, and in the darkness fall foul of one another. Midian is scattered: Israel is free.

In quiet contemplation let us now play the part of spies. With all our wits about us, let us thread our way among the sleepers, and listen to this dream and the interpretation thereof.

I. The first thing that I shall bring under your observation is *the striking providence* which must have greatly refreshed Gideon.

Just as he and Phurah stealthily stole up to the tent, the Midianite was telling a dream, bearing an interpretation so appropriate to Gideon. It may appear to be a little thing, but an occurrence is nonetheless wonderful because it appears to be insignificant. The microscope reveals a world of marvels quite as surprising as that which is brought before us by the telescope. God is as divine in the small as in the stupendous, as glorious in the dream of a soldier as in the flight of a seraph.

Now observe, first, the providence of God that this man should have dreamed just then, and that he should have dreamed that particular dream. Dreamland is chaos, but the hand of the God of order is here. What strange romantic things our dreams are!—fragments of this, and broken pieces of the other, strangely joined together in absurd fashion.

> How many monstrous forms in sleep we see,
> That neither were, nor are, nor e'er can be!

Yet observe that God holds the brain of this sleeping Arab in his hand, and impresses it as he pleases. Dreams often come of previous thoughts; see then the providence which had taken this man's mind to the hearth and the cake baking. The Lord prepares him when he is awake to dream aright when he is asleep. God is omnipotent in the world of mind as well as in that of matter: he rules it when men are awake, and does not lose his power when men fall asleep. The heathen ascribed dreams to their gods; we read of one, that

> Pallas poured sweet slumbers on his soul,
> And balmy dreams, the gift of soft repose.

Thin as the air, inconstant as the wind, the stuff that dreams are made of is vanity of vanities; and yet the Lord fashions it according to his own good pleasure. The man must dream, must dream then and there, and dream that dream which should convey confidence and courage to Gideon. Oh, believe it, God is not asleep when we are asleep: God is not dreaming when we are. I admire the providence of God in this; do not you? Is it not specially well ordered that this man shall dream, and therein declare a truth as deep as any in the compass of philosophy?

Further, I cannot but admire *that this man should be moved to tell his dream to his fellow.* It is not everybody that tells his dream at night; he usually waits till the morning. We are grossly foolish sometimes, but we are not always so: and hence we do not hurry to tell such disjointed visions as that which this Arab had just seen. What was there in it? Many a time, no doubt, this son of the desert would have cried, "I have had a dream—past the wit of man to say what dream it was." But this time he cannot shake it off. It burdens him, and he must tell it to his comrade by the campfire. Look you into the face of Gideon as he catches every syllable.

Now, if this dream telling had been arranged by military authority, and if it had been part of a program that Gideon should be present at the nick of time to hear it, there would have been a failure somehow or other. If the man had known that he had a listener, he might not have been punctual with his narrative; but he did not know a word about being overheard, and yet he was punctual to the tick of a clock. God rules men's idle tongues as well as their dreaming brains, and he can make a talkative soldier in the camp say just as much and just as little as will subserve the purposes of wisdom. It is remarkable that *the man should tell his dream just when Gideon and Phurah had come near.* Just think a minute of the many chances against such a thing. We are on the side of the hill, and we glide down among the trees and the great rocks till we are nearly in the grasslands in the valley. Here lie the Midianites in their long lines of black tents, and the hush of deep slumber is over all, save where a few maintain a sleepy watch. Why does Gideon go to that particular part of the camp? Going there, why does he happen to drop on this particular spot where two men are talking? If he was spying out the camp, he would naturally wander along where there was most quiet, in order that he might not be discovered; for if the warriors had suddenly started up and snatched their spears these two men would have had small chance of life. It was singular that out of tents so countless Gideon should alight upon the very one in which were the two wakeful sentinels, and that he should come just as they were talking to one another about Gideon the son of Joash, a man of Israel. Considering that there were fifty thousand other things that they might have talked of, and considering that there were fifty thousand other persons upon whom Gideon might have lighted, there were so many chances against Gideon's hearing that singular talk, that I do not hesitate to say, this is the finger of God. If this were but one instance of the accuracy of Providence it might not so much surprise us; but history bristles with such instances: I mean not only public history, but our own private lives. Men sometimes make delicate machines where everything depends upon the touching of a certain pin at a certain instant, and their machinery is so arranged that nothing fails. Now our God has so arranged the whole history of men, and angels, and the regions of the dead, that each event occurs at the right moment so as to effect another event, and that other event brings forth a third, and all things work together for good.

I think if I had been Gideon, I should have said to myself, "I do not so much rejoice in what this dreamer says as I do in the fact that he has told his dream at the moment when I was lurking near him: I see the hand of the Lord in this, and I am strengthened by the sight. Verily, I perceive that the Lord works all things with unfailing wisdom, and fails not in his designs. He that has ordered this matter can order all things else." O child of God, when you are troubled it is because you fancy that you are alone; but you are not alone; the eternal Worker is with you. Listen, and you will hear the revolution of those matchless wheels which are forever turning according to the will of the Lord. These wheels are high and dreadful, but they move with fixed and steady motion, and they are all "full of eyes roundabout." Their course is no blind track of a car of juggernaut, but the eyes see, the eyes look toward their end, the eyes look upon all that comes within the circuit of the wheels. Oh, for a little heavenly eye salve to touch our eyes that we may perceive the presence of the Lord in all things! Then shall we see the mountain to be full of horses of fire and chariots of fire around about the prophets of the Lord. The stars in their courses are fighting for the cause of God. Our allies are everywhere. God will summon them at the right moment.

II. But now, second, I want to say something to you about *the comfortable trifle* which Gideon had thus met with.

It was a dream, and therefore a trifle or a nothing, and yet he took comfort from it. He was solaced by a dream, a gipsy's dream, and a poor dream at that. He took heart from an odd story of a barley bannock [cake] which overturned a tent. It is a very curious thing that some of God's servants do draw a very great deal of consolation from comparatively trivial things. We are all the creatures of sentiment as well as of reason, and hence we are often strongly affected by little things. Gideon is cheered by a dream of a barley cake. When Robert Bruce had been frequently beaten in battle, he despaired of winning the crown of Scotland; but when he lay hidden in the loft among the hay and straw, he saw a spider trying to complete her web after he had broken the thread many times. As he saw the insect begin again, and yet again, until she had completed her net for the taking of her prey, he said to himself, "If this spider perseveres and conquers, so will I persevere, and succeed." There might not be any real connection between a spider and an aspirant to a throne; but the brave heart made a connection, and thereby the man was cheered. If you and I will but look about us, although the adversaries of God are as many as grasshoppers, yet we shall find consolation. I hear the birds sing, "Be of good cheer," and the leafless trees bid us trust in God and live on, though all visible signs of life be withered. If a dream was sufficient to encourage Gideon, an everyday fact in nature may equally well serve the same purpose to us.

But what a pity it is that we should need such little bits of things to cheer us up, when we have matters of far surer import to make us glad! Gideon had already received, by God's own angel, the word, "Surely I will be with thee, and thou shalt smite the Midianites as one man." Was not this enough for him? Whence is it that a boy's dream comforts him more than God's own word. O child of God, how you degrade yourself and your Master's word, when you set so much store by a small token! Your Lord's promise—is that little in your eyes? What surer pledge of love do you desire than the blood of Jesus spilled for you? When Jesus says, "Verily, verily, I say unto you," what more can you require? Is not the word of the Lord absolute truth? What seal do you want to the handwriting of God? The Lord may grant us further tokens for good, but we ought not to require them.

I have said that our gracious God does condescendingly grant us even trifles, when he sees that they will cheer us, and this, I think, calls for adoring gratitude, and also for practical use of this comfort. God grant us grace to do great things, as the result of that which to others may seem a trifle. Let us not make a sluggard's bed out of our tokens; but let us hasten to the fight as Gideon did. If you have received a gleam of comfort, hasten to the conflict before the clouds return; go to your consecrated labor before you have lost the fervor of your spirit. May the Holy Ghost lead you so to do.

III. I have been brief upon that point, because I want you to notice, third, *the cheering discovery.*

Gideon had noticed a striking providence, he had received a comfortable trifle, but he also made a very cheering discovery; which discovery was that the enemy dreamed of disaster. You and I sometimes think about the hosts of evil, and we fear we shall never overcome them, because they are so strong, and so secure. Hearken: we overestimate them. The powers of darkness are not so strong as they seem to be. The subtlest infidels and heretics are only men. What is more, they are bad men; and bad men at bottom are weak men. You fret because in this war you are not angels; be comforted to think that the adversaries of the truth are men also. You sometimes grow doubtful; and so do they. You half despair of victory; and so do they. You are at times hard put to it; so are they. You sometimes dream of disaster; so do they. It is natural to men to fear, and doubly natural to bad men. It must have been a great comfort to Gideon to think that the Midianites dreamed about him, and that their dreams were full of terror to themselves. He did not think much of himself; he reckoned himself to be the least of all his father's house, and that his father's house was little in Israel—but the foes of Israel had taken another gauge of Gideon—they had evidently the notion that he was a great man, whom God might use to smite them; and they were afraid of him. He that interpreted the dream made use of the name of "Gideon the son of Joash," evidently knowing a great deal more about Gideon than Gideon might have expected. "This," said the soldier, "is the sword of Gideon the son of Joash, a man of Israel: for into his hand hath God delivered Midian, and all the host." Notice how his words tallied with those which the Lord had spoken to Gideon. The enemy had begun to dream, and to be afraid of him who now stood listening to their talk. A dread from the Lord had come upon them. Let us say to ourselves, "Why should we be afraid of sinners? They are afraid of us." A Christian man, the other day, was afraid to speak about his Lord to one whom he met. It cost him a deal of trouble to screw his courage up to speak to a skeptic; but when he had spoken, he found that the skeptic had all along been afraid that he would be spoken to. It is a pity when we tremble before those who are trembling because of us. By want of faith in God we make our enemies greater than they are.

Behold the host of doubters and heretics and revilers who, at the present time, have come up into the inheritance of Israel, hungry from their deserts of rationalism and atheism! They are eating up all the corn of the land. They cast a doubt upon all the verities of our faith. But we need not fear them; for if we heard their secret counsels, we should perceive that they are afraid of us. Their loud blusterings and their constant sneers are the index of real fear. Those who preach the cross of our Lord Jesus are the terror of modern thinkers. In their heart of hearts they dread the preaching of the old-fashioned gospel, and they hate what they dread. On their beds they dream of the coming of some evangelist into their neighborhood. What the name of Richard was to the Saracens, that is the name of Moody to these boastful intellects. They wish they could stop those Calvinistic fellows and those evangelical old fogies. Brethren, so long as the plain gospel is preached in England, there will always be hope that these brigands will yet be scattered, and the church be rid of their intrusion. Rationalism, Socinianism, ritualism, and universalism will soon take to their legs, if the clear, decided cry of "the sword of the LORD and of Gideon" be once more heard.

There is nothing of which a child of God need be afraid either on the earth or under it. I do not believe that in the lowest depths of hell we should hear or see anything that need make a believer in the Lord Jesus to be afraid. On the contrary, tidings of what the Lord has worked have made the enemy to tremble. Goodness wears in her innocence a breastplate of courage, but sin genders to cowardice. Those who follow after falsehood have a secret monitor within, which tells them that theirs is a weak cause, and that truth must and will prevail over them. Let them alone; the beating of their own hearts will scare them. The Lord lives, and while he lives let none that trust in his word suffer his heart to fail him; for the mountains shall depart, and the hills be removed, but the word of the Lord endureth forever. Our adversaries are neither so wise, nor so brave, nor so influential as we think them to be. Only have courage and rely upon God, and you will overcome them. David, you need not fear the giant because of his size; the vastness of his shape will only make him an easier target for your smooth stone. His very bulk is his weakness; it were hard to miss so huge a carcass. Be not afraid, but run to meet him; the Lord has delivered him into your hand. Why should the servants of the Lord speak doubtfully when their God pledges his honor that he will aid them? Let us change our manner of speech, and say with the psalmist, "Ascribe ye strength unto God: his excellency is over Israel. Let God arise, let his enemies be scattered; let them also that hate him flee before him." We have received a kingdom which cannot be moved. We have believed the faith once delivered unto the saints, and we will display it as a banner because of the truth. Yet shall this song be sung in our habitations: "The LORD gave the word: great was the company of those that published it. Kings of armies did flee apace: and she that tarried at home divided the spoil."

IV. Last, and most important of all, let us think for a little of *the dream itself and of its interpretation.*

The Midianite in his dream saw a barley cake. Barley cakes were not much valued as food in those days, any more than now. People ate barley when they could not get wheat; but they would need to be driven to such food by poverty or famine. Barley meal was rather food for dogs or cattle than for men; and therefore the barley cake would be the emblem of a thing despised. A barley cake was generally made upon the hearth. A hole was made in the ground and paved with stones; in this a fire was made, and when the stones were hot, a thin layer of barley meal was laid upon them, covered over with the ashes, and thus quickly and roughly baked. The cake itself was a mere biscuit. You must not interpret the dream as having in it a large quarter loaf of barley bread, tumbling down the hill and smashing up the tent with its own weight. No, it was only a cake, that is to say, a biscuit, of much the same form and thinness as we see in the Passover cakes of the Jews. It may have been a long piece of thin crust, and it was seen in the dream moving onward and waving in the air something like a sword. It came rolling and waving down the hill till it came crash against the pavilion of the prince of Midian, and turned the tent completely over, so that it lay in ruins. Perhaps driven by a tremendous wind, this flake of barley bread cut like a razor through the chief pole of the pavilion, and over went the royal tent. That was his vision: an odd, strange dream enough. His fellow answered, "The dream means mischief for our people. One of those barley cake eaters from the hills will be upon us before long. That man Gideon, whom we have heard of lately, may fall upon us on a sudden, and break down our power." That was the interpretation: the barley biscuit the ruin of the pavilion.

Now, what we have to learn from it is just this, *God can work by any means.* He can never be short of instruments. For his battles he can find weapons on the hearth, weapons in the kneading trough, weapons in the poor man's basket. Omnipotence has servants everywhere. For the defense of his cause God can enlist all the forces of nature, all the elements of society, all the powers that be. His kingdom cannot fail, since the Lord can defend it even by the cakes which are baking upon the coals. Gideon, who threshes corn today, will thresh the Lord's enemies tomorrow. Preachers of the Word are being trained everywhere.

God can work by the feeblest means. He can use a cake which a child can crumble to smite Midian, and subdue its terrible power. Alas, sirs! we often consider the means to be used, and forget to go onward to him who will use them. We often stop at the means and begin to calculate their natural force, and thus we miss our mark. The point is to get beyond the instruments, to the God who uses the instruments. I think I have heard that a tallow candle fired from a rifle will go through a door: the penetrating power is not in the candle, but in the force impelling it. So in this case, it was not the barley biscuit, but the almighty impulse which urged it forward, and made it upset the pavilion. We are nothing; but God with us is everything. "He giveth power to the faint; and to them that have no might he increaseth strength."

By using weak means our Lord gets to himself all the glory, and hides pride from men. The Lord had said to Gideon in the early part of this chapter, "The people are yet too many for me to give the Midianites into their hands, lest Israel vaunt themselves against me, saying, 'Mine own hand hath saved me.'" Their oppression was a punishment for sin, and their deliverance must be an act of mercy. They must be made to see the Lord's hand, and they cannot see it more clearly than by being delivered by feeble means. Out of jealousy for his own glory it often pleases God to set aside likely means and use those which we looked not for. Now I know how it is today: men think that if the world is to be converted it must be done by learned men, men of noble family, or at least of eminent talent. But is this the Lord's usual way? Is there anything in the Acts of the Apostles, or in the life of Christ, that should lead us to look to human wisdom or talent or prestige? Does not everything look in the contrary direction? The lake of Galilee was Christ's apostolic college. Has not God always acted upon his own declaration that he has hid these things from the wise and prudent and has revealed them unto babes? Is it not still true that the Lord has chosen the weak things of the world to confound the things which are mighty; and base things of the world, and things which are despised has God chosen, yes, and things which are not, to bring to naught things that are? Are we not on the wrong track altogether when we look to men, and means and measures, instead of considering the right hand of the most High? Brethren, let us never forget that out of the mouth of babes and sucklings has the Lord ordained strength because of his enemies, that he might still the enemy and the avenger.

The Lord employs feeble means, that so he may have an opening for you and for me. If he used only the great, the wise, the strong, we should have to lie in the corner. Then might the men of one talent be excused for hiding it. But now the least among us may through God's grace aspire to usefulness. Brothers, let not your weakness keep you back from the Lord's work: you are at least as strong as barley cakes. I find that the original text suggests a noise, such as might be made by chestnuts or corn when roasting in the fire. The dreamer marked that it was a noisy cake which tumbled into the host of Midian. More noise than force, one would say. It was like a coal which dies out of the fire, makes a little explosion, and is never more heard of. Thus have many of God's most useful servants been spoken of at the first. They were nine-day wonders, mere flashes in the pan, much ado about nothing, and so forth. And yet the Lord smites his enemies by their feeble means. My brother, perhaps you have begun to make a little stir by faithfully preaching the gospel, and this has opened the mouths of the adversaries, who are indignant that such a nobody as you should be useful. "Why, there is nothing in the fellow: it is sheer impudence for him to suppose that he has any right to speak." Never mind. Go on with your work for the Lord. Cease not because you are of such small account, for by such as you are God is pleased to work.

Never are his adversaries so shamefully beaten as when the Lord uses feeble instrumentality. The Lord smote the hosts of Jabin by the hand of a woman, and the hosts of Philistia by the hand of Shamgar the plowman. It was to their everlasting reproach that the Lord put his foes to the rout with pitchers and trumpets in the hand of the little band who followed the thresher of Abiezer. The Lord will tread Satan under our feet shortly, even under our feet, who are less than the least of all saints.

Note, next, *God uses unexpected means*. If I wanted to upset a tent, I certainly should not try to overturn it by a barley cake. If I had to cannonade an encampment, I should not bombard it with biscuits. Yet how wonderfully God hath wrought by the very persons whom we should have passed over without a thought. O paganism, your gigantic force and energy, with Caesar at their head, shall be vanquished by fishermen from the sea of Galilee! God willed it so, and so it was done. Rome's papal met a singular downfall from reformers rude of speech and poor in estate. Expect the unexpected. Thus the Lord works to call men's attention to what he does. If he does what men commonly reckon upon, they take no notice of his doings, however splendid they may be in themselves; but if he steps aside and does that which none could have looked for, then is their attention arrested, and they consider that the hand of the Lord is in it. Then also they admire and feel somewhat of awe of him. For the tent to fall seems nothing, but for the tent to fall by being smitten with a barley cake is something to be marveled at. For souls to be saved is in itself remarkable, but for them to be saved by some simple childlike evangelist who can scarcely speak grammatically, this is the talk of the town. For the Lord to call out a thief or a blasphemer and speak by his lips, is a thing to make men feel the greatness of God. Then they cry, "How unsearchable are his ways!" For an error to be blasted and dried up is a blessed thing—and yet it is all the more miraculous when this is done, not by reasoning, nor by eloquent argument, but by the simple declaration of gospel truth. O sirs, we never know what the Lord will do next. He can raise up defenders of the faith from the stones of the river. I despair not for the grand old cause. No, I hope against hope. Driven back as we may be, I see the very dust breeding warriors, and the grass of the field hardening into spears. Courage! Courage! Stand still, and see the salvation of God!

But the dream has more in it than this: *God uses despised means*. This man Gideon is likened to a cake, and then only to a barley cake; but the Lord styles him "a mighty man of valor." God loves to take men whom others despise, and use them for his glorious ends. "He is a fool," they say, "an uneducated man, one of the very lowest class of minds. He has no taste, no culture, no thought. He is not a person of the advanced school." My dear brother, I hope no one among you will be influenced by this kind of silly talk. The "mashers" in our churches talk in this fashion; but who cares for their proud nonsense? It is time that men who despise others should be themselves despised, and be made to know that they are so. Those who boast their intellect are of small account with God. The whole tenor of this inspired Book is that way; it speaks kindly of things that are despised, but it has no word of reverence for the boastful and pretentious. Therefore, you despised ones, let the proud unbelievers laugh at you, and sing concerning you their song of a barley cake; but do you in patience possess your souls, and go on in the service of your Lord. They think to render you contemptible; but the scorn shall return upon the scorners. You shall yet by the Lord's strength have such force and vigor put into you, that you shall put to flight the armies of the aliens. Say you with Paul, "When I am weak, then am I strong." "Fear not, little flock; for it is your Father's good pleasure to give you the kingdom." "He hath put down the mighty from their seats, and exalted them of low degree."

But, then, *God ever uses effectual means*. This cake of barley bread came unto a tent and smote it, that it fell, and overturned it, that the tent lay along. The Lord never does his work by halves. Even if he works by barley cakes, he makes a clean overthrow of his enemy. A cannonball could not have done its work better than did this barley cake. Friend, if the Lord uses you for his own purpose, he will do his work by you as effectually and surely as if he had selected the best possible worker. He lifts our weakness out of itself, and elevates it to a level of power and efficacy little dreamed of by us. Wherefore, be not afraid, you servants of God, but commit yourselves into the hands of him who, out of weakness, can bring forth strength.

I shall be done when I have made an application of all this to certain practical purposes. Brethren, do you not think that this smiting of the tent of Midian by the barley cake, and afterward the actual overthrow of the Midianite hordes by the breaking of the pitchers, the blazing of the torches, and the blowing of the trumpets, all tends to comfort us as to those powers of evil which now cover the world? I am appalled sometimes as I think of the power of the enemy, both in the matter of impurity and falsehood. At this present moment you seem as if you could do nothing: you cannot get in to strike a blow. Sin and error have so much the upper hand that we know not how to strike them. The two great parties in England, the Puritan and the Cavalier, take turn about, and just now the Cavalier rules most powerfully. At one time sound doctrine and holy practice had sway; but in these days loose teaching and loose living are to the fore. But our duty clearly lies in sticking to the Word of the Lord and the gospel of our fathers. God forbid that we should glory save in the cross of our Lord Jesus Christ. By this sign we shall conquer yet. The impurity of the age will never be cleansed except by the prevalence of the gospel; and the infidelity of the period will never die before any assault but that of the pure truth of the living Lord. We must tell of pardon bought with blood, of free forgiveness according to the riches of divine grace, and of eternal power changing fallen human nature, and making men new creatures in Christ Jesus. They call this a worn-out doctrine: let us put its power to the test on the largest scale, and we shall see that it is the power of God unto salvation to everyone that believeth.

As for me, I shall preach the gospel of the grace of God, and that only, even if I be left alone. The hosts of Israel are melting away, and they will melt much more. As in Gideon's day, out of the whole host twenty and two thousand have gone altogether away from true allegiance to the cause, and many more have no stomach for the fight. Let them go. The thousands and the hundreds. Let the thirty thousand who came at the trumpet call decrease to the three hundred men that lap in haste as a dog laps, because they are eager for the fray. When we are thinned out, and made to see how few we are, we shall be hurled upon the foe with a power not our own. Our weapon is the torch of the old gospel, flaming forth through the breaking of our earthen vessels. To this we add the trumpet sound of an earnest voice. Ours is the midnight cry: "Behold he cometh!" We cannot get victory by any might or skill of ours, and yet in the end the foe shall be defeated, and the Lord alone shall be exalted. Were things worse than they are, we would still cry, "The sword of the Lord and of Gideon," and stand each man in his place till the Lord appeared in strength.

Another lesson would I draw from the text as to our inward conflicts. Dear friend, you are feeling in your heart the great power of sin. The Midianites are encamped in your soul; in the little valley of Esdraelon [Jezreel] which lies within your bosom, there are countless evils, and these, like the locusts, eat up every growing thing, and cause comfort and strength and joy to cease from your experience. You sigh because of these invaders. I counsel you to try what faith can do. Your own earnest efforts appear to make you worse; try faith. Neither tears nor prayers nor vows nor self-denials have dislodged the foe; try the barley cake of faith. Believe in the Lord Jesus Christ. In him you are saved; in him you have power to become a child of God. Believe this and rejoice. Poor sinner! try faith. Poor backslider! try faith. Poor desponding heir of heaven! try faith. This barley cake of faith will smite the power of sin and break the dominion of doubt, and bring you victory. Remember that ancient Scripture, "Call upon me in the day of trouble, and I will deliver thee, and thou shalt glorify me." Make bold to believe. Say at once,

> I do believe, I will believe,
> That Jesus died for me.

This seems a very poor means of getting the victory, as poor as the barley cake baked on the coals—but God has chosen it, and he will bless it, and it will overthrow the throne of Satan within your heart, and work in you holiness and peace.

Once again, still in the same vein: let us, dear friends, try continually the power of prayer for the success of the gospel, and the winning of men's souls. Prayer will do anything—will do everything. It fills the valleys and levels the mountains. By its power men are raised from the door of hell to the gate of heaven. What is to become of London? What is to become of heathen nations? I listen to a number of schemes, very visionary, and very hard to work out. But I put these aside. There remains to believers but one scheme: our Lord has said, "Go ye into all the world and preach the gospel to every creature." This, therefore, we must do, and at the same time we must cry mightily unto God by prayer that his Holy Spirit may attend the proclamation of the Word. Let us more and more prove the power of prayer, resting assured that the Lord is able to do exceeding abundantly above what we ask or even think. Let each man stand with the flaming torch of truth in his hand, and the trumpet of the gospel at his lips, and so let us compass the army of the aliens. This is our war cry—Christ and him crucified! God forbid that we should know anything else among men, but the death, the blood, the resurrection, the reign, the coming, the glory of Christ. Let us not lose faith in our calling, nor in our God; but rest assured that the Lord reigns and his cause must triumph. Where sin abounded grace doth much abound. We shall see better and brighter days than these. Grant it, O Lord, for thy Son's sake. Amen.

Samuel: An Example of Intercession

Delivered on Lord's Day morning, May 9, 1880, at the Metropolitan Tabernacle, Newington. No. 1537.

Moreover as for me, God forbid that I should sin against the LORD in ceasing to pray for you: but I will teach you the good and the right way.
—1 SAMUEL 12:23

It is a very great privilege to be permitted to pray for our fellowmen. Prayer in each man's case must necessarily begin with personal petition, for until the man is himself accepted with God, he cannot act as an intercessor for others; and herein lies part of the excellence of intercessory prayer, for it is to the man who exercises it aright a mark of inward grace, and a token for good from the Lord. You may be sure that your King loves you when he will permit you to speak a word to him on behalf of your friend. When the heart is enlarged in believing supplication for others, all doubts about personal acceptance with God may cease; he who prompts us to love has certainly given us that love, and what better proof of his favor do we desire? It is a great advance upon anxiety for our own salvation when we have risen out of the narrowness of dread about ourselves into the broader region of care for a brother's soul. He who in answer to his intercession has seen others blessed and saved may take it as a pledge of divine love, and rejoice in the condescending grace of God. Such prayer rises higher than any petition for ourselves, for only he who is in favor with the Lord can venture upon pleading for others.

Intercessory prayer is an act of communion with Christ, for Jesus pleads for the sons of men. It is a part of his priestly office to make intercession for his people. He has ascended up on high to this end, and exercises this office continually within the veil. When we pray for our fellow sinners we are in sympathy with our divine Savior, who made intercession for the transgressors.

Such prayers are often of unspeakable value to those for whom they are offered. Many of us trace our conversion, if we go to the root of it, to the prayers of certain godly persons. In innumerable instances the prayers of parents have availed to bring young people to Christ. Many more will have to bless God for praying teachers, praying friends, praying pastors. Obscure persons confined to their beds are often the means of saving hundreds by their continual pleadings with God. The book of remembrance will reveal the value of these hidden ones, of whom so little is thought by the mass of Christians. As the body is knit together by bands and sinews, and interlacing nerves and veins, so is the whole body of Christ converted into a living unity by mutual prayers; we were prayed for, and now in turn we pray for others. Not only the conversion of sinners, but the welfare, preservation, growth, comfort, and usefulness of saints are abundantly promoted by the prayers of their brethren; hence apostolic men cried, "Brethren, pray for us"; he who was the personification of love said, "Pray one for another that ye may be healed," and our great Lord and Head ended his earthly career by a matchless prayer for those whom the Father had given him.

Intercessory prayer is a benefit to the man who exercises it, and is often a better channel of comfort than any other means of grace. The Lord turned again the captivity of Job when he prayed for his friends. Even where such prayer does not avail for its precise object, it has its results. David tells us that he prayed for his enemies: he says, in PSALM 35:13, "As for me, when they were sick, my clothing was sackcloth: I humbled my soul with fasting." And he adds, "my prayer returned into mine own bosom." He sent forth his intercession, like Noah's dove, but as it found no rest for the sole of its foot, and no blessing came of it, it returned to him who sent it, and brought back with it an olive leaf plucked off, a sense of peace to his own spirit; for nothing is more restful to the heart than to have prayed for those who despitefully use us and persecute us. Prayers for others are pleasing to God and profitable to ourselves; they are no waste of breath, but have a result guaranteed by the faithful Promiser.

I. Let us first dwell upon *his habit of intercession,* for it was most manifest in Samuel.

We gather this from the text. He says, "God forbid that I should sin against the LORD in ceasing to pray for you." It is clear, therefore, that he had been in the continual habit and practice of praying for Israel; he could not speak of ceasing to pray if he had not hitherto continued in prayer. Samuel had become so rooted in the habit of prayer for the people that he seems to start at the very thought of bringing his intercession to an end. The people, measuring the prophet by themselves, half suspected that he would be irritated with them, and would, therefore, deny them his prayers; therefore in verse 19 we read, "All the people said unto Samuel, 'Pray for thy servants unto the LORD thy God, that we die not.'" They greatly valued his prayers, and felt as if their national life, and perhaps their personal lives, depended upon his pleadings:

therefore they urged him as men who plead for their lives that he would not cease to pray for them, and he replied, "God forbid that I should." The denial of his prayers does not seem to have entered his thoughts. To my mind the words represent him as astonished at the idea, horrified and half indignant at the suggestion—"What I, Samuel, I who have been your servant from my childhood, since the day when I put on the little ephod, and waited for you in the house of the Lord; I that have lived for you and have loved you, and was willing to have died in your service, shall I ever cease to pray for you?" He says, "God forbid." It is the strongest expression that one can well imagine, and this, together with his evident surprise, shows that the prophet's habit of intercession was rooted, constant, fixed, abiding, a part and parcel of himself.

If you will read his life you will see how truly this was the case. Samuel was born of prayer. A woman of a sorrowful spirit received him from God and joyfully exclaimed, "For this child I prayed." He was named in prayer, for his name Samuel signifies, *"asked of God."* Well did he carry out his name and prove its prophetic accuracy, for having commenced life by being himself asked of God, he continued asking of God, and all his knowledge, wisdom, justice, and power to rule were things which came to him because "asked of God." He was nurtured by a woman of prayer at the first, and when he left her it was to dwell in the house of prayer all the days of his life. His earliest days were honored by a divine visitation, and he showed even then that waiting, watchful spirit which is the very knee of prayer. "Speak, LORD, for thy servant heareth" is the cry of a simple, sincere heart, such as the Lord ever accepts.

We all think of Samuel under that little figure so often painted and sculptured, in which a sweet child is seen in the attitude of prayer. We all seem to know little Samuel, the praying child: our boys and girls know him as a familiar friend, but it is as kneeling with clasped hands. He was born, named, nurtured, housed, and trained in prayer, and he never departed from the way of supplication. In his case the text was fulfilled, "Out of the mouth of babes and sucklings thou hast perfected praise"; and he so persevered in prayer that he brought forth fruit in old age, and testified of God's power to those who came after him. So famous did Samuel become as an intercessor that, if you will turn to the Ninety-ninth Psalm, at the sixth verse, you will read a short but very fragrant eulogy of him: "Moses and Aaron among his priests, and Samuel among them that call upon his name." If Moses and Aaron are selected as being consecrated men, leaders of God's Israel in service and sacrifice, Samuel is selected as the praying man, the man who calls upon God's name. All Israel knew Samuel was an intercessor as well as they knew Aaron as a priest. Perhaps even more notably you get the same inspired estimate of him in Jeremiah 15, at the first verse, where he is again classed with Moses: "Then said the LORD unto me, 'Though Moses and Samuel stood before me, yet my mind could not be toward this people: cast them out of my sight, and let them go forth.'" Here there is no doubt an allusion to the prevalent prayer of Moses, when in the agony of his heart he cried, "If not, blot me, I pray thee, out of thy book which thou hast written." This was a high form of pleading, but such is God's valuation of Samuel as an intercessor that he puts him side by side with Moses, and by way of threatening to sinful Israel he tells Jeremiah that he would not even listen to Moses and Samuel if they stood before him. It is well to learn the art of prayer in our earliest days, for then we grow up to be proficient in it. Early prayer grows into powerful prayer.

Hear this, you young people, and may the Lord now make Samuels of you. What an honor to be called to intercede for others, to be the benefactor of our nation, or even the channel of blessing to our own households. Aspire to it, my dear young friends. Perhaps you will never preach, but you may pray. If you cannot climb the pulpit, you may bow before the mercy seat, and be quite as great a blessing.

As to the success of Samuel's prayers, read his life, and you will find that wrought great deliverances for the people. In the seventh chapter of this book we find that the Philistines grievously oppressed Israel, and Samuel bravely called the people together, to consider their condition, and bade them turn from idolatry, and worship the only true God, and promised them his prayers as a boon which they greatly valued. These are his words: "Gather all Israel to Mizpeh, and I will pray for you unto the LORD." He then took a lamb, and offered it up for a burnt offering wholly unto the Lord, "and Samuel cried unto the LORD for Israel, and the LORD heard him." This is one of the grand events of his life, and yet it is fairly descriptive of his whole career. He cried, and the Lord heard. In this instance the Israelites marched to battle, but Jehovah went before them, in answer to the prophet's prayer. You could hear the rolling of the drums in the march of the God of armies, and see the glittering of his spear, for so is the history of the battle recorded: "And as Samuel was offering up the burnt offering, the Philistines drew near to battle against Israel: but the LORD thundered with a great thunder on that day upon the Philistines, and discomfited them; and they were smitten before Israel. And the men of Israel went out of Mizpeh, and pursued the Philistines, and smote them." The conclusion of the whole is "So the Philistines were subdued"; that is to say, the prayer of Samuel was the conquering weapon, and Philistia crouched beneath its power. O you who know the power of prayer, write this on your banners, "So the Philistines were subdued."

Samuel's prayers were so prevalent that the very elements were controlled by him. Oh, the power of prayer! It has been ridiculed: it has been represented as an unscientific and an unpractical thing, but we who daily try it know that its power cannot be exaggerated, and do not feel even a shadow of doubt concerning it. There is such power in prayer that it "moves the arm that moves the world." We have but to know how to pray, and the thunder shall lift up its voice in answer to our cry, and Jehovah's arrows shall be scattered abroad to the overthrowing of his adversaries. How should those be able to judge of prayer who never ask at all, or never ask in faith? Let those bear witness to whom prayer is a familiar exercise, and to whom answers from God are as common as the day. Over a father's heart no power has so great a control as his child's necessity, and in the case of our Father who is in heaven it is especially so. He must hear prayer, for he cannot dishonor his own name or forget his own children.

When in his old age the people began to turn against Samuel, and to express dissatisfaction with his unworthy sons, it is beautiful to notice how Samuel at once resorted to prayer. Look at the eighth chapter, the fifth verse: the people "said unto him, 'Behold, thou art old, and thy sons walk not in thy ways: now make us a king to judge us.'" The old man was sorely grieved; it was natural that he should be. But look at the next words. Did Samuel scold the people? Did he send them home in a huff? No. It is written, "And Samuel prayed unto the LORD." He told his Master about them, and his Master said to him, "Hearken unto the voice of the people in all that they say unto thee: for they have not rejected thee,"—do not lay it to heart as if it were a personal affront to you—"but they have rejected me, that I should not reign over them." This slight upon God's servant was a rejection of God himself, and he would not have Samuel lay to heart their ingratitude to him, but think of their wicked conduct to the Lord their God.

Thus, you see, Samuel was a man of abundant prayer, and in the twenty-first verse we read that, after he had entered his protest, and told the people of all that they would have to suffer from a king, how he would tax them and oppress them and take their sons to be soldiers and their daughters to wait in his palace, and take their fields and vineyards, though they still persisted in saying, "Nay, but we will have a king," he made no angry answer but returned to his God in secret communion, "Samuel heard all the words of the people, and he rehearsed them in the ears of the LORD." Oh, that we were wise enough to do the like! Instead of going about and telling one and another of the opprobrious things that have been said about us, it were well to go straight away to our closet and rehearse them in the ears of the Lord. Samuel was thus, you see, throughout his whole official life, a man mighty in prayer, and when the people left him and followed after their new-made king, our text shows that he did not cease to intercede for them. He says, "God forbid that I should cease to pray to God for you."

Nor was this all, when Saul had turned aside and become a traitor to his divine Lord, Samuel made intercession for him. One whole night he spent in earnest entreaty, though it was all in vain; and many a time and often did he sigh for the rejected prince. The old man had been, from his youth up, an intercessor, and he never ceased from the holy exercise till his lips were closed in death. Now, beloved, you are not judges of the land, else would I plead with you to pray much for the people whom you rule. You are not all pastors and teachers, else would I say that if we do not abound in prayer the blood of souls will be upon our skirts. Some of you, however, are teachers of the young: do not think that you have done anything for your classes till you have prayed for them. Be not satisfied with the hour or two of teaching in the week, be frequent in your loving supplications. Many of you are parents. How can you discharge your duty toward your children except you bear their names upon your hearts in prayer? Those of you who are not found in these relationships have nevertheless some degree of ability, some measure of influence, some position in which you can do good to your fellows, and these demand your dependence upon God. You cannot discharge your responsibilities as relatives, as citizens, as neighbors, no, as Christian men, unless you often make supplication for all ranks and conditions. To pray for others must become to you a habit from which you would not cease even if they provoked you to the utmost degree; for you would only cry out, God forbid that I should cease to pray for you, for it would be a great sin in the sight of the most High.

II. Now, second, I call you to notice in Samuel's case *his provocation to cease from intercession,* **which provocation he patiently endured.**

The first provocation was *the slight which they put upon himself.* The grand old man who had all the year round made his circuit from place to place to do justice had never looked at a bribe. He had done everything for them without fee or reward. Though he had a right to his stipend, yet he did not take it; in the generosity of his spirit he did everything gratuitously, like Nehemiah in after days who said, "The former governors that had been before me were chargeable unto the people, and had taken of them bread and wine, beside forty shekels of silver; yea, even their servants bare rule over the people: but so did not I, because of the fear of God." Samuel throughout a long life had kept the land in peace, and innumerable blessings had come to Israel through his leadership; but now he was getting old and somewhat infirm, though he was far from being worn out, and they seized on this excuse for setting up a king. The old man felt that there was life and work in him yet; but they clamored for a king, and therefore their aged friend must give up his office and come down from his high position. It displeases him when he first hears their demand, but after a little time spent in prayer he resigns his position very pleasantly, and all his anxiety is to find the right man for the throne. When the man is found he is full of care that the Lord's anointed shall be guided aright in the kingdom; and without a thought about himself he rejoices at the sight of one whose opening days promised so well. His deposition was a hard thing, mark you, an unkind, ungenerous thing; but he did not pray one atom the less for the people because of it; probably he prayed much more; for as his mother prayed most when the sorrow of her heart was greatest, so was it with him.

Beyond the provocation which came from slight upon himself he felt wounded *by their utter rejection of his solemn protest*. He stood before them and reasoned with them in the clearest possible manner: "What do you want a king for?" he seemed to say. "This will be the manner of the king that shall reign over you: he will take your sons and appoint them for himself, for his chariots, and to be his horsemen; and some shall run before his chariots. He will take your daughters to be confectionaries, and to be cooks, and to be bakers; and he will take your fields, and your vineyards, and your olive yards, even the best of them, and give them to his servants. He will take the tenth of your seed, and of your vineyards, and give to his officers, and to his servants; and he will take your menservants, and your maidservants, and your goodliest young men, and your asses, and put them to his work. He will take the tenth of your sheep; and ye shall be his servants; and ye shall cry out in that day because of your king which ye shall have chosen you; and the LORD will not hear you in that day." There was sound common sense in all these, and every word turned out to be true in fact before long, and yet they would not listen. They said, "Nay, but we will have a king over us; that we also may be like all the nations; and that our king may judge us, and fight our battles." Despite their rejection of his warning, the venerable man did not grow testy. It is sometimes the infirmity of wise men of years and weight, that when they have presented a clearer case, presented it earnestly in all simplicity of heart, and the thing looks as plain as that twice two make four, then if their hearers deliberately persist in defying their warning they grow peevish, or perhaps it is more fair to say they exhibit a justifiable indignation. Samuel is always hopeful, and if they will not do the best thing possible, he will try to lead them to do the second best. If they will not abide under the direct rule of the Lord, as their King, he hopes that they will do well under a human king who shall be a viceroy under God, and so he continues hopefully to pray for them, and to make the best he can of them.

At last it came to this, that the nation must have a king, and their king must be crowned. They must go to Gilgal to settle the kingdom, and then Samuel stood up and in the words which I read to you just now he declared how he had dealt with them, how he had never defrauded nor oppressed, nor taken anything from them, and he told them that their choice of a king was to some extent a rejection of God, that they were putting aside the best of rules and the most honorable of governments to go down to the level of the nations. Still, *they rejected his last appeal,* and it is beautiful to my mind to see how calmly he drops the question when he has given his last address, and made his most solemn appeal to heaven. Their obstinate adherence to their whim did not cause him to restrain prayer on their behalf.

The practical lesson of this is that when you are tempted to cease from pleading for certain persons you must not yield to the suggestion. They have ridiculed your prayers: they tell you that they do not want them: they have even made a taunt and a jest of your pious wishes on their behalf. Never mind. Retaliate by still greater love. Do not cease to wrestle with God for them. It may be you have been very much disappointed in them; your heart breaks to see how they have gone aside, yet go with your deep anxieties to the mercy seat, and cry out again for them. What will become of them if you leave them to themselves? Do not leave off interceding, though you are provoked to do so in ten thousand ways.

It may be that you think, partly in unbelief, and partly through trembling anxiety, that really their doom is sealed, and they will go on to perdition. Let this rather increase the intensity of your prayer than in the least degree diminish it. Till sinners are in hell cry to God for them. As long as there is breath in their bodies and your body cause the voice of our supplication to be heard. Your husband, good woman, what if he does grow more drunken and more profane, pray for him still; for God, who can draw out leviathan as with a hook, can yet take this great sinner and make a saint of him. What if your son does seem to be more profligate than ever, follow him with many entreaties, and weep before God about him still. Loving mother and gracious father, join your fervent cries day and night at the mercy seat and you shall yet obtain your desire.

III. I come, in the third place, briefly to notice Samuel in his *persevering intercession.*

Though the people thus provoked him, he did not cease from prayer for them; for, first, there and then, he offered fresh supplication for them, and that cry was heard, and Saul was dowried with a rich measure of favor to start with. Samuel did not cease his prayer for Saul when Saul had gone far astray, for we find this passage: "Then came the word of the LORD to Samuel, saying, 'It repenteth me that I have set up Saul to be king, for he has turned back from following me, and hath not performed my commandment'; and it grieved Samuel, and he cried unto the LORD all night." *All night.* I think I see the old man in an agony for Saul, whom he loved. Old men need sleep, but the prophet forsook his bed, and in the night watches poured out his soul unto the Lord. Though he received no cheering answer, he still continued to cry; for we read, a little further on, that the Lord said to him, "How long wilt thou mourn for Saul?" He was pushing the case as far as ever he could push it, till the Lord gave him warning that there was no use in it. "How long wilt thou mourn for Saul?"

It is to be admired in Samuel, that, even though Saul may have committed the sin which is unto death, and Samuel had some fear that his fate was fixed, yet he prayed on in desperate hope. The apostle John puts the case thus: "If any man see his brother sin a sin which is not unto death, he shall ask, and he shall give him life for them that sin not unto death. There is a sin unto death: I do not say that he shall pray for it." He does not in such a case forbid our prayers, neither does he encourage them, but I take it that he gives us a permit to pray on. We do not know for certain that the most guilty person has indeed passed the bound of mercy, and therefore we may intercede with hope. If we have a horrible dread upon us that possibly our erring relative is beyond hope, if we are not commanded to pray, we are certainly not forbidden, and it is always best to err on the safe side, if it be erring at all. We may still go to God, even with a forlorn hope, and cry to him in the extremity of our distress. We are not likely to hear the Lord say to us, "How long wilt thou mourn for Saul?" We are not likely to hear him say, "How long will you pray for your boy? How long will you mourn over your husband? I do not intend to save them."

When the prophet knew that Saul was hopelessly rejected, he did not cease to pray for the nation, but went down to Bethlehem and anointed David, and when David was pursued by the malice of Saul we find him harboring David at Ramah, and exhibiting the power of prayer in his own house and in the holy place; for when Saul came down thinking to seize David, even in the seer's house, there was a prayer meeting being held, and Saul was so struck with it that he took to prophesying himself, and lay down all night among them disrobed and humbled. Men exclaimed, "Is Saul also among the prophets?" The malicious king could not venture to touch Samuel. The prophet was a gentle, mild, loving man; and yet the black-hearted Saul always had an awe of him, so that he took hold of his skirts for protection, and after he was dead wickedly sought to his supposed spirit for guidance. The man of God had evidently impressed the tall reprobate with the weight of his holy character. It is written that God was with him, and did let none of his words fall to the ground; and this was because he was a praying man. He who can prevail with God for man can always prevail with man for God. If you can overcome heaven by prayer, you can overcome earth by preaching: if you know the art of speaking to the Eternal, it will be a small thing to speak to mortal men. Rest assured that the very essence of all true power over men for their good must lie in power with God in secret: when we have waited upon the Lord, and prevailed, our work is well-nigh done.

I pray you, therefore, still persevere in supplication, and be supported in your perseverance by the knowledge that it would be a sin to cease to pray for those who have been the subjects of your petitions. Samuel confesses that it would have been sinful on his part to abstain from intercession. How so? Why, if he ceased to pray for that people, he would be neglecting his office, for God had made him a prophet to the nation, and he must intercede for them or neglect his duty. It would show a want of love to the Lord's chosen people if he did not pray for them. How could he teach them if he was not himself taught of God? How could he possibly hope to sway them if he had not enough affection for them to cry to God on their behalf? It would be in his case, too, a sin of anger. It would look as if he were in a pet [petulance] with them and with God too, because he could not be all that he would wish to be. "God forbid," he said, "I should harbor such anger in my bosom as to cease to pray for you." It would have been a neglect of the divine glory; for whatever the people might be, God's name was wrapped up in them, and if they did not prosper, the Lord would not be glorified in the eyes of the heathen. He could not give up praying for them, for their cause was the cause of God. It would have been a cruelty to souls if he who possessed such power in prayer had restrained it. Now, brethren and sisters, it will be sin on your part if you neglect the mercy seat. You will grieve the Holy Spirit, you will rob Christ of his glory, you will be cruel to souls dead in sin, and you will be false and traitorous to the Spirit of grace, and to your sacred calling.

IV. Our last point is that Samuel showed *his sincerity in intercession* by corresponding action.

For he says in the words of the text, "God forbid that I should sin against the LORD in ceasing to pray for you: but I will teach you the good and the right way." So far from leaving off praying, he would be doubly diligent to teach them: and he did so. He taught them by reminding them of God's promises, that he would not forsake his people: by directing them how to act—"serve God in truth with all your heart"; by urging motives upon them—"consider the great things he hath done for you"; and by adding a solemn warning, "if you shall still do wickedly, ye shall be consumed, both ye and your king." After praying for your friends, do try as well as you can to answer your own prayer by using the means which God ordinarily blesses. Some persons make idle prayers, for they use no effort for obtaining their requests. If a husbandman asks for a harvest, he also plows and sows, for else his supplications would be hypocritical. If we wish to see our neighbors converted, we shall labor for it in all ways. We shall invite them to go with us where the gospel is faithfully preached, or we shall place a good book in their way, or we shall speak with them personally about eternal things. If I knew where gold was to be had for the picking up, and I wanted my neighbor to be rich, I would tell him of the precious deposit and ask him to come and gather some of the treasure with me. But many never think of inviting a neighbor or a friend who is a Sabbath breaker to go with them to the house of God; and there are thousands in London who only want an invitation and they would be sure to come, once, at any rate, and who can tell but that once might lead to their conversion?

If I desire the salvation of anyone, I ought to tell him as best as I can what his condition is, and what the way of salvation is, and how he may find rest. All men are approachable at some time or in some way. It is very imprudent to rush at everybody as soon as you see them, without thought or ordinary prudence, for you may disgust those whom you wish to win: but those who earnestly plead for others, and bestir themselves to seek them, are generally taught of God, and so they are made wise as to time, manner, and subject. A man who wishes to shoot birds will, after a while, become expert in the sport, because he will give his mind to it: he will after a little practice become a noted marksman and know all about guns and dogs. A man who wants to catch salmon has his heart set upon his angling, and becomes absorbed in the pursuit. He soon learns how to use his rod and how to manage his fish. So he who longs to win souls, and puts his heart into it, finds out the knack of it by some means, and the Lord gives him success. I could not teach it to you, you must practice in order to find out; but this I will say, no man is clear of his fellows' blood simply because he has prayed to be so. Suppose we had around this parish of Newington a number of people who were dying of hunger, and we were to have a prayer meeting that God would relieve their wants: would it not be hypocrisy worthy to be ridiculed and held up to reprobation if, after having prayed for these people, we all went home and ate our own dinners and did not give them a farthing's worth of bread? The truly benevolent man puts his hand in his pocket and says, "What can I do that my prayer may be answered?" I have heard of one who prayed in New York for a certain number of very poor families that he had visited, and he asked the Lord that they might be fed and clothed. His little son said, "Father, if I were God I should tell you to answer your own prayer, for you have plenty of money." Thus the Lord might well say to us when we have been interceding, "Go and answer your own prayer by telling your friends of my Son." Do you sing, "Fly abroad, thou mighty gospel"? Then give it wings covered with silver. Do you sing, "Waft, waft, ye winds, his story"? Then spend your breath for it. There is a power in your gifts; there is a power in your speech; use these powers. If you cannot personally do much, you can do a great deal by helping another to preach Christ: but chief and first you ought to do somewhat by your own hand, heart, and tongue. Go and teach the good and right way, and then shall your prayers be heard.

David: Encouraging Himself in God

≺≻

Delivered on Lord's Day morning, June 26, 1881, at the Metropolitan Tabernacle, Newington. No. 1606.

> *And David was greatly distressed; for the people spake of stoning him, because the soul of all the people was grieved, every man for his sons and for his daughters: but David encouraged himself in the LORD his God. . . . And David inquired at the LORD, saying, "Shall I pursue after this troop? shall I overtake them?" And he answered him, "Pursue: for thou shalt surely overtake them, and without fail recover all."*—1 SAMUEL 30:6, 8

We ought to be deeply grateful to God for the inspired history of the life of his servant David. It was a great life, a vigorous life, a life spent in many positions and conditions. I almost rejoice that it was not a faultless life, for its failings and errors are instructive. It is the life of a man after God's own heart; but still, the life of one who went astray, like a lost sheep, and was recovered by the great Shepherd's grace. By this fact he comes all the nearer to us poor, faulty men and women. I would venture to apply to David the description which has been applied to the world's own poet—

> *A man so various, that he seemed to be*
> *Not one, but all mankind's epitome.*

Each one may find something like himself in the long, eventful, and checkered life of the son of Jesse. Among other things we learn this, that where there is faith there is sure to be trial; for David, though he trusted God so heartily, had good need of all the faith he possessed. In his early days he was hunted like a partridge upon the mountains by Saul and was constantly in jeopardy of his life. He had so choice a treasure of faith about him, that Satan was forever trying to plunder him of it. Still, the worst trials that David suffered arose not out of his faith, but out of his want of it. That which he did to avoid trouble brought him into deeper distress than ordinary providences ever caused him. He left the country where he was so ill at ease, which was, nevertheless, your land, O Emmanuel, and he went away into the land of the Philistines, expecting there to escape from further turmoil. In so doing he transgressed, and fresh trials came upon him, trials of a worse kind than those which had happened to him from the hand of Saul. Brethren, the poet said—

> The path of sorrow, and that path alone,
> Leads to the land where sorrow is unknown,

and he spoke truly; for "in the world ye shall have tribulation." If you have faith, it must be tried, and should that faith fail, you must be tried still more. There is no discharge from this war: difficulties must be faced. This is the day of battle, and you must fight if you would reign. You are like men thrown into the sea, you must swim or drown. It is useless to expect ease where your Lord had none. If you adopt the paltry shifts suggested by unbelief, not even then shall you avoid affliction; the probabilities are that you will be taken among the thorns and scourged with the briars of the wilderness. However rough the king's highway may be, the bypaths are far worse; therefore keep the way of the commandment and bravely face its trials.

Another lesson is this: though we shall be tried, yet faith in God is an available resource at all times. Faith is a shield which you may use for warding off every kind of arrow, yes, even the fiery darts of the great enemy; for this shield cannot be penetrated even by javelins of fire. You cannot be cast into a condition in which faith shall not help you. There is a promise of God suitable for every state, and God has wisdom and skill and love and faithfulness to deliver you out of every possible jeopardy; and therefore you have only to confide in God, and deliverance is sure to come. Mainly note this: that *even when your trouble has been brought upon you by your own fault, faith is still available.* When your affliction is evidently a chastisement for grievous transgression, still trust in the Lord. The Lord Jesus prayed for erring Peter that his faith might not fail him: his hope of recovery lay there. Faith under a sense of guilt is one of those noble kinds of faith at which some are staggered. To my mind the faith of a saint is comparatively easy; it is the faith of a sinner that is hard. When you know that you have walked uprightly before God, and have not stained your garments, then you can trust him without difficulty: but, oh, when you have stepped aside, and when at last the heavenly Father makes you smart under his rod—to cast yourself upon him then is faith indeed. Do not fail to exercise it, for this is the faith which saves. What faith is that which first of all brings men into possession of a good hope but the faith of a sinner? Often in life, when our sinnership becomes more manifest to us than usual, we shall be driven to that first sort of faith, in which, being unworthy, we trust entirely in pardoning grace. It would be wise always to live by this same faith.

If any of you at this time are in great distress, and are conscious that you richly deserve all your troubles because of your folly, still trust in the mercy of the Lord. Do not doubt the Lord your Savior, for he invites his backsliding children to return unto him. Though you have fallen by your iniquity, yet take with you words and return unto the Lord. May the Holy Spirit give you renewed trust in the Lord, who forgives iniquity, transgression, and sin, and retains not his anger forever, because he delights in mercy.

Let this stand as our preface, and the whole of the sermon will tend to illustrate it. We notice: first, David's distress—"David was greatly distressed"; second, David's encouragement—"David encouraged himself in the LORD his God"; third, David's inquiry—"And David inquired at the LORD"; and then, fourth, David's answer of peace—the Lord said, "Pursue: for thou shalt surely overtake them, and without fail recover all."

I. First, then, let us look at *David's distress*—"David was greatly distressed."

His city was burned, his wives were gone, the sons and daughters of his comrades were all captive, and little Ziklag, where they had made a home, smoked before them in blackened ruins. The men of war, wounded in heart, mutinied against their leader, and were ready to stone him. David's fortunes were at their lowest ebb. To understand his position we must go a little further back in his history.

David was greatly distressed for *he had been acting without consulting his God*. It was his general habit to wait upon the Lord for direction, for even as a shepherd lad it was his joy to sing, "He leadeth me"; but for once David had gone without leading, and had chosen a bad road. Worn out by the persecution of Saul, in an evil moment his heart failed him, and he said, "I shalt surely fall one day by the hand of Saul." This was a dangerous mood. Always be afraid of being afraid. Failing faith means failing strength. Do not regard despondency as merely a loss of joy, view it as draining away your spiritual life. Struggle against it, for it often happens that when faith ebbs sin comes to the flood. He who does not comfortably trust God will soon seek after comfort somewhere else, and David did so: without asking divine direction he fled to the court of the Philistine chieftain Achish, hoping to be quiet there. See what came of it! When he stood among the ashes of Ziklag, he began to understand what an evil and bitter thing it is to lean to our own understanding, to forget God who guides us, and to become a law unto ourselves. Perhaps some of you are in distress in the same way: you have chosen your own path, and now you are caught in the tangled bushes which tear your flesh. You have carved for yourselves, and you have cut your own fingers; you have obtained your heart's desire, and while the meat is yet in your mouth a curse has come with it. You say you "did it for the best"; yes, but it has turned out to be for the worst. David never made a heavier rod for himself than when he thought to avoid all further discomfort by leaving his true place.

Worse than this, if worse can be, *David had also followed policy instead of truth.* The Oriental mind was, and probably still is, given to lying. Easterners do not think it wrong to tell an untruth; many do it habitually. Just as an upright merchant in this country would not be suspected of a falsehood, so you would not in the olden time have suspected the average Oriental of ever speaking the truth if he could help it, because he felt that everybody else would deceive him and so he must practice great cunning. The golden rule in David's day was, "Do others, for others will certainly do you." David in his early days was not without the taint of his times. He became the commander of the bodyguard of Achish, king of Gath, and he lived in the royal city. As he found himself rather awkwardly situated in that idolatrous town, he said to the king, "If I have now found grace in thine eyes, let them give me a place in some town in the country, that I may dwell there: for why should thy servant dwell in the royal city with thee?" Achish appears to have been almost a convert to the worship of Jehovah, and certainly shines brilliantly in the narrative before us. At David's request he gave him the town of Ziklag.

David and his men warred with the various tribes of Canaanites who dwelled in the south of Palestine, and took from them great spoil; but he greatly erred in making Achish believe that he was fighting against Judah. We read, "And Achish believed David, saying, 'He hath made his people Israel utterly to abhor him; therefore he shall be my servant forever.'" This was the result of David's acted and uttered lie, and lest the falsehood should be found out, David spared none of those whom he conquered, saying "Lest they should tell on us, saying, 'So did David.'" So that beginning with policy he went on to falsehood, and from one falsehood he was driven to another, and his course became far other than that which a man of God should have pursued. How different was such false conduct from the usual character of the man who said, "He that worketh deceit shall not dwell within my house: he that telleth lies shall not tarry in my sight." See the fruit of his falsehood! Ziklag is burned with fire: his wives are captives; and his men speak of stoning him.

If you and I ever get away from living by straightforward truth, we shall wander into a maze from which it will be hard to extricate ourselves. We should each feel that we can die but we cannot lie, we can starve but we cannot cheat, we can be ground into the dust but we cannot do an unrighteous thing. If it be so, we may count upon the help of God, and may go bravely on under every difficulty. David had left the highway of righteousness, and was stumbling among the dark mountains of craft and deceit. He was plotting and scheming like the worst of worldlings, and he must be made to see his error, and taught to abhor the way of lying; hence in one moment the Lord launches at him bereavement, plunder, mutiny, danger of life, that he might be driven to his God, and made to hate the way of cunning. What wonder that David was greatly distressed?

Yet was his distress the more severe on another account, for *David had sided with the enemies of the Lord's people.* He had gone to the Philistines, and their prince had said to him, "I will make thee keeper of mine head forever." Think of David keeping the head of a Philistine! When Achish gathered the Philistine army to battle with Israel, we read with shame, "And the lords of the Philistines passed on by hundreds, and by thousands: but David and his men passed on in the reward with Achish." How dreadfully troubled David must have felt in this false position. Think of David, who was ordained to be king of Israel, marching his armed band to fight his own countrymen! How gracious was the Lord in bringing him out of that perilous position. The Philistine princes suspected him, as well they might, and said to Achish, "What do these Hebrews here?" They were jealous of the high office to which David had been promoted, and fearful of his turning against them during the fight. "And the princes of the Philistines were wroth with Achish; and the princes of the Philistines said unto him, 'Make this fellow return, that he may go again to his place which thou hast appointed him, and let him not go down with us to battle, lest in the battle he be an adversary to us: for wherewith should he reconcile himself unto his master? should it not be with the heads of these men? Is not this David, of whom they sang, one to another in dances, saying, "Saul slew his thousands, and David his ten thousands?"'" Though the Philistine king, like the true man that he was, smoothed it down, he was forced to send David away. What a relief David must have felt! Well might he pen the words of Psalm 124, "Our soul is escaped as a bird out of the snare of the fowlers: the snare is broken, and we are escaped." What a horror would have been upon him if he had actually gone with the Philistines to the battle in which Saul and Jonathan were slain. It would have been a stain upon David all his life. The Lord delivered him, but he made him to feel his rod at the same time, for no sooner had David reached Ziklag, than he saw that the hand of the Lord was gone out against him, desolation smoked around him, and we do not marvel that David was greatly distressed.

Picture the position of David, in the center of his band. He has been driven away by the Philistine lords with words of contempt; his men have been sneered at—"What do these Hebrews here? Is not this David?" When he walked with God he was like a prince, and no man dared to sneer at him, but now he has been flouted by the uncircumcised Philistines, and has been glad to sneak back to his little city, ashamed of himself. It is terrible when a man of God falls into such a position that he gives the enemy opportunity to blaspheme God, and to despise his servant. It is terrible when even worldlings scout the inconsistency of the professed follower of Jesus. "What do these Hebrews here?" is the sarcastic question of the world. "How comes a professing Christian to be acting as we do? Look, he is trying to cultivate our acquaintance, and pass for one of ourselves, and yet he calls himself a servant of God!" They begin to point, as they did at Peter—"Thou also wast with Jesus of Nazareth, for thy speech betrayeth thee." "What doest thou here, Elijah?" is the voice which comes from God's mouth, and the lips of his adversaries repeat it. When the child of God feels that he is in that predicament, and in great trouble too, it is not strange that he is greatly distressed.

At the back of this came *bereavement*. His wives were gone. He was a man of a large, affectionate, tender heart, and what grief it must have been to him! Nor was he a solitary mourner; but all those brave fellows who were joined with him were bereaved too. Hark to the common chorus of grief! They weep, until they have no more power to weep. It must have been a dread day for their leader to feel his own personal sorrow merged and drowned in the flood of grief which swept over his companions. As for his worldly possessions, he was now as *poor* as he possibly could be; for all that he had was taken away, and his habitation was burned with fire, and the rovers were gone he knew not whither. Worst of all, he was now *forsaken* by his followers. Those who had been with him in his worst fortunes now upbraided him with their calamity. Why did he leave the city to go off to help these enemies of the Lord, the uncircumcised Philistines? He might have known better; and they grew indignant, and one said, "Let us stone him"; to which others answered, "Let us do it at once." They were evidently in a great rage. He stands there faint with weeping, a friendless, forsaken man, with *his very life in danger* from furious mutineers. Do you wonder that it is written, "And David was greatly distressed"? He is surrounded with sorrow; but he has no need to gather ashes as the emblems of his woe; for ashes are everywhere about him, the whole place is smoking. He mourns greatly for his wives, and his soldiers mourn for their children, for they are as if they were slain with the sword. It is a case of deep distress, with this added sting—that he had brought it upon himself.

There is the picture before you: now let us see a fairer scene as we observe what David did under the circumstances. When he was at his worst he was seen at his best.

II. Second, let us consider *David's encouragement*: "And David encouraged himself."

That is well, David! He did not at first attempt to encourage anybody else; but he encouraged *himself.* Some of the best talks in the world are those which a man has with himself. He who speaks to everybody except himself is a great fool. I think I hear David say, "Why art thou cast down, O my soul, and why art thou disquieted within me? hope thou in God; for I will yet praise him." David encouraged himself. But he encouraged himself "in the LORD his God," namely, in Jehovah. That is the surest way of encouraging yourself. David might have drawn, if he had pleased, a measure of encouragement from those valiant men who joined him just about this particular time; for it happened, according to 1 Chronicles 12:19–22, that many united with his band at that hour. Let us read the passage. "And there fell some of Manasseh to David, when he came with the Philistines against Saul to battle; but they helped them not: for the lords of the Philistines upon advisement sent him away, saying, 'He will fall to his master Saul to the jeopardy of our heads.' As he went to Ziklag, there fell to him of Manasseh, Adnah, and Jozabad, and Jediael, and Michael, and Jozabad, and Elihu, and Zilthai, captains of the thousands that were of Manasseh. And they helped David against the band of the rovers: for they were all mighty men of valor, and were captains in the host. For at that time day by day there came to David to help him, until it was a great host, like the host of God." These newcomers had not lost their wives and children, for they had not been in Ziklag; but David did not look around to them and beg them to stand by him, and put down the mutiny. No, he had by this time become sick of men, and weary of trusting to himself. God was beginning to cure his servant by a bitter dose of distress, and the evidence of the cure was that he did not encourage himself by his new friends, or by the hope of others coming; but he encouraged himself in the Lord his God.

Do you not feel a wind from the hills? The air blows strong and fresh from the everlasting mountains, now that the man of God is looking to God alone. Before, David was down there in the valleys, with his policy and his craft, in the stagnant atmosphere of self-trust and worldliness; but now he stands in Ziklag, a friendless man, but free and true. How grand he is amid the rains! He rises to his full height, while his fortunes fall! He reminds you of his youthful days when he said, "The LORD that delivered me out of the paw of the lion, and out of the paw of the bear, he will deliver me out of the hand of this Philistine." He is no longer in bondage to craft, but he is a man again, strong in the strength of God; for he casts himself away from all earthly trusts, and encourages himself in the Lord.

He did not sit down in sullen despair, nor did he think, as Saul did, of resorting to wrong means for help; but he went, sinner as he was, confessing all his wrongdoing, straightaway to his God, and asked for the priest to come that he might speak with him in the name of the most High. Brothers and sisters, if you are in trouble, and your trouble is mixed with sin, if you have afflicted yourselves by your backslidings and perversities, nevertheless I pray you look nowhere else for help but to the God whom you have offended. When he lifts his arm, as it were, to execute vengeance, lay hold upon it and he will spare you. Does he not himself say, "Let him lay hold on my strength"? I remember old Master Quarles has a strange picture of one trying to strike another with a flail, and how does the other escape? Why, he runs in and keeps close, and so he is not struck. It is the very thing to do. Close in with God. Cling to him by faith; hold fast by him in hope. Say, "Though he slay me, yet will I trust in him." Resolve, "I will not let thee go." Guilty as you are, it is good for you to draw nigh unto God.

Let us try to conceive of the way in which David would encourage himself in the Lord his God. Standing amid those ruins, he would say, "Yet the Lord does love me, and I love him. Though I have wandered, yet my heart cannot rest without him. Though I have had but little fellowship with him of late, yet he has not forgotten to be gracious, nor has he in anger shut up his bowels of compassion." He would look back upon those happy days when he kept sheep, and sang psalms unto the Lord his God amid the pastures of the wilderness. He would recollect those peaceful hours of happiest communion and long to have them over again. His own psalms would tend to comfort him as he saw how his heart had once been glad. He would say to himself: "My experience of divine love is not a dream. I know it is not a myth or a delusion. I have known the Lord, and I have had near and dear intercourse with him, and I know that he changes not, and therefore he will help me. His mercy endureth forever. He will put away my transgression." Thus he encouraged himself in the Lord his God.

Then he went further, and argued, "Hath not the Lord chosen me? Has he not ordained me to be king in Israel? Did he not send his prophet Samuel, who poured oil upon my head, and said, 'This is he'? Surely the Lord will not change his appointment or suffer his word to fail. I have been separated from my kinsfolk and hunted by Saul and driven from rock to cave and from cave to wilderness, and I have known no rest, and all because I was ordained to be king in Saul's place; surely the Lord will carry out his purpose, and will set me on the throne. He has not chosen and ordained and anointed me in mockery."

Brethren, do you need an interpretation of this parable? Can you not see its application to yourselves? Are you not saying, "The Lord called me by his grace, brought me out from my love of the world, and made me a priest and a king unto himself, and can he leave me? Is not the oil of his Spirit still upon me? Can he cast me off? He separated me to himself, and gave me to know that my destiny was not like that of the ungodly world, but that he had ordained me and chosen me to be his servant forever—will he leave me to perish? Shall his enemy rejoice over me?" Thus may you encourage yourself in God.

Then he would go over all the past deliverances which he had experienced. I see the picture which passed like a panorama before David's eye. He saw himself when he slew the lion and the bear. Did God deliver him then, and will he not deliver him now? He pictured himself going out to meet the giant Goliath, with nothing but a sling and a stone, and coming back with the monster's head in his hand; and he argued, "Will he not rescue me now?" He saw himself in the courts of Saul, when the mad king sought to pin him to the wall with a javelin, and he barely escaped. He saw himself let down by the kindness of Michal from the window, when her father sought to slay him in his bed.

He saw himself in the cave of Engedi, and upon the tracks of the wild goats, pursued by his remorseless adversary, but always strangely guarded from his cruel hand. He cheers himself, as one had done before him, with the inference, "If the Lord had meant to destroy me, he would not have showed me such things as these."

Come, now, dear children of God, take down your diaries and refer to the days when the Lord helped you again and again. How many times has he blessed you? You could not count them, for God has been so gracious and tender that he has aided you ten thousand times already. Has he changed in love, in faithfulness, in power? God forbid that we should indulge such a wicked thought. He is still the same, and so let us encourage ourselves in him.

"Alas," say you, "I have done wrong." I know you have; but *he* has not. If your confidence were in yourself, that wrong of yours might crush your hope; but since your confidence is in God, and he has not changed, why should you fear? "Oh, but I am so sinful." Yes; I know you are, and so you were when he first looked upon you in love. If his love had sought to come to you by the way of merit, it never would have reached you; but it comes to you by way of free, rich, sovereign grace, and therefore it will come to you evermore. Do you not feel refreshed this morning as you think of what the Lord has done? And do you not feel that after doing so much it would be wrong now to distrust him? Will you not even now encourage yourself in your God?

Perhaps David at that moment perceived that this crushing blow was sent in infinite tenderness to clean him right out of the condition into which he had fallen. The Lord seems to say to David, "All that you have ever got of Achish is this village of Ziklag, and I have caused it to be burned up, so that you have nothing left to be a tie between you and Philistia. The princes said, 'I send this fellow away,' and they have sent you away; and now the town that Achish gave you is utterly destroyed; there is no link left between you and the Philistines, and you have come back to your natural standing." The hardest blow that our God ever strikes, if it puts us right and separates us from self and sin, and carnal policy, is a coup de grâce, a blow of love. If it ends our life of selfishness, and brings us back into the life of trust, it is a blessed blow. When God blesses his people most it is by terrible things in righteousness. He smote David to heal him. He fetched him out from the snare of the Philistine fowler, and delivered him from the noisome pestilence of heathen association, by a way that brought the tears into his eyes till he had no more power to weep. Now the servant of the Lord begins to see the wonderful hand of God, and he shall yet say, "Before I was afflicted I went astray, but now have I kept thy word."

I, the preacher of this hour, beg to bear my little witness that the worst days I have ever had have turned out to be my best days, and when God has seemed most cruel to me he has then been most kind. If there is anything in this world for which I would bless him more than for anything else, it is for pain and affliction. I am sure that in these things the richest, tenderest love has been manifested toward me. I pray you, dear friends, if you are at this time very low and greatly distressed, encourage yourselves in the abundant faithfulness of the God who hides himself. Our Father's wagons rumble most heavily when they are bringing us the richest freight of the bullion of his grace. Love letters from heaven are often sent in black-edged envelopes. The cloud that is black with horror is big with mercy. We may not ask for trouble, but if we were wise we should look upon it as the shadow of an unusually great blessing. Dread the calm, it is often treacherous, and beneath its wing the pestilence is lurking. Fear not the storm, it brings healing in its wings, and when Jesus is with you in the vessel the tempest only hastens the ship to its desired haven. Blessed be the Lord, whose way is in the whirlwind, and who makes the clouds to be the dust of his feet. May some such thoughts as these help you to encourage yourself in God as David did.

III. And now, third, we have *David inquiring of God.*

"And David inquired at the LORD, saying, 'Shall I pursue after this troop? Shall I overtake them?'"

Note well that as soon as David had come to be right with God, he longed to know the Lord's mind as to his next action. You and I would have said, "Let us hasten after these marauders; let us not stop an instant, we can pray as we march, or at some other time. Haste! haste! for the lives of our wives and children are at stake." It was a time for hurry if ever there was; but, as the good proverb says, "Prayer and provender hinder no man's journey." David wisely stops. "Bring hither the ephod," cries he, and he waits till the oracle answers his inquiries. He will not march till the Lord shall give the word of command. This is well. It is a sweet frame of mind to be in to be brought to feel that you must now wait the Lord's bidding, that your strength is to sit still till God bids you go forward. Oh, that we could always keep up this submission of heart! Oh, that we never leaned to our own understanding, but trusted solely in God!

Observe that David takes it for granted that his God is going to help him. He only wants to know how it is to be done. "Shall I pursue? Shall I overtake?" When you, my brother, are inquiring of the Lord, do not approach him as if he would not help you, or could hardly be expected to aid you. You would not like your children to ask a favor of you as if they were afraid of their lives to speak to you. I am sure you would not like a dear child, whatever wrong he had been doing, to feel a suspicion of your love, and doubt your willingness to help; for whatever he has done he is your child still. David has encouraged himself in his God, and he is sure that God is ready to save him; all that he wants to know is how he is himself to act in the business.

It is to be remarked, however, that David does not expect that God is going to help him, without his doing his best. He inquires, "Shall I pursue? Shall I overtake?" He means to be up and doing. Sad as he is, and faint as he is, he is ready for action. Many who get into trouble seem to expect an angel to come and lift them up by the hair of their heads; but angels have other matters in hand. The Lord generally helps us by enabling us to help ourselves, and it is a way which does us double good. It was more for David's benefit that he should himself smite the Amalekites than that God should hurl hailstones out of heaven upon them, and destroy them. David will have their spoil for the wage of battle, and be rewarded for the forced march and the fight. Brother, you will have to work and labor to extricate yourself from debt and difficulty, and so the Lord will hear your prayer. The rule is to trust in God to smite the Amalekites, and then to march after them, as if it all depended upon yourself. There is a God-reliance which arouses all our self-reliance and yokes it to the chariot of providence, making the man ready for action because God is with him. It is instructive to notice that, although David was thus ready for action, trusting in God, he greatly distrusted his own wisdom; for he asked, "Shall I pursue them?" That man is wise who counts his own wisdom to be folly; and he who lays his judgment down at Jesus' feet is a man of soundest judgment. He who tarries till the divine wisdom shall guide him, he shall be expert and prudent in all things.

David also distrusted his own strength though quite ready to use what he had; for he said, "Shall I overtake?" Can my men march fast enough to overtake these robbers? And what a blessed state of heart that is when we have no strength of our own, but seek unto God! It is good to be insufficient, and to find God all-sufficient. I pause here a minute and pray God ever to keep you and me in just the condition into which he brought his servant David. I do not care so much about his overtaking the robbers, and all that: the glory was to have overtaken his God and to be waiting at his feet. He could not be brought to this without his city being burned, without his being bereaved, robbed, and ready to die by the hands of his own warriors; but it was worth all the cost to be brought to rest on the bare arm of God, and to wait in childlike dependence at the great Father's door. Let the proud lift up their heads, but let me rest mine on Jesus' bosom. Let the mighty raise their shields on high; as for me, the Lord is my Shield and my Defense, and he alone. When I am weak, then I am strong. "They that wait upon the Lord shall renew their strength." The old song of Hannah is still true: "He hath showed strength with his arm; he hath scattered the proud in the imagination of their hearts. He hath put down the mighty from their seats, and exalted them of low degree."

IV. We close our sermon with the fourth note, which is a note of jubilate and praise unto God, who helped his servant—*David's answer of peace.*

The Lord heard his supplication. He says, "In my distress I cried unto the Lord and he heard me." But mark this, he was not delivered without further trial. David marched with his six hundred men on foot after the foe, with all speed, and the band became so worn and weary that one third of them could not ford the brook Besor, which, though usually dry, was probably at that time flowing with a strong stream. Many a leader would have given up the chase with one out of three of his troop in hospital, but David pursued with his reduced force. When God means to bless us, he often takes away a part of the little strength we thought we had. We did not think our strength equal to the task, and the Lord takes away a portion even of the little power we had. Our

God does not fill till he has emptied. Two hundred men must be rent away from David's side before God could give him victory, for he meant to have David's whole force to be exactly equal to the four hundred Amalekites who fled, that he might make the victory the more memorable and renowned. Expect then, O troubled one, that you will be delivered, but know that your sorrow may yet deepen, that you may have all the greater joy by and by.

Leaving the two hundred men behind, David dashes ahead, and by forced marches overtakes the enemy; finds them feasting; smites them hip and thigh, and destroys them, and takes the spoil, but in such a way that manifestly it was the gift of God. He speaks of the spoil as "that which the LORD hath given us, who hath preserved us, and delivered the company that came against us into our hand." God will help his servants who trust him, but he will have all the honor of the victory. He will deliver them in such a way that they shall lift their psalms and hymns unto God alone, and this shall be the strain: "Sing unto the LORD, for he hath triumphed gloriously. We were unworthy, we were faint, we were distressed, but God has made us more than conquerors through his great love."

David's victory was perfect. We are told over and over again that "David recovered all." Nothing was lost: not a piece of money nor a garment, not an ox nor a sheep, much less a child, or one of womankind—"David recovered all." How well the Lord works when he once lays his hand to it. "He will perfect that which concerneth me." Salvation is of the Lord, and it is an everlastingly complete salvation. Trust in the Lord forever, for in the Lord Jehovah there is everlasting strength. He will work, and work perfectly, till he shall say, "It is finished." The battle is the Lord's, and his saints shall be more than conquerors.

Not only did God give David complete rescue, but he awarded him great spoil. "And they said, 'This is David's spoil.'" David became rich and able to send presents to his friends; but he was also the better man, the holier man, the stronger man, the more fit to wear that crown which was so soon to adorn his brow. O brothers and sisters, the deeper your trouble, the louder will be your song, if you can but trust in God and walk in fellowship with Jesus. Little skiffs that keep near the land carry but small cargoes, and their masters see little save the shore; but they that go down to the sea in ships, that do business in great waters, these see the works of the Lord and his wonders in the deep. It is something to be out on the wide main in a terrific storm, when the ship is tossed to and fro like a ball, when the heavens are mixed up with the ocean, and all is uproar. Then great thunder contends with the roaring of the sea, and the lightning flames are quenched by the boiling of the mighty waves. When you reach the shore again, you know a gladness which the landsman cannot feel, and you have a tale to tell to your children, and your children's children, of what you have seen in the deep, such as lubberly landsmen scarce can understand. As for those who dwell at ease, what do they see? You who have been in the battle can sing of victory, and, pointing to your experience, can exclaim, "This is David's spoil."

Trust in the Lord your God. Believe also in his Son Jesus. Get rid of sham faith, and really believe. Get rid of a professional faith, and trust in the Lord at all times, about everything. "What, trust him about pounds, shillings, and pence?" Assuredly. I dread the faith that cannot trust God about bread and garments—it is a lying faith. Depend upon it, that is not the solid, practical faith of Abraham, who trusted God about his tent and his cattle, and about a wife for his son. That faith which made David trust God about the sons and daughters and the spoil, that is the sort of faith for you and for me. If God cannot be trusted about loaves and fishes how shall he be trusted about the things of eternity and the glories which are yet to be revealed? Stay yourself on God with an everyday faith. Faith in God is the exercise of sanctified common sense. Somebody called me "superstitious" for trusting God as to his answering prayer, but I reply that he is superstitious who does not trust the living God. He who believes in the power of the greatest of all forces and trusts in the surest of all truths, is but acting rationally. The purest reason approves reliance upon God. The end shall declare the wisdom of believing God. At the last, when we with all believers shall lift up the great hallelujah unto the Lord God of Israel who reigns over all things for his people, it shall be known by all that faith is honorable and unbelief contemptible.

God bless you, brethren, and if any of you have never trusted God at all, nor rested in his dear Son, may you be brought to do so at once. May you see your self-righteousness burned like Ziklag, and all your carnal hopes carried away captive, and may you then encourage yourselves in Christ, for he will recover all for you, and give you spoil besides, and there shall be joy and rejoicing. The Lord be with you. Amen.

Job: The Turning of Job's Captivity

Delivered at the Metropolitan Tabernacle, Newington. Published in 1875. No. 1262.

> The LORD *turned the captivity of Job, when he prayed for his friends: also the* LORD *gave Job twice as much as he had before.*—JOB 42:10

Since God is immutable he acts always upon the same principles, and hence his course of action in the olden times to a man of a certain sort will be a guide as to what others may expect who are of like character. God does not act by caprice, nor by fits and starts. He has his usual modes and ways. The psalmist David uses the expression, "Then will I teach transgressors *thy ways,*" as if God had well-known ways, habits, and modes of action; and so he has, or he would not be the unchangeable Jehovah. In that song of Moses the servant of God, and the song of the Lamb, which is recorded in the fifteenth chapter of the Revelation, we read, "Just and true are thy ways, thou King of saints."

The Lord has ways as high above our ways as the heavens are above the earth, and these are not fickle and arbitrary. These ways, although very different if we view them superficially, are really always the same when you view them with understanding. The ways of the Lord are right, though transgressors fall therein by not discerning them; but the righteous understand the ways of the Lord, for to them he makes them known, and they perceive that grand general principles govern all the actions of God. If it were not so, the case of such a man as Job would be of no service to us. It could not be said that the things which happened aforetime happened unto us for an example, because if God did not act on fixed principles we could never tell how he would act in any fresh case, and that which happened to one man would be no rule whatever, and no encouragement whatever, to another. We are not all like Job, but we all have Job's God. Though we have neither risen to Job's wealth, nor will, probably, ever sink to Job's poverty, yet there is the same God above us if we be high, and the same God with his everlasting arms beneath us if we be brought low; and what the Lord did for Job he will do for us, not precisely in the same form, but in the same spirit, and with like design. If, therefore, we are brought low tonight, let us be encouraged with the thought that God will turn again our captivity; and let us entertain the hope that after the time of trial shall be over, we shall be richer, especially in spiritual things, than ever we were before. There will come a turning point to the growing heat of affliction, and the fire shall cool. When the ebb has fallen to its lowest, the sea will return to its strength; when midwinter has come, spring will be near, and when midnight has struck, then the dawning will not be far away. Perhaps, too, the signal of our happier days shall be the very same as that of the patient patriarch, and when we pray for our friends, blessings shall be poured into our own bosoms.

Our text has in it three points very clearly; first, *the Lord can soon turn his people's captivity*: "The LORD turned the captivity of Job." Second, *there is generally some point at which he does this*: in Job's case he turned his captivity when he prayed for his friends. And, third, *believers shall never be losers by God*, for he gave Job twice as much as he had before.

I. First, then, *the Lord can soon turn his people's captivity.*

That is a very remarkable expression—"captivity." It does not say, "God turned his poverty," though Job was reduced to the extremity of penury, having lost all his property. We do not read that the Lord turned his sickness, though he was covered with sore boils. It does not say that he turned away the sting of bereavement, reproach, and calumny, although all those are included. But there is something more meant by the word *captivity.* A man may be very poor, and yet not in captivity; his soul may sing among the angels when his body is on a dunghill and dogs are licking his sores. A man may be very sick, and yet not be in captivity; he may be roaming the broad fields of covenant mercy though he cannot rise from his bed; and his soul may never enjoy greater liberty than when his body is scarcely able to turn from side to side. Captivity is bondage of mind, the iron entering into the soul. I suspect that Job, under the severe mental trial which attended his bodily pains, was, as to his spirit, like a man bound hand and foot and fettered, and then taken away from his native country, banished from the place which he loved, deprived of the associations which had cheered him, and confined in darkness. I mean that, together with the trouble and trial to which he was subjected, he had lost somewhat the presence of God; much of his joy and comfort had departed; the peace of his mind had gone, and the associations which he had formed with other believers were now broken: he was in all these respects like a lone captive. His three friends had condemned him as a hypocrite, and would not have association with him except to censure him, and thus he felt like one who had been carried into a far country, and banished both from God and man. He could only follow the occupation of a captive, that is, to be oppressed, to weep, to claim compassion, and to pour out a dolorous complaint. He hung his harp on the willows, and felt that he could not sing the Lord's song in a strange land. Poor Job! He is less to be pitied for his bereavements, poverty, and sickness than for his loss of that candle of the Lord which once shone about his head.

That is the worst point of all when trouble penetrates to the heart. All the bullets in the battle, though they fly thick as hail, will not distress a soldier like one which finds a lodging in his flesh. "To take arms against a sea of troubles, and by opposing end them" is a grand and manly thing; but when that sea of trouble fills the cabin of the heart, puts out the fires of inward energy, washes the judgment from the wheel, and renders the pumps of resolution useless, the man becomes very nearly a wreck. "A wounded spirit who can bear?" Touch a man in his bone, and in his flesh, and yet he may exult; but touch him in his mind—let the finger of God be laid upon his spirit—and then, indeed, he is in captivity. I think the term includes all the temporal distress into which Job came, but it chiefly denotes the bondage of spirit into which he was brought, as the combined result of his troubles, his sickness, the taunts of his friends, and the withdrawal of the divine smile. My point is that God can deliver us out of that captivity; he can both from the spiritual and the temporal captivity give us a joyful release.

The Lord can deliver us out of spiritual captivity, and that very speedily. I may be addressing some tonight who feel everything except what they want to feel. They enjoy no sweetness in the means of grace, and yet for all the world they would not give them up. They used at one time to rejoice in the Lord; but now they cannot see his face and the utmost they can say is, "Oh, that I knew where I might find him!" It little matters that some live in perpetual joy; the triumphs of others cannot cheer a man who is himself defeated. It is idle to tell a distressed soul that it ought to rejoice as others do. What one ought to do and what one can do are sometimes very different, for how to perform that which we would we find not. In vain do you pour your glad notes into a troubled ear. Singing songs to a sad heart is like pouring vinegar upon niter; the elements are discordant, and cause a painful effervescence. There are true children of God who walk in darkness and see no light; yes, some who are the excellent of the earth nevertheless are compelled to cry aloud, "My God, my God, why hast thou forsaken me?" Throughout all time some of these have been in the church, and there always will be such, let our perfect brethren condemn them as they please. The Lord will always leave his mourners; his church shall always have an afflicted and poor people in her midst. Let us all take warning, for we also may be tried and cast down before our day is over; it may be that the brightest eye among us may yet be dimmed, and the boldest heart may yet be faint, and he that dwells nearest to his God at this moment nary yet have to cry out in bitterness of soul, "O God, return unto me, and lift up the light of thy countenance upon me."

Therefore mark well this cheering truth, God can turn your captivity, and turn it at once. Some of God's children seem to think that to recover their former joy must occupy a long period of time. It is true, dear brother, that if you had to work your passage back to where you came from, it would be a weary voyage. There would have to be most earnest searchings of heart and purgings of spirit, struggling with inbred lusts and outward temptations, and all that, if joy were always the result of inward condition. There must needs be a great deal of scrubbing and cleansing and furbishing up of the house, before you could invite your Lord to come, if he and you dwelled together on terms of law. But albeit, that all this cleansing and purifying will have to be done, it will be done far better when you have a sense of his love than it ever can be if you do it in order to make yourself fit for it.

Do you not remember when first you sought him you wanted him to deal with you on the legal ground of making yourself better, and you prepared the house for him to come and dwell in it? But he would not come on such terms. He came to you just as you were, and when he came he himself drove out the intruders which profaned the temple of your soul, and he dwelled with you, in order to perfect the cleansing. Now he will vouchsafe to you the conscious enjoyment of his presence on the same terms as at first, that is, on terms of free and sovereign grace. Did you not at that time admit the Savior to your soul because you could not do without him? Was not that the reason? Is it not a good reason for receiving him again? Was there anything in you when you received him which could commend you to him? Say, were you not all over defilement and full of sin and misery? And yet you opened the door and said, "My Lord, come in, in your free grace, come in, for I must have you or I perish." My dear friend, dare you invite him now on other terms? Having begun in the Spirit, would you be made perfect in the flesh? Having begun to live by grace, would you go on to live by works? When you were a stranger, did you trust in his love, and now that you are his friend, will you appeal to the law? God forbid. O brother, Jesus loves you still, and in a moment he will restore you. O sister, Jesus would fain come back to your heart again, and that in an instant. Have you never read that joyful exclamation of the spouse, "Or ever I was aware, my soul made me like the chariots of Amminadib"? Why, can he not do the same with you now, and quicken and inspirit you even in a moment? After all, you are not worse than you were when he first visited you;

you are not in so sorry a plight after all, as your first natural state, for then you were dead in trespasses and sins altogether, and he quickened you, and now, though you say you feel dead, yet the very expression proves that there is some life lingering in you. Did I not hear you say,

> Return, O Sacred Dove, return,
> Sweet messenger of rest,
> I hate the sins that made thee mourn,
> And drove thee from my breast.

Why, friend, those sighs and groans are sweet to the Lord, and they would not have been in you if he had not put them there; they are sure tokens that his grace has not been altogether taken from thee. Know you not, O child of God, that the grace of God is intended to meet all your sins after conversion as well as before conversion? Do you not know that the Lord loved you of old, despite your sins, and he loves you still? Understand you not that the ground of your salvation is not your standing or your character, but the standing of Christ before God, and the character and work of Christ in the presence of God? Believe you firmly that still he loves you, for so indeed he does. Cast your eyes upon those dear wounds of his, and read his love still written there. O unbelieving Thomas, do not put your finger into your own wounds, for that will not help you, but place them in the wounds of Jesus. Come close to him, and you shall cry with ecstasy of spirit, "My Lord and my God."

Well do I know what it is to feel this wondrous power of God to turn our captivity. When one is constantly engaged in ministry, it sometimes happens that the mind wanders, the spirit flags, and the energy is damped, yet, all in a minute, the Lord can quicken us into vigorous activity; the tow catches fire and blazes gloriously, when the Holy Spirit applies the fire. We have heard a hymn sung, and we have said, "I cannot join in that as I could wish," and yet, on a sudden, a mighty rushing wind has borne us away with the song right into heaven. The Lord does not take days, months, weeks, or even hours, to do his work of revival in our souls. He made the world in six days, but he lit it up in an instant with one single word. He said, "light be," and light was, and cannot he do the same for us, and chase away our gloom before the clock ticks again? Do not despair, no, do not even doubt your God. He can turn your captivity as the streams in the south.

Beloved, *he can do the same as to our temporal captivity.* We do not often say much about temporals when we are preaching; I fear we do not say enough about them, for it is wonderful how the Old Testament is taken up with the narration of God's dealings with his people as to temporal things. Many people imagine that God has a great deal to do with their prayer closet, but nothing to do with their store closet; it would be a dreadful thing for us if it were so. Indeed, my brethren, we ought to see as much the hand of our Lord on the table in the kitchen when it is loaded as we do at the communion table, for the same love that spreads the table when we commemorate our Savior's dying love, spreads the table which enables us to maintain the bodily life without which we could not come to the other table at all. We must learn to see God in everything, and praise him for all that we have.

Now it may be I address some friend who has been a great sufferer through pecuniary losses. Dear friend, the Lord can turn your captivity. When Job had lost everything, God readily gave him all back. "Yes," say you, "but that was a very remarkable case." I grant you that, but then we have to do with a remarkable God, who works wonders still. If you consider the matter, you will see that it was quite as remarkable a thing that Job should lose all his property as it was that he should get it back again. If you had walked over Job's farm at first and seen the camels and the cattle, if you had gone into his house and seen the furniture and the grandeur of his state—if you had seen how those who passed him in the street bowed to him, for he was a highly respected man, and if you had gone to his children's houses, and seen the comfort in which they lived, you would have said, "Why, this is one of the best-established men in all the land of Uz." There was scarcely a man of such substance to be found in all that region, and if somebody had foretold that he would in one day lose all this property—all of it—and lose all his children, why you would have said, "Impossible! I have heard of great fortunes collapsing, but then they were built on speculations. They were only paper riches, made up of bills and the like; but in the case of this man, there are oxen, sheep, camels, and land, and these cannot melt into thin air. Job has a good substantial estate, I cannot believe that ever he will come to poverty." Why, when he went out into the gate where the magistrates sat to administer justice, they rose up and gave him the chief seat on the bench. He was a man whose flocks could not be counted, so great were his possessions—possessions of real property, not of merely nominal estate: and yet suddenly, marvelously, it all took to itself wings and disappeared. Surely, if God can scatter, he can gather. If God could scatter such an estate as that, he could, with equal ease, bring it back again. But this is what we do not always see. We see the destructive power of God, but we are not very clear about the upbuilding power of God. Yet, my brethren, surely it is more consonant with the nature of God that he should give than take, and more like him that he should caress than chastise. Does he not always say that judgment is his strange work? I feel persuaded that it was strange work with God to take away all Job's property from him and bring him into that deep distress; but when the Lord went about to enrich his servant Job again, he went about that work, as we say, *con amore*—with heart and soul. He was doing then what he delights to do, for God's happiness is never more clearly seen than when he is distributing the largesses of his love. Why can you not look at your own circumstances in the same light? It is more likely that God will bless you and restore to you than it was ever likely that he would chasten you and take away from you. He can restore you all your wealth, and even more.

This may seem to be a very trite observation, commonplace, and such as everybody knows, but, beloved, the very things that everybody knows are those which we need to hear, if they are most suitable to our case. Those old things which we did not care about in our prosperity are most valued when we are cast down by the terrible blows of tribulation. Let me then repeat the truism, the Lord who takes away can as easily restore. "The Lord maketh sore, *and bindeth up*; he woundeth, *and his hands make whole*. He killeth, *and he maketh alive.*" Believe that he will put forth his right hand soon if the left has been long outstretched, and, if you can believe it, it will not be long before you will be able to say, "He hath regarded the low estate of his servant. He hath lifted the poor from the dunghill and set him among princes, even the princes of his people. For the Lord putteth down the mighty from their seat, but he exalteth them that are of low degree." I leave with you this simple truth: The Lord can turn the captivity of his people. You may apply the truth to a thousand different things. You Sunday school teachers, if you have had a captivity in your class, and no good has been done, God can change that. You ministers, if for a long time you have plowed and sowed in vain, the Lord can turn your captivity there. You dear wives who have been praying for your husbands, you fathers who have been pleading for your children, and have seen no blessing yet, the Lord can turn your captivity in those respects. No captivity is so terrible but God can bring us back from it; no chain is so fastened but God can strike it off, and no prison house is so strong but God can break the bars and set his servants free.

II. I pass on to our second remark, which is this: *there is generally some point at which the Lord interposes to turn the captivity of his people.*

In Job's case, I have no doubt, the Lord turned his captivity, as far as the Lord was concerned, because *the grand experiment which had been tried on Job was now over.*

The suggestion of Satan was that Job was selfish in his piety—that he found honesty to be the best policy, and, therefore, he was honest—that godliness was gain, and therefore he was godly. "Hast thou not set a hedge about him and all that he hath?" said the old accuser of the brethren. The devil generally does one of two things. Sometimes he tells the righteous that there is no reward for their holiness, and then they say, "Surely, I have cleansed my heart in vain and washed my hands in innocence"; or else he tells them that they only obey the Lord because they have a selfish eye to the reward. Now it would be a calamity if the devil could charge the Lord with paying his servants badly: it would have been an ill thing if the fiend had been able to say, "There is Job, a perfect and an upright man, but thou hast set no hedge about him. Thou hast given him no reward whatever." That would have been an accusation against the goodness and justice of God; but, as the devil cannot say that, he takes the other course and says—"Thou hast set a hedge about him and all that he has; he serves thee for gain and honor; he has a selfish motive in his integrity."

By God's permission the matter was tested. The devil had said, "Put forth now thy hand and touch his bone and his flesh, and he will curse thee to thy face." But Job had done no such thing. In his extremity he said, "The LORD gave and the LORD hath taken away; blessed be the name of the LORD." God puts his servants sometimes into these experiments that he may test them, that Satan himself may know how truehearted God's grace has made them, and that the world may see how they can play the man. Good engineers, if they build a bridge, are glad to have a train of enormous weight go over it. You remember when the first Great Exhibition was built, they marched regiments of soldiers, with a steady tramp, over the girders, that they might be quite sure that they would be strong enough to bear any crowd of men; for the regular tramp of well-disciplined soldiers is more trying to a building than anything else. So our wise and prudent Father sometimes marches the soldiery of trouble right over his people's supports, to let all men see that the grace of God can sustain every possible pressure and load. I am sure that if any of you had invented some implement requiring strength, you would be glad to have it tested, and the account of the successful trial published abroad. The gunsmith does not object to a charge being fired from the barrel at the proof house far greater than any strain which it ought ordinarily to bear; for he knows that it will endure the proof. "Do your worst or do your best; it is a good instrument; do what you like with it"; so the maker of a genuine article is accustomed to speak; and the Lord seems to say the same concerning his people. "My work of grace in them is mighty and thorough. Test it, Satan; test it, world; test it by bereavements, losses, and reproaches; it will endure every ordeal." And when it is tested, and bears it all, then the Lord turns the captivity of his people, for the experiment is complete.

Most probably there was, in Job's character, some fault from which his trial was meant to purge him. If he erred at all, probably it was in having a somewhat elevated idea of himself and a stern manner toward others. A little of the elder-brother spirit may, perhaps, have entered into him. A good deal that was sour came out of Job when his miserable comforters began to tease him—not a hundredth part as much as would come out of me, I warrant you, or, perhaps, out of you; but, still, it would not have come out if it had not been in. It must have been in him or otherwise all the provocation in the world would not have brought it out; and the Lord intended by his trials to let Job have a view of himself from another standpoint, and discover imperfections in his character which he would never have seen if he had not been brought into a tried condition. When through the light of trial, and the yet greater light of God's glorious presence, Job saw himself unveiled, he abhorred himself in dust and ashes. Probably Job had not humbled himself of late, but he did it then, and now, if any sort of selfishness lurked in him, it was put away, for Job began to pray for his cruel friends. It would take a good deal of grace to bring some men to pray for such friends as they were. To pray for one's real friends, I hope, comes natural to us; but to pray for that Bildad and the other two, after the abominable things they had spoken and insinuated—well, it showed that there was a large amount of sweetness and light in Job's character, and abounding grace deep down in his soul, or he would scarcely have interceded for such ungenerous tramplers upon a fallen friend. Now, behold, Job has discovered his fault, and he has put it away, and the grand old man bows his knee to pray for men who called him hypocrite—to pray for men who cut him to the very soul. He pleads with God that he would look in mercy upon men who had no mercy upon him, but had pitilessly heaped all kinds of epithets upon him, and stung him in his tenderest places, just when they ought to have had pity upon him. His misery alone ought to have stopped their mouths, but it seems as if that misery egged them on to say the most cruel things that could possibly have been conceived—the more cruel because they were, all of them, so undeserved. But now Job prays for his friends. You see the trial had reached its point. It had evidently been blessed to Job, and it had proved Satan to be a liar, and so now the fire of the trial goes out, and like precious metal the patriarch comes forth from the furnace brighter than ever.

Beloved friends, the point at which God may turn your captivity may not be the same as that at which he turned Job's, for yours may be a different character. I will try and indicate, briefly, when I think God may turn your trial.

Sometimes he does so *when that trial has discovered to you your special sin.* You have been putting your finger upon diverse faults, but you have not yet touched the spot in which your greatest evil is concentrated. God will now help you to know yourself. When you are in the furnace, you will begin to search yourself, and you will cry, "Show me wherefore thou contendest with me." You will find out three or four things, perhaps, in which you are faulty, and you will commit yourself to the Lord and say, "Give me grace, good Lord, to put away these evil things." Yes, but you have not come to the point yet, and only a greater trial will guide you to it. The anger of the Lord smokes against your house, not for this or that, but for another evil, and you have need to institute another search, for the images may be under the seat whereon a beloved Rachel sits. The evil in your soul may be just at the point where you think that you are best guarded against temptation. Search, therefore, and look, dear brother, for when the sin has been found out, and the Achan has been stoned, then the valley of Achor shall be a door of hope, and you shall go up to victory, the Lord going with you.

Perhaps, too, your turning point will be *when your spirit is broken.* We are by nature a good deal like horses that want breaking in, or, to use a scriptural simile, we are as "bullocks unaccustomed to the yoke." Well, the horse has to go through certain processes in the ménage until at last it is declared to be "thoroughly broken in," and we need similar training. You and I are not yet quite broken in, I am afraid. We go very merrily along, and yield to the rein in certain forms of service; but if we were called to other sorts of work, or made to suffer, we should need the kicking strap put on, and require a sharper bit in our mouths. We should find that our spirit was not perfectly broken. It takes a long time of pain and sickness to bring some down to the dust of complete resignation to the divine will. There is something still in which they stick out against God, and of many it is true, "Though thou shouldest bray a fool in a mortar among wheat with a pestle, yet will not his foolishness depart from him." We have been brayed in that mortar, and with that pestle day after day, and week after week, and yet we are still foolish. When our soul shall cheerfully say, "Not as I will, but as thou wilt," then our captivity will be almost over, if not quite. While we cry, "It must not be so, I will not have it so," and we struggle and rebel, we shall only have to feel that we are kicking against the pricks, and wounding our foot every time we kick; but when we give up all that struggling, and say, "Lord, I leave it entirely with thee, thy will be done"—then will the trial cease, because there will be no necessity for it any longer. That is with some the culmination and turning point of trouble. Their Gethsemane ends when, like the Lord Jesus, they cry, "Nevertheless, not as I will, but as thou wilt."

Sometimes, again, trial may cease *when you have learned the lesson which it was intended to teach you, as to some point of gospel truth.* I think I have sometimes said that many truths of the gospel are like letters written with sympathetic ink. If you have ever had a letter written with that preparation, when you look at it you cannot see anything whatever: it is quite illegible. The proper thing to do is to hold the writing up to the fire. As it warms at the fire, the acid writing becomes manifest, and the letters are before you. Many of God's promises need to be held before the scorching fires of adversity and personal trouble, and then we read the precious secret of the Spirit's consolation. You cannot see the stars in the daytime upon the surface of the earth, but if you go down into a well you can, and when you go down the deep well of trouble it often happens that you see a beauty and luster in the promise which nobody else can see, and when the Lord has brought you into a certain position in which you can see the glory of his grace as you never could have seen it anywhere else, then he will say, "It is enough; I have taught my child the lesson, and I will let him go."

I think, too, it may be with some of us that *God gives us trouble until we obtain a sympathetic spirit.* I should not like to have lived forty years in this world without ever having suffered sickness. "Oh," you say, "that would have been very desirable." I grant you it appears so. When I met with a man that never had an ache or a pain or a day's sickness in his life, I used to envy him, but I do not now because I feel very confident that he is a loser by his unvarying experience. How can a man sympathize with trouble that he never knew? How can he be tender in heart if he has never been touched with infirmity himself? If one is to be a comforter to others, he must know the sorrows and the sicknesses of others in his measure. It was essential to our Lord, and, certainly, what was essential to him is necessary to those who are to be shepherds of others, as he was. Now it may be that by nature some of us are not very sympathetic; I do not think Job was: it is possible that though he was kind, and generous to the poor, yet he was rather hard, but his troubles taught him sympathy. And, perhaps, the Lord may send you trouble till you become softer in heart, so that afterward you will be one who can speak a word in season to the weary. As you sit down by the bedside of the invalid, you will be able to say, "I know all the ins and outs of a sick man's feelings, for I have been sore sick myself." When God has worked that in you, it may be he will turn your captivity.

In Job's case, the Lord turned his captivity *when he prayed for his friends.* Prayer for ourselves is blessed work, but for the child of God it is a higher exercise to become an intercessor, and to pray for others. Prayer for ourselves, good as it is, has just a touch of selfishness about it: prayer for others is delivered from that ingredient. Herein is love, the love which God the Holy Spirit delights to foster in the heart, when a man's prayers go up for others. And what a Christlike form of prayer it is when you are praying for those who have ill-treated you and despitefully used you. Then are you like your master. Praying for yourselves, you are like those for whom Jesus died; but praying for your enemies, you are like the dying Jesus himself. "Father, forgive them, for they know not what they do" has more of heaven in it than the songs of seraphs, and your prayer when offered for those who have treated you ill is somewhat akin to the expiring prayer of your Lord. Job was permitted to take a noble revenge, I am sure the only one he desired, when he became the means of bringing them back to God. God would not hear them, he said, for they had spoken so wrongly of his servant Job, and now Job is set to be a mediator, or intercessor, on their behalf: thus was the contempt poured upon the patriarch turned into honor. If the Lord will only save the opposer's soul through your prayer, it will be a splendid way of returning bitter speeches. If many unkind insinuations have been thrown out, and wicked words said, if you can pray for those who used such words, and God hears you and brings them to Jesus, it will be such a triumph as an angel might envy. My brother, never use any other weapon of retaliation than the weapon of love. Avenge not yourself in anywise by uttering anything like a curse, or desiring any hurt or mischief to come to your bitterest foe, but inasmuch as he curses, overwhelm him with blessings. Heap the hot coals of your good wishes and earnest prayers upon his head, and if the Lord give you to bring him to a state of salvation, he shall be praised, and you shall have happiness among the sons of men.

Perhaps some of you are in trouble now because you cannot be brought sincerely to pray for your enemies. It is a grievous fault when Christian men harbor resentments; it is always a sad sign when a man confesses, "I could not heartily pray for So-and-So." I would not like to live an hour at enmity with any man living, be he who he may; nor should any Christian man, I think. You should feel that however treacherous, dishonorable, unjust, and detestable the conduct of your enemy may have been to you, yet still it is forgiven, quite forgiven in your heart, and, as far as possible, forgotten, or wherein remembered, remembered with regret that it should have occurred, but with no resentment to the person who committed the wrong. When we get to that state, it is most probable that the Lord will smile upon us and turn our captivity.

III. The last word I have to say—the third word—is this: that *believers shall not be losers for their God.*

God, in the experiment, took from Job all that he had, but at the end he gave him back twice as much as he had—twice as many camels and oxen, and twice as many of everything, even of children. I heard a very sweet remark about the children the other day, for somebody said, "Yes, God did give him twice as many children, because his first family were still his. They were not lost but gone before." So the Lord would have his people count their children that are gone to heaven, and reckon them as belonging to the family still, as the child did in Wordsworth's pretty poem, "Master, we are seven." And so Job could say of his sons and daughters, as well as of all the other items, that he had twice as many as before. True, the first family were all gone, but he had prayed for them in the days of their feasting, he had brought them together and offered sacrifice, and so he had a good hope about them, and he reckoned them as still his own. Tried brother, the Lord can restore to you the double in temporal things if he pleases. If he takes away, he can as certainly give, and that right early. He certainly can do this in spiritual things; and if he takes away temporals and gives spirituals we are exceedingly great gainers. If a man should take away my silver and give me twice the weight in gold in return, should I not be thankful? And so, if the Lord takes away temporals and gives us spirituals, he thus gives us a hundred times more than he takes away.

Dear brethren, you shall never lose anything by what you suffer for God. If, for Christ's sake, you are persecuted, you shall receive in this life your reward; but if not, rejoice and be glad, for great is your reward in heaven. You shall not lose anything by God's afflicting you. You shall, for a time, be an apparent loser; but a real loser in the end you shall never be. When you get to heaven you will see that you were a priceless gainer by all the losses you endured. Shall you lose anything by what you give to God? Never. Depend on it, he will be no man's debtor. There dwells not in earth or heaven any man who shall be creditor to the most High. The best investment a man makes is that which he gives to the Lord from a right motive. Nothing is lost which is offered to the cause of God. The breaking of the alabaster box of precious ointment was not a wasteful thing, and he who should give to the Lord all that he had would have made a prudent use of his goods. "He that giveth to the poor lendeth to the Lord," and he that giveth to the Lord's church and to the Lord himself lays up his treasure in heaven, where it shall be his forever.

Beloved, we serve a good Master, and if he chooses to try us for a little we will bear our trial cheerfully, for God will turn our captivity before long. In closing, I wish I could feel that this subject had something to do with you all, but it is not the case. Oh no, there are some of you who have felt no captivity, but you have a dreadful captivity to come, and there is no hope of God's ever turning that captivity when once you get into it. Without God, without Christ, strangers from the commonwealth of Israel, you are in bondage until now, and there will before long come upon you bondage that will never end. You cannot pray for your friends: you have never prayed for yourself. God would not hear you if you did pray for others, for, first of all, you must be yourself reconciled to him by the death of his Son. Oh, that you would mind these things and look to Jesus Christ alone for your salvation, for if you do he will accept you, for he has promised to cast out none who come to him. And then look at this: after all is right between God and your soul, you need not fear what happens to you in the future, for, come sickness or health, come poverty or wealth, all is right, all is safe, all is well. You have put yourself into the hand of God, and wherever God may lift that hand, you are still within it, and therefore always secure and always blessed; and, if not always consciously happy, yet you have always the right to be so, seeing you are true to God, and he delights in you. God bless you, and give you all salvation, for Jesus Christ's sake. Amen.

Isaiah: Messengers Wanted

—∞∞—

Delivered on Sunday morning, April 22, 1866, at the Metropolitan Tabernacle, Newington. No. 687.

> *Also I heard the voice of the* Lord, *saying, "Whom shall I send, and who will go for us?" Then said I, "Here am I; send me."*
> —Isaiah 6:8

God's great remedy for man's ruin of man is the sacrifice of his dear Son. He proclaims to the sons of men that only by the atonement of Jesus can they be reconciled unto himself. In order that this remedy should be of any avail to any man, he must receive it by faith, for without faith men perish even under the gospel dispensation. There is at the present moment great lack of men to tell out the story of the cross of Jesus Christ, and many considerations press that lack upon our hearts. Think how many voices all mingle into this one—"Who will go for us?" Listen to the wounds of Jesus, as they plaintively cry, "How shall we be rewarded? How shall the precious drops of blood be made available to redeem the souls of men, unless loving lips shall go for us to claim by right those who have been redeemed by blood?" The blood of Jesus cries like Abel's blood from the ground, "Whom shall I send?" and his wounds repeat the question, "who will go for us?" Does not the purpose of the eternal Father also join with solemn voice in this demand? The Lord has decreed a multitude unto eternal life. He has purposed, with a purpose which cannot be changed or frustrated, that a multitude whom one man can number shall be the reward of the Savior's travail; but how can these decrees be fulfilled except by the sending forth of the gospel, for it is through the gospel, and through the gospel alone, that salvation can come to the sons of men. I think I hear the awful voice of the purpose mingling with the piercing cry of the cross, appealing to us to declare the word of life. I see the handwriting of old Eternity bound in one volume with the crimson writing of Calvary, and both together write out most legibly the pressing question: who shall go for us to bring home the elect and redeemed ones?

The very sins of men, horrible as they are to think upon, may be made an argument for proclaiming the gospel. Oh, the cruel and ravenous sins which destroy the sons of men, and rend their choicest joy in pieces! When I see monstrous lusts defiling the temple of God, and gods many and lords many usurping the throne of the Almighty, I can hear aloud the cry, "Who will go for us?" Do not perishing souls suggest to us the question of the text? Men are going down to the grave, perishing for lack of knowledge; the tomb engulfs them, eternity swallows them up, and in the dark they die without a glimmer of hope. No candle of the Lord ever shines upon their faces. By these perishing souls we implore you this morning to feel that heralds of the cross are wanted, wanted lest these souls be ruined everlastingly; wanted that they may be lifted up from the dunghill of their corruption, and made to sit among princes redeemed by Christ Jesus. The cry wells into a wail of mighty pathetic pleading; all time echoes it, and all eternity prolongs it, while heaven and earth and hell give weight to the chorus.

Beloved, there are two forms of missionary enterprise, conducted by two classes of agents. I so divide them merely for the occasion; they are really not divided by any rigid boundary. The first is the agency of those specially dedicated to the ministry of the word, who give themselves wholly to it, who are able by the generous effort of the Christian church, or by their own means, to set their whole time apart for the great work of teaching the truth. As there are but few in this assembly who can do this, I shall not translate my text in its reference to ministers, although it has a loud voice to such, but I shall rather refer to another and equally useful form of agency, namely, the Christian church as a whole; the believers who, while following their secular avocations, are heralds for Christ and missionaries for the cross. Such are wanted here, such are needed in our colonies, such might find ample room in the great world of heathendom, men and women, who, if they did not stand up beneath the tree to address the assembled throng, would preach in the workshop; who, if they did not teach the hundreds, would at the fireside instruct the twos and threes.

We want both sorts of laborers, but I may do more good on this present occasion by stirring up this second sort. You may all be teachers of Christ in another sense; you can all give yourself to the work of God in your own calling, and promote your Master's glory perseveringly in your daily avocations. I lift up an earnest cry in God's name for consecrated men and women, who, not needing to wait till the church's hands can support them, shall support themselves with their own hands, and yet minister for Christ Jesus wherever Providence may have cast their lot.

I. *The person wanted,* as described in the questions, "Whom shall I send? Who will go for us?"

The person wanted is viewed from two points. He has a character bearing two aspects. The person wanted has a divine side; "whom shall *I* send?" Then he has a human aspect; "who will go *for us?*" But the two meet together—the human and divine unite in the last words *for us.* Here is a man, nothing more than a man of human instincts, but clad through divine grace with superhuman, even with divine, authority.

Let us look, then, at this two-sided person. He is *divinely chosen*—"Whom shall *I* send?" As if in the eternal counsels this had once been a question, "Who shall be the chosen man, who shall be the object of my eternal love, and in consequence thereof shall have this grace given him that he should tell to others the unsearchable riches of Christ?" Beloved, what a mercy it is to us who are believers that *to us* this is no more a question; for sovereignty has pitched upon us and eternal mercy, not for anything good in us, but simply because God would have it so, has selected us that we may bring forth fruit unto his name. As we hear the question, let us listen to the Savior's exposition of it. "Ye have not chosen me, but I have chosen you and ordained you that ye should go and bring forth fruit, and that your fruit should remain." The workers for the living God are a people chosen by the most High. He sends whom he wills, he makes choice of this man and not another, and in every case exercises his own sovereign will.

This question indicates a person *cheerfully willing,* and this is what I meant by the human side of the messenger. "Who will *go for us?*" The man sought for is one who will go with ready mind; there would be no need to ask, "who will go?" if a mere slave, or machine without a will could be sent. Beloved, the purpose of God does not violate the free agency, or even the free will of man. Man is saved by the will of God, but man is made willing to be so saved. The fault is not in the hyper-Calvinist that he insists upon sovereignty, nor in the Arminian that he is so violent for free agency; the fault is in both of them, because they cannot see more truths than one, and do not admit that truth is not the exclusive property of either, for God is a sovereign, and, at the same time, man is a responsible free agent. Many among us are perpetually seeking to reconcile truths which probably never can be reconciled except in the divine Mind. I thank God that I believe many things which I do not even wish to understand. I am weary and sick of arguing and understanding and misunderstanding. I find it true rest and joy, like a little child, to believe what God has revealed, and to let others do the puzzling and the reasoning. If I could comprehend the whole of revelation, I could scarcely believe it to be divine; but inasmuch as many of its doctrines are too deep for me, and the whole scheme is too vast to be reduced to a system, I thank and bless God that he has deigned to display before me a revelation far exceeding my poor limited abilities. I believe that every man who has Jesus has him as a matter of his own choice; it is true it is caused by grace, but it is there—it is there. Ask any man whether he is a Christian against his will, and he will tell you certainly not, for he loves the Lord, and delights in his law after the inward man. Thy people are not led unwillingly to thee in chains, O Jesus, but thy people shall be *willing* in the day of thy power. We willingly choose Christ, because he has from of old chosen us.

In the matter of holy work, every man who becomes a worker for Jesus is so because he was chosen to work for him; but he would be a very poor worker if he himself had not chosen to work for Jesus. I can say that I believe God ordained me to preach the gospel, and that I preach it by his will, but I am sure I preach it with my own; for it is to me the most delightful work in all the world, and if I could exchange with an emperor, I would not consent to be so lowered. To preach the gospel of Jesus Christ is one of the sweetest and noblest employments, and even an angel might desire to be engaged in it. The true worker for God must be impelled by divine election, but yet he must make and will make, by divine grace, his own election of his work.

The two meet together in this—the man is sent by the Three in One, who here asks, "Who will go for us?" Every faithful Christian laborer labors for God. Brethren, when we tell others the story of the cross, we speak of *God the Father.* It is through our lips that the prodigal son must be reminded that the hired servants have bread enough and to spare. It may be through us that he will be shown his rags and his disgrace; through us he will discover more clearly the disgrace of feeding swine. The Spirit of God is the efficient agent, but it is by us that he may work. It is by us that the divine Father falls upon the neck of his prodigal child. *He* does it, but it is through the teaching of his Word in some form or other. The promises are spoken by our lips, the sweet invitations are delivered by our tongues. We, as though God did beseech them by us, are to pray them in Christ's stead to be reconciled to God. God the Father says to you who know and love him, "Will you go for me and be an ambassador for me?" Nor must we forget our tender *Redeemer.* He is not here, for he is risen. He will come again, but meanwhile he asks for someone to speak for him, someone to tell Jerusalem that her iniquity is forgiven; to tell his murderers that he prays for them, "Father, forgive them"; to assure the blood-bought that they are redeemed; to proclaim liberty to the captive, and the opening of the prison doors to them that are bound. Jesus from his throne of glory says, "Who will go for me and be a speaker for me?" Moreover, that blessed *Spirit,* under whose dispensatorial power we live at the present hour, has no voice to speak to the sons of men audibly except by his people; and though he works invisibly and mysteriously in the saints, yet he chooses loving hearts and compassionate lips and tearful eyes to be the means of benediction. The Spirit descends like the cloven tongue, but he sits *upon* disciples; there is no resting place for the Spirit of God nowadays within walls, and even the heaven of heavens contains him not, but he enthrones himself within his people. He makes us God-bearers, and he speaks through us as through a trumpet to the sons of men. So that the adorable Trinity cry to you, you blood-bought, blood-redeemed sons of God, and say, "Are you seeking to promote our glory? Are you effecting our purposes? Are you winning those purchased by our eternal sacrifice?" Turning to the church here assembled, the Lord pronounces those ancient questions, "Whom shall I send? Who will go for us?"

II. By God's help, we would say a little upon *the person offering himself.* "Here am I; send me."

The person offering himself is described in the chapter at very great length—he must be an Isaiah. Being an Isaiah, he must in the first place *have felt his own unworthiness.* My brother, my sister, if you are to be made useful by God in soul winning, you must pass through the experience which Isaiah describes in the chapter before us. You must have cried in bitterness of spirit, "Woe is me, for I am a man of unclean lips!" God will never fill you with himself until he has emptied you of your own self. Till you feel that you are weak as water, you shall not see the splendor of the divine power. May I ask then those of you who feel desirous to serve God this experimental question, "Have you been made fully conscious of your own utter unfitness to be employed in any work for God, and your own complete unworthiness of so great an honor as to become a servant of the living God? If you have not been brought to this you must begin with yourself; you cannot do any good to others: you must be born again; and one of the best evidences of your being born again will be a discovery of your own natural depravity and impurity in the sight of God.

Now, beloved, I want you to notice how it was that Isaiah was made to feel his unworthiness. It was first by *a sense of the presence of God.* "I saw the Lord sitting upon a throne, high and lifted up." Have you ever had a consciousness of the presence of God? The other day I was prostrated in soul, utterly prostrated, with this one word "I AM!" There is everything in that title, the I AM! God is the truest of all existences. With regard to all other things, they may or may not be, but I AM! It came with such power to me. I thought, "Here am I sitting in my study, whether I am, or whether that which surrounds me really is, may be a question, but, God is—God is here. And when I speak God's word in his name, though I am nothing, God is everything, and as to whether or not his word shall be fulfilled there cannot be any question, because he still is called not "I was," but "I AM," infinite, omnipotent, divine. Think of the reality of the divine presence, and the certainty of that divine presence, everywhere, close here, just now! "I AM!" O God, if we be not, yet thou art! I scarcely think that any man is fitted to become a teacher of others till he has had a full sense of the glory of God crushing him right down into the dust, a full sense of that word, "I AM." You know a man cannot pray without it, for we must believe that he is, and that he is the rewarder of them that diligently seek him; and if a man cannot pray for himself, much less can he rightly teach others. There must be the fullest conviction of the reality of God, an overwhelming sight and sense of his glory, or else you cannot benefit your fellows.

The source of Isaiah's sense of nothingness was this, that Isaiah saw the glory of Christ. Have you ever sat down and gazed upon the cross till, having read your own pardon there, you have seen that cross rising higher and higher till it touched the heavens and overshadowed the globe? Then you have seen and felt the glory of him who was lifted up, and have bowed before the regal splendor of divine love, incarnate in suffering humanity, and resplendent in agony and death. If you have ever beheld the vision of the crucified, and felt the glory of his wounds, you will then be fit to preach to others. I have sometimes thought that certain brethren who preach the gospel with such meager power and such lack of unction have no true knowledge of it. There is no need to talk of it with bated breath. It is sneered at as being such a very simple tale—"Believe and live"; but after all, no philosopher ever made such a disclosure; and if a senate of discoverers could sit through the ages, they could not bring to light any fact equal to this, that God was in Christ reconciling the world unto himself. Well may you open your mouth boldly when you have such a subject as this to speak upon; but if you have never perceived its glory, you are utterly incapable of fulfilling God's errand. Oh, to get the cross into one's heart, to bear it upon one's soul, and above all, to feel the glory of it in one's whole being, is the best education for a Christian missionary whether at home or abroad.

It will strike you too, dear friends, that the particular aspect in which this humiliation may come to us will probably be a sense of the divine holiness, and the holiness of those who see his face. "Holy, holy, holy, Lord God of hosts!" was the song which overawed the prophet. What messengers are those who serve so holy a God? From earth and all its grossness free, like flames of fire they flash at his command. Who then am I, a poor creature, cribbed, cabined, and confined within this house of clay? Who am I, a sinful worm of the dust, that I should aspire to the service of so thrice holy a God? Oh, let us serve the Lord with fear and rejoice with trembling; fearful lest we should do mischief while seeking to do good, and pollute the altar while attempting to offer sacrifice upon it.

The next preparation for Christian work is, we must possess *a sense of mercy.* Then flew one of the seraphims and took a live coal from off the altar. We explained in our reading that the altar is for sacrifice, and that the lip must be touched with a coal of that sacrifice; then, being so touched, it derives two effects therefrom. In the first place, *the lip is purged* of iniquity; and in the next place, *it feels the influence of fire,* enabling it to speak with vehemence and force. Beloved hearer, you say perhaps in zeal, "I desire to serve Christ and to tell abroad the story of his cross." Have you proved that story to be true? Were you ever washed in the fountain? How can you bid others come if you have never come yourself? Have your sins been put away? "I hope so." Do you know it? I question if you can preach with any power till you have a full assurance of your own salvation. To teach the gospel with "but" and "if" is a poor teaching. You Sunday school teachers cannot hope to do much good to others while you doubt your own acceptance in the Beloved. You must know that you are saved. O beloved, you must feel the touch of that live coal, you must feel that Christ gave himself for you. You Little Faiths may get to heaven, but you must keep in the back rank while here; we cannot put you in the front of the battle. Though God may make you of service, we cannot expect you to be eminently of service. The man who would serve God must know himself to be saved.

The effect of that live coal will be to fire the lip with heavenly flame. "Oh," says one man, "a flaming coal will burn the lip so that the man cannot speak at all." That is just how God works with us; it is by consuming the fleshly power that he inspires the heavenly might. O let the lip be burned, let the fleshly power of eloquence be destroyed, but, oh, for that live coal to make the tongue eloquent with heaven's flame—the true divine power which urged the apostles forward, and made them conquerors of the whole world.

According to the text, *the man who will be acceptable must offer himself cheerfully.* "Here am I." Though how few of us have in very deed given ourselves to Christ. It is with most professors, "Here is my half guinea; here is my annual contribution"; but how few of us have said, "Here am I." No; we sing of consecration as we sing of a great many other things which we have not realized, and when we have sung it, we do not wish to be taken at our word. It is not

"Here am I." The man whom God will use must in sincerity be a consecrated man. I have explained that he may keep still to his daily work, but he must be consecrated to God in it; he must sanctify the tools of his labor to God, and there is no reason why they should not be quite as holy as the brazen altar or the golden candlestick.

You will observe that the person who thus volunteered for sacred service gave himself *unreservedly*. He did not say, "Here am I; use me where I am," but, "send me." Where to? No condition as to place is so much as hinted at. Anywhere, anywhere, anywhere—send me. Some people are militia-Christians—they serve the King with a limitation and must not be sent out of England; but others are soldier-Christians, who give themselves wholly up to their Lord and Captain; they will go wherever he chooses to send them. Oh, come, my Master, and be absolute Lord of my soul! Reign over me, and subdue my every passion to do and be, and feel all that your will ordains. Blessed prayer! May we never be content till we get all that is to be got by way of joyful experience and holy power, nor until we yield all that is to be yielded by mortal man to the God whose sovereign right to us we claim.

Notice one more thought, that while the prophet gives himself unreservedly, he gives *obediently*, for he pauses to ask directions. It is not "Here am I; away I will go," but "Here am I; send me." I like the spirit of that prayer. Some people get into their head a notion that they must do something uncommon and extraordinary, and though it may be most unreasonable and most irrational, it is for that very reason that the scheme commends itself to their want of judgment. Because it is absurd, they think it to be divine; if earthly wisdom does not justify it, then certainly heavenly wisdom must be called in to endorse it. Now, I conceive that you will find that whenever a thing is wise in God's sight, it is really wise, and that a thing which is absurd is not more likely to be adopted by God than by man; for though the Lord does use plans which are called foolish, they are only foolish to fools, but not actually foolish; there is a real wisdom in their very foolishness, there is a wisdom of God in the things which are foolish to man. When a project is evidently absurd and ridiculous, it may be my own but it cannot be the Lord's, and I had better wait until I can yield up my whims, and subject myself to divine control, saying, "Here am I; send me."

III. In the last place, *the work which such persons will be called to undertake.*

Isaiah's history is a picture of what many and many a true Christian laborer may expect. Isaiah was sent to preach very unpleasant truth, but like a true hero he was very bold in preaching it. "Isaiah is very bold," says the apostle. Now if you are called of God either to preach or teach, or whatever it is, remember the things you have to preach or teach will not be agreeable to your hearers. Scorn on the man who ever desires to make truth palatable to unhallowed minds. If he modulates his utterances or suppresses the truth which God has given him even in the slightest possible degree to suit the tastes of men, he is a traitor and a coward: let him be drummed out of God's regiment, and driven from the army of God altogether. God's servants are to receive God's message, and whether men will hear or whether they will forbear, they are to deliver it to them in the spirit of old Micaiah, who vowed, "As the LORD my God liveth, whatsoever the LORD saith to me, that will I speak."

But this is not the hardest task; the severest labor is this: we may have to deliver unpleasant truth to people who are resolved not to receive it, to people who will derive no profit from it, but rather will turn it to their own destruction. You see in the text that ancient Israel was to hear but not to receive; they were to be preached to, and the only result was to be that their heart was to be made fat, and their ears dull of hearing. What! Is that ever to be the effect of the gospel? The Bible tells us so. Our preaching is a savor of death unto death, as well as of life unto life. "Oh," says one, "I should not like to preach at that rate." But remember, brother, that the preaching of the cross is a sweet savor of Christ either way. The highest object of all to a Christian laborer is not to win souls, that is a great object; but *the* great object is to glorify God; and many a man has been successful in this who did not succeed in the other. If Israel be not gathered, yet, if we bear our testimony for God, our work is done. No farmer thinks of paying his men in proportion to the harvest. He pays his workers for work done, and so will it be with us, by God's grace, and if I happen to be a very successful laborer here, I boast not, nor claim any large reward on that account. I believe that had I preached the gospel with earnestness and waited upon God, if he had denied me conversions, my reward would be as great at the last, in some respects, because the Master would not lay to my door a nonsuccess which could not be attributed to myself.

Now it would be a very pleasant thing for me to ask you whether you would go for God in your daily vocation and tell of Jesus to sinners who are willing to hear of him; you would all be glad to do that. If I were to ask which sister here would take a class of young women, all anxious to find Christ, why you would all hold up your hands. If I could say, "Who will take a class of boys who long to find the Savior?" you might all be glad of such an avocation; but I have to put it another way, lest you should afterward be dispirited. Who among you will try and teach truth to a drunken husband? Who among you will carry the gospel to despisers and profligates, and into places where the gospel will make you the object of rage and derision? Who among you will take a class of ragged roughs? Who among you will try and teach those who will throw your teaching back upon you with ridicule and scorn? You are not fit to serve God unless you are willing to serve him anywhere and everywhere. You must with the servant be willing to take the bitter with the sweet; you must be willing to serve God in the winter as in the summer. If you are willing to be God's servant at all, you are not to pick and choose your duty and say, "Here am I; send me where there is pleasant duty." Anybody will go then; but if you are willing to serve God, you will say today, "Through floods and flames if Jesus leads, I will by the Holy Spirit's aid be true to my following."

Now, though I have said nothing particularly with regard to foreign missions, I have preached this sermon with the view that God will stir you all up to serve his cause, and particularly with the hope that the missionary feeling being begotten may show itself in a desire also to carry the gospel into foreign parts. Pastor Harms has lately been taken to his rest, but those of you who know the story of his life must have been struck with it; how an obscure country village, on a wild heath in Germany, was made to be a fountain of living waters to South Africa. The poor people had little care for the name of Jesus till Harms went there; and, notwithstanding that I have no sympathy with his Lutheran high-churchism and exclusiveness, I may say he went there to preach Christ with such fire that the whole parish became a missionary society, sending out its own men and women to preach Christ crucified. That ship, the *Candace,* purchased by the villagers of Hermansburgh with their own money, went to and from South Africa, taking the laborers to make settlements, and to undertake Christian enterprise in that dark continent. The whole village was saturated with a desire to serve God and preach the gospel to the heathen, and Harms at the head of it acted with a simple faith worthy of apostolic times. I would that my God would give me what I should consider the greatest honor of my life, the privilege of seeing some of the brethren and sisters of this church devoted to the Lord, and going forth into foreign parts. One gave his farm for students to be educated, another gave all he had, until throughout Hermansburgh it became very much like apostolic days when they had all things in common, the grand object being that of sending the gospel to the heathen. The day may come when we who have been able to do something for this heathen country of England may do something for other heathen countries in sending out our sons and daughters.

Jonah: Sleepers Aroused

-ᴧ〜ᴧ-

Published on Thursday, September 29, 1904; delivered on Thursday evening, July 27, 1876, at the Metropolitan Tabernacle, Newington. No. 2903.

> *But Jonah was gone down into the sides of the ship; and he lay, and was fast asleep.*—JONAH 1:5

We are told, before this fact is mentioned, that the Lord sent out a great wind into the sea to overtake the bark in which Jonah was sailing for Tarshish. The great wheels of Providence are continually revolving in fulfillment of God's purposes concerning his own people. For them, winds blow, and tempests rise. It is a wonderful thing that the whole machinery of nature should be made subservient to the divine purpose of the salvation of his redeemed. I was in a diamond-cutting factory at Amsterdam, and I noticed that there were huge wheels revolving, and a great deal of power being developed and expended; but when I came to look at the little diamond—in some cases a very small one indeed—upon which that power was being brought to bear, it seemed very remarkable that all that power should be concentrated upon such a little yet very precious object. In a similar style, all the wheels of providence and nature, great as they are, are brought to bear, by divine skill and love, upon a thing which appears to many people to be of trifling value, but which is to Christ of priceless worth; namely, a human soul. Here is this common-looking Jew, Jonah, named, according to the general rule that names go by contraries, "a dove," for, at any rate, on this occasion he looked more like the raven that would not come back to the ark; and for this one man—this altogether unamiable prophet—the sea must be tossed in tempest, and a whole shipful of people must have their lives put in jeopardy. This truth is a very far-reaching one. You cannot well exaggerate it. The vast universe is but a platform for the display of God's grace, and all material things that now exist will be set aside when the great drama of grace is completed. The material universe is but scaffolding for the church of Christ. It is but the temporary structure upon which the wonderful mystery of redeeming love is being carried on to perfection. See then, that as the great wind was raised to follow Jonah and to lead to his return to the path of duty, so all things work together for the good of God's people, and all things that exist are being bowed and bent toward God's one solemn eternal purpose—the salvation of his own.

But note also that, while God was awake, Jonah was asleep. While storms were blowing, Jonah was slumbering. It is a strange sight, O Christian, that you should be an important item in the universe, and yet that you should not know it, or care about it; that for you all things are keeping their proper place and time, and yet that you are the only one who does not seem to perceive it; and therefore you fall into a dull, lethargic, sleepy state. Everything around you is awake for your good, yet you yourself are slumbering even as the fugitive prophet was while the storm was raging.

I am going to speak upon the case of Jonah, first, as we may regard it as a useful lesson to the people of God; and, second, as it may be considered as *an equally valuable warning to the unconverted.*

I. First, then, I shall use the case of Jonah as *a useful lesson to the people of God;* and I may very fairly do so when we remember who Jonah was.

First, *Jonah was a believer in God*. He worshiped no false god; he worshiped only the living and true God. He was a professed and avowed believer in Jehovah. He was not ashamed to say—even when his conduct had laid him open to blame, and when there was nobody to support him—"I am a Hebrew; and I fear the Lord, the God of heaven, which hath made the sea and the dry land." Yet, though he was a believer in God, he was in the sides of the ship, fast asleep. O Christian man—a real Christian man, too—if you are in a similar condition, how is it that you can be slumbering under such circumstances? Should not the privileges and the honor, which your being a believer has brought to you by divine grace, forbid that you should be a slumberer, inactive, careless, indifferent? I may be addressing dozens of Jonahs, those who are really God's people, but who are not acting as if they were, chosen of the most High; but are forgetful of their election, their redemption, their sanctification, the life they have begun to live here below and the eternal glory that awaits them hereafter.

Besides being a believer, or as a natural consequence of being a believer, *Jonah was a man of prayer.* Out of the whole company on board that ship, he was the only man who knew how to pray to the one living and true God. All the mariners "cried every man unto his god." But those were idle prayers because they were offered to idols; they could not prevail because they were presented to dumb, dead deities. But here was a man who could pray—and who could pray aright, too—yet he was asleep. Praying men and praying women—you who have the keys of the kingdom of heaven swinging at your girdle—you who can ask what you will, and it shall be done for you—you who have many a time in the past prevailed with God in wrestling prayer—you who have received countless blessings in answer to your supplications—can you be, as Jonah was, sleeping in the time of storm? Can it be possible that he, who knows the power of prayer, is restraining it; that he, to whom God has given this choice privilege, is not availing himself of it? I fear that this may be the case with some of you; and looking at Jonah, a praying man sinfully asleep, I cannot help feeling that I may be speaking to many others who are in exactly the same condition.

More than this, Jonah was not merely a believing man, and a praying man, but *he was also a prophet of the Lord.* He was one to whom God had spoken, and by whom God had spoken. He was a minister; that is to say, one of God's own sent servants, though he was not in his proper place when he was in the ship sailing toward Tarshish. But can God's ministers neglect their duty like this? If I had been asked at that time, "Where is the prophet of the Lord?"—perhaps the only prophet of his age; at any rate, a man who was the very foremost in his time—if I had been asked, "Where is he?" I should have said that he must be looked for amid the masses of the dense population of Nineveh, carrying out his Master's commission with unstaggering faith; or else that he might be looked for amid the thousands of Israel, denouncing their idol gods and their wicked ways. But who would have thought of finding Jonah asleep on board such a ship as that? He is a seer, yet he sees not, for he is sound asleep. He is a watchman, but he is not watching, for he is slumbering and sleeping. Everything is in confusion; yet this man, upon whom rests the divine anointing, and into whose mouth God has put a message to multitudes of his fellow creatures, is sleeping instead of witnessing. Come, Mr. Preacher, see to yourself while I am talking about Jonah, and I will take the message to myself while I am talking to you; for this is a matter which ought to come home to all of us upon whom such great responsibilities are laid, and to whom such high privileges are given. But all of you, who love the Lord, are witnesses for Christ in some capacity or other; and it would be a very sad thing if you, who are called to speak in the name of the Lord, though it should only be in your Sunday school class, or in a little cottage meeting, or to your own children, should be asleep when you ought to be wide awake and active. May the Lord awaken you; for you are the wrong person to be asleep! You, above all others, are bound to have both your eyes open, and to watch day and night to hear what

God the Lord will speak to you, and what he would have you say to the ungodly or to his own chosen people in his name.

It is also worthy of notice that, at the very time when Jonah was asleep in the ship, he was not only a prophet, but he was *a prophet under a special commission*. He was not on furlough; he was, on the contrary, empowered by special warrant, under the King's seal and sign manual, to go at once to a certain place, and there to deliver the King's message; and yet there he is, asleep in this ship, and going in the very opposite direction to the one given him! When prophets sleep, it should be when their errand has been done, and their message has been delivered; but Jonah had not been on his Lord's errand, nor had he delivered his Lord's message; no, he had refused to obey his Lord, and had run away from the path of duty and here he lies, fast asleep, in the sides of the ship. O dear brothers and sisters, if we could truthfully say that our own work for the Lord was done, we might be somewhat excused if we took our rest. But is our life-work done? Mine is not, that I feel certain; it seems to be scarcely begun. Is yours finished, my brother, my sister? Have you so lived that you can be perfectly content with what you have done? Would it not be a cause of grief to you if you were assured that you would have no more opportunities of glorifying God upon the earth? I think you would feel that very much. Well, then, how can you be willing to be indifferent, cold, and dead, when so much of God's work lies before you scarcely touched as yet? All that you and I have done, so far, has been like apprentice work; we have been just getting our hand in, we have not become journeymen in God's great workshop yet; certainly we cannot claim to be wise master builders yet. Few of us, if any, have attained to that degree; so let us not go to sleep. O sir, shame on you! Asleep in the early morning? A man may take his rest when he gets weary after a long day's toil; but not yet, with all that work to be done—with the King's commission pressing upon us. With the call of the myriads of Nineveh sounding in his ears, Jonah, God's appointed messenger, should not have been found asleep in the sides of the ship.

This, then, is who the man was. He was a believing man and a praying man, and a prophet, and a prophet under a special commission. But where was he? Where had he got to?

Well, he had gone down into the sides of the ship; that is to say, *he had gone where he hoped he should not be observed or disturbed*. He had gone down into the sides of the ship—not among the cargo; the mariners threw that overboard, yet the noise did not wake the sleeping prophet. He was not upon the deck, ready to take a turn at keeping watch; but he had got as much out of the way as ever he could; and I have known Christian people try, as far as they could, to get out of the way. Possibly, they are not living inconsistently, or doing, as far as others can see, anything that is glaringly sinful; but they have just retired from their Master's business. They have got into a little quiet place where nobody notices them. I wonder whether there is a Christian man who has gone to live in a country village, where he has not yet said anything for Christ, although, when he lived in London, he was a busy worker for God. He has, like Jonah, gone down into the sides of the ship, into a quiet place where nobody can see him. Around him there are very few Christian people—perhaps hardly any—and he does not want anybody to know that he is a Christian. He would like now to live in quite a private way. If he were asked about himself, he would answer, as Jonah did, "I fear God"; but he does not wish to be asked anything about himself. He does not want people to fix their eyes upon him; he is afraid of being too conspicuous. He says that he always was of a retiring disposition, like the soldier, who ran away as soon as the first shot of the battle was fired, and so was shot as a deserter. He says that he is like Nicodemus, who came to Jesus by night, or like Joseph of Arimathea, a disciple, but secretly, for fear of the Jews. He has gone down into the sides of the ship, though, at one time, he was one of the foremost workers for Christ.

He has gone, too, *where he will not lend a hand in any service that needs to be done*. He was in the Sunday school once, but he says that he has had his turn at that, and does not intend to do anything more. He used to be, perhaps, a deacon of a church, but now he does not wish for such a position as that. He says there is a great deal of trouble and toil in connection with such offices, and he intends, for the future, to avoid everything that will give him trouble, or cause him the slightest toil. Once he took delight in preaching the Word; and, in those days, if anybody had said that he would live to be silent, and not speak in Christ's name, he would have been very angry at the man who made such a statement; but it has come true now. Jonah is not up on deck helping to hold the rudder or to set a sail or to do anything, not even a hand's turn to help the poor laboring vessel. He has gone to sleep in the sides of the ship where nobody inquires about him, at least for the present, and where there is nothing for him to do.

Observe, too, that *Jonah was stopping away from the prayer meeting*. Do you ask, "What prayer meeting?" Why, every other man on board that ship was crying unto his god, but Jonah was asleep in the sides of the ship. He was not praying; he was sleeping, and perhaps dreaming, but he was certainly not praying; and it is a very bad thing when a true servant of God, a praying man, and one by whom God has spoken aforetime, begins to get into such a spiritually sleepy state that he not only does nothing to help the church, but he does not even join in prayer in the time of danger. Do you know anybody in such a state as that, my brother? "Yes," you reply, "several." Are you in that state yourself, brother? If so, let charity for people who are doing wrong begin at home; it may extend to others afterward. But if this cap fits you, wear it, and wear it till you wear it out, and have improved yourself through wearing it.

This man, asleep in the sides of the ship, *represents one who cannot even take any notice of what was going on around him.* At first, he did not wish to be himself observed; but now, he does not care to observe others. What is the condition of the millions of heathen in foreign lands? That is a subject that he avoids; he is of opinion that they will be converted in the millennium, or that, even if they are not converted, their future lot may be a happy one. At any rate, it is a subject about which he does not concern himself. Jonah is asleep in the sides of the ship, and he appears quite content to let the millions of heathen perish. Then, with regard to the church of Christ at home, sometimes he is told that everything is prospering, but from other quarters he is informed that we are all going to the bad. Well, he does not know which report is the true one, and he does not particularly care; and, as for the church of which he is a member, does he not care for that?

Well, yes, in a certain fashion; but he does not care enough for the Sunday school, for instance, to lend a hand there, or for the preaching society to lend a hand there. He never encourages the minister's heart by saying that the love of Christ constrains him to take his share of holy service. Jonah is asleep in the sides of the ship. He is not much noticed, if at all, for those around him have come to the conclusion that he is good for nothing; and he himself, as I have shown you, does not take much notice of what is going on, though all the while he is a man of God, a man of prayer, and one whom God has used in times past. I wonder whether these descriptions are at all applicable to any of my hearers. At any rate, I know that they represent, as in a mirror, the lives of many professors of religion. We trust they are sincere in heart in the sight of God; but to us their sleepiness is more apparent than their sincerity.

Now, further, what was Jonah doing at that time? *He was asleep—asleep amid all that confusion and noise.* What a hurly-burly shore was outside that vessel—storms raging, billows roaring—and Jonah was not a sailor, but a landsman, yet he was asleep. Certainly he must have been in a remarkable state to be able to sleep through such a storm as that. And what a noise there was inside the ship as well as outside! Everybody else was crying to his god; and the mariners had been throwing the cargo out of the ship, so they must have stirred the whole place up from one end to the other. There seems to have been scarcely any opportunity for anybody to rest, yet Jonah could sleep right through it all, no matter what noise the men made as they pulled the ropes or threw out their wares, or what outcries they made as they presented their prayers to their idol gods. Jonah was asleep amid all that confusion and noise; and, O Christian man, for you to be indifferent to all that is going on in such a world as this, for you to be negligent of God's work in such a time as this is just as strange. The devil alone is making noise enough to wake all the Jonahs if they only want to awake. Then there are the rampant errors of the times, the sins of the times, the confusions of the times, the controversies of the times, all these things ought to wake us. And then, beyond the times, there is eternity, with all its terrors and its glories. There is the dread conflict that is going on between Christ and Belial—between the true and the false— between Jesus and antichrist. All around us there is tumult and storm, yet some professing Christians are able, like Jonah, to go to sleep in the sides of the ship. I think, brethren and sisters, if we are spiritually awake, if we only look at the condition of religion in our own country, we shall often be obliged at night to lie awake literally, and toss to and fro, crying, "O God, have mercy upon this distracted kingdom, and let your truth triumph over the popery which many are endeavoring to bring back among us!" But, alas! the great multitude of believers have little or no care about this matter; they do not even seem to notice it, for they are sound asleep in the midst of a storm.

Notice, also, that *Jonah was asleep when other people were awake.* All around us people seem to be wide awake, whether we are asleep or not. When I see what is being done by Romanists, and observe the zeal and self-denial of many persons who have dedicated themselves to the propagation of their false faith, I am astonished that we are doing so little for the true faith. Is it really the case that God has the dullest set of servants in the whole world? It is certain that men are all alive in the service of Satan; then we should not be half alive in the service of our God. Are the worshipers of Baal crying aloud, "O Baal, hear us," and the devotees of Ashtaroth shouting, "Hear us, O mighty Ashtaroth"; and yet the prophet of Jehovah is lying asleep in the sides of the ship? Is it so? Does everything else seem to arouse all a man's energies, but does true religion paralyze them? I have really thought, when I have been reading some books written by very good men, that the best thing for sending a man to sleep was a book by an evangelical writer; but that the moment a man becomes unsound in the faith, it seems as if he woke up, and had something to say which people were bound to hear. It is a great pity that it should be so, just as it was a great pity that everybody should have been awake on that vessel with the exception of Jonah; yet I fear that it is still only too true that those who serve the living God are not half filled with the arousing fervor which ought to possess them for the honor of the Lord most High.

Jonah was asleep, next, not only in a time of great confusion, and when others were awake, but also *in a time when he was in great danger*, for the ship was likely to sink. The storm was raging furiously, yet Jonah was asleep. And, believer, when you and those about you are in danger of falling into great sin through your careless living; when your family is in danger of being brought up without the fear of God; when your servants are in danger of concluding that religion is all a farce because you act as if it were; when those who watch you in business are apt to sneer at Christian profession because they say that your profession is of very little worth to you; when all this is taking place, and there is imminent danger to your own soul, and to the souls of others, can you still sleep in unconcern?

And Jonah was asleep *when he was wanted to be awake*. He, above all other men, was the one who ought to awake, and call upon his God. If anybody goes to sleep nowadays, it certainly ought not to be the believer in the Lord Jesus Christ. All things demand that Christians should be in real earnest. I know of no argument that I could gather from time or eternity, from heaven or earth or hell, to allow a Christian man to be supine and careless, but if I am asked for reasons why Christians are wanted to be in downright earnest and full of consecrated vigor in the service of God, those arguments are so plentiful that I have no time to mention them all. The world needs you; careless souls need to be awakened; inquiring souls need to be directed; mourning souls need to be comforted; rejoicing souls need to be established; the ignorant need to be taught; the desponding need to be cheered. On all sides, for a very Christian man, there is an earnest cry; and certainly, in these days, God has made a truly godly man to be more precious than the gold of Ophir; and that man, who keeps himself back from earnest service for God in such a time as this, surely cannot expect the Lord's blessing to rest upon him. Verily, the old curse of Meroz may well be pronounced upon the man who, in this age, and under present circumstances, like Jonah, goes down into the sides of the ship, lies down, and goes to sleep.

Jonah was asleep, with all the heathens around him, upbraiding him by their actions. They were praying while he was sleeping; and, at last, it came to this— that the shipmaster sternly addressed the prophet of God, and said, "What meanest thou, O sleeper?" It is sad indeed when things have come to such a pass that a heathen captain rebukes a servant of God; and yet I am afraid that the church of God, if she does not mend her ways, will have a great many similar rebukes from heathen practices and heathen utterances. Look at the enormous sums that the heathen spend upon their idols and their idol temples and worship, and then think how little we spend upon the service of the living God. One is amazed to read of the lakhs [hundreds of thousands] of rupees that are given by Indian princes for the worship of their dead deities, and yet our missionary societies languish, and the work of God in a thousand ways is stopped, because, God's stewards are not using what he has entrusted to them as they should. Think, too, of the flaming zeal with which the votaries of false faiths compass sea and land to make one proselyte, while we do so little to bring souls to Jesus Christ. One of these days you will have Hindus and Brahmins talking to us in this fashion: "You profess that the love of Christ constrains you, but to what does it constrain you?" They even now ask us what kind of religion must ours be that forces opium upon the poor Chinese. They quote our great national sins against us, and I do not wonder that they do. I only wish that they could be told that Christians reprobate those evils, and that they are not Christians who practice them. But we must do more than even the best Christians are now doing or else we shall have the heathen saying, as the semiheathen at home do say, "If we believed in eternal punishment, we should be earnest day and night to rescue souls from it"—which is to me a strong corroboration of the truth of that doctrine.

We do not want any doctrine that can make us less zealous than we are. We certainly do not want any doctrine that can give us any excuse for want of zeal. Still there is great force in the remark I quoted just now. We are not as earnest to save men from going down to the pit as we ought to be if we do indeed believe that they are hastening to that doom. The shipmasters are again rebuking the Jonahs. Those who believe in error, those who worship false gods, turn round upon us and ask us what we mean. O Jonah, sleeping Jonah, is it not time that you were awake?

But why was Jonah asleep? I suppose that it was partly the reaction after the excitement through which his mind had passed in rebelling against God. He had wearied himself with seeking his own evil way; so now, after the disobedience to God of which he had been guilty, his spirit sinks, and he sleeps. Besides, it is according to the nature of sin to give—not physical sleep, I grant you—but to give spiritual slumber. There is no opiate like the commission of an evil deed. A man who has done wrong is so much less able to repent of the wrong, so much the less likely to do so. Jonah's conscience had become hardened by his willful rejection of his Lord's commands, and therefore he could sleep when he ought to have been aroused and alarmed.

Besides, he wished to get rid of the very thought of God. He was trying to flee from God's presence. I suppose he could not bear his own thoughts;

they must have been dreadful to him. So, being in a pet against his God, and altogether in a wrong spirit, he hunts about for a snug corner of the ship, stretches himself out and there falls asleep, and sleeps on right through the storm. O sleepy Christian, there is something wrong about you too! Conscience has been stupefied. There is some darling sin, I fear, that you are harboring. Search it out, and drive it out. Sin is the mother of this shameful indifference. God help you to get rid of it! Brother, I am speaking to you with as much directness as I possibly can, yet not with more than I use toward myself. Have I, in my preaching, been slumbering and sleeping? If you find that I am not in earnest, I charge you, my brother in Christ, tell me of it, and wake me out of my sleep if you can, as I now tell you of it, and say, by all that God has done to you in saving you by his grace, and in making you his servant, give not up your soul to slumber, but awake, awake, put on strength, and arouse yourself, by the power of the Holy Spirit, to prayer and to the service of your God.

Thus I have spoken, perhaps at too great length, to Christians.

II. Now, more briefly, I want to give *a warning to the unconverted.*

Jonah, asleep on board that ship, is a type of a great number of unconverted people who come to our various places of worship. Jonah was in imminent danger, for God had sent a great storm after him: and, my unconverted hearer, *your danger, at this present moment, is beyond description.* There is nothing but a breath between you and hell. One of our beloved elders was with us here last Sabbath day; he is now with the spirits of just men made perfect; but if it had been the lot of any unconverted person here to suffer and to expire in the same manner, alas, how sad it would have been for you, my hearer! Driven from the presence of God, you would be cast in the outer darkness where there is weeping and wailing and gnashing of teeth. The sword of divine justice is already furbished, will you yet make mirth? Can you laugh and jest when there is but a step between you and death—but a step between you and hell? An enemy to God, unforgiven, the angel of justice seeking you out as the storm sought out Jonah in that ship, "What meanest thou, O sleeper," when the peril of everlasting wrath is so near thee?

You are asleep, too, *when there are a great many things to awake you.* As I have already said, there was a great noise in the vessel where Jonah was, a great noise inside and outside the ship, yet he did not awake. I do believe that many of you, unconverted people, find it hard to remain as you are. You get hard blows sometimes from the preacher. At family prayer often your conscience is touched. When you hear a passage from the Bible read, or when you hear of a friend who has died, you get somewhat aroused. Why, the very conversion of others should surely awaken you. If nothing else had awoke Jonah, the prayers of the mariners ought to have awakened him; and the earnestness of your mother and father, the pleading of your sister, the cries of new converts, the earnest anxieties of inquirers, ought to have—and if you were not so deeply sunken in slumber, would have some influence over you to arouse you.

You are asleep, brother, *while prayer could save you.* If your prayers could not be heard, I think I should say, "Let him sleep on." If there were no possibility of your salvation, I do not see why you should be aroused from your slumbers. Despair is an excellent excuse for sloth; but you have no reason to despair. "Arise, call upon thy God," said the shipmaster to Jonah; and we say to you, "Friend, how is it that you are so indifferent, and do not pray, when it is written, 'Ask, and it shall be given you; seek, and ye shall find'; and when the facts prove the truth of the words of Jesus, 'for he that asketh receiveth, and he that, seeketh findeth'?" Heaven is within your reach, yet you will not stretch out your hand. Eternal life is so near to you that Paul writes, "If thou shalt confess with thy mouth the Lord Jesus, and shalt believe in thine heart that God hath raised him from the dead, thou shalt be saved." Assuredly, that man who has food heaped up before him, but who sits down and goes to sleep with his head in Benjamin's mess [largest share, from Genesis 43:34], and yet will not eat of it, deserves to be starved. He who can slumber when the river runs up to his very lip; he who is dying of thirst, yet will not drink, deserves to die; does he not? With such wondrous blessings set before you in the gospel—with heaven itself just yonder, and the pearly gates set wide open, yet you are so indifferent that you despise the good land, and murmur, and refuse to accept the Savior who would lead you to it—why, surely, you must be sleeping the sleep of death! You are sleeping while God's people are wondering at you, just as those mariners in the ship wondered at Jonah; and while they are weeping over you and praying for you. There are some, in this place, who are the constant subjects of prayer. Some of you, who are seated here, do not perhaps know it, but there are those who love you and who mention your name day and night before God; and yet, while they are concerned about you, you are not concerned about yourself. O God, if storms cannot awaken these sleeping Jonahs, awaken them by some other means, even though it be by one like themselves, or one even worse than themselves! Send a message that shall upbraid them. Set some blasphemer to ask them how they can attend the means of grace, and yet be undecided. I have known that to happen. I have known a coarse, vile-living man to accost a moral and excellent attendant on the means of grace, and say to him, "Why are you not either one thing or the other? If religion is all a lie, why don't you be as I am; but if it is true, why don't you become a Christian?" And verily may they put such questions as those to some of you.

O friends, I pray you, if you are out of Christ, do not pretend to be happy! Do not accept any happiness till you find it in him. To some of you, I would speak very pointedly. Are you sick? Do you feel that your life is very precarious? O my dear friend, you are like Jonah when the ship was like to be broken. Do not delay. Are there the beginnings of consumption about you? Is it supposed to be so? Do not delay. Has some relative been taken away, and does there seem some likelihood that you may have the same disease? Oh, do not sleep, but awake! Are you getting old, friend? Are the gray hairs getting thick around your brow? Oh, do not delay! For unsaved young people, it is wrong to sleep, for he that sleeps when he is young sleeps during a siege; but he that slumbers when he is old sleeps during the attack, when the enemy is actually at the breach, and storming the walls. Do any of you work in dangerous trades? Do you have to eat your bread where an accident might easily happen, as it has often happened to others? Oh, be prepared to meet your God!

But having begun this list, I might continue it almost indefinitely; but I will end it in a sentence or so. *Are you a mortal man? Can you die? Will you die? May you die now?* May you drop dead in the street? May you go to sleep and never wake up again on earth? May your very food or drink become the vehicle of death to you? May there be death in the air you breathe? May it be so? Will you one day, at any rate, have to be carried to your long home, like others, and lie asleep in the grave? Will you give account to God for the things done in the body? Will you have to stand before the great, white throne, to make one of that innumerable throng, and to be there put into the balance to be weighed for eternity? If so, sleep not, I beseech you, as do others; but bestir yourself. May God's Holy Spirit bestir you to make your calling and election sure! Lay hold on Jesus Christ with the grip of an earnest, humble faith, and surrender yourself, henceforth, to the service of him who has bought you with his precious blood. God grant to all of us the grace to awake, and arise, that Christ may give us life and light, for his dear name's sake! Amen.

Daniel: Undaunted Courage

Delivered on Sunday morning, June 14, 1868, at the Metropolitan Tabernacle, Newington. No. 815.

> *Now when Daniel knew that the writing was signed, he went into his house; and his windows being open in his chamber toward Jerusalem, he kneeled upon his knees three times a day, and prayed, and gave thanks before his God, as he did aforetime.*—DANIEL 6:10

Daniel had been exalted to very great worldly prosperity, but his soul had prospered too. Oftentimes outward advancement means inward decline. Tens of thousands have been intoxicated by success. Though they bade fair in starting in the race of life to win the prize, they were tempted to turn aside to gather the golden apples, and so they missed the crown. It was not so with Daniel—he was as perfect before God in his high estate as in his lowlier days; and this is to be accounted for by the fact that he sustained the energy of his outward profession by constant secret communion with God. He was, we are told, a man of an excellent spirit, and a man abundant in prayer; hence his head was not turned by his elevation, but the Lord fulfilled in him his promise to "make his servant's feet like hinds' feet, that they may stand upon their high places." Yet, although Daniel preserved his integrity, he did not find a position of greatness to be one of rest. As the birds peck at the ripest fruit, so his envious enemies assailed him; and as the most conspicuous warriors most attract the arrows of the foe, so the honors of Daniel brought upon him the enmities of many.

Seek not then, beloved, seek not then, with an excess of desire, or an unrest of ambition, to be great among the great ones of the earth. There are more precious things than honor and wealth. A Persian king, wishing to give two of his courtiers a token of his regard, gave to one of them a golden cup and to the other a kiss: he who had obtained the golden cup considered that he was hardly done by, and envied the courtier who received the kiss from the monarch's own mouth. And let me say, let who will receive the wealth and honors of the world, which make up her golden cup, if you receive a kiss of favor from the lip of God and feel the sweetness of it in your inmost soul, you have received more than they; you have no reason whatsoever to repine though that kiss should come to you in poverty and sickness, but rather to rejoice that God has counted you worthy, in his infinite grace, to receive the more of spirituals though you have the less of temporals.

Luther declared that all the greatness of the world was but a bone which God threw to a dog. "For," says he, "he gives more to the pope and to the Turk than to all his saints put together," and so verily it is. To be great, distinguished, and wealthy may be the lot of a Haman, who shall be hanged upon a gallows, while God's true servant may sit at the gate and bear contempt as did Mordecai. Better to pine with Lazarus than feast with Dives, for the love of God more than compensates for temporary disadvantages. Better an ounce of divine grace than a ton of worldly goods. Though the good things come not as the left-handed blessings of outward prosperity, be more than content if you win the right-handed benediction of spiritual joy.

The example of Daniel I present you for your observation today, believing that these are times when we need to be as firm and resolute as he, and that at any rate, occasions will come to every one of us before we win our crown, when we shall need to put our foot down firmly, and be steadfast and unflinching for the Lord and his truth.

I. First, let me invite your attention to *Daniel's habitual devotion:* it is worthy of our study. We might never have known of it if he had not been so sorely tried, but fire reveals the hidden gold.

Daniel's habitual devotion. We are told that aforetime, before the trial, he had been in the constant habit of prayer. He prayed much. There are some forms of spiritual life which are not absolutely essential, but prayer is of the very essence of spirituality. He that has no prayer lacks the very breath of the life of God in the soul. I will not say that every man who prays is a Christian, but I will say that every man who prays sincerely is so; for, recollect, men may pray after a fashion, and even practice private prayer too, and yet may be deceiving themselves; for as the frogs of Egypt came up into the bedchambers, so does hypocrisy intrude itself even into the private places where men pretend to worship God; but I do say that a cheerful constancy in sincere private devotion is such a mark of grace, that he who has it may fairly conclude himself to be one of the Lord's family.

Daniel always had subjects for prayer and reasons for prayer. He prayed for himself that in his eminent position he might not be uplifted with pride, might not be taken in the snares of those who envied him, might not be permitted to fall into the usual oppressions and dishonesties of Eastern rulers. He prayed for his people. He saw many of the house of Judah who were not in such prosperous circumstances as himself. He remembered those who were in bonds, as being bound with them. Those who were bone of his bone and flesh of his flesh, he brought in the arms of faith before his God. He interceded for Jerusalem. It grieved him that the city was laid waste, that still the brand of the Chaldean destroyer was upon Mount Zion, so beautiful, and once the joy of the whole earth. He pleaded for the return from the captivity, which he knew was ordained of his God. He prayed for the glory of his God, that the day might come when the idols should be utterly abolished, and when the whole earth should know that Jehovah rules in heaven, and among the sons of men. It would have been a delightful thing to have listened at the keyhole of Daniel's closet, and to have heard the mighty intercessions which went up to the Lord God of hosts.

We read next, that with all his prayers he mingled thanksgiving. Do observe it, for so many forget this, "He prayed and gave thanks to God." Surely, it is poor devotion which is always asking and never returning its gratitude! Am I to live upon the bounty of God, and never to thank him for what I receive? Surely, prayers in which there is no thanksgiving are selfish things: they rob God; and will a man rob God—rob God even in his prayers and yet expect that his prayers should be successful? Have I not often said in this place that prayer and praise resemble the process by which we live? We breathe in the atmospheric air, and then breathe it out again: prayer takes in deep drafts of the love and grace of God, and then praise breathes it out again.

> *Prayer and praise, with sins forgiven,*
> *Bring down to earth the bliss of heaven.*

Good Daniel had learned to praise as well as to pray, and to offer to God that sweet incense which was made of diverse spices, of earnest desires and longings mingled with thanksgivings and adorations.

It is worthy of notice, that the text says, "Daniel prayed and gave thanks before his God." This enters into the very soul of prayer—this getting before God. O brethren, do you not often catch yourselves praying to the wind, and in private uttering words as though you were only to be heard by the four walls which bound your little room? But prayer, when it is right, comes before God, in realizing the majesty of the throne of his grace, and seeing the blood of the eternal covenant sprinkled thereon; in discerning that God is gazing right through you, reading every thought and interpreting every desire; in feeling that you yourself are speaking into the ear of God, and are now, as it were,

Plunged in the Godhead's deepest sea,
And lost in his immensity.

This is praying, when we draw near to God. I shall not care if you do not use a single word, if you feel the majesty of God to be so overwhelming that words are out of place; and silence becomes far more expressive when you bow with sobs and tears and groanings that cannot be uttered. That is the prayer which wins its suit of God, and is dear to the majesty of heaven. Thus Daniel prayed and gave thanks, not before men to be seen of them, nor yet in private before himself to satisfy his conscience, but "before God," of whom he had an audience thrice each day.

That little word *his* I must not let slip, however. He prayed and gave thanks before his God. He spoke not to God merely as God who might belong to any man and every man, but unto his God, whom he had espoused by a solemn determination that he would not turn aside from his service, that determination having resulted from God's having determined to select him and to make him his own man, peculiarly set apart unto his own praise. "*His* God." Why, it seems to me to bring up that word *covenant*—his "covenant God," as though he had entered into covenant with God according to the language of the most High, "I will be their God, and they shall be my people." True son of Abraham and Isaac and Jacob was this Daniel when he looked upon God as being his own, his property, could claim him, could say as we sometimes sing in that sweet psalm, "Yea, mine own God is he!" Oh, to feel that the Lord belongs wholly to me! My God, my God, if no other man can claim him; my Father, my Shepherd, my Friend, my Lord, and my God! Yes, here lies power in prayer, when a man can talk with God as his covenant God. That man cannot miss; every arrow sticks in the center of the target when he pleads "before his God." That man must conquer the angel at Jabbok's brook who grips him with both hands by a faith which knows its heaven-wrought claims. It is not winning mercies from another's God, nor pleading outside the covenant, but the believer feels that he is asking of his own God mercies already promised and made sure to him by oaths and covenant and blood.

Some other particulars in the text are not quite so important; nevertheless, observe that he prayed *three times a day.* That does not tell you how often he prayed, but how often he was in the posture of prayer. Doubtless he prayed three hundred times a day if necessary—his heart was always having commerce with the skies; but thrice a day he prayed formally. It has been well said that we usually take three meals in the day, and that it is well to give the soul as many meals as the body. We want the morning's guidance, we need the eventide's forgiveness, do we not also require the noontide's refreshment? Might we not well say at noontide, "Tell me, O thou whom my soul loveth, where thou feedest, where thou makest thy flock to rest at noon." If you find from morn till eve too long an interval between prayer, put in another golden link at midday. There is no rule in Scripture as to how often you should pray, and there is no rule as to when you should pray; it is left to the man's own gracious spirit to suggest season. We need not come back to the bondage of the Mosaic covenant, to be under rule and rubric; we are left to that free Spirit who leads his saints aright. Yet three times a day is a commendable number.

Notice, also, *the posture.* That, also, is of little consequence, since we read in Scripture of men who prayed on the bed, with their face to the wall. We read of David sitting before the Lord. How very common and acceptable a posture was that of *standing* before God in prayer! Yet there is a peculiar appropriateness, especially in private prayer, in the posture of kneeling. It seems to say, "I cannot stand upright before thy majesty; I am a beggar, and I put myself in the position of a beggar; I pursue of thee, great God, on bended knee, in the posture of one who owns that he deserves nothing, but humbles himself before thy gracious majesty." The reason why he kneeled on the particular occasion mentioned in the text was, no doubt, because he always had kneeled, and therefore always would kneel, and he would not be driven from the posture, little as that might be, at a tyrant's word. No, if all earth and hell should be against him, if he had found it more to God's honor to kneel, then kneel still he would, even though he should be cast into the lions' den for it.

One more observation. We are told that Daniel kneeled upon his knees *with his windows open toward Jerusalem.* This was not done with any view to publicity. It may be that nobody could see him, even when his windows were open, except the servants in the court. I suppose the house to have been erected as most Eastern houses were, with an open square in the center; and though he would be looking toward Jersualem, the windows would be looking into the court, where he could only be observed by those who might be residents in the house or visitors on business. Probably his fellow counselors knew the hour which he usually set apart for devotion, and therefore called in so as to find him in the act. Besides, you must recollect that, though it would be strange here for a man to pray with his windows open, where he could be heard, it was not at all strange among the Orientals, since you will find the Pharisees and others not at all slow to perform their devotions in any place, when the hour of prayer comes, and therefore it would not be regarded at all as being of a Pharisaic nature, that he should pray with his windows open.

The windows being open toward Jerusalem may have been suggested by the prayer of Solomon, when he asked that if the Lord's people were banished at any time, when they sought the Lord with their faces toward that holy place, God would hear them. It may have helped him also to recollect that dear city toward which every Jew's heart turns with affection, even as the needle trembles toward its pole. The thought of its ruin assisted his earnestness, the recollection of its sin humbled him, and the promises concerning it comforted him. He turned toward Jerusalem. And what does this say to us? Men and brethren, it tells us that we ought to take care when we pray, to have our windows open toward Calvary. Neither turn you to the east, nor to the west, but let your spirits turn toward the cross of Christ. That is the great point toward which all the faces of the faithful must continually be turned, where Jesus died, where Jesus rose, where Jesus intercedes before the throne of mercy. There it is that the eyes of faith must look. With your windows open toward Calvary always pray; look upon the precious blood; gaze steadfastly upon the risen Lord; behold the authority of his plea, as before his Father he wins his suit for his people, and you will grow strong to wrestle until you prevail.

II. We must now turn to a second consideration, *Daniel's action under trial.*

There is nothing that kings and queens are much fonder of than meddling with religion. Though the Prussian king tried to make a number of watches all tick together, and could not do it, yet notwithstanding the experiment and its failure, there are always evil counselors who would force men's consciences to keep stroke. Folly is in the throne when monarchs patronize or oppress religion. Caesar always muddles when he meddles with the things of God. In Daniel's day there was an act of uniformity passed in some respects similar to the famous act which was thrust upon this land. Darius ordained that no man should pray for thirty days: the other Act of Uniformity commanded that no man should pray at any time in public without his book. There is not very much to prefer between the two. When this act of uniformity was passed, several courses were open to Daniel. He might, for instance, have said, "This does not answer my purpose. I have a high position in society. I am chief president over all these dominions, and though I am willing to suffer something for my religion, yet gold may be bought too dear, and therefore I shall cease to pray." He might have found many precedents and many companions. What crowds, when it has come to a question between life and truth, between honor and Christ, have made the evil choice and perished infamously? Daniel does not seem to have raised that question. Yet he might have said, "Well, well, we must be prudent; God must be worshiped certainly, but there is no particular reason for my worshiping him in the usual room, nor even in the city where I live; I can retire in the evening, or find some more secret spot in my own house, and especially there is no occasion to open the window. I can pray with the window shut, and I shall be just as acceptable before God. I think, therefore, I shall keep my conscience clear, but not obtrude my religion in these evil days."

Daniel did not so reason; he was a lionlike man, and scorned to lower his standard in the presence of the foe; for see, in his position, if he had not prayed as before, it would have been a scandal to the weak and a scorn to the wicked; for the weak would have said, "See, Daniel is cowed by the decree." Then every poor Jew throughout the realm would have found excuse for forsaking his principles; and the wicked would have said, "Note, he serves his God when all goes well, but see where he drifts when trouble comes!" He would not seek the secrecy which prudence might have suggested. Still it might have suggested to him that he could pray inwardly. Prayers without words are just as acceptable to God: could he not do this? He felt he could not, inasmuch as the decree was not inward, and the king's opposition to religion was not inward. He did not believe in opposing outward falsehood by an inward truth. He did, in the language of the hymn we were singing, "strength to strength oppose." He would give distinct outward avowal of his own convictions in opposition to the outward persecuting edict.

As Daniel did not happen to have one of those rotating, double-acting consciences, he did not try to import a new meaning into the terms of the decree or invent a compromise between it and his own convictions, but he went straightforward in the plain path. He knew what the edict meant, and therefore down on his knees he went before his God in direct defiance of it. Whether the edict might be read in a milder sense or not, did not trouble him; he knew what Darius meant by it, and what the captains and the counselors meant by it, and he knew also what he himself intended to do, and therefore he did the right thing, and before his God he dared the lions, rather than soil his conscience with aught of ill.

Observe with care what Daniel did. He made up his mind to act as he had done aforetime. Note how *quietly* he acted. He did not say to any of his enemies, "I mean to carry out my convictions." Not at all; he knew that talk was lost upon them, so he resorted to actions instead of words. He quietly went home when he found the law was passed—though grieved that such a thing was done—without a single word of repining or caviling he sought his chamber. I do not find that he was at all distracted or disturbed. The words "as he had done aforetime" seem to imply that he went upstairs as calmly as he had been accustomed to do. His servants would not have known from his behavior that any law had been made. He always had gone at that hour to pray, and they could hear him pray just as earnestly as he ever had done. He was stayed on God, therefore continued at perfect peace.

Note again, how he acted unhesitatingly—*immediately*! He did not pause; he did not ask for time to consider what he should do. In matters of perilous duty, our first thoughts are best. When there is anything to be lost by religion, follow out the first thought of conscience, namely, "Do the right." Who needs to question where duty points the way? Where God commands, there is no room for reason to raise cavils. Yet I have no doubt, if the devil could have whispered into the prophet's ear, he would have said, "Now Daniel, you had better consider a little while. You are in a position where you can materially help your friends. You are of very great authority in this court; you may be of assistance to the true religion. You do not know how many may be converted by your example. You ought not lightly to give up a position where you can do so much good." That argument I have heard hundreds of times when people have been urged to come out of false positions and do the right. But what have you and I to do with maintaining our influence and position at the expense of truth? It is never right to do a little wrong, to obtain the greatest possible good. Your duty is to do the right: consequences are with God; and after all it never can be, in the long run, a good thing either for you or for others to do wrong.

You will observe also, that Daniel did not act under excitement, but *with a full knowledge of the result*. The record expressly has it: "when Daniel knew that the writing was signed." Many people will do right in a hurry, and under strong excitement will go further than they would have done in cold blood; but Daniel, probably shut out from the council by some crafty device of the counselors, no sooner heard that the statute stood good than, without parley, his resolution was formed and his mind made up. It was not for him to delay and to hesitate; he had all the data before him, and obedience made her determination known. Count the cost, young man, before you profess to be a Christian; do not espouse, upon a sudden, an enterprise for which you will be unequal. Devote yourselves to the Lord your God by his grace, but let it be according to the command of Christ, after having first made an estimate of that which will be required of you, and seek grace from on high that you may accomplish what otherwise will be impossible.

I like that word, and must go back to it again, *"as he had done aforetime."* Here he makes no alteration; he takes not the slightest possible notice of the king's decree. At the same place, at the same hour, in the same posture, and in the same spirit, the prophet is found. This indicates to us the Christian's duty under persecution—he should act under persecution as he would have done if none had arisen. If you have worshiped God under the smile of your Christian friends, worship him under the crown of the ungodly. If you have, as a tradesman, pursued a course of honest action in more prosperous times, do not for God's sake, for Christ's sake, tamper with that honest course because the times have changed. What has been right is right, and therefore abide by it. What you have done sincerely still do, and God will give you a blessing in it. Daniel could not have performed that act of praying, when the lions' den was to be the penalty, if he had not fallen into the habit of constant prayer beforehand. It was his secret communion with God which gave him strength and vigor to push on. Because he was right, he found it easier to keep right, whatever the penalty might be. I dare say I address some young man who has come from the country from a godly family where true religion has been daily set before him, and now he is placed in a workshop where he is startled to find that Jesus is ridiculed, and religion is a byword. Now friend, so as you used to do at home, make no difference to please vain men; take care that you begin as you mean to go on. I would not say merely, "Do not give up the spirit of religion," but, "Do not even yield the form." The devil never gives up to us; do not give up to him. He takes care to fight us with all his might; let us do the same to him.

I believe hundreds of Christian men make a hard lot to themselves by little yieldings at first, for generally is it so in this world, that if a man is determined and makes up his mind, after a while the world will let him alone. In the barrack room, when the soldier kneels to pray, how often has he been the subject of a thousand ribald jests, and so has given up all thought of bowing the knee! Yet we have heard of a real convert, who, when he came into the regiment, having been converted, knelt down to pray, and as he persisted in so doing, his comrades said, "Ah! he's one of the plucky ones; he's a genuine fellow"; and they left him alone afterward; whereas, if he had once sneaked into his bed without prayer, he would never after that have dared to kneel. There is nothing like following Daniel's example, by never giving in, for thus you will win the respect of those who otherwise would have sneered at you. How soon the world will find out our real meaning! We may think we are playing our game so prettily that they cannot make us out, and that we shall be pleasing the world and pleasing God too, but it always comes to a dead failure, and then, while the world despises, we have not the comfort of our conscience to sustain us.

Oh, if our fathers, the Puritans, would but have yielded a little; if they could have made but a nick in their consciences, as some are now doing, then, instead of being cast out of house and home, and prevented from opening their mouths to preach Christ, their yielding and consenting would have kept them in ease and honor; but where, then, would have been that gospel light which gladdens the nations? Where those pure and sacred institutions which they have handed down to us? Now, at this hour, through their intrepid resolution, they remain among the blessed, and men honor them. Let us not, the sons of brave fathers, let us not be craven. Recollect the days of Cromwell, and the times when the godless Cavaliers felt the edge of the Roundheads' sword, and though we take not carnal weapons, but eschew them utterly, let us show our foemen that the manhood of England is in us still, and we are of the same mettle as our sires.

III. Let us turn to the third point, with which we conclude, *the secret support of Daniel.*

There was something in the man which gave him this backbone; there was a secret something which made him so magnanimous. What was it? It resulted from several things. It sprang from the fact that *Daniel's religion was not the offspring of passion, but of deep-seated principle.*

There are some men whose religion is like the flower which lives upon the surface—they soon dry up when the sun of persecution burns; but there are others who, like the forest trees, send down their roots into the deep soil of principle, who know what they know, have learned thoroughly what they have learned, and hold fast what they have received, and these, in the time of trial, are sustained by springs of secret grace, and their leaf is not withered. Because the Holy Ghost had worked into Daniel's' spirit the principles of faith, he was sustained in the time of trial; but I doubt not that Daniel was also supported *by what he had read of the works of God* in the olden times. He was a great searcher of books, and he had found that in olden times Jehovah was always victorious. The prophet's eye gleamed as he thought of Pharaoh and the Red Sea, as he remembered Og, king of Basham, and the brooks of Arnon, and as his mind flew on to Sennacherib and the hook put into leviathan's jaws to turn him back by the way which he came. Recollecting the works of the Lord, for which his spirit made diligent search, he felt quite certain that the living God would prove himself true to his own.

Besides, the prophet's spirit was sustained *by what he had himself seen.* He had been brought in close contact with the three holy children who were brought before Nebuchadnezzar. Where Daniel was at that time we do not precisely know, but he must have been well aware of that heroic deed. He had seen King Nebuchadnezzar defied, had beheld the Son of God walking in the furnace with the three heroes, and had seen them come forth with not so much as the smell of fire passed upon them: here was grand encouragement. Besides, *Daniel had personal* experience of his God. He stood before Nebuchadnezzar to tell him the dream, and the interpretation thereof; yes, on a yet more dread occasion, without fear and trembling, he had faced the king Belshazzar, when the thousands of his guests were shouting to their gods, and the king and his wives and concubines in gorgeous state were drinking wine out of the bowls consecrated to Jehovah. That lone man stood erect amid the ribald crew, and pointing to the mysterious letters, read the terrible sentence, "Mene, Mene, Tekel, Upharsin," a monarch's doom proclaimed in his presence by a man unarmed! Was such a one likely now to be afraid! He that trembled not before tens of thousands of fierce soldiery, shall he fear now, when nothing but lions are in his way? Not he. He had looked into the face of his God, and would not fear the face of a lion; Jehovah had overshadowed him, and the den into which he would be cast had nothing in it terrible to him. His own experience helped to strengthen him. He had this conviction, that God could deliver him, and that if God did not deliver him, yet still such was *his love to the God of Israel* that he would be content to give himself to die.

It is blessed to have such a confidence as this. You good people who are tried, and who may expect to be tried yet more, you will never stand unless you come to this: "God can deliver me; but if he does not deliver me, still I am well content to be a sacrifice for Jesus' sake." Ah! some of you would fain be Christians, but in the time of trial you give it up; like the freshwater sailor, who, seeing the ship decked with all her colors, and her fair white sails bellying to the wind, thinks it must be a fine thing to be a mariner, but he is not far out to sea before qualms have come upon him; he dreads the storm, and vows, "*If* I can but once get safe to shore, I had done with sailoring forever." Many have said, "We will follow the Lord with Daniel." Yes, and well content they are to be with Daniel at Shushan, in the king's palace, but when it comes to the lions' den, then, "Daniel, good-bye." Take heed to yourselves that you be not deceived with a fair profession which shall afterward fail you. Daniel failed not, because his love to his God rested deep in his inmost heart: it had become part and parcel of himself, and sustained by the two hands of love and faith, he was graciously upborne over the rough and thorny places.

Remember that Daniel is a type of our Lord Jesus Christ. Jesus had enemies who sought to destroy him; they could find nothing against him except "touching his God." They accused him of blasphemy, and then afterward, as they did Daniel, they brought a charge of sedition. He was cast into the den, into the grave: his soul was among the lions. They sealed his tomb with their signet, lest any should steal him by night, but he arose as Daniel did, alive and unhurt, and his enemies were destroyed. Now if Daniel is a type of Christ, and the Lord Jesus is the great representative Man for all who are in him, you, believer, must expect that there will be those who will attack you, who will assail you especially in your religion. You must expect, too, that they will prevail against you for a time, so that you may be cast into the den, that they will seek to fasten you in as though you were destroyed forever; but there will be a resurrection not only of bodies but of reputations, and you shall arise. When the trumpet shall sound, not merely the corporeal particles, which make the man, but the man's memory shall rise; his good name, which has been buried beneath the clods of slander, shall rise to life, while as to his enemies, they and their reputations shall find devouring destruction from the presence of the Lord. Oh, to be a follower of Jesus, the great Daniel! To tread in his footsteps wherever he goes! To be much with him, whether in private or public! This is a thing to be desired, and though I exhort you to it, I do not expect you to attain to it in your own strength, but I point you to the Holy Ghost, who can work this in you, and make you to be greatly beloved as was this prophet of old.

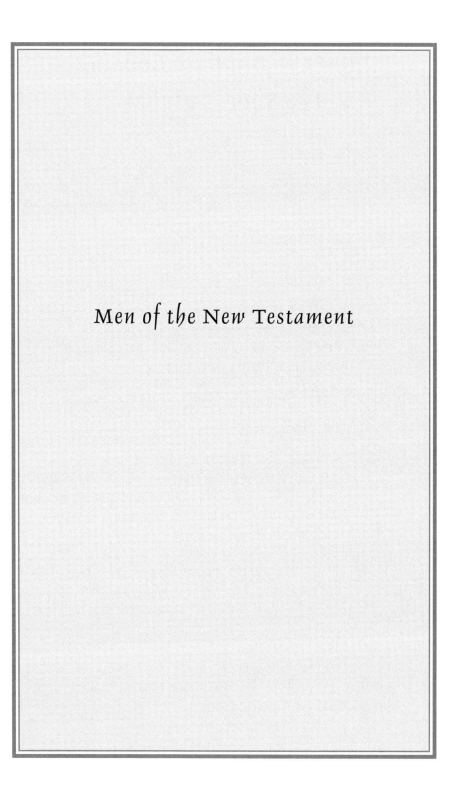

Men of the New Testament

John the Baptist: Loosing the Shoe-Latchet

~~~

Delivered on Lord's Day morning, March 31, 1872, at the Metropolitan Tabernacle, Newington. No. 1044.

One mightier than I cometh, the latchet of whose shoes I am not worthy to unloose.—LUKE 3:16

It was not John's business to attract followers to himself but to point them to Jesus, and he very faithfully discharged his commission. His opinion of his Master, of whom he was the herald, was a very high one; he reverenced him as the anointed of the Lord, the King of Israel, and, consequently, he was not tempted into elevating himself into a rival. He rejoiced to declare, "he must increase but I must decrease." In the course of his self-depreciation, he uses the expression of our text, which is recorded by each one of the Evangelists, with some little variation. Matthew words it "whose shoes I am not worthy to bear"; he was not fit to fetch his Lord his shoes. Mark writes it "whose shoes I am not worthy to stoop down and unloose"; and John has it very much as in Luke. This putting on and taking off and putting away of sandals was an office usually left to menial servants; it was not a work of any repute or honor, yet the Baptist felt that it would be a great honor to be even a menial servant of the Lord Jesus. He felt that the Son of God was so infinitely superior to himself that he was honored if only permitted to be the meanest slave in his employ. He would not allow men to attempt comparisons between himself and Jesus; he felt that none could, for a moment, be allowed. Now this honest estimate of himself as less than nothing in comparison with his Master is greatly to be imitated by us. John is to be commended and admired for this, but better still he is to be carefully copied.

Remember that John was by no means an inferior man. Among all that had been born of women before his time there had not been a greater than he. He was the subject of many prophecies, and his office was a peculiarly noble one; he was the friend of the great Bridegroom and introduced him to his chosen bride. He was the morning star of the gospel day, but he counted himself no light in the presence of the Sun of Righteousness whom he heralded. The temperament of John was not that which bowed or cringed; he was no reed shaken by the wind, no man of courtly habits fitted for a king's palace. No. We see in him an Elijah, a man of iron, a son of thunder; he roared like a young lion on his prey, and feared the face of none. Some men are so naturally meek spirited, not to say weak-minded, that they naturally become subservient and set up others as their leaders. Such men are apt to err in depreciating themselves; but John was every inch a man, his great soul bowed only before that which was worthy of homage; he was in God's strength as an iron pillar and a brazen wall, a hero for the cause of the Lord, and yet he sat down in the presence of Jesus as a little child on a stool sits at his master's feet, and he cried, "whose shoe-latchet I am not worthy to stoop down and to unloose."

Recollect, moreover, that John was a man endowed with great abilities, and these are very apt to make a man proud. He was a prophet, yes, and more than a prophet. When he stood in the wilderness to preach, his burning eloquence soon attracted the people from Jerusalem and from all the cities round about, and the banks of Jordan saw a vast multitude of eager hearers crowding around the man clothed with a garment of camel's hair. Thousands gathered together to listen to the teaching of one who had not been brought up at the feet of the rabbis, neither had been taught eloquence after the fashion of the schools. John was a man of bold, plain, telling, commanding speech; he was no second-rate teacher, but a master in Israel, yet he assumed no airs of self-conceit, but accounted the lowest place in the Lord's service as too high for him. Note, too, that he was not only a great preacher, but he had been very successful not only in attracting the crowds but in baptizing them. The whole nation felt the effects of John's ministry and knew that he was a prophet: they were swayed to and fro by his zealous words, as the corn of autumn is moved in the breath of the wind. A man is very apt when he feels that he has power over masses of his fellow creatures to be lifted up and exalted above measure, but not so John. It was safe for the Lord to trust him with a great popularity and a great success, for though he had all those honors he laid them meekly down at Jesus' feet, and said, "I am not worthy to be even the lowest slave in Messiah's household."

Recollect, also, moreover, that John was a religious leader, and he had the opportunity, if he had pleased, of becoming the leader of a powerful sect. The people were evidently willing to follow him. There were some, no doubt, who would not have gone over to Christ himself if John had not bidden them go, and testified, "Behold the Lamb of God," and confessed over and over again, saying, "I am not the Christ." We read of some who years after the Baptist was dead still remained his disciples, so that he had the opportunity of leading away a multitude who would have become his followers, and so of setting up his own name among men; but he scorned it; his elevated view of his Master prevented his entertaining any desire for personal leadership and, putting himself down not in the place of a captain of the lord's hosts, but as one of the least soldiers in the army, he says, "His shoe-latchets I am not worthy to unloose." What was the reason, do you think, of John's always retaining his proper position? Was it not because he had a high idea of his Master and a deep reverence for him? Ah, brethren, because of our little estimate of Christ, it is often unsafe for the Lord to trust us in any but the very lowest positions. I believe many of us might have been ten times as useful, only it would not have been safe for God to have allowed us to be so; we should have been puffed up, and like Nebuchadnezzar we should have boasted, "Behold this great Babylon that I have built." Many a man has had to fight in the back ranks, and serve his Master but little, and enjoy but little success in that service, because he did not reverence Christ enough, did not love his Lord enough, and consequently self would soon have crept in to his own overturning, to the grief of the church, and to the dishonor of his Lord. Oh, for high thoughts of Christ, and low thoughts of ourselves! Oh, to see Jesus as filling all in all, and to be ourselves as less than nothing before him.

Having thus introduced the subject, our object this morning is to draw instruction from the expression which John here and elsewhere used with regard to himself and his Lord: "whose shoe-latchet I am not worthy to unloose."

I gather from this, first, that no form of holy service is to be lightly set by: second, that our unworthiness is apparent in the presence of any sort of holy work: but that, third, this unworthiness of ours, when most felt, should rather stimulate us to action than discourage us, for so it doubtless operated in the case of John the Baptist.

I. First, then, note *that no form of holy service is to be lightly set by.*

To unloose the latchets of Christ's shoes might seem very trivial; it might even seem as if it involved the loss of self-respect for a man of position and influence to stoop to offices which a servant might quite as well perform. Why should I bring myself down to that? I will learn of Christ; I will distribute bread among the multitude for Christ; I will have my boat by the seashore ready for Christ to preach in, or I will go and fetch the ass upon which he shall ride in triumph into Jerusalem; but what need can there be for the disciple to become a mere menial? Such a question as that is here forever silenced, and the spirit which dictates it is practically rebuked. Nothing is dishonorable by which Jesus may be honored. Nothing lowers a man if thereby he honors his Lord. It is not possible for any godly work to be beneath our dignity; rather ought we to know that the lowest grade of service bestows dignity upon the man who heartily performs it. Even the least and most obscure form of serving Christ is more high and lofty than we are worthy to undertake.

Now note that little works for Christ, little shoe bearings and latched loosings, often *have more of the child's spirit in them than greater works*. Outside in the streets, a man's companion will do him a kindness, and the action performed is friendly; but for filial acts you must look inside the house. There the child does not lend money to its father or negotiate business, yet in his little acts there is more sonship. Who is it that comes to meet father when the day is over? And what is the action which often indicates childhood's love? See the little child comes tottering forward with father's slippers, and runs off with his boots as he puts them off. The service is little, but it is loving and filial, and has more of filial affection in it than the servant's bringing in the meal, of preparing the bed, or any other more essential service. It gives the little one great pleasure, and expresses his love. No one who is not my child, or who does not love me in something like the same way, would ever dream of making such a service his specialty. The littleness of the act fits it to the child's capacity, and there is also something in it which makes it a suitable expression of a child's affection. So also in little acts for Jesus. Oftentimes men of the world will give their money to the cause of Christ, putting down large sums for charity or for missions, but they will not weep in secret over other men's sins, or speak a word of comfort to an afflicted saint. To visit a poor sick woman, teach a little child, reclaim a street urchin, breathe a prayer for enemies, or whisper a promise in the ear of a desponding saint, may show more of sonship than building a row of almshouses or endowing a church.

In little acts for Christ it is always to be remembered that the *little things are as necessary to be done as the greater acts*. If Christ's feet be not washed, if his sandals be not unloosed, he may suffer, and his feet may be lamed, so that a journey may be shortened, and many villages may miss the blessing of his presence. So with other minor things. There is as much need for the quiet intercessions of saints as for the public delivery of God's truth before the assembled thousands. It is as needful that babes be taught their little hymns as that monarchs be rebuked for sin. We remember the old story of the losing of the battle through the missing of a single nail in a horseshoe, and peradventure up to this moment the church may have lost her battle for Christ, because some minor work which ought to have been done for Jesus has been neglected. I should not wonder if it should turn out that many churches have been without prosperity because, while they have looked to the public ministry and the visible ordinances, they have been negligent of smaller usefulnesses. Many a cart comes to grief through inattention to the linchpin. A very small matter turns an arrow aside from the target. To teach a child to sing "Gentle Jesus," and to point its young heart to the Redeemer, may seem a trifle, but yet it may be a most essential part of the process of that gracious work of religious education by which that child shall afterward become a believer, a minister, and a winner of souls. Omit that first lesson, and it may be you have turned aside a life.

Take another instance. A preacher once found himself advertised to preach in an obscure village; the storm was terrible, and therefore, though he kept his appointment, he found only one person present in the place of meeting. He preached a sermon to that one hearer with as much earnestness as if the house had been crowded. Years after he found churches all over the district, and he discovered that his audience of one had been converted on that day and had become the evangelist of the whole region. Had he declined to preach to one, what blessings might have been withheld. Brethren, never neglect the loosing of the shoe-latchet for Christ, since you do not know what may hang upon it. Human destiny often turns upon a hinge so small as to be invisible. Never say within yourself, "This is trivial"—nothing is trivial for the Lord. Never say, "But this surely might be omitted without much loss." How do you know? If it be your duty, he who allotted you your task knew what he did. Do not in any measure neglect any portion of his orders, for in all his commands there is consummate wisdom, and on your part it will be wisdom to obey them, even to the jots and tittles.

Little things for Christ again are *often the best tests of the truth of our religion.* Obedience in little things has much to do with the character of a servant. You engage a servant in your own house, and you know very well whether she be a good or bad servant that the main duties of the day are pretty sure to be attended to; the meals will be cooked, the beds will be prepared, the house will be swept, the door will be answered; but the difference between a servant who makes the house happy and another who is its plague lies in a number of small matters, which, peradventure, you could not put down on paper, but which make up a very great deal of domestic comfort or discomfort, and so determine the value of a servant. So I believe it is in Christian life; I do not suppose that the most of us here would ever omit the weightier matters of the law; as Christian men we endeavor to maintain integrity and uprightness in our actions, and we try to order our households in the fear of God in great matters; but it is in the looking to the Lord upon minor details that the spirit of obedience is most displayed; it is seen in our keeping our eye up to the Lord, as the eyes of the handmaidens are to their mistresses for daily orders about this step and that transaction. The really obedient spirit wishes to know the Lord's will about everything, and if there be any point which to the world seem trifling, for that very reason the obedient spirit says, "I will attend to it to prove to my Lord that even in the minutiae I desire to submit my soul to his good pleasure." In small things lie the crucibles and the touchstones. Any hypocrite will come to the Sabbath worship, but it is not every hypocrite that will attend prayer meetings, or read the Bible in secret, or speak privately of the things of God to the saints. These are less things, so they judge, and therefore they neglect them, and so condemn themselves. Where there is deep religion prayer is loved: where religion is shallow only public acts of worship are cared for. You shall find the same true in other things. A man who is no Christian will very likely not tell you a downright lie by saying that black is white, but he will not hesitate to declare that whitish-brown is white— he will go that length. Now the Christian will not go halfway to falsehood, no, he scorns to go an inch on that road. He will no more cheat you out of two-pence farthing, than he would out of £2000. He will not rob you of an inch any more than of an ell [unit of length, about 45 inches]. It is in the little that the genuineness of the Christian is made to appear; the goldsmith's hallmark is a small affair, but you know true silver by it. There is a vast deal of difference between the man who gladly bears Christ's shoes, and another who will not stoop to anything which he thinks beneath him. Even a Pharisee will ask Christ to his house to sit at meat with him; he is willing to entertain a great religious leader at his table; but it is not everyone who will stoop down and unloose his shoes, for that very Pharisee who made the feast neither brought him water to wash his feet, nor gave him the kiss of welcome; he proved the insincerity of his hospitality by forgetting the little things. I will be bound to say Martha and Mary never forgot to unloose his shoe-latchets, and that Lazarus never failed to see that his feet were washed. Look then, I pray you, as Christians to the service of Christ in the obscure things, in the things that are not recognized by men, in the matters which have no honor attached to them, for by this shall your love be tried.

Mark, also, with regard to little works that very often *there is about them a degree of personal fellowship with Christ which is not seen in greater work*. For instance, in the one before us, to unloose the latchets of his shoes brings me into contact with himself, though it be only his feet I touch; and I think if I might have the preference between going forth to cast out devils and to preach the gospel and to heal the sick, or to stay with him and always loose the latchets of his shoes, I should prefer this last; because the first act Judas did—he went with the twelve and saw Satan like lightning fall from heaven, but he perished because he failed in the acts that came into contact with Christ—in keeping Christ's purse he was a thief, and in giving Christ the kiss he was a traitor. He who does not fail in things relating personally to Christ is the sound man; he has the evidence of righteousness of heart. There was never a grander action done beneath the stars than when the woman broke her alabaster box of precious ointment and poured it upon him; though the poor did not get anything out of it, though no sick man was the better for it, the act was done distinctly unto him, and therefore there was a peculiar sweetness in it. Oftentimes similar actions, because they do not encourage other people for they do not know of them, because they may not be of any very great value to our fellowmen, are lightly esteemed, yet seeing, they are done for Christ, they have about them a peculiar charm as terminating upon his blessed person. True, it is but the loosing of shoe-latchets, but then, they are his shoes, and that ennobles the deed.

Dear fellow Christians, you know what I mean, though I cannot put it into very good language this morning—I mean just this, that if there is some little thing I can do for Christ, though my minister will not know about it, though the deacons and elders will not know, and nobody will know, and if I leave it undone nobody will suffer any calamity because of it, but, if I do it, it will please my Lord, and I shall enjoy the sense of having done it to him, therefore will I attend to it, for it is no slight work if it be for him.

Mark, also, once more, concerning those gracious actions which are but little esteemed by the most of mankind, that we know *God accepts our worship in little things.* He allowed his people to bring their bullocks, others of them to bring their rams, and offer them to him; and these were persons of sufficient wealth to be able to afford a tribute from their herds and flocks, but he also permitted the poor to offer a pair of turtledoves, or two young pigeons, and I have never found in God's Word that he cared less for the turtledove offering than he did for the sacrifice of the bullock. I do know, too, that our ever blessed Lord himself, when he was here, loved the praise of little children. They brought neither gold nor silver like the wise men from the East, but they cried, "Hosanna," and the Lord was not angry with their hosannas, but accepted their boyish praise. And we remember that a widow woman cast into the treasury two mites, which only made a farthing, but, because it was all her living, he did not reject the gift, but rather recorded it to her honor. We are now quite familiar with the incident, but for all that, it is very wonderful. Two mites that make a farthing given to the infinite God! A farthing accepted by the King of kings! A farthing acknowledged by him who made the heavens and the earth, who said, "If I were hungry I would not tell thee, for the cattle on a thousand hills are mine." Two mites received with pleasure by the Lord of all! It was scarcely so much as a drop thrown into the sea, and yet he thought much of it. Measure not little actions by human scales and measures, but estimate them as God does, for the Lord has respect unto the hearts of his people; he regards not so much their deeds in themselves as the motives by which they are actuated. Therefore, value the loosing of the Savior's shoe-latchets, and despise not "the day of small things."

II. Now, brethren and sisters, I wish to conduct you, in the second place, to the consideration of *our own unworthiness*, **which is sure to be felt by us whenever we come practically into contact with any real Christian service.**

I believe that a man who does nothing at all thinks himself a fine fellow, as a general rule. You shall usually find that the sharpest critics are those who never write; and the best judges of battles those who keep at a prudent distance from the guns. Christians of the kid-gloved order, who never make an attempt to save souls, are marvelously quick to tell us when we are too rough or too light in our speech; and they readily detect us if our modes of action are irregular or too enthusiastic. They have a very keen scent for anything like fanaticism or disorder. For my part, I feel pretty safe when I have the censures of these gentlemen; we are not far wrong when they condemn us. Let a man begin earnestly to work for the Lord Jesus, and he will soon find out that he is unworthy of the meanest place in the employ of one so glorious. Let us turn over that fact a minute.

Dear brothers and sisters, when we recollect what we used to be, I am sure we must feel unworthy to do the very least thing for Christ. You know how Paul describes the wickedness of certain offenders, and he adds, "But such were some of you." What hardness of heart some of us exhibited toward God! What rebellion! What obstinacy! What quenching of his Spirit! What love of sin! Why, if I might stoop down to unloose the latchet of the shoe of that foot which was crucified for me, I must bedew the nail print with my tears, and say, "My Savior, can it be that I am ever allowed to touch your feet?" Surely, the prodigal, if he ever unloosed his father's shoes, could say to himself, "Why, these hands fed the swine, these hands were often polluted by the harlots; I lived in uncleanness and was first a reveler, and then a swineherd, and it is amazing love which permits me now to serve so good a father." Angels in heaven might envy the man who is permitted to do the least thing for Christ, and yet they never sinned. Oh, what a favor that we who are defiled with sin should be called to serve the sinless Savior.

But, then, another reflection comes at the back of it—we *recollect what we are as well as what we were*—I say, what we are, for though washed in Jesus' blood and endowed with a new heart and a right spirit, yet we start aside like a deceitful bow, for corruption dwells in us. It is sometimes hard work to maintain even a little faith, we are so double-minded, so unstable, so hot, so cold, so earnest, and then so negligent: we are so everything except what we ought to be, that we may well wonder that Christ allows us to do the least thing for him. If he were to shut us in prison and keep us there, so long as he did not actually execute us, he would be dealing with us according to mercy, and not giving us our full deserts; yet he calls us out of prison, and puts us in his service, and therefore we feel that we are unworthy to perform the least action in his house.

Besides, beloved, even *small services we feel require a better state of heart than we often have.* I am sure the service of preaching the gospel here often brings to my sight my unworthiness far more than I should otherwise see it. If it be a gracious thing to see one's sinfulness, I may thank God I preach the gospel, for it makes me see it. Sometimes we come to preach about Jesus Christ and glorify him, and yet our heart is not warm toward him, and we do not value him aright; while the text we are preaching from seats him on a high throne, our heart is not setting him there; and, oh, then we think we could tear our heart out of our very body, if we could get rid of the black drops of its depravity which prevent our feeling in unison with the glorious truth before us. Another time, perhaps, we have to invite sinners and seek to bring them to Christ, and that wants so much sympathy that if Christ were preaching our sermon he would bedew it with his tears; but, we deliver it with dry eyes, almost without emotion, and then we flog our hard heart that it will not stir and cannot be made to feel.

It is just the same in other duties. Have you not felt "I have to go and teach my class this afternoon, but I am not fit; I have been worried all the week with cares, and my mind is not up to the mark now; I hope I love my Lord, but I hardly know whether I do or not. I ought to be earnest about these boys and girls; but it is very likely I shall not be earnest; I shall sit down and go through my teaching as a parrot would go through it, without life, without love"? Yes, then you painfully feel that you are not worthy to unloose the latchets of your Lord's shoes. Possibly, you are going this afternoon to visit a dying man, and you will try and talk to him about the way to heaven. He is unconverted. Now you want a tongue of fire to speak with, and instead of that, you have a tongue of ice; you feel, "O God, how can it be that I shall sit by that bedside and think of that poor man, who will be in the flames of hell, perhaps, within a week, unless he receive Christ, and yet I shall coolly treat his tremendously perilous condition as though it were a matter of the very slightest consequence?" Yes, yes, yes, we have had hundred of times to feel that we are in and of ourselves not fit for anything. If the Lord wanted scullions in his kitchen, he could get better than we are; and if he needed someone to shovel out the refuse of his house, he could find better men than we are for that. To such a Master we are unworthy to be servants.

The same feeling arises in another way. Have we not to confess, brethren and sisters, in looking upon what we have done for Christ, that *we have far too much eye to self in our conduct*. We pick and choose our work, and the picking and choosing is guided by the instinct of self-respect. If we are asked to do that which is pleasant to ourselves, we do it. If we are requested to attend a meeting where we shall be received with acclamation, if we are asked to perform a service which will lift us up in the social scale or that will commend us to our fellow Christians, we jump at it like a fish at a fly; but suppose the work would bring us shame, suppose it would discover to the public rather our inefficiency than our ability, we excuse ourselves. The spirit which Moses felt a little of, when the Lord called him, is upon many of us. "If I were to speak for Christ," says one, "I should stutter and stammer." As if God did not make stuttering mouths as well as intent mouths; and as if, when he chose a Moses, he did not know what he was at. Moses must go and stammer for God and glorify God by stammering, but Moses does not like that; and many in similar cases have not had grace enough to go to the work at all. Why, if I cannot honor the Lord with ten talents, shall I refuse to serve him with one? If I cannot fly like a strong-winged angel through the midst of heaven and sound the shrill-mouthed trumpet so as to wake the dead, shall I refuse to be a little bee and gather honey at God's bidding? Because I cannot be a leviathan, shall I refuse to be an ant? What folly and what rebellion if we are so perverse.

And, if you have performed any holy work, have you not noticed that pride is ready to rise? God can hardly let us succeed in any work but what we become toplofty. "Oh, how well we have done it!" We do not want anybody to say, "Now that was very cleverly, and nicely, and carefully, and earnestly done," for we say all that to ourselves, and we add, "Yes, you were zealous about that work, and you have been doing what a great many would not have done, and you have not boasted of it either. You do not call in any neighbor to see it; you have been doing it simply out of love to God, and, therefore, you are an uncommonly humble fellow, and none can say you are vain." Alas!

What flattery, but truly "the heart is deceitful above all things, and desperately wicked." We are not worthy to unloose the latchets of Jesus' shoes, because, if we do, we begin to say to ourselves, "What great folks are we; we have been allowed to loose the latchets of the Lord's sandals." If we do not tell somebody else about it with many an exultation, we at least tell ourselves about it and feel that we are something after all, and ought to be held in no small repute.

My brethren, we ought to feel that we are not worthy to do the lowest thing we can do for Christ, because, *when we have gone to the lowest, Jesus always goes lower down than we have gone.* Is it a little thing to bear his shoes? What, then, was his condescension when he washed his disciples' feet? To put up with a cross-tempered brother, to be gentle with him, and feel, "I will give way to him in everything because I am a Christian," that is going very low; but then, our Lord has borne far more from us; he was patient with his people's infirmities and forgave even to seventy times seven. And, suppose we are willing to take the lowest place in the church, yet Jesus took a lower place than we can, for he took the place of the curse: he was made sin for us, even he that knew no sin, that we might be made the righteousness of God in him. I have sometimes felt willing to go to the gates of hell to save a soul; but the Redeemer went further, for he suffered the wrath of God for souls. If there should be any Christian here who is so humble that he has no lofty thoughts about himself, but prefers to be least among his brethren, and so proves his graciousness, yet, my dear brother, you are not so lowly as Christ made himself, for he "made himself of no reputation," and you have some reputation left; and he took upon himself the form of a servant, and he became obedient to death—you have not come to that yet—even the death of the cross—the felon's death upon the gibbet, you will never be brought to that. Oh, the stoop of the Redeemer's amazing love! Let us, henceforth, contend how low we can go side by side with him, but remember, when we have gone to the lowest, he descends lower still, so that we can truly feel that the very lowest place is too high for us, because he has gone lower still.

Beloved friends, to put these things in a practical shape, it may seem to be a very small duty for any of you to do, to speak to one person alone about his soul. If you were asked to preach to a hundred, you would try it. I ask you solemnly, in God's name, not to let the sun go down today till you have spoken to one man or woman alone about his or her soul. Will you not do that? Is it too little for you? Then I must be plain with you, and say you are not worthy to do it. Speak today to some little child about his soul. Do not say, "Oh, we cannot talk to children, we cannot stoop to them." Let no such feeling occupy any of our minds, for if this work be as the loosing of the Master's shoe-latchets, let us do it. Holy Brainerd, when he was dying and could no longer preach to the Indians, had a little Indian boy at his bedside, and taught him his letters; and he remarked to one who came in, "I asked God that I might not live any longer than I could be of use, and so, as I cannot preach anymore, I am teaching this poor little child to read the Bible." Let us never think that we are stooping when we teach children, but if it be stooping let us stoop.

There are some of you, perhaps, who have the opportunity to do good to fallen women. Do you shrink from such work? Many do. They feel as if they could do anything rather than speak to such. Is it the loosing of the latchet of your Master's shoe? It is, then, an honorable business; try it, brother. It is not beneath you if you do it for Jesus; it is even above the best of you, you are not worthy to do it. Possibly there is near your house a district of very poor people. You do not like going in among them. They are dirty and perhaps infected with disease. Well, it is a pity that poor people should so often be dirty, but pride is dirty too. Do you say, "I cannot go there"? Why not? Are you such a mighty fine gentleman that you are afraid of soiling your hands? You will not unloose your Master's shoe-latchet then. The Lord lived among the poor and was poorer even than they; for he had not where to lay his head. Oh, shame on you, you wicked and proud servant of a condescending, loving Lord! Go about your business and unloose the latchets of his shoes directly! Instead of imagining that you would be lowered by such work for Jesus, I tell you, it would honor you; indeed, you are not fit for it; the honor is too great for you and will fall to the lot of better men.

It comes to this, beloved, anything that can be done for Christ is too good for us to do. Somebody wanted to keep the door! Somebody wanted to rout out the back lanes! Somebody wanted to teach ragged roughs! Somebody wanted to ask people to come to the place of worship, and to lend them their seats, and stand in the aisle while they sit. Well, be it what it may; I had rather be a doorkeeper in the house of the Lord, or the doormat either, than I would be accounted among the noblest in the tents of wickedness. Anything for Jesus, the lower the better; anything for Jesus, the humbler the better; anything for Jesus. The more going down into the deeps, the more thrusting the arms up to the elbows in the mud to find out precious jewels, the more of that the better. This is the true spirit of the Christian religion. Not the soaring up there to sit among the choristers and sing in grand style, not the putting on of apparel and preaching in lawn sleeves; not the going through gaudy and imposing ceremonies—all that is of Babylon: but to strip yourself to the shirtsleeves to fight the battle for Christ, and to go out among men as a humble worker, resolved by any means to save some, this is what your Lord would have you to do, for this is the unloosing of the latchets of his shoes.

III. And, now, our last remark shall be that *all this ought to stimulate us and not discourage us.*

Though we are not worthy to do it, that is the reason why we should avail ourselves of the condescending grace which honors us with such employ. Do not say, "I am not worthy to unloose the latchets of his shoes, and, therefore, I shall give up preaching." Oh, no, but preach away with all the greater vigor. John did so, and to his preaching he added warning. Warn people as well as preach to them. Tell them of the judgment to come and separate between the precious and the vile. We should perform our work in all ways, not omitting the more painful part of it, but going through with whatever God has appointed to us. John was called to testify of Christ, he felt unworthy to do it, but he did not shirk the work. It was his lifelong business to cry, "Behold, behold, behold the Lamb of God!" and he did it earnestly; he never paused in that cry. He was busy in baptizing too. It was the initiatory rite of the new dispensation, and there he stood continually immersing those who believed. Never a more indefatigable worker than John the Baptist; he threw his whole soul into it, because he felt he was not worthy to do the work. Brethren and sisters, your sense of unworthiness will, if you be idle, sadly hamper you but if the love of God be in your soul you will feel, "Since I do so badly when I do my best, I will always do my utmost. Since it comes to so little when the most is done, I will at least do the most." Could I give all my substance to him, and give my life, and then give my body to be burned, it would be a small return for love so amazing, so divine, as that which I have tasted: therefore, if I cannot do all that, at any rate, I will give the Lord Jesus all I can, I will love him all I can, I will pray to him all I can, I will talk about him all I can, and I will spread his gospel all I can; and no little thing will I count beneath me if his cause require it.

Brethren, John lived hard, for his meat was locusts and wild honey; his dress was not the soft raiment of men who live in palaces, he wrapped about him the rough camel's skin; and as he lived hard he died hard too, his boldness brought him into a dungeon, his courageous fidelity earned him a martyr's death. Here was a man who lived in self-denial and died witnessing for truth and righteousness, and all this because he had a high esteem of his Master. May our esteem of Christ so grow and increase, that we may be willing to put up with anything in life for Christ, and even to lay down our lives for his name's sake!

Certain Moravian missionaries, in the old times of slavery, went to one of the West Indian islands to preach, and they found they could not be permitted to teach there unless they themselves became slaves; and they did so, they sold themselves into bondage, never to return, that they might save slaves' souls. We have heard of another pair of holy men who actually submitted to be confined in a lazar house, that they might save the souls of lepers, knowing as they did that they would never be permitted to come out again; they went there to take the leprosy and to die, if by so doing they might save souls. I have read of one, Thomé de Jesu, who went to Barbary among the Christian captives, and there lived and died in banishment and bondage, that he might cheer his brethren, and preach Jesus to them. Brethren, we have never reached to such devotion; we fall far short of what Jesus deserves. We give him little, we give him what we are ashamed not to give him. Often we give him our zeal for a day or two and then grow cool; we wake up suddenly and then sleep all the more soundly. We seem today as if we would set the world on fire, and tomorrow we scarce keep our own lamp trimmed. We vow at one time that we will push the church before us and drag the world after us, and by-and-by we ourselves are like Pharaoh's chariots with the wheels taken off, and drag along right heavily. Oh, for a spark of the love of Christ in the soul! Oh, for a living flame from off Calvary's altar, to set our whole nature blazing with divine enthusiasm for the Christ who gave himself for us that we might live! Henceforth, take upon yourselves in the solemn intent of your soul this deep resolve: "I will unloose the latchets of his shoes; I will seek out the little things, the mean things, the humble things, and I will do them as unto the Lord and not unto men, and may he accept me even as he has saved me through his precious blood." Amen.

Matthew: "A Man Named Matthew"

⟨✦⟩

Intended for reading on Lord's Day, November 29, 1896; delivered on Lord's Day evening, April 12, 1885, at the Metropolitan Tabernacle, Newington. No. 2493.

> *As Jesus passed forth from thence, he saw a man, named Matthew, sitting at the receipt of custom: and he saith unto him, "Follow me." And he arose, and followed him.*—MATTHEW 9:9

This is a little bit of autobiography. Matthew wrote this verse about himself. I can fancy him, with his pen in his hand, writing all the rest of this gospel; but I can imagine that, when he came to this very personal passage, he laid the pen down a minute, and wiped his eyes. He was coming to a most memorable and pathetic incident in his own life, and he recorded it with tremulous emotion. "As Jesus passed forth from thence, he saw a man, named Matthew." The Evangelist could not have said much less about himself than this. "He saw a man, named Matthew, sitting at the receipt of custom: and he saith unto him, 'Follow me.' And he arose, and followed him." I do not think there is any part of Matthew's gospel that touched him more than this portion in which he was writing down the story of divine love to himself, and of how he himself was called to be a disciple of Christ.

I notice a very grave distinction between Matthew's way of recording his call and the very general style of converts relating their experience nowadays. The man seems to come boldly forth, with a springing step and a boastful air, and shouts out that he was the biggest blackguard who ever lived, and he tells with great gusto how he used to curse and to swear, and he talks as if there was something to be proud of in all that evil. Sit down, sir; sit down, and give us the story in this style, "As Jesus passed forth from thence, he saw a man, named Matthew"—that is about as much as we care to know. Tell us as briefly as you can how the Lord called you, and enabled you to follow him. There is a modesty about this narrative—not a mock modesty, by any means; there is no concealment of the facts of the case, there is no obscuration of the grace of Christ, but there is a concealment of Matthew himself. He mentions that he was a publican; in the list that he gives of the apostles he calls himself "Matthew the publican." The other Evangelists hardly ever call him a publican;

they do not even call him "Matthew," as a rule; they give his more respectable name "Levi," and they have more to say of him than he says of himself. It is always best for us, if there is anything to be said in our praise, not to say it ourselves, but to let somebody else say it. Brother, if your trumpeter is dead, put the trumpet away. When that trumpet needs to be blown, there will be a trumpeter found to use it; but you need never blow it yourself.

This verse reads to me so tenderly that I do not know how to communicate to you just how I feel about it. I have tried to imagine myself to be Matthew, and to have to write this story; and I am sure that, if I had not been inspired as Matthew was, I should never have done it so beautifully as he has done it, for it is so full of everything that is touching, tender, timid, true, and gracious: "As Jesus passed forth from thence, he saw a man, named Matthew, sitting at the receipt of custom: and he saith unto him, 'Follow me.' And he arose, and followed him."

Please notice—perhaps you did notice in our reading—whereabouts Matthew has put this story: it is placed immediately after a miracle. Some question has been raised, in a harmony of the Gospels, as to the exact position of this fact; whether it did occur just where Matthew tells it or whether he rather studied effect than chronology. Sometimes the Evangelists seem to overlook the chronological position of a statement, and put it out of its proper place that it may be more in its place for some other purpose. Well, I do not know about the chronology of this event; but it seems to me very beautiful on Matthew's part to record his call just here. "There," said he, "I will tell them one miracle about the Savior having made the palsied man take up his bed and walk, and then I will tell them of another miracle—a greater miracle still—how there was another man who was more than palsied, chained to his gains and to an injurious traffic, yet who, nevertheless, at the command of Christ, quit that occupation and all his gains, that he might follow his divine Master." Whenever you think about your own conversion, dear friend, regard it as a miracle, and always say within yourself, "It was a wonder of grace. If the conversion of anybody was ever a miracle of mercy, it was my conversion; it was extraordinary condescension on Christ's part to look on such a sinner as I was, and nothing but a miracle of grace could have saved me."

So Matthew tells his own story very tenderly, but he tells it very suggestively, putting it just after a most notable miracle; and I think that the Evangelist thought there was some similarity between the miracle and his own conversion, for there is nothing that palsies a man toward spiritual things like the lust of gold. Let a man be engaged in oppression and extortion, as the publicans were, and the conscience becomes seared as with a hot iron, and the extortioner is not likely to feel or desire that which is right. Yet here was a man, up to his neck in an evil occupation, but in a moment, at the divine call, he is made to part with all his hopes of gain that he may follow Christ. It was a miracle similar and equal to the raising of the palsied man who took up his bed and walked. You, too, dear friend, can trace a parallel, perhaps, between your conversion and some miracle of the Master. Was it, in your case, the casting out of devils? Was it the opening of the eyes of the blind? Was it the unstopping of deaf ears, and the loosing of a silent tongue? Was it the raising of the dead, or even more than that, was it the calling forth of corruption itself out of the grave, as when Jesus cried, "Lazarus, come forth," and Lazarus came forth? In any case, I invite you who know the Lord, in the silence of your souls just to sit down and think, not about Matthew, but about ourselves. I shall think about "a man named Spurgeon," and you can think about "a man named John Smith" or "Thomas Jones" or whatever your name may happen to be. If the Lord has looked upon you in love, you can just put your own name into the text, and say, "As Jesus passed forth from thence, he saw a man named James" or "John" or "Thomas," and you women may put in your names, too, you Marys and Janes, and so forth. Just sit and think how Jesus said to each one of you, "Follow me," and how in that happy moment you did arise and follow him, and from that hour you could truly sing, as you have often sung since—

> 'Tis done! the great transaction's done:
> I am my Lord's, and he is mine:
> He drew me, and I followed on,
> Charmed to confess the voice divine.
>
> High heaven, that heard the solemn vow,
> That vow renew shall daily hear:
> Till in life's latest hour I bow,
> And bless in death a bond so dear.

With some degree of rapidity, I will try to conduct your thoughts to various points of this interesting and instructive narrative.

I. The first is, that *this call of the man named Matthew seemed accidental and unlikely.*

"As Jesus passed forth from thence," just as he was going about some work or other, going away from Capernaum, perhaps, or merely going down one of its streets, it was as he "passed forth" that this event happened. As he passed, "he saw a man, named Matthew." That is the way we talk when we speak of things that, as we say, "happen" we scarcely know why. Now, dear friend, was that how you were converted? I do not know how long ago it was; but it did so happen, did it not? Yet it did not seem to you to be a very likely event ever to occur.

Looking back at the case of Matthew, it does seem now to have been a very unlikely thing that he should become a follower of Jesus. *Capernaum was Christ's own city, so he had often been there, yet Matthew remained unsaved.* Christ had not seen that "man, named Matthew," in the special way in which he saw him on this particular occasion; and you, dear friend, went to a place of worship a great many times before you were converted; perhaps you had been there regularly since you were a child. Yet it was not till that one particular day of grace that anything special happened to you, even as it was not till the time recorded in our text that something very special happened to the man named Matthew.

Further, at that time, *Jesus seemed as if he was about other business*; for, we read, "as Jesus passed forth from thence." And perhaps it seemed to you that the preacher was aiming at something else when his word was blessed to you. He was, maybe, comforting believers, yet God sent the message home to you, a poor unconverted sinner. Strange, was it not, both in Matthew's case, and your own?

At that time, also, *there are many other people in Capernaum, yet Christ did not call them.* He saw them, but not in the particular way in which he saw the man named Matthew. And, in like manner, on that day of mercy when you received the blessing of salvation, perhaps there was a crowded congregation, but, as far as you know, the blessing did not reach anybody but yourself. Why, then, did it come to you? You do not know, unless you have learned to look behind the curtains in the holy place, and to see by the light of the lamp within the veil. If you have looked there, you know that, when Jesus Christ is passing by, what men call his accidents are all intentional, the glances of his eye are all ordained from eternity; and when he looks upon anyone, he does it according to the everlasting purpose and the foreknowledge of God. The Lord had looked long before on that man named Matthew, so, in the fullness of time, Jesus Christ must needs pass that way, and he must look in love and mercy upon that man named Matthew. He saw him then because, long before, he foresaw him.

I cannot tell how you happen to be here, my dear friend—a stranger in London, perhaps, and a total stranger to this tabernacle; yet I believe you are brought here that my Lord and Master may see you—*you*, "a man, named

Matthew" or "John" or "James" or "Thomas" or whatever your name may be. And, oh! I pray that this may be the time when you shall see him, and hear him say, "Follow me," and you shall feel a blessed constraint to follow him without question or hesitancy, but at once leave whatever your sinful life may have been, and become a follower of Christ.

So, in the first place, this call of Matthew seemed accidental and unlikely, yet it was according to the purpose of God, and therefore it was duly given and answered.

II. In the second place, *this call of the man named Matthew was altogether unthought of and unsought.*

Matthew was not engaged in prayer when Christ called him. *He was in a degrading business*: "sitting at the receipt of custom." He was not listening to the Savior's preaching; he was taking from the people, against their will, the taxes for their Roman conqueror. As far as I can see, he had not even thought about Christ. I do not believe that he had been called before to be a disciple of Christ, and that he was on this occasion called to be an apostle; for I cannot imagine one who had been saved by Christ, returning to the publican business. It was an extortioner's occupation all through, and he who is called to be Christ's follower does not practice extortion from his fellowmen. If that is his employment before his conversion, he quits it when he comes to Christ.

Matthew was, further, *in an ensnaring business.* Nothing is more likely to hold a man fast than the love of gain. Sticky stuff is that gold and silver of which many are so fond; it has birdlimed many a soul for the best fowler, the devil, and many have been destroyed by it. The publicans usually made a personal profit by extorting more than was due; and, at this time, Matthew was not paying away money, but "sitting at the receipt of custom."

I do not know that, *even if Matthew has wished to follow Christ, he would have dared to do so.* He must have thought that he was too unworthy to follow Christ; and if he had dared to attempt it, I should suppose that *he would have been repulsed by the other apostles.* They would have snubbed him, and asked, "Who are you, to come among us?" They dared not do so after Christ himself had said to Matthew, "Follow me," but certainly there is no indication that this man named Matthew was seeking Christ, or even thinking about him; yet, while he sat taking his tolls and customs, Jesus came to him, and said, "Follow me."

O my dear hearer, if you have been converted, it may be that something like this was true in your case! At any rate, this I know is true; you were not the first to seek Christ, but Christ was the first to seek you. You were a wandering sheep and did not love the fold; but his sweet mercy went out after you.

His grace made you thoughtful and led you to pray; the Holy Spirit breathed in you your first breath of spiritual life, and so you came to Christ. It was so, I am sure; you did not first seek Christ, but he first sought you. Let us who are saved present the prayer to God now, that many here who have never sought the Lord may nevertheless find him; for it is written, "'I am found of them that sought me not': I said, 'Behold me, behold me, unto a nation that was not called by my name.'" See, then, the freeness of the grace of God, the sovereignty of his choice. Admire it in the man named Matthew; admire it still more in yourself, whatever your name may be.

III. Third, *this call of Matthew was given by the Lord Jesus with full knowledge of him.*

It is not said that Matthew first saw the Lord; but, "as Jesus passed forth from thence, he saw a man, named Matthew." I like to dwell upon those words, "He saw a man, named Matthew," because they seem to me to have a great deal of instruction in them.

Christ probably stopped opposite where Matthew was sitting, and looking at him, *he saw all the sin that had been in him, and all the evil that still remained in him.* "He *saw* a man, named Matthew." Christ has a searching look, a discerning look, a detecting look. He looked Matthew up and down, and he saw all that was in him. All that was secret to others was manifest before his piercing eyes. "He saw a man, named Matthew," and I believe that Jesus saw more in Matthew than was really in Matthew; I mean, that his love looked goodness into Matthew, and then saw it; his love looked grace into Matthew, and then saw it.

I do not know, but as far as I can see, Matthew had always been called "Levi" before. The Lord Jesus Christ did not see "a man named Levi." That was his old name; but, *he saw Matthew as he was to be*: "He saw a man, named Matthew." O beloved, when the Lord looked upon you even while you were a sinner, he saw a saint in you; though it was only his own eyes that could see so much as that. What he meant to make of you, he already saw in you, and he loved you as one who should yet be one of his redeemed servants.

I believe also that when the Lord Jesus Christ saw Matthew with the pen in his hand, he said to himself, "See what a nimble pen he has; *he is the man to write the first of the four Gospels.*" Jesus saw Matthew figuring away, as he put down the people's names, and how much they paid, and he said to himself, "That is the man to write one of the most regular and orderly of the Gospels; there is a clerkly habit about him, he is a good account keeper, that is the man for my service."

I do not know, dear friend, what the Lord may happen to see in you. I do not know all that he saw when he looked upon me. I fear that he saw nothing in me but sin and evil and vanity; but I believe that he did say to himself concerning me, "I see one to whom I can teach my truth, and who, when he gets a hold of it, will grip it fast, and never let it go, and one who will not be afraid to speak it wherever he is." So the Lord saw what use he could make of me, and I wonder what use he can make of you. Sit still, dear child of God, and wonder that the Lord should have made such use of you as he has made. And you who are just beginning to think of the Lord Jesus Christ, sit still, and each one of you say, "I wonder what use he can make of me."

There is an adaptation in men, even while they are unconverted, which God has put into them for their future service. Luke, you know, was qualified to write his gospel because he had been a physician; and Matthew was qualified to write the particular gospel which he has left us because he had been a publican. There may be a something about your habits of life, and about your constitution, and your condition, that will qualify you for some special niche in the church of God in years to come. Oh, happy day, when Jesus shall look upon you, and call you to follow him! Happy day, when he did look upon some of us, and saw in us what his love meant to put there, that he might make of us vessels of mercy meet for the Master's use!

IV. Pressing on a little further, I want you to notice, in the fourth place, that *Matthew's call was graciously condescending*: "As Jesus passed forth from thence, he saw a man, named Matthew, sitting at the receipt of custom: and he saith unto him, 'Follow me.'"

Christ had the choice of his followers, but *how came he to choose a publican?* The Roman yoke was so detestable to the freeborn son of Abraham that he could not bear the fact that the Roman, the idolater, should be lord in the Holy Land; so, if the Romans wanted Jews to collect the taxes, they could only get persons who had lost all care about public repute. They might be no worse than other people; perhaps they were not, but they were esteemed as being the very offscouring and pariahs of their race. But the Lord Jesus Christ sees this publican, and says to him, "Follow me." Not much of a credit will he be to his Master; so at least those around him will say. "See how this man, Jesus Christ, goes about, and picks up the scum of the people, the *residuum*. He is taking a publican as his follower—the man who has given himself up to be the servant of the oppressors and who has been himself an oppressor—he is going to have *him*. Now, if the Nazarene had passed by, and seen a learned rabbi or a Pharisee with his phylacteries, one who had made broad the borders of his garment, if Jesus had called *him*, it would have given a respectability to the community." Yes, but it so happens that the Lord Jesus Christ does not care about that sort of respectability at all. He is so respectable himself, in the highest sense of being respected, that he has honor enough and to spare for all his people, and he can condescend, without hazard, to call into his immediate company, to be one of his personal followers, "a man, named Matthew," even though he is a collector of the Roman taxes.

"Oh!" says one, "but I cannot think that he will ever call me." Yes, but I can think that he will! You remember John Newton, who had been a slave dealer, and more, who had been himself a slave, literally a slave, as well as a slave to the worst passions. Yet, let the church of St. Mary Woolnoth tell how from its pulpit there sounded through long years the glorious gospel of the blessed God from one who had been an African blasphemer, but who became a minister of Christ of the highest and noblest kind. Yes, the Lord Jesus Christ loves to look out for the *publicans*, the very lowest of the low, and to say to them, "Follow me. Come into my company. Walk behind me. Become my servant. Be entrusted with my gospel. I will make use of you." He still takes such as these to become the proclaimers of his Word; oh, that he may thus call some of you!

"Well," say you, "it was great condescension when the Lord called Matthew, the publican." Yes, but was it not equal condescension when he called you and me? O man or woman, whatever your name, sit and wonder and adore the condescending love that chose even you to be Christ's follower!

V. Again, dear friends—I hope I do not weary you while I try to bring this case of Matthew fully before you, wishing always that you may see yourself in it—observe next, that *this call of Matthew was sublimely simple*. Here it is in a nutshell: "He saith."

It was not John who said it or James or any of the apostles; but, *"He* saith." And it is not my preaching or your preaching or an archbishop's preaching, that can save souls; it is, *"He* saith," and it is when the Lord Jesus Christ, by the divine Spirit, says to a man, *"Follow me,"* that then the decisive work is done. Did he not say to the primeval darkness, "Light be!" and light was? And God, the omnipotent and eternal, has but to speak to man, and a like result will follow. "He saith unto him, 'Follow me'"; and then immediately, just as simply as possible, the record says, *"he arose, and followed him."* There is no palaver, no priestcraft, no sacramentalism. "He saith, 'Follow me.' And he arose, and followed him." That is the way of salvation; Christ bids you, while you are at your sin, leave it, and you leave it. He bids you trust him, and you trust him;

and trusting him, you are saved, for "he that believeth on the Son hath ever-lasting life."

Is that how you were saved, dear friend? I know it is; yet you used to fuss and fret and fume, and say to yourself, "I want to feel, I want to see, I want to experience." Now you have got clear of all those mistakes, I hope there is nothing more sublime than your conversion, but there is nothing more simple. And as for you, dear friends, who are looking for signs and wonders, or else you will not believe, I wish you would give up that foolish notion, for there is no sign and no wonder which is equal to this, that Christ should say to the dead heart, "Live," and it lives; that he should say to the unbelieving heart, "Believe," and it believes. In the name of Jesus Christ of Nazareth, I say to you, sinner, "Believe on the Lord Jesus Christ"; and if he is really speaking by me, you will believe in him, and you will arise and follow him.

So Matthew's call to follow Christ was sublimely simple.

VI. Notice, also, that it was immediately effectual. The Lord Jesus Christ said to him, "Follow me," and "he arose, and followed him." *Matthew followed at once.*

Some might have waited and put the coins away; but it does not appear that Matthew did so: "he arose, and followed him." He did not say to Christ, "I must enter the amounts to the end of this page; here is a lot of people with fish baskets, I must just see how much I can get out of them, and so finish up my reckoning." No, "he arose, and followed him." I believe that, when a man is converted, he is converted outright, and he will come right out from whatever wrong thing he has been doing. I have heard of a publican (I mean the other sort of publican, not a tax gatherer) who was very fond of drink, and he had by means of the drink sent many to perdition; but the day he was converted, he smashed his signboard, and had done with the evil traffic forever. When there is anything else that is wrong, whatever it is, I like to see men smash it up, and have done with it. Clear every trace of it out of your house; do not try to keep even a little piece of it or to do a wrong thing, and say, "I will give the profits to the Lord Jesus Christ." He will not take the money that is stained with the blood of souls. Quit the evil trade, and have done with it. Every kind of sin and every sort of evil, whatever it may be, will be left as soon as effectual grace comes to a man. I do not believe that anyone ever repents a little bit at a time; it is once for all that he does it, he turns straight around immediately, and obeys the Lord's call, "Follow me." Jesus said to Matthew. "'Follow me,' and he arose, and followed him."

"Oh!" says one, "was it so?" Yes, it was; I am not talking about things that are matters of question; I am speaking about facts. "As Jesus passed forth from thence, he saw a man, named Matthew, sitting at the receipt of custom, and he saith unto him, 'Follow me.' And he arose, and followed him." I know another man, not named "Matthew," but "Charles," and the Lord said to him, "Follow me"; and he also arose, and followed him. If I were to ask all the Christian men here now—John, James, Samuel, or whatever their names, who heard Jesus Christ say, "Follow me," and who followed him—to stand up, there would not be many of you left sitting, I hope. And you godly women, too, know that it was just the call of the Lord Jesus Christ to you that brought you to him there and then.

The call to Matthew was the call of effectual grace. "Where the word of a king is, there is power"; and Jesus Christ spoke to Matthew the word of *the* King. He said, "Follow me," and Matthew did follow him. I have heard that when the queen sends to anybody to come and see her, she does not "request the pleasure of his company," but she sends her command to him to come. That is the way kings and queens talk; and that is just the way with the Lord Jesus Christ, the King of kings, and Lord of lords. He says, "Follow me." And preaching to you in his name, we do not say, "Dear friend, do be converted, if you will"; but we say, "Thus saith the Lord: believe on the Lord Jesus Christ, and thou shalt be saved"; and with that command goes the power of the word of a king, and so sinners are saved. Jesus said to Matthew, "'Follow me,' and he arose, and followed him."

VII. Now, lastly, *Matthew's call was a door of hope for other sinners.*

I have been speaking mostly about personal conversion, and perhaps somebody says, "You know, sir, we are to think about other people as well as ourselves." Precisely so, and there is never a man who is saved who wants to go to heaven alone. So, when the Lord Jesus Christ saw "a man, named Matthew," and bade the publican follow him, *his salvation encouraged other publicans to come to Jesus.* Christ saw a great many other publicans and sinners whom he intended to draw to himself by means of that "man, named Matthew." He was to become a decoy duck for a great multitude of others like himself.

Next, *his open house gave opportunity to his friends to hear Jesus.* No sooner was Matthew called, and led to follow the Lord Jesus, than he said to himself, "Now, what can I do for my new Master? I have a good big room, where I have been accustomed to lock up the people's goods till they have paid their dues—

the *douane*, the customhouse, where I put away their goods in bond. Here, John, Thomas, Mary, come and clean out this room! Put a long table right down the middle. I am going to have in all my old friends; they have known what kind of man I have been, I am going to invite them all to supper; and it will not be a mean supper, either; it shall be the best supper they have ever had." Levi made a great feast in his own house, and he said to the Lord Jesus, "You have bidden me follow you, and I am trying to do so; and one way in which I am following you is that I am going to have a great feast in my house tonight, and to fetch in all my old companions. Will you, my Lord, be so good as to come and sit at the head of the table, and talk with them? They will be in a better humor for listening after I have fed them well. Will you come; and when they are all happy around my table, will you do for them what you have done for me? Maybe, Lord, if you will say that Matthew has become your follower, they will say, 'What! Matthew? Does he follow Christ? Well, then, who must this Christ be, that he will have such a follower as Matthew? Surely, he will have us, too, for we are like Matthew, and we will come to him as Matthew has come to him, if he will but speak the word of power to us as he did to Matthew.'" So the call of Matthew was Christ's way of bringing numbers of lost ones to a knowledge of the truth and to eternal salvation.

Now, has it been as with you, dear friend? Man, named John, Thomas, Samuel—woman, named Mary, Jane, or whatever it may be—have *you* brought any others to Jesus? Have you brought your children to Jesus? Have your prayers brought your husband to Jesus? Have your entreaties brought your brethren to Jesus? If not, you have failed as yet in accomplishing that which should be your life-work. Ask the Lord to help you now to begin with somebody or other of your own circle and your own standing, to whom you will be most likely to speak with the largest measure of influence and power of any man. The day you are converted, try to talk with those who were your schoolmates. Were you converted in a factory? Do not hesitate to speak to your fellow workmen. Are you a person of position? Do you occupy a high station in the fashionable world? Do not be ashamed of your Master, but introduce Christ into the drawing room, and let him have a footing among the highest of the land. Let each man, according to his calling, feel, "He who bade me follow him has bidden me do so that others may, through my instrumentality, be led to follow him too." God bless you in this holy service!

I feel as if I must close my discourse by just saying that, as the Lord saw "a man, named Matthew," and as he saw you, try now to return that look of love and see him; consider how great this man was; and, as Christ came to

Matthew's table, I now invite you who are believers in the Lord Jesus Christ to come to his table; and though you are not now numbered with publicans and sinners, but with his redeemed people, still it shall be your great joy to wonder as you sit here that your Master does still condescend to eat with publicans and sinners. God bless you, and save the whole of this great company, for his dear name's sake! Amen.

Simeon: "Nunc Dimittis"

Delivered on Lord's Day morning, January 15, 1871, at the Metropolitan Tabernacle, Newington. No. 1014.

Lord, now lettest thou thy servant depart in peace, according to thy word: for mine eyes have seen thy salvation.—LUKE 2:29–30

Blessed were you, O Simeon, for flesh and blood had not revealed this unto you; neither had it enabled you so cheerfully to bid the world farewell. The flesh clings to the earth; it is dust and owns affinity to the ground out of which it was taken; it loathes to part from mother earth. Even old age, with its infirmities, does not make men really willing to depart out of this world. By nature we hold to life with a terrible tenacity; and even when we sigh over the evils of life, and repine concerning its ills, and fancy that we wish ourselves away, it is probable that our readiness to depart lies only upon the surface, but down deep in our hearts we have no will to go.

Flesh and blood had not revealed unto Simeon that he saw God's salvation in that babe which he took out of the arms of Mary and embraced with eager joy. God's grace had taught him that this was the Savior, and God's grace at the same time loosened the cords which bound him to earth, and made him feel the attractions of the better land. Blessed is that man who has received by grace a meetness for heaven, and a willingness to depart to that better land: let him magnify the Lord who has worked so great a work in him. As Paul says, "Thanks be unto the Father, which hath made us meet to be partakers of the inheritance of the saints in light." Certainly none of us were meet by nature—not even Simeon; the fitness of the venerable man was all the handiwork of God, and so, also, was his anxiety to obtain the inheritance for which God had prepared him. I trust, brethren, while we consider this morning the preparedness of the saints for heaven, and turn over in our mind those reflections which will make us ready to depart, God's Holy Spirit, sent forth from the Father, may make us also willing to leave these mortal shores, and launch upon the eternal sea at the bidding of our Father, God.

We shall note, this morning, first, that *every believer may be assured of departing in peace*; but that, second, *some believers feel a special readiness to depart now*: "Now lettest thou thy servant depart in peace"; and, third, that *there are words of encouragement to produce in us the like readiness*: "according to thy word." There are words of Holy Writ which afford richest consolation in prospect of departure.

I. First, then, let us start with the great general principle, which is full of comfort; namely, this, that *every believer may be assured of ultimately departing in peace.*

This is no privilege peculiar to Simeon, it is common to all the saints, since the grounds upon which this privilege rests are not monopolized by Simeon, but belong to us all.

Observe, first, that *all the saints have seen God's salvation*, therefore, should they all depart in peace. It is true, we cannot take up the infant Christ into our arms, but he is "formed in us, the hope of glory." It is true, we cannot look upon him with these mortal eyes, but we have seen him with those eyes immortal which death cannot dim—the eyes of our own spirit which have been opened by God's Holy Spirit. A sight of Christ with the natural eye is not saving, for thousands saw him and then cried, "Crucify him, crucify him." After all, it was in Simeon's case the spiritual eye that saw, the eye of faith that truly beheld the Christ of God; for there were others in the temple who saw the babe; there was the priest who performed the act of circumcision, and the other officials who gathered round the group; but I do not know that any of them saw God's salvation. They saw the little innocent child that was brought there by its parents, but they saw nothing remarkable in him; perhaps, Simeon and Anna, alone of all those who were in the temple, saw with the inward eye the real Anointed of God revealed as a feeble infant. So, though you and I miss the outward sight of Christ, we need not regret it, it is but secondary as a privilege; if with the inner sight we have seen the incarnate God, and accepted him as our salvation, we are blessed with holy Simeon. Abraham saw Christ's day before it dawned, and even thus, after it has passed, we see it, and with faithful Abraham we are glad. We have looked unto him, and we are lightened. We have beheld the Lamb of God which taketh away the sins of the world. In the "despised and rejected of men" we have seen the anointed Savior; in the crucified and buried One, who afterward arose again, and ascended into glory, we have seen salvation, full, free, finished. Why, therefore, should we think ourselves less favored than Simeon? From like causes like results shall spring: we shall depart in peace, for we have seen God's salvation.

Moreover, believers already enjoy peace as much as ever Simeon did. No man can depart in peace who has not lived in peace; but he who has attained peace in life shall possess peace in death, and an eternity of peace after death.

"Being justified by faith we have peace with God through our Lord Jesus Christ." Jesus has bequeathed us peace, saying, "Peace I leave with you, my peace I give unto you." "For he is our peace," and "the fruit of the Spirit is peace." We are reconciled unto God by the death of his Son. Whatever peace flowed in the heart of Simeon, I am sure it was not of a diviner nature than that which dwells in the bosom of every true believer. If sin be pardoned, the quarrel is ended; if the atonement is made, then is peace established, a peace covenanted to endure forever. We are now led in the paths of peace; we walk the King's highway, of which it is written, "no lion shall be there"; we are led beside the still waters, and made to lie down in green pastures. We feel no slavish fear of God, though he be "a consuming fire" even to us; we tremble no longer to approach into his presence, who deigns to be our Father. The precious blood upon the mercy seat has made it a safe place for us to resort at all times; boldness has taken the place of trembling. The throne of God is our rejoicing, though once it was our terror.

> Once 'twas a seat of dreadful wrath,
> And shot devouring flame;
> Our God appeared "consuming fire,"
> And vengeance was his name.

Therefore, brethren, having peace with God, we may be sure that we shall "depart in peace." We need not fear that the God of all consolation, who has already enriched us in communion with himself, and peace in Christ Jesus, will desert us at the last. He will help us to sing a sweet swan song, and our tabernacle shall be gently taken down, to be rebuilt more enduringly in the fair country beyond Jordan.

Furthermore, we may rest assured of the same peace as that which Simeon possessed, since we are, if true believers, equally *God's servants*. The text says, "Lord, now lettest thou *thy servant* depart in peace." But, in this case, one servant cannot claim a privilege above the rest of the household. The same position toward God, the same reward from God. Simeon, a servant; you also, my brother, a servant; he who says to Simeon, "depart in peace," will say also the same to you. The Lord is always very considerate toward his old servants and takes care of them when their strength fails. The Amalekite of old had a servant who was an Egyptian, and when he fell sick he left him, and he would have perished if David had not had compassion on him; but our God is no Amalekite slave owner, neither doth he cast off his worn-out servants. "Even to your old age I am he; and even to hoar hairs will I carry you: I have made, and I will bear; even I will carry, and will deliver you." David felt this, for he prayed to God, and said, "Now, also, when I am old and gray-headed, O God, forsake me not." If you have been clothed in your Lord's livery of grace, and taught to obey his will, he will never leave you, nor forsake you; he will not sell you into the hands of your adversary, nor suffer your soul to perish. A true master counts it a part of his duty to protect his servants, and our great Lord and Prince will show himself strong on the behalf of the very least of all his followers, and will bring them every one into the rest which remains for his people. Do you really serve God? Remember, "his servants ye are to whom ye obey." Are you taught of the Spirit to obey the commandments of love? Do you strive to walk in holiness? If so, fear not death; it shall have no terrors to you. All the servants of God shall depart in peace.

There is also another reflection which strengthens our conviction that all believers shall depart in peace, namely, this: that up till now *all things in their experience have been according to God's word*. Simeon's basis of hope for a peaceful departure was "according to thy word"; and, surely, no Scripture is of private interpretation, or to be reserved for one believer to the exclusion of the rest? The promises of God, which are "Yea and amen in Christ Jesus," are sure to all the seed: not to some of the children is the promise made, but all the grace-born are heirs. There are not special promises hedged round and set apart for Simeon and a few saints of old time, but with all who are in Christ, their federal head, the covenant is made, and stands "ordered in all things and sure." If, then, Simeon, as a believer in the Lord, had a promise that he should depart in peace, I have also a like promise if I am in Christ. What God hath said in his Word, Simeon lays hold of, and none can say him no; but if, with the same grace-given faith, I also grasp it for myself, who shall challenge my right? God will not violate his promise to one of his people anymore than to another, and, consequently, when our turn shall come to gather up our feet in the bed and to resign our spirit, some precious passage in sacred Writ shall be as a rod and a staff to us that we may fear no evil.

These four considerations, gathered out of the text itself, may give fourfold certainty to the assurance that every believer, at the hour of his departure, shall possess peace.

For a moment, review attentively the words of the aged saint: they have much instruction in them. Every believer shall in death depart in the same sense as Simeon did. The word here used is suggestive and encouraging: it may be applied either to escape from confinement or to deliverance from toil. The Christian man in the present state is like a bird in a cage: his body imprisons his soul. His spirit, it is true, ranges heaven and earth, and laughs at the limits of matter, space, and time; but for all that, the flesh is a poor scabbard unworthy of the glittering soul, a mean cottage unfit for a princely spirit, a clog, a burden, and a fetter. When we would watch and pray, we find full often that the spirit is willing but the flesh is weak. "We that are in this body do groan." The fact is, we are caged birds; but the day comes when the great Master shall open the cage door, and release his prisoners. We need not dread the act of unfastening the door, for it will give to our soul the liberty for which it only pines, and then, with the wings of a dove, covered with silver, and its feathers with yellow gold, though aforetime it had lain among the pots, it will soar into its native air, singing all the way with a rapture beyond imagination. Simeon looked upon dying as a mode of being let loose—a deliverance out of durance vile, an escape from captivity, a release from bondage. The like redemption shall be dealt unto us. How often does my soul feel like an unhatched chick, shut up within a narrow shell, in darkness and discomfort! The life within labors hard to chip and break the shell, to know a little more of the great universe of truth, and see in clearer light the infinite of divine love. O happy day, when the shell shall be broken, and the soul, complete in the image of Christ, shall enter into the freedom for which she is preparing! We look for that, and we shall have it. God, who gave us to aspire to holiness and spirituality and to likeness to himself, never implanted those aspirations in us out of mockery. He meant to gratify these holy longings, or, else, he would not have excited them. Before long we, like Simeon, shall depart—that is, we shall be set free to go in peace.

I said that the word meant also a release from toil. It is as though Simeon had been standing at the table of his Master like a servant waiting on his Lord. You know the parable in which Christ says that the master does not first bid his servant sit down and eat bread, but commands him thus, "Gird thyself, and serve me." See then, Simeon stands yonder, girded and serving his Master; but by and by, when the Master sees fit, he turns around and says to Simeon, "Now you may depart, and take your own meat, your work is done." Or, we may use another simile, and picture Simeon sitting at the king's gate, like Mordecai, ready for any errand which may be appointed him, but at length his time of attendance expires, and the great monarch bids him depart in peace. Or, yet again, we may view him as a reaper toiling amid the harvest beneath a burning sun, parched with thirst and wearied with labor, and lo! the great Boaz comes into the field, and, having saluted his servant, says to him, "You have fulfilled like a hireling your day: take your wage, and depart in peace." The like shall happen to all true servants of Christ; they shall rest from their labors where no weariness shall vex them, "neither shall the sun light on them, nor any heat." They shall enter into the joy of their Lord, and enjoy the rest which remains for them. There is much of comfortable thought if we meditate upon this.

But note the words again. You perceive that the departure of the child of God is *appointed* of the Lord. "Now *lettest thou* thy servant depart." The servant must not depart from his labor without his master's permission, else would he be a runaway, dishonest to his position. The good servant dares not stir till his master says, "Depart in peace." Simeon was content to wait till he received permission to depart, and it becomes us all to acquiesce cheerfully in the Lord's appointment, whether he lengthens or shortens, our life. It is certain that without the Lord's will no power can remove us. No wind from the wilderness shall drive our souls into the land of darkness, no fiends with horrid clamor can drag us down to the abyss beneath, no destruction that wasteth at noonday, or pestilence waiting in darkness can cut short our mortal career. We shall not die till God shall say to us, "My child, depart from the field of service, and the straitness of this your tabernacle, and enter into rest." Till God commands us we cannot die, and when he bids us go it shall be sweet for us to leave this world.

Note, further, that the words before us clearly show that the believer's departure is attended with *a renewal of this divine benediction*. "Depart in peace," says God. It is a farewell, such as we give to a friend: it is a benediction, such as Aaron, the priest of God, might pronounce over a suppliant whose sacrifice was accepted. Eli said unto Hannah, "Go in peace: and the God of Israel grant thee thy petition that thou hast asked of him." Around the sinner's deathbed the tempest thickens, and he hears the rumblings of the eternal storm: his soul is driven away, either amid the thunderings of curses loud and deep, or else in the dread calm which evermore forebodes the hurricane. "Depart, ye cursed" is the horrible sound which is in his ears. But not so the righteous. He feels the Father's hand of benediction on his head, and underneath him are the everlasting arms. The best wine with him is kept to the last. At eventide it is light; and, as his sun is going down, it grows more glorious, and lights up all the surroundings with a celestial glow, whereat bystanders wonder, and exclaim, "Let me die the death of the righteous, and let my last end be like his." That pilgrim sets out upon a happy journey to whom Jehovah says, "Depart in peace." This is a sole finger laid upon the closing eyelid by a tender father, and it ensures a happy waking, where eyes are never wet with tears.

I cannot detain you longer over these words: suffice it to add, that whatever belonged to Simeon in this benediction must not be regarded as peculiar to him alone, but as, in their measure, the possession of all believers. "'This is

the heritage of the servants of the Lord, and their righteousness is of me,'
saith the Lord."

II. But now, second, we remind you, that *some believers are conscious
of a special readiness to depart in peace.*

When do they feel this? Answer: first, *when their graces are vigorous.* All the
graces are in all Christians, but they are not all there in the same proportion,
nor are they at all times in the same degree of strength. In certain believers
faith is strong and active. Now, when faith becomes "the evidence of things
not seen," and "the substance of things hoped for," then the soul is sure to say,
"Lord, now lettest thou thy servant depart in peace." Faith brings the clusters
of Eshcol into the desert, and makes the tribes long for the land that flows
with milk and honey. When the old Gauls had drunk of the wines of Italy, they
said, "Let us cross the Alps, and take possession of the vineyards which yield
such generous draughts." So when faith makes us realize the joys of heaven,
then it is that our soul stands waiting on the wing, watching for the signal
from the glory land.

The same is true of the grace of *hope,* for hope peers into the things invisible. She brings near to us the golden gates of the Eternal City. Like Moses,
our hope climbs to the top of Pisgah, and beholds the Canaan of the true
Israel. Moses had a delightful vision of the Promised Land when he gazed
from Nebo's brow, and saw it all from Dan to Beersheba: so also hope drinks
in the charming prospect of the goodly land and Lebanon, and then she
exclaims exultingly, "Lord, now lettest thou thy servant depart in peace."
Heaven realized and anticipated by hope renders the thought of departure
most precious to the heart.

And the like, also, is the effect of the grace of love upon us. Love puts the
heart, like a sacrifice, on the altar, and then she fetches heavenly fire and kindles it; and, as soon as ever, the heart begins to burn and glow like a sacrifice;
what is the consequence? Why, it ascends like pillars of smoke up to the throne
of God. It is the very instinct of love to draw us nearer to the person whom we
love; and, when love toward God pervades the soul, then the spirit cries, "Make
haste, my beloved, be thou like a roe or a young hart upon the mountains of
separation." Perfect love, casting out all fear, cries, "up, and away."

> *Let me be with thee, where thou art,*
> *My Savior, my eternal rest!*
> *Then only will this longing heart*
> *Be fully and forever blest.*

I might thus mention all the graces, but suffer one of them to suffice, one which is often overlooked, but is priceless as the gold of Ophir—it is the grace of *humility*. Is it strange that the lower a man sinks in his own esteem the higher does he rise before his God? Is it not written, "Blessed are the poor in spirit, for theirs is the kingdom of heaven"? Simeon had no conceit of his own importance in the world, else he would have said, "Lord, let me stay, and be an apostle. Surely I shall be needed at this juncture to lend my aid in the auspicious era which has just commenced." But no, he felt himself so little, so inconsiderable, that now that he had attained his heart's wish and seen God's salvation, he was willing to depart in peace. Humility by making us lie low helps us to think highly of God and, consequently, to desire much to be with God. Oh, to have our graces always flourishing, for then shall we always be ready to depart and willing to be offered up. Lack of grace entangles us, but to abound in grace is to live in the suburbs of the New Jerusalem.

Another time, when believers are thus ready to go, is when their assurance is clear. It is not always so with even the most mature Christians, and some true saints have not yet attained to assurance; they are truly saved and possess a genuine faith, but as assurance is the cream of faith, the milk has not stood long enough to produce the cream; they have not yet come to the flower of assurance, for their faith is but a tender plant. Give a man assurance of heaven, and he will be eager to enjoy it. While he doubts his own security, he wants to linger here. He is like the psalmist when he asked that God would permit him to recover his strength before he went hence, and was no more. Some things were not yet in order with David, and he would stay a while till they were. But when the ship is all loaded, the crew on board, and the anchor heaved, the favoring breeze is desired that the bark may speed on its voyage. When a man is prepared for his journey, ready to depart, he does not care to linger long in these misty valleys, but pants for the sunny summits of the mount of God, whereon stands the palace of the great King. Let a man know that he is resting upon the precious blood of Christ, let him by diligent self-examination perceive in himself the marks of regeneration, and by the witness of his own spirit and by the infallible witness of the Holy Ghost bearing witness with his own spirit, let him be certified that he is born of God, and the natural consequence will be that he will say, "Now let me loose from all things here below and let me enter into the rest which is assuredly my own." O you that have lost your assurance by negligent living, by falling into sin, or by some other form of backsliding, I do not wonder that you hug the world, for you are afraid you have no other portion; but with those who read their titles clear to mansions in the skies it will be otherwise.

They will not ask to linger in this place of banishment, but will sing in their hearts, as we did just now:

> Jerusalem my happy home,
> Name ever dear to me;
> When shall my labors have an end,
> In joy and peace and thee?

Beloved, furthermore, saints feel most their readiness to go when *their communion with Christ is near and sweet*; when Christ hides himself we are afraid to talk of dying, or of heaven; but when he only shows himself through the lattices, and we can see those eyes which are "as the eyes of doves by the rivers of water, washed with milk and fitly set"; when our own soul melts even at that hazy sight of him, as through a glass darkly. Oh, then we fain would be at home, and our soul cries out for the day when her eyes shall see the King in his beauty, in the land that is very far off. Have you never felt the heavenly homesickness? Have you never pined for the home bringing? Surely, when your heart has been full of the Bridegroom's beauty, and your soul has been ravished with his dear and ever precious love, you have said: "When shall the day break, and the shadows flee away? Why are his chariots so long in coming?" You have swooned, as it were, with lovesickness for your precious Savior, thirsting to see him as he is, and to be like him. The world is black when Christ is fair; it is a poor heap of ashes when he is altogether lovely to us. When a precious Christ is manifested to our spirits, we feel that we could see Jesus and die. Put out these eyes, there is nothing more for them to see when they have seen *him*. "Black sun," said Rutherford, "black moon, black stars, but inconceivably bright and glorious Lord Jesus." How often did that devout man write words of this sort:

"Oh, if I had to swim through seven hells to reach him, if he would but say to me, like Peter, 'Come unto me,' I would go unto him not only on the sea, but on the boiling floods of hell, if I might but reach him, and come to him." I will pause here and give you his own words: "I profess to you I have no rest, I have no ease, till I be over head and ears in love's ocean. If Christ's love (that fountain of delight) were laid as open to me as I would wish, oh, how I would drink, and drink abundantly! I half call his absence cruel; and the mask and veil on Christ's face a cruel covering that hideth such a fair, fair face from a sick soul. I dare not upbraid him, but his absence is a mountain of iron upon my heavy heart. Oh, when shall we meet? Oh, how long is it to the dawning of the marriage day? O sweet Lord Jesus, take wide steps; O my Lord, come over the mountains at one stride! O my Beloved, be like a roe, or a young hart, on the mountains of separation. Oh, if he would fold the heavens together like an old cloak, and shovel time and days out of the way, and make ready in haste the Lamb's wife for her Husband! Since he looked upon me my heart is not mine; he hath run away to heaven with it."

When these strong throes, these ardent pangs of insatiable desire come upon a soul that is fully saturated with Christ's love, through having been made to lean its head upon his bosom, and to receive the kisses of his mouth, then is the time when the soul says, "Lord, now lettest thou thy servant depart in peace."

So again, beloved, saints have drawn their anchor up and spread their sails, when they have been *made to hold loose by all there is in this world*; and that is generally when they hold fastest by the world to come. To many this world is very sweet, very fair, but God puts bitters into the cup of his children; when their nest is soft, he fills it with thorns to make them long to fly. Alas, that it should be so, but some of God's servants seem as if they had made up their minds to find a rest beneath the moon. They are moonstruck who hope to do so.

All the houses in this plague-stricken land are worm-eaten and let in the rain and wind: my soul longs to find a rest among the ivory palaces of your land, O Emmanuel.

Brethren, it often happens that the loss of dear friends, or the treachery of those we trusted, or bodily sickness, or depression of spirit, may help to unloose the holdfasts which enchain us to this life; and then we are enabled to say with David in one of the most precious little psalms in the whole Book—131: "I have behaved and quieted myself, as a child that is weaned of his mother: my soul is even as a weaned child." I have often thought that if David had said, "my soul is even as a weaning child," it would have been far more like most of God's people. But to be weaned, quite weaned from the world, to turn away from her consolations altogether, this it is which makes us cry, "Lord, now lettest thou thy servant depart in peace." Even as the psalmist when he said, "And now, Lord, what wait I for? my hope is in thee."

Again, saints are willing to depart when their work is almost done. This will not be the case with many here present, perhaps, but it was so with Simeon. Good old man! He had been very constant in his devotions, but on this occasion he came into the temple, and there, it is said, he took the child in his arms, and blessed God. Once more he delivered his soul of its adoration—once more he blended his praise with the songs of angels. When he had done that, he openly confessed his faith: another important work of every believer, for he said, "mine eyes have seen thy salvation." He bore public testimony to the child Jesus and declared that he should be "a light to lighten the gentiles." Having done that, he bestowed his fatherly benediction upon the child's parents, Joseph and his mother; he blessed them, and said unto Mary, "Behold, this child is set for the fall and rising again of many in Israel." Now we read that David, after he had served his generation, fell on sleep; it is time for man to sleep when his life's work is finished. Simeon felt he had done all: he had blessed God; he had declared his faith; he had borne testimony to Christ; he had bestowed his benediction upon godly people; and so he said, "Now, Lord, lettest thou thy servant depart in peace." Ah, Christian people, you will never be willing to go if you are idle. You lazy lie-a-beds, who do little or nothing for Christ, you sluggish servants, whose garden is overgrown with weeds, no wonder that you do not want to see your master! Your sluggishness accuses you and makes you cowards. Only he who has put out his talents to good interest will be willing to render an account of his stewardship. But when a man feels, without claiming any merit, that he has fought a good fight, finished his course, and kept the faith, then will he rejoice in the crown which is laid up for him in heaven, and he will long to wear it. Throw your strength into the Lord's work, dear brethren, all your strength; spare none of your powers: let body, soul, and spirit be entirely consecrated to God and used at their utmost stretch. Get through your day's work, for the sooner you complete it, and have fulfilled like a hireling your day, the more near and sweet shall be the time when the shadows lengthen, and God shall say to you, as a faithful servant, "Depart in peace!"

One other matter, I think, helps to make saints willing to go, and that is *when they see or foresee the prosperity of the church of God.* Good old Simeon saw that Christ was to be a light to lighten the gentiles, and to be the glory of his people Israel; and, therefore, he said, "Lord, now lettest thy servant depart in peace." I have known many a godly deacon who has seen a church wither and decay, its ministry become unprofitable, and its membership become divided; the dear old man has poured out his soul in agony before God, and when at last the Lord has sent a man to seek the good of Israel, and the church has been built up, he has been overjoyed, and he has said, "now lettest thou thy servant depart in peace." It must have reconciled John Knox to die when he had seen the Reformation safely planted throughout all Scotland. It made dear old Latimer, as he stood tied to the stake, feel happy when he could say, "Courage, brother, we shall this day light such a candle in England as shall never be blown out." "Pray for the peace of Jerusalem." Yes, that we do, and we vehemently desire her prosperity, and if we can see Christ glorified, error defeated, truth established, sinners saved, and saints sanctified, our spirit feels she has all she wishes. Like dying David, when we have said, "Let the whole earth be filled with his glory," we can fall back upon the pillows and die, for our prayers like those of David the son of Jesse are ended. Let us pray for this peace and this prosperity, and when we see it come, it shall bring calm and rest to our spirits, so that we shall be willing to depart in peace.

III. I shall call your attention now, for a little while, to the third point, that *there are words to encourage us to the like readiness to depart.*

"*According to thy word.*" Now let us go to the Bible, and take from it seven choice words all calculated to cheer our hearts in the prospect of departure, and the first is Psalm 23:4: "Yea, though I walk through the valley of the shadow of death, I will fear no evil: for thou art with me; thy rod and thy staff they comfort me." "We walk"—the Christian does not quicken his pace when he dies; he walked before, and he is not afraid of death, so he calmly walks on. It is a walk through a "shadow." There is no substance in death, it is only a shade. Who needs fear a shadow? It is not a lonely walk—"thou art with me." Neither is it a walk that need cause us terror; "I will fear no evil": not only is there no evil, but no fear shall cloud my dying hours. It shall be a departure full of comfort: "thy rod and thy staff"—a duplicate means shall give us a fullness of consolation. "Thy rod and thy staff they comfort me."

Take another text, and so follow the direction, "according to thy word." Psalm 37:37: "Mark the perfect man, and behold the upright: for the end of that man is peace." If we are perfect, that is sincere; if we are upright, that is honest in heart; our end then shall assuredly be peace.

Take another word, Psalm 116:15: "Precious in the sight of the LORD is the death of his saints." It is no ordinary thing for a saint to die; it is a spectacle which the eyes of God are delighted with. As kings delight in their pearls and diamonds, and count them precious, so the deathbeds of the saints are God's precious things.

Take another, Isaiah 57:2: "He shall enter into peace: they shall rest in their beds, each one walking in his uprightness." Here is an entrance into peace for the saint, rest on his dying bed, rest for his body in the grave, rest for his spirit in the bosom of his Lord, and a walking in his uprightness in the immortality above. "According to thy word." O what force there is in these few syllables! When you can preach the Word of God you must prevail. Nothing has such marrow and fatness in it as a text of Scripture. It has a force of comfort all its own. Consider also 1 Corinthians 3:21–22: "For all things are yours; whether Paul, or Apollos, or Cephas, or the world, or life, or death, or things present, or things to come; all are yours." Now, if death is yours, there can be no sort of reason why you should be afraid of that which is made over to you as a part of your inheritance.

Take 1 Corinthians 15:54–57: "So when this corruptible shall have put on incorruption, and this mortal shall have put on immortality, then shall be brought to pass the saying that is written, Death is swallowed up in victory. O death, where is thy sting? O grave, where is thy victory? The sting of death is sin; and the strength of sin is the law. But thanks be to God, which giveth us the victory through our Lord Jesus Christ." With such a text we need not fear to depart.

And so that other word, the seventh we shall quote, and in that number seven dwells perfection of testimony. Revelation 14:13: "And I heard a voice from heaven saying unto me, 'Write, Blessed are the dead which die in the Lord from henceforth.' 'Yea,' saith the Spirit, 'that they may rest from their labors; and their works do follow them.'"

Now, I dare say, many of you have said, "I wish I had a word from God, just like Simeon had, to cheer me in my dying moments." You have it before you; here are seven that I have read to you, most sure words of testimony, unto which you do well to take heed, as unto a light shining in a dark place. These promises belong to all believers in our precious Lord and Savior, Jesus Christ. Fear not, then, be not afraid, but rather say, "Now lettest thou thy servant depart in peace."

I have done the sermon, but we must put a rider to it. Just a word or two to those of you who cannot die in peace because you are not believers in Christ: you have never seen God's salvation, neither are you God's servants. I must deal with you as I have dealt with the saints. I have given them texts of Scripture, for the text says, "according to thy word"; and I will give you also two passages of Scripture, which will show you those who may not hope to depart in peace.

The first one is negative: it shows who cannot enter heaven, and, consequently, who cannot depart in peace—1 Corinthians 6:9–10: "Know ye not that the unrighteous shall not inherit the kingdom of God?" the unjust, the oppressive, cheats, rogues, "the unrighteous shall not inherit the kingdom of God." I will read these words. I need not explain them, but let everyone here who comes under their lash submit to God's Word. "Be not deceived: neither fornicators"—plenty of them in London—"nor idolaters"—and you need not worship a God of wood and stone to be idolaters, worship anything but God, you are an idolater—"nor adulterers, nor effeminate, nor abusers of themselves with mankind, nor thieves, nor covetous, nor drunkards"—alas, some of these come to this house regularly—"nor revilers," that is, backbiters, cavilers, talebearers, swearers, and such like, "nor extortioners"—you fine 20 percent gentlemen! You who grind poor borrowers with usurious interest. None of you shall inherit the kingdom of God, not one of you. If you come within this list, except God renew your hearts and change you, the holy gates of heaven are shut in your face.

Now, take another text, of a positive character, from the book of Revelation 21:7–8: "He that overcometh shall inherit all things; and I will be his God, and he shall be my son. But the fearful"—that means the cowardly, those that are ashamed of Christ, those that dare not suffer for Christ's sake, those who believe everything, and nothing, and so deny the truth, because they cannot endure to be persecuted; "the fearful, and unbelieving"—that is, those who do not trust a Savior—"and the abominable"—and they are not scarce, some among the poor are abominable, and there are right honorables who ought to be called right abominables; yes, and greater than that, too, whose vices make them abominable to the nation; "and murderers"—"he that hateth his brother is a murderer"; and "whoremongers, and sorcerers"; those who have or pretend to have dealings with devils and spirits, your spirit rappers, the whole batch of them; "and idolaters, and all liars," and these swarm everywhere, they lie in print, and they lie with the voice; ". . . all liars, shall have their part in the lake which burneth with fire and brimstone: which is the second death."

Now these are no words of mine, but the words of God; and if they condemn you, you are condemned; but, if you be condemned, fly to Jesus. Repent and be converted, as says the gospel, and forgiveness shall be yours, through Jesus Christ. Amen.

John: "The Disciple Whom Jesus Loved"

⋙⋘

Delivered on Lord's Day morning, May 23, 1880, at the Metropolitan Tabernacle, Newington. No. 1539.

The disciple whom Jesus loved following; which also leaned on his breast at supper.—JOHN 21:20

Our Lord loved all his disciples—"having loved his own which were in the world, he loved them unto the end." He said to all the apostles, "I call you not servants; for the servant knoweth not what his Lord doeth: but I have called you friends; for all things that I have heard of my Father I have made known unto you."

And yet within that circle of love there was an innermost place in which the beloved John was favored to dwell: upon the mountain of the Savior's love there was a knoll, a little higher than the rest of the mount, and there John was made to stand, nearest to his Lord. Let us not, because John was specially loved, think less, even in the slightest degree, of the love which Jesus Christ gave forth to the rest of his chosen. I take it, brethren, that those who display an extraordinary love to one are all the more capable of great affection to many; and therefore, because Jesus loved John most, I have an enhanced estimate of his love to the other disciples. It is not for a moment to be supposed that anyone suffered from his supreme friendship for John. John was raised, and they were not lowered, but raised with him. All believers are the dear objects of the Savior's choice, the purchase of his blood, his portion and inheritance, the jewels of his crown. If in John's case one is greater in love than another, yet all are eminently great, and therefore if it should so happen that you dare not hope to reach the height of John, and cannot look to be distinguished above others as "the disciple whom Jesus loved," yet be very thankful to be among the brotherhood who can each say, "He loved me, and gave himself for me." If you have not attained unto the first three, be happy to belong to the host of those who follow the Son of David. It is a matchless privilege, and an unspeakable honor, to enjoy the love of Jesus, even if you march among the rank and file of the armies of love. Our Lord's love to each of us has in it heights immeasurable and depths unfathomable; it passes knowledge.

Yet would I not utter this word of good cheer to make you remain at ease in a low state of grace; far rather would I excite you to rise to the highest point of love; for if already the Lord has loved you with an everlasting love, if already he has chosen you and called you, and kept you and instructed you, and forgiven you, and manifested himself to you, why should you not hope that another step or two may yet be taken, and that so you may climb to the very highest eminence? Why should you not before long be styled like Daniel, a "man greatly beloved," or like John, "that disciple whom Jesus loved"?

To be loved as John was, with a special love, is an innermost form of that same grace with which all believers have been favored. You must not imagine when I try to exhibit some of the lovable traits of John's character, that I would have you infer that the love of Christ went forth toward John in any other way than according to the law of grace; for whatever there was that was lovable in John, it was worked in him by the grace of God. Under the law of works John would have been as surely condemned as any of us, and there was nothing legally deserving in John. Grace made him to differ, just as truly as grace separates the vilest sinner from among the ungodly. Though it be granted that there were certain natural characteristics which made him amiable, yet God is the Creator of all that is estimable in man, and it was not till the natural had been by grace transformed and transfigured into the spiritual that these things became the subject of the complacency of Christ Jesus.

Brethren, we do not speak of John today as if he were loved because of his works or stood higher in the heart of Christ on the ground of personal merit, whereof he might glory. He, like all the rest of his brethren, was loved of Jesus because Jesus is all love and chose to set his heart upon him. Our Lord exercised a sovereignty of love and chose John for his own name's sake; and yet at the same time there was created in John much that was a fit object for the love of Christ. The love of Jesus was shed abroad in John's heart, and thus John himself was made fragrant with delightful odors. It was all of grace: the supposition of anything else is out of place. I look upon this special form of our Lord's love as one of those "best gifts" which we are bidden earnestly to covet—but a gift most emphatically, and not a wage or a purchasable commodity. Love is not bought. It never talks of price or claim. Its atmosphere is free favor. "If a man would give all the substance of his house for love, it would utterly be condemned." The supremest love is to be sought for, then, after the analogy of grace, as gracious men seek greater grace, and not as legalists chaffer and bargain for reward and desert. If ever we reach the upper chambers of love's palace, love herself must lead us up the stairs, yes, and be to our willing feet the staircase itself. Oh, for the help of the Holy Spirit while we speak upon such a theme.

I. And now, to come nearer to the text, first, dear friends, *let us consider the name itself,* "the disciple whom Jesus loved."

Our first observation upon it is—*it is a name which John gives to himself.* I think he repeats it five times. No other writer calls John "the disciple whom Jesus loved": John has thus surnamed himself, and all the early writers recognize him under that title. Do not suspect him, however, of egotism. It is one of the instances in which egotism is quite out of the question. Naturally, you and I would be rather slow to take such a title, even if we felt it belonged to us, because we should be jealous for our repute and be afraid of being thought presumptuous; but with a sweet naïveté which makes him quite forget himself, John took the name which he knew most accurately described him, whether others caviled at it or no. So far from there being any pride in it, it just shows the simplicity of his spirit, the openness, the transparency of his character, and his complete self-forgetfulness. Knowing it to be the truth, he does not hesitate to say it: he was sure that Jesus loved him better than others, and, though he wondered at it more than anyone else did, yet he so rejoiced in the fact that he could not help publishing it whatever the consequences to himself might be. Often there is a deal more pride in not witnessing to what God has done for us than in speaking of it. Everything depends upon the spirit which moves us. I have heard a brother with the deepest humility speak with full assurance of the divine love, and while some have thought that he was presumptuous, I have felt within myself that his positive testimony was perfectly consistent with the deepest humility, and that it was his simple modesty which made the man so utterly forget himself as to run the risk of being thought forward and egotistical. He was thinking of how he should glorify God, and the appearance of glorifying himself did not alarm him, for he had forgotten himself in his Master. I wish we could bear to be laughed at as proud for our Lord's sake. We shall never have John's name till like John we dare wear it without a blush.

It is a name in which John hides himself. He is very chary of mentioning John. He speaks of "another disciple," and "that other disciple," and then of "that disciple whom Jesus loved." These are the names by which he would travel through his own gospel "incognito." We find him out, however, for the disguise is too thin, but still he intends to conceal himself behind his Savior; he wears his Master's love as a veil, though it turns out to be a veil of light. He might have called himself if he had chosen "that disciple who beheld visions of God," but he prefers to speak of love rather than of prophecy. In the early church we find writings concerning him, in which he is named "that disciple who leaned on Jesus' bosom," and this he mentions in our text. He might have been called "that disciple who wrote one of the Gospels" or "that disciple who knew more of the very heart of Christ than any other"; but he gives the preference to love. He is not that disciple who did anything, but who received love from Jesus; and he is not that disciple who loved Jesus, but "whom Jesus loved." John is the man in the silver mask; but we know the man and his communications, and we hear him say, "We have known and believed the love that God hath to us. God is love, and he that dwelleth in love dwelleth in God, and God in him."

The name before us is *a name in which John felt himself most at home.* No other title would so well describe him. His own name, "John," means the "gift of God," and he was a precious gift from God the Father to his suffering Son, and a great comfort to the Savior during the years of his abode among men. Jesus doubtless counted him to be his Jonathan, his John, his God gift, and he treasured him as such; but John does not so much think of his being of any service to his Lord, as of that which his Lord had been to him. He calls himself "that disciple whom Jesus loved," because he recognized the delightful obligation which springs out of great love, and wished ever to be under its royal influence. He looked on Jesus' love as the source and root of everything about himself which was gracious and commendable. If he had any courage, if he had any faithfulness, if he had any depth of knowledge, it was because Jesus had loved these things into him. All the sweet flowers which bloomed in the garden of his heart were planted there by the hand of Christ's love, so when he called himself "that disciple whom Jesus loved," he felt that he had gone to the root and bottom of the matter, and explained the main reason of his being what he was.

This endearing name was very precious to him, because it evoked the sunniest memories of all his life. Those short years in which he had been with Jesus must have been looked upon by him in his old age with great transport, as the crown and glory of his earthly existence. I do not wonder that he saw Christ again in Patmos, after having seen him once in Palestine as he did see him; for such sights are very apt to repeat themselves. Such sights, I say; for John's view of his Lord was no ordinary one. There is at times an echo to sights as well as to sounds; and he who saw the Lord with John's eagle eye, with his deep-seated inner eye, was the likeliest man in all the world to see him over again in vision as he did see him amid the rocks of the Aegean Sea. All the memories of the best part of his life were awakened by the name which he wore, and by its power he often renewed that intimate communion with the living Christ which had lived on during the horrors of the crucifixion and lasted to the end of his days. That charming name set all the bells of his soul a-ringing: does it not sound right musically—"the disciple whom Jesus loved"?

That name was a powerful spring of action to him as long as he lived. How could he be false to him who had loved him so? How could he refuse to bear witness to the gospel of the Savior who had loved him so? What leagues of journeying could be too long for the feet of that disciple whom Jesus loved? What mobs of cruel men could cow the heart of the disciple whom Jesus loved? What form of banishment or death could dismay him whom Jesus loved? No, henceforth in the power of that name John becomes bold and faithful, and he serves his loving Friend with all his heart. I say, then, that this title must have been very dear to John, because he felt himself most at home in it; the secret springs of his nature were touched by it, he felt his whole self, heart, soul, mind, memory, all comprehended within the compass of the words "the disciple whom Jesus loved."

It was a name which was never disputed. You do not find anyone complaining of John for thus describing himself. General consent awarded him the title. His brethren did quarrel with him a little when his fond mother, Salome, wanted thrones for her two sons on the right and the left hand of the Messiah; but the love of Jesus to John never caused any ill will among the brethren, nor did John take any undue advantage of it. I believe that the apostles tacitly acknowledged that their Lord was perfectly right in his choice. There was something about John which made his brethren love him, and therefore they did not marvel that their Lord should make him his most intimate friend. The truly loved one of God generally receives the love of his brethren, yes, and even the love of the ungodly after a sort; for when a man's ways please the Lord, he makes even his enemies to be at peace with him. While David walked with God, all Israel loved him, and even Saul was forced to cry, "Thou art more righteous than I." John was so loving that he gained love everywhere. We may well be eager after this choice blessing, since it alone of all known treasures excites no envy among the brethren, but the rather makes all the godly rejoice. Inasmuch as saints wish to be greatly loved themselves, they are glad when they meet with those who have obtained that blessing. If we would ourselves smell of myrrh and aloes and cassia, we are glad to meet with those whose garments are already fragrant. You never find John lecturing his brethren or acting as a lord over God's heritage, but in all gentleness and lowliness he justified the affection which our Lord manifested toward him.

II. Thus much, then, with regard to the name. Second, *let us look at the character which lay below it.*

I can only give a miniature of John: it is quite impossible in the few moments of a sermon to draw a full-length portrait; and, indeed, I am not artist enough to accomplish it if I should attempt the task. In the character of John we see much that is admirable.

First, let us look at *his personality as an individual.* His was a large and warm heart. Perhaps his main force lies in the intensity of his nature. He is not vehement, but deep and strong. Whatever he did he did right heartily. He was simpleminded, a man in whom there was no guile: there was no division in his nature, he was one and indivisible in all that he felt or did. He did not entertain questions, he was not captious, he was not apt to spy out faults in others, and as to difficulties, mental or otherwise, he seems to have been happily without them. Having pondered and come to a conclusion, his whole nature moved in solid phalanx with forceful march; whichever way he went he went altogether, and right resolutely. Some men go two ways, or they tack about, or they go toward their object in an indirect manner; but John steams straight forward, with the fires blazing and the engine working at full speed. His whole soul was engaged in his Lord's cause, for he was a deep thinker, a silent student, and then a forceful actor. He was not impetuous with the haste of Peter, but yet he was determined and thoroughgoing, and all on fire with zeal.

He was exceedingly livid in his beliefs, and believed to the utmost what he had learned of his Lord. Read his epistle through, and see how many times he says, "we know," "we know," "we know." There are no "ifs" about him; he is a deep and strong believer. His heart gives an unfeigned assent and consent.

Withal there was an intense warmth about John. He loved his Lord; he loved his brethren; he loved with a large heart, for he had a grand nature. He loved constantly, and he loved in such a way as to be practically courageous for his Master, for he was a bold man, a true son of thunder. He was ready to go to the front if he was bound to do so, but it is in quite a quiet way, and not with a rush and a noise: his is not the dash of a cataract, but the still flow of a deep river.

Putting all together that we know about his personality, we look upon him as a man who was the reverse of your cold, calculating, slow-moving son of diffidence. You know the sort of persons I mean, very good people in their way, but by no means fascinating or much to be imitated. He was quite the reverse of those dried, juiceless brethren who have no human nature in them—men who are somewhere about perfect, for they have not life enough to sin, they do no wrong, or they do nothing at all. I know a few of those delightful people, sharp critics of others and faultless themselves, with this one exception, that they are heartless. John was a hearty man: a man of brain, but of soul too—a soul which went out to the tips of his fingers, a man who was permeated with intense but quiet life: a man to be loved. His life was not that of an ice plant, but of the red rose. He carried summer in his countenance, energy in his manner, steady force in all his movements. He was like that other John of whom he was once a disciple, "a burning and a shining light." There was warmth as well as light in him. He was intense, sincere, and unselfish by nature, and a fullness of grace came upon him and sanctified these virtues.

Let us now view him *in his relation to his Lord*. The name he takes to himself is *"the disciple* whom Jesus loved." Jesus loved him as a disciple. What sort of disciples do masters love? You that have ever been teachers of youth know that if teachers had their choice certain persons would be selected before others. If we teach we love teachable people: such was John. He was a man quick to learn. He was not like Thomas, slow, argumentative, cautious; but having once assured himself that he had a true teacher, he gave himself right up to him, and was willing to receive what he had to reveal.

He was a disciple of very keen eye, seeing into the soul of his instructor's teaching. His emblem in the early church was the eagle—the eagle which soars, but also the eagle which sees from afar. John saw the spiritual meaning of types and emblems; he did not stop at the outward symbols, as some of the disciples did, but his penetrating soul read into the depths of truth. You can see this both in his gospels and in his epistles. He is a spiritually minded man; he stays not in the letter, but he dives beneath the surface. He pierces through the shell and reaches the inner teaching. His first master was John the Baptist, and he was so good a disciple that he was the first to leave his teacher. You hint that this did not show that he was a good disciple. Indeed it did, for it was the Baptist's aim to send his followers to Jesus. The Baptist said, "Behold the Lamb of God, which taketh away the sin of the world," and John was so good a follower of the forerunner that he immediately followed the Lord himself, to whom the forerunner introduced him. This he did without a violent jerk: his progress was natural and even. Paul came to Jesus with a great start and twist, when he was put upon the lines on the road to Damascus: but John glided gently to the Baptist and then from the Baptist to Jesus. He was not obstinate, neither was he weak, but he was teachable, and so he made steady progress in his learning: such a disciple is one that a teacher is sure to love, and John was therefore "the disciple whom Jesus loved."

He was full of faith to accept what he was taught. He believed it, and he believed it really and thoroughly. He did not believe as some people do, with the fingertips of their understanding, but he gripped the truth with both hands, laid it up in his heart, and allowed it to flow from that center and saturate his whole being. He was a believer in his inmost soul; both when he saw the blood and water at the cross, and the folded grave clothes at the sepulcher, he saw and believed.

His faith worked in him a strong and enduring love, for faith works by love. He believed in his Master in a sweetly familiar way, "for there is no fear in love; but perfect love casteth out fear." Such a trustful, confiding disciple is sure to be loved of his teacher.

John had great receptiveness. He drank in what he was taught. He was like Gideon's fleece, ready to be saturated with the dew of heaven. His whole nature absorbed the truth as it is in Jesus. He was not a great talker: I should think he was almost a silent disciple. So little did he say that we have only one saying of his recorded in the Gospels. "Why," one might say, "I remember two or three." Do you remind me that he asked that he might sit on the right hand of Christ? I have not forgotten that request, but I answer that his mother, Salome, spoke on that occasion. Again, you tell me that at the supper he asked, "Lord, who is it?" Yes, but it was Peter who put that question into his mouth. The only utterance that I remember in the gospel which was altogether John's, is that at the sea of Tiberias, when he said to Peter, "It is the Lord." This was a very significant little speech—a recognition of his Lord such as the quick eye of love is sure to make. He who lived nearest to Jesus could best discern him as he stood upon the shore. "It is the Lord," is the gladsome cry of love, overjoyed at the sight of its Beloved. It might have served John as his motto—"It is the Lord." Oh, that we were able amid darkness and tossing to discern the Savior, and rejoice in his presence. "Blessed are the pure in heart, for they shall see God"; and such was the beloved disciple.

One great trait in John's character as a disciple was his intense love for his teacher; he not only received the truth, but he received the Master himself. I take it that the leaning of a man's faults often betrays his heart more than his virtues. It may seem a strange observation to make, but it is true. A true heart may as well be seen in its weakness as in its excellence. What were the weak points about John, as some would say? On one occasion he was intolerant. Certain persons were casting out devils, and he forbade them because they followed not with the disciples. Now, that intolerance, mistaken as it was, grew out of love to his Lord; he was afraid that these interlopers might set up as rivals to his Lord, and he wanted them to come under the rule of his beloved Jesus. At another time the Samaritans would not receive them, and he asked his Master that he might call down fire from heaven on them. One does not commend him, but still it was love to Jesus which made him indignant at their ungenerous conduct to their best friend. He felt so indignant that men should not entertain the Savior who had come into the world to bless them that he would even call fire from heaven: it showed his burning love for Jesus. Even when his mother asked that he and the brother might sit upon thrones at the right hand and the left hand of Christ, it was a deep and thoughtful faith in Jesus which suggested it. His idea of honor and glory was bound up with Jesus. If he gives way to ambition it is an ambition to reign with the despised Galilean. He does not want a throne unless it be at his Leader's side. Moreover, what faith there was in that request! I am not going to justify it, but I am going to say something to moderate your condemnation. Our Lord was going up to Jerusalem to be spat upon, and to be put to death, and yet John so thoroughly threw himself into his Lord's career that he would fain share in the fortune of his great Caesar, assured that it must end in his enthronement. He is content, he says, to be baptized with his baptism, and to drink of his cup; he only asks to share with Jesus in all things. As a good writer says, it reminds one of the courage of the Roman who when Rome was in the hands of the enemy purchased a house within the walls: John heroically asks for a throne at the side of one who was about to die on the cross, for he feels sure that he will triumph. When the cause and kingdom of Christ seemed ready to expire, yet so wholehearted was John in his faith in God and his love to his beloved Lord, that his highest ambition was still to be with Jesus and take shares with him in all that he would do and be. So, you see, all through he loved his Lord with all his heart, and therefore Jesus Christ loved him: or let me turn it the other way—the Lord loved John, and therefore he loved the Lord Jesus. It is his own explanation of it: "We love him because he first loved us."

I must ask you to look at John once more, as an instructed person. He was a beloved disciple, and remained a disciple, but he grew to know more and more, and in that capacity I would say of him, that doubtless our Lord Jesus loved him because of the tenderness which was produced by grace out of his natural warmth. How tender he was to Peter, after that apostle's grievous fall, for early in the morning John goes with him to the sepulcher. He is the man who restored the backslider. He was so tender that our Lord did not say to John, "Feed my lambs"; for he knew he would be sure to do it; and he did not even say to him, "Feed my sheep," as he did to Peter; he knew that he would do so from the instincts of his loving nature. He was a man who under the tutorship of Christ grew, moreover, to be very spiritual and very deep. The words he uses in his epistles are mostly monosyllables, but what mighty meanings they contain. If we may compare one inspired writer with another, I should say that no other Evangelist is at all comparable to him in depth. The other Evangelists give us Christ's miracles, and certain of his sermons, but his profound discourses, and his matchless prayer, are reserved for that disciple whom Jesus loved. Where the deep things of God are concerned, there is John, with sublime simplicity of utterance, declaring unto us the things which he has tasted and handled. Of all the disciples John was most Christlike. Like will to like. Jesus loved John for what he saw of himself in him, created by his grace. Thus I think you will see that, without supposing John to have possessed any merit, there were points in his personal character, in his character as a disciple, and in his character as an educated, spiritual man, which justified our Savior in making him the object of his most intimate affection.

III. Very briefly, in the third place, *let us review the life which grew out of this extraordinary love of Christ.*

What was the life of John? First, it was a life of *intimate communion.* John was wherever Christ was. Other disciples are put away, but Peter and James and John are present. When all the disciples sit at the table, even Peter is not nearest to the Lord Jesus, but John leans his head upon his bosom. Their intercourse was very near and dear. Jesus and John were David and Jonathan over again. If you are a man greatly beloved you will live in Jesus, your fellowship will be with him from day to day.

John's was a life of *special instruction.* He was taught things which no others knew, for they could not bear them. At the latter end of his life he was favored with visions such as even Paul himself, though not a whit behind the chief of the apostles, had never seen. Because of the greatness of his Lord's love to him he showed him future things, and lifted up the veil so that he might see the kingdom and the glory. They shall see most who love most; they shall be taught most who most completely give up their hearts to the doctrine.

John henceforth became a man in whose life there was *amazing depth.* If he did not say much as a rule while his Lord was with him, he was taking it all in for future use. He lived an inner life. He was a son of thunder, and could boldly thunder out the truth, because, as a thundercloud is charged with electricity, so had he gathered up the mysterious force of his Lord's life, love, and truth. When he did break out there was a voice like the voice of God in him;

a deep, mysterious, overwhelming power of God was about him. What a flash of lightning is the Apocalypse! What awful thunders sleep within the voils and the trumpets! His was a life of divine power because of the great fire which burned within; his was not the flash of crackling thorns beneath a pot, but the glow of coals in a furnace when the whole mass is molten into a white heat. John is the ruby among the twelve, he shines with a warm brilliance reflecting the love which Jesus lavished on him.

Hence his life was one of *special usefulness.* He was entrusted with choice commissions involving high honor. The Lord gave him to do a work of the most tender and delicate kind, which I am afraid he could not commit to some of us. As the Redeemer hung upon the tree dying he saw his mother standing in the throng, and he did not commit her to Peter, but to John. Peter would have been glad of the commission, I am sure, and so would Thomas, and so would James; but the Lord said to John, "Behold thy mother!" and to his mother, "Woman, behold thy son!" And from that hour that disciple took her to his own home. So modest, so retiring, I was going to say so gentlemanly, was John, that he was the man to take charge of a brokenhearted mother. Said I wrong that he was a true gentleman? Divide the word, and surely he was the gentlest of men. John has a delicate air and considerate manner, needful to the care of an honored woman. Peter is good, but he is rough; Thomas is kind, but cold; John is tender and affectionate. When you love Jesus much he will trust his mother to you; I mean his church and the poorest people in it, such as widows and orphans, and poor ministers. He will trust them to you because he loves you much. He will not put everybody into that office. Some of his people are very hard and stony of heart, and fitter to be tax collectors than distributors of alms. They would make capital officers in an army, but not nurses in a hospital. If you love Jesus much you shall have many delicate offices to perform which shall be to you proofs of your Lord's trust in you, and renewed tokens of his love.

John's life was, moreover, one of *extraordinary heavenliness.* They call him John the Divine, and he was so. His eagle wings bore him aloft into the heavenly places, and there he beheld the glory of the Lord. Whether in Jerusalem or in Antioch, in Ephesus or in Patmos, his conversation was in heaven. The Lord's Day found him in the spirit, waiting for him that cometh with clouds, so waiting that he who is the Alpha and Omega hastened to reveal himself to him. It was the love of his Lord which had thus prepared him for visions of the glory. Had not that love so enkindled his own love as to hold him faithfully at the cross all through the agony, he might never have been able to gaze upon the throne. He had lovingly followed him who had been pointed out to him as the "Lamb of God," and therefore he was made meet to see him as the Lamb in the midst of the throne, adored of angels and redeemed saints, whose harps and viols are engrossed with his praise. Oh, that we, too, could be freed from the grossness of earth, and borne aloft into the purer atmosphere of spiritual and heavenly things.

IV. We close by saying, very briefly, *let us learn lessons for ourselves* **from that disciple whom Jesus loved. May the Holy Spirit speak them to our inmost hearts.**

First, I speak to those of you who are still young. If you wish to be "the disciple whom Jesus loved," *begin soon.* I suppose that John was between twenty and twenty-five when he was converted; at any rate, he was quite a young man. All the representations of him which have been handed down to us, though I attach no great value to them, yet unite in the fact of his youth. Youthful piety has the most profitable opportunity of becoming eminent piety. If you begin soon to walk with Christ, you will improve your pace, and the habit will grow upon you. He who is only made a Christian in the last few years of his life will scarcely reach to the first and highest degree, for lack of time, and from the hampering influence of old habits; but you who begin soon are planted in good soil, with a sunny aspect, and should come to maturity.

Next, if we would be like John in being loved by Christ, let us *give our heart's best thoughts to spiritual things.* Brethren and sisters, do not stop in the outward ordinance, but plunge into its inner sense. Never allow your soul, on the Lord's Day for instance, to be thankful and happy merely because you have been to the place of worship. Ask yourself, "Did I worship? Did my soul commune with God?" In the use of the two ordinances of baptism and the Supper, content not yourself with the shell, but seek to get at the kernel of their inner meaning. Rest not unless the Spirit of God himself dwell within you. Recollect that the letter kills; it is the spirit that gives life. The Lord Jesus Christ takes no delight in those who are fond of broad phylacteries and multiplied sacraments and holy performances and superstitious observances. The Father seeks those to worship him who worship him in spirit and in truth. Be spiritual, and you are among those who are likely to be men greatly beloved.

Next to that, *cherish a holy warmth.* Do not repress your emotions and freeze your souls. You know the class of brethren who are gifted with refrigerating power. When you shake hands with them, you would think that you had hold of a fish: a chill goes to your very soul. Hear them sing. No, you cannot hear them! Sit in the next pew, and you will never hear the gentle hiss or mutter which they call singing. Out in their shops they could be heard a quarter of a mile off, but if they pray in the meeting, you must strain your ears. They do all Christian service as if they were working by the day for a bad master and at scanty wages: when they get into the world, they work by the piece as if for dear life. Such brethren cannot be affectionate. They never encourage a young man, for they are afraid that their weighty commendation might exalt him above measure. A little encouragement would help the struggling youth mightily, but they have none to offer. They calculate and reckon and move prudently; but anything like a brave trust in God they set down as rashness and folly. God grant us plenty of rashness, I say, for what men think imprudence is about the grandest thing under heaven. Enthusiasm is a feeling which these refrigerators do not indulge. Their chant is, "As it was in the beginning, is now, and ever shall be, world without end. Amen"; but anything like a dash for Christ and a rush for souls they do not understand. Mark this, if you trace such brethren home, you will find that they have little joy themselves and make very little joy for others. They are never quite certain that they are saved, and if they are not sure of it we may readily guess that other people are not. They spend in anxious thought the strength which ought to have gone in hearty love. They were born at the north pole and live amid perpetual frost: all the furs of Hudson's Bay could not warm them. About them you see none of the rich tropical flowers which bedeck the heart upon which the Sun of Righteousness shines with perpendicular beams. These chilly mortals have never traversed the sunny regions of heavenly love where the spices of holy delight load all the air, and apples of gold are everywhere within the reach of glowing hearts. The Lord bring us there!

Jesus Christ loves warm people; he never shines on an iceberg except to melt it. His own life is so full of love that its holy fire kindles the like flame in others, and thus he has fellowship with those whose hearts burn within them. The fitness for love is love. To enjoy the love of Jesus we must overflow with love. Pray for earnest, eager, intense affection. Lay your hearts among the coals of juniper till they melt and glow.

Dear brother, if you want to be the man that Jesus loves, cultivate strong affection and *let your nature be tender and kind*. The man who is habitually cross, and frequently angry, cannot walk with God. A man of a quick, hot temper who never tries to check it, or a man in whom there is a malicious remembrance of injuries, like a fire smoldering amid the embers, cannot be the companion and friend of Jesus, whose spirit is of an opposite character. A pitiful, compassionate, unselfish, generous heart is that which our Lord approves. Forgive your fellow as if you never had anything to forgive. When brethren injure you, hope that they have made a mistake, or else feel that if they knew you better they would treat you worse. Be of such a mind toward them that you will neither give nor take offense. Be willing to lay down, not only your comfort, but even your life for the brethren. Live in the joy of others, even as saints do in heaven. Love others so as to forget your own sorrows. So shall you become a man greatly beloved.

Last of all, may the Spirit of God help you to rise to heavenliness. Do not be miserable money-grubbers, or sordid earthworms; do not be pleasure hunters and novelty seekers, do not set your affection upon these children's toys, which will be so soon broken up. Be no more children, but men of God. Oh, to find your joy in Christ, your wealth in Christ, your honor in Christ, your everything in Christ—this is peace. To be in the world but not to be of it: to linger here as if you were an angel sent from heaven to dwell for a while among the sons of men, to tell them of heaven, and point them the way—this is to abide in Christ's love. To be always ready to fly, to stand on tiptoe, waiting for the heavenward call, to expect to hear the trumpet ring out its clarion note, the trumpet of the coming of your Lord—this is to have fellowship with Christ. Sit loose, I pray you, by this world; get a tighter grip of the world to come—so shall Jesus' love be shed abroad within you. Throw your anchor upward, into the placid sea of divine love, and not like the seamen, downward, into a troubled ocean. Anchor yourselves to the eternal throne, and never be divided even in thought from the love of God, which is in Christ Jesus our Lord. May it be my privilege and yours, brothers and sisters, to lean these heads of ours on Jesus' bosom, till the day break and the shadows flee away. Amen and amen.

Andrew: Everyday Usefulness

❧

Delivered on Lord's Day morning, February 14, 1869, at the Metropolitan Tabernacle, Newington. No. 855.

And he [Andrew] brought him [Peter] to Jesus.—JOHN 1:42

We have a most intense desire for the revival of religion in our own midst, and throughout all the churches of our Lord Jesus. We see that error is making great advances, and we would fain lift up a banner for the cause of truth; we pity the mighty populations among whom we dwell, for they are still godless and Christless, and the things of their peace are hid from their eyes, therefore would we fain behold the Lord performing miracles of grace. Our hope is that the set time to favor Zion is come, and we intend to be importunate in prayer that God will reveal his arm and do great things in these latter days. Our eager desire, of which our special services will be the expression, is a right one. Challenge it who will, be it ours to cultivate it, and prove by our zeal for God that the desire is not insincere or superficial.

But, my brethren, it is very possible that in addition to cultivating a vehement desire for the revival of religion, we may have been daydreaming, and forecasting in our minds a conception of the form which the divine visitation shall take. Remembering what we have heard of former times of refreshing, you expect a repetition of the same outward signs, and look for the Lord to work as he did with Livingstone at the Kirk of Shotts or with Jonathan Edwards in New England or Whitefield in our own land. Perhaps you have planned in your mind that God will raise up an extraordinary preacher whose ministry will attract the multitude, and while he is preaching, God the Holy Spirit will attend the word, so that hundreds will be converted under every sermon; other evangelists will be raised up of a like spirit, and from end to end this island shall hear the truth and feel its power.

Now it may be that God will so visit us. It may be that such signs and wonders as have frequently attended revivals may be again witnessed—the Lord may rend the heavens and come out and make the mountains to flow down at his feet; but it is just possible that he may select quite another method. His Holy Spirit may reveal himself like a mighty river swollen with floods, and sweeping all before its majestic current; but if so he wills, he may rather unveil his power as the gentle dew which, without observation, refreshes all the earth. It may happen unto us as unto Elijah when the fire and the wind passed before him, but the Lord was not in either of those mighty agencies: he preferred to commune with his servant in a still, small voice. Perhaps that still, small voice is to be language of grace in this congregation. It will be useless then for us to be mapping out the way of the eternal God, idle for us to be rejecting all the good which he may be pleased to give us because it does not happen to come in the shape which we have settled in our own minds to be the proper one. Idle, did I say? Such prejudice would be wicked in the extreme.

It has very frequently happened that while men have been sketching out imaginary designs, they have missed actual opportunities. They would not build because they could not erect a palace; they therefore shiver in the winter's cold. They would not be clothed in homespun, for they looked for scarlet and fine linen before long; they were not content to do a little, and therefore did nothing. I want, therefore, to say this morning to every believer here, it is vain for us to be praying for an extensive revival of religion, and comforting each other in the hope of it, if meanwhile we suffer our zeal to effervesce, and sparkle, and then to be dissipated: our proper plan is, with the highest expectations, and with the largest longings, to imitate the woman of whom it is written, "She hath done what she could," by laboring diligently in such holy works as may be within our reach, according to Solomon's precept, "Whatsoever thy hand findeth to do, do it with thy might." While believers are zealously doing what God enables them to do, they are in the high road to abundant success; but if they stand all the day idle, gaping after wonders, their spiritual want shall come upon them as an armed man. I have selected the text before us in order that I may speak upon matters which are practical and efforts within the reach of all. We shall not speak of the universal triumph of the gospel, but of its victory in single hearts; nor shall we deal with the efforts of an entire church, but with the pious fervor of individual disciples. If the Christian church were in a proper and healthy state, the members would be so studious of the word of God, and would themselves have so much of the Spirit of Christ, that the only thing they would need in the great assemblies, over and above worship, would be a short encouraging and animating word of direction addressed to them, as to well-drilled and enthusiastic soldiers, who need but the word of command, and the deed of valor is straightaway performed. So would I speak, and so would I have you hear at this hour.

Coming then, to the subject, Andrew was converted by Christ to become his disciple. Immediately he sets to work to recruit the little army by discipling others. He finds his brother Peter, and he brings him to Jesus.

I. First, I shall call your attention, this morning, to *the missionary disciple.*

Andrew is the picture of what all disciples of Christ should be. To begin, then. This first successful Christian missionary *was himself a sincere follower of Jesus.* Is it needful to make that observation? No, will it ever be needless while so many make a profession of a faith which they do not possess? While so many will wantonly thrust themselves into the offices of Christ's church, having no concern for the glory of his kingdom, and no part or lot in it, it will be always needful to repeat that warning, "Unto the wicked God saith, 'What hast thou to do to declare my statutes?'" Men who have never seen the beauties of Emmanuel are not fit persons to describe them to others. An experimental acquaintance with vital godliness is the first necessity for a useful worker for Jesus. That preacher is accursed who knows not Christ for himself. God may, in infinite sovereignty, make him the means of blessing to others, but every moment that he tarries in the pulpit he is an impostor; every time he preaches he is a mocker of God, and woe unto him when his Master calls him to his dread account. You unconverted young people who enter upon the work of Sunday school instruction, and so undertake to teach to others what you do not know yourselves, do place yourselves in a position of unusual solemnity and of extraordinary peril. I say "of extraordinary peril," because you do by the fact of being a teacher profess to know, and will be judged by your profession, and I fear condemned out of your own mouths. You know the theory only of religion, and of what use is that while you are strangers to its power? How can you lead others along a way which you yourself refuse to tread?

Besides, I have noticed that persons who become active in church work before they have first believed in Christ are very apt to remain without faith, resting content with the general repute which they have gained. O dear friends, beware of this. In this day hypocrisy is so common, self-deceit is so easy, that I would not have you place yourselves where those vices become almost inevitable. If a man voluntarily puts himself where it is taken for granted that he is godly, his next step will be to mimic godliness, and by and by he will flatter himself into the belief that he really possesses that which he so successfully imitates. Beware, dear hearers, of a religion which is not true; it is worse than none. Beware of a form of godliness which is not supported by the fervor of your heart and soul. This age of shams presents but few assistances to self-examination, hence am I the more earnest that every one of us, before he shall seek to bring others to Christ, should deliberately ask himself, "Am I a follower of Christ myself? Am I washed in his blood? Am I renewed by his

Spirit?" If not, my first business is not in the pulpit, but on my knees in prayer: my first occupation should not be in the Sunday school class, but in my closet, confessing my sin and seeking pardon through the atoning sacrifice.

Andrew was earnest for the souls of others, though he was but a young convert. So far as he can gather, he appears to have beheld Jesus as the Lamb of God one day, and to have found out his brother Peter the next. Far be it from us to forbid you who but yesterday found joy and peace, to exert your newborn zeal and youthful ardor. No, my brethren and sisters, delay not, but make haste to spread abroad the good news which is now so fresh and so full of joy to you. It is right that the advanced and the experienced should be left to deal with the captious and the skeptical, but you, even you, young as you are, may find some with whom you can cope; some brother like Simon Peter, some sister dear to you who will listen to your unvarnished tale, and believe in your simple testimony. Though you be but young in grace, and but little instructed, begin the work of soul winning, and

> Tell to sinners 'round
> What a dear Savior you have found.

If the religion of Jesus Christ consisted in abstruse doctrines, hard to be understood, if the saving truths of Christianity were metaphysical points, difficult to handle, then a matured judgment would be needed in every worker for God, and it would be prudent to say to the young convert, "Hold back till you are instructed"; but, since that which saves souls is as simple as A, B, C, since it is nothing, but this, "He that believeth and is baptized, shall be saved," he that trusts the merit of Christ shall be saved. You who have trusted him know that he saves you, and you know that he will save others; and I charge you before God, tell it, tell it right and left, but especially tell it to your own kinsfolk and acquaintance, that they also may find eternal life.

Andrew was a disciple, a new disciple, and, I may add, *a commonplace disciple,* a man of average capacity. He was not at all the brilliant character that Simon Peter his brother turned out to be. Throughout the life of Jesus Christ, Andrew's name occurs, but no notable incident is connected therewith. Though in afterlife he no doubt became a most useful apostle, and according to tradition sealed his life's ministry by death upon a cross, yet at the first Andrew was, as to talent, an ordinary believer, one of that common standard and nothing remarkable. Yet Andrew became a useful minister, and thus it is clear that servants of Jesus Christ are not to excuse themselves from endeavoring to extend the boundaries of his kingdom by saying, "I have no remarkable talent or singular ability." I very much disagree with those who decry ministers of slender gifts, sneering at them, as though they ought not to occupy the pulpit at all. Are we, after all, brethren, as servants of God, to be measured by mere oratorical ability? Is this after the fashion of Paul, when he renounced the wisdom of words lest the faith of the disciples should stand in the wisdom of man, and not in the power of God? If you could blot out from the Christian church all the minor stars, and leave nothing but those of the first magnitude, the darkness of this poor world would be increased sevenfold. How often the eminent preachers, which are the church's delight, are brought into the church by those of less degree, even as Simon Peter was converted by Andrew! Who shall tell what might have become of Simon Peter if it had not been for Andrew? Who shall say that the church would ever have possessed a Peter if she had closed the mouth of Andrew? And who shall put their finger upon the brother or sister of inferior talent and say, "These must hold their peace"? No, brother, if you have but one talent, the more zealously use it. God will require it of you: let not your brethren hold you back from putting it out to interest. If you are but as a glowworm's, lamp, hide not your light, for there is an eye predestinated to see by your light, a heart ordained to find comfort by your faint gleam. Shine, and the Lord accept you.

I am putting it in this way that I may come to the conclusion that every single professor of the faith of Christ is bound to do something for the extension of the Redeemer's kingdom. I would that all the members of this church, whatever their talents were, would be like Andrew in *promptness.* He is no sooner a convert than he is a missionary; no sooner taught than he begins to teach. I would have them like Andrew, *persevering,* as well as prompt. He first finds Peter—that is his first success, but how many afterward he found, who shall tell? Throughout a long life of usefulness it is probable that Andrew brought many stray sheep to the Redeemer's fold, yet certainly that first one would be among the dearest to his heart. "He first" found Peter: he was the spiritual father of many sons, but he rejoiced most that he was the father of his own brother Peter—his brother in the flesh, but his son in Christ Jesus.

Could it be possible for me to come to every one of you personally, and grasp you by the hand, I would with most affectionate earnestness—yes, even with tears—pray you, by him to whom you owe your souls, awake and render personal service to the Lover of your souls; make no excuse, for no excuse can be valid from those who are bought with so great a price. Your business, you will tell me, requires so much of your thoughts, I know it does; then use your business in such a way as to serve God in it. Still there must be some scraps of time which you could devote to holy service; there must be some opportunities for directly aiming at conversions. I charge you, avail yourselves of such occasions, lest they be laid to your door. To some of you the excuse of "business" would not apply, for you have seasons of leisure. Oh, I beseech you, let not that leisure be driveled away in frivolities, in mere talk, in sleep and self-indulgence! Let not time slip away in vain persuasions that you can do nothing, or in mere preparations for grand experiments, but now, like Andrew, hasten at once to serve Jesus; if you can reach but one individual, let him not remain unsought.

Time is hastening, and men are perishing. The world is growing old in sin. Superstition and idolatry root themselves into the very soil of human nature. When, when will the church become intent upon putting down her Master's foes? Possessing such little strength, we cannot afford to waste a jot of it. With such awful demands upon us, we cannot afford to trifle. Oh, that I had the power to stir the heart and soul of all my fellow Christians by a description of this huge city wallowing in iniquity, by a picture of the graveyards and cemeteries fattening on innumerable corpses; by a portrayal of that lake of fire to which multitudes yearly descend.

Surely sin, the grave, and hell are themes which might create a tingling even in the dull cold ear of death. Oh, that I could set before you the Redeemer upon the cross dying to ransom souls! Oh, that I could depict the heaven which sinners lose, and their remorse when they shall find themselves self-excluded! I would, I could even set before you in vivid light the cases of your own sons and daughters, the spiritual condition of your own brothers and sisters, without Christ, and therefore without hope, unrenewed, and therefore "heirs of wrath, even as others," then might I expect to move each believer here to an immediate effort to pluck men as brands from the burning.

II. Having described the missionary disciple, we shall now speak briefly in the second place upon *his great object.*

The great object of Andrew seems to have been to bring Peter to Jesus. This, too, should be the aim of every renewed heart—to bring our friends to Jesus, not to convert them to a party. There are certain unbrotherly sectarians, called Brethren, who compass sea and trod land to make proselytes from other churches. These are not merchants seeking goodly pearls in a legitimate fashion, but pirates who live by plunder; they must not excite our wrath so much as our pity, though it is difficult not to mingle with it something of disgust. While this world remains so wicked as it is, we need not be spending our strength as Christian denominations in attacking one another: it will be better for us to go and fight with the Canaanites than with rival tribes which should be one united Israel.

I should reckon it to be a burning disgrace if it could be said, "The large church under that man's pastoral care is composed of members whom he has stolen away from other Christian churches." No, but I value beyond all price the godless, the careless, who are brought out from the world into communion with Christ. These are true prizes, not stealthily removed from friendly shores, but captured at the edge of the sword from an enemy's dominions. We welcome brethren from other churches if in the providence of God they are drifted to our shores, but we would never hang out the wrecker's beacon to dash other churches in pieces in order to enrich ourselves with the wreck. Far rather would we be looking after perishing souls than cajoling unstable ones from their present place of worship. To recruit one regiment from another is no real strengthening of the army; to bring in fresh men should be the aim of all.

Furthermore, the object of the soul winner is not to bring men to an outward religiousness merely. Little will you have done for a man if you merely make the Sabbath breaker into a Sabbath keeper, and leave him a self-righteous Pharisee. Little will you have done for him if you persuade him, having been prayerless, to be a mere user of a form of prayer, his heart not being in it. You do but change the form of sin in which the man lives; you prevent him being drowned in the salt water, but you throw him into the fresh; you take one poison from him, but you expose him to another. The fact is, if you would do real service to Christ, your prayer and your zeal must follow the person who has become the object of your attention, till you bring him absolutely to close with grace and lay hold on Jesus Christ, and accept eternal life as it is found in the atoning sacrifice. Anything short of this may have its usefulness for this world, but must be useless for the world to come. To bring men to Jesus—Oh, be this your aim and mine!—not to bring them to baptism, nor to the meetinghouse, nor to adopt our form of worship, but to bring them to his dear feet who alone can say, "Go in peace; your sins which are many are all forgiven you."

Brethren, as we believe Jesus to be the very center of the Christian religion, he who gets not to Christ gets not to true godliness at all. Some are quite satisfied if they get to the priest and obtain his absolution; if they get the sacraments, and eat bread in the church; if they get to prayers, and pass through a religious routine; but we know that all this is less than nothing and vanity, unless the heart draws near to Jesus. Unless the soul accepts Jesus as God's appointed sin offering and rests alone in him, it walks in a vain show and disquiets itself in vain. Come then, brethren, nerve yourselves to this point, that from this day forth let your one ambition be in dealing with your fellowmen, to bring them to Jesus Christ himself. Be it determined in your spirit that you will never cease to labor for them till you have reason to believe that they are trusting in Jesus, loving Jesus, serving Jesus, united to Jesus, in the hope that they shall be conformed to the image of Jesus and dwell with him, world without end.

But some will say, "We can very clearly understand how Andrew brought Peter to the Lord, because Jesus was here among men, and they could walk together till they found him." Yes, but Jesus is not dead, and it is a mistake to suppose that he is not readily to be reached. Prayer is a messenger that can find Jesus at any hour. Jesus is gone up on high as to his body, but his spiritual presence remains to us, and the Holy Ghost as the Head of this dispensation is always near at hand to every believer.

Intercede, then, for your friends. Plead with Christ on their account; mention their names in your constant prayers; set apart special times in which you plead with God for them. Let your dear sister's case ring in the ears of the Mediator; let your dear child's name be repeated again and again in your intercessions. As Abraham pleaded for Ishmael, so let your cry come up for those who are round about you, that the Lord would be pleased to visit them in his mercy. Intercession is a true bringing of souls to Christ, and this means will avail when you are shut out from employing any other. If your dear ones are in Australia, in some settler's hut where even a letter cannot reach them, prayer can find them out; no ocean can be too wide for prayer to span, no distance too great for prayer to travel. Far off as they are, you can take them up in the arms of believing prayer, and bear them to Jesus and say, "Master, have mercy upon them." Here is a valuable weapon for those who cannot preach or teach; they can wield the sword of all-prayer. When hearts are too hard for sermons, and good advice is rejected, it still remains to love to be allowed to plead with God for its wayward one. Tears and weepings are prevalent at the mercy seat, and if *we* prevail there, the Lord will be sure to manifest his prevailing grace in obdurate spirits.

To bring men to Jesus you can adopt the next means, with most of them, namely, that of instructing them, or putting them in the way of being informed concerning the gospel. It is a very wonderful thing that while to us the light of the gospel is so abundant, it should be so very partially distributed in this country. When I have expounded my own hope in Christ to two or three in a railway carriage, I have found myself telling my listeners perfect novelties. I have seen the look of astonishment upon the face of many an intelligent Englishman when I have explained the doctrine of the substitutionary sacrifice of Christ; persons who have even attended their parish church from their youth up, I have met with, who were totally ignorant of the simple truth of justification by faith; yes, and some who have been to Dissenting places of worship do not seem to have laid hold of the fundamental truth that no man is saved by his own doings, but that salvation is procured by faith in the blood and righteousness of Jesus Christ.

This nation is steeped up to the throat in self-righteous doctrine, and the Protestantism of Martin Luther is very generally unknown. The truth is held by as many as God's grace has called, but the great outlying world still talk of doing your best, and then hoping in God's mercy, and I know not what beside, of legal self-confidence, while the master doctrine that he who believes in Jesus is saved by Jesus' finished work, is sneered at as enthusiasm, or attacked as leading to licentiousness. Tell it, then, tell it on all sides, take care that none under your influence shall be left in ignorance of it; I can bear personal witness that the statement of the gospel has often proved in God's hand enough to lead a soul into immediate peace.

Not many months ago I met with a lady holding sentiments of almost undiluted popery, and in conversing with her I was delighted to see how interesting and attractive a thing the gospel was to her. She complained that she enjoyed no peace of mind as the result of her religion, and never seemed to have done enough. She had a high idea of priestly absolution, but it had evidently been quite unable to yield repose to her spirit. Death was feared, God was terrible, even Christ an object of awe rather than love. When I told her that whosoever believeth on Jesus is perfectly forgiven, and that I knew I was forgiven—that I was as sure of it as of my own existence; that I feared neither to live nor to die, for it would be the same to me, because God had given me eternal life in his Son, I saw that a new set of thoughts were astonishing her mind. She said, "If I could believe that, I should be the happiest person in the world." I did not deny the inference, but claimed to have proved its truth, and I have reason to believe that the little simple talk we had has not been forgotten. You cannot tell how many may be in bondage for want of the simplest possible instruction upon the plainest truths of the gospel of Jesus Christ.

Many, too, may be brought to Christ through your example. Believe me, there is no preaching in this world like the preaching of a holy life. It shames me sometimes, and weakens me in my testimony for my Master, when I stand here and recollect that some professors of religion are a disgrace not only to their religion, but even to common morality. It makes me feel as though I must speak with bated breath and trembling knees, when I remember the damnable hypocrisy of those who thrust themselves into the Church of God, and by their abominable sins bring disgrace upon the cause of God and eternal destruction upon themselves. In proportion as a church is holy, in that proportion will its testimony for Christ be powerful. Oh! Were the saints immaculate, our testimony would be like fire among the stubble, like the flaming firebrand in the midst of the sheaves of corn. Were the saints of God less like the world, more disinterested, more prayerful, more godlike, the tramp of the armies of Zion would shake the nations, and the day of the victory of Christ would surely dawn. Freely might the church barter her most golden-mouthed preacher if she received in exchange men of apostolic life. I would be content that the pulpit should be empty if all the members of the church would preach Jesus by their patience in suffering, by their endurance in temptation, by exhibiting in the household those graces which adorn the gospel of Jesus Christ. Oh, so live, I pray you, in God's fear and by the Spirit's power, that they who see you may ask, "Whence hath this man this holiness?" and may follow you till they are led by you to Jesus Christ to learn the secret by which men live unto God.

You can bring men to Jesus by your example, then. And once again, let me say, before I close this point, our object should be to bring men to Jesus, having tried intercession, and instruction, and example, by occasionally, as time and opportunity may serve us, giving a word of importunate entreaty. Half a dozen words from a tender mother to a boy who is just leaving home for an apprenticeship may drop like gentle dew from heaven upon you. A few sentences from a kind and prudent father given to the daughter, still unconverted, as she enters upon her married life, and to her husband, kindly and affectionately put, may make that household forever a house for God. A kind word dropped by a brother to a sister, a little letter written from a sister to her brother, though it should be only a line or two, may be God's arrow of grace. I have known even such little things as a tear or an anxious glance work wonders.

You perhaps may have heard the story of Mr. Whitefield, who made it his wont wherever he stayed to talk to the members of the household about their souls—with each one personally; but stopping at a certain house with a colonel, who was all that could be wished except a Christian, he was so pleased with the hospitality he received and so charmed with the general character of the good colonel and his wife and daughters, that he did not like to speak to them about decision as he would have done if they had been less amiable characters. He had stopped with them for a week, and during the last night, the Spirit of God visited him so that he could not sleep. "These people," said he, "have been very kind to me, and I have not been faithful to them; I must do it before I go; I must tell them that whatever good thing they have, if they do not believe in Jesus they are lost." He arose and prayed. After praying he still felt contention in his spirit. His old nature said, "I cannot do it," but the Holy Spirit seemed to say, "Leave them not without warning." At last he thought of a device, and prayed God to accept it; he wrote upon a diamond-shaped pane of glass in the window with his ring these words: "One thing thou lackest." He could not bring himself to speak to them, but went his way with many a prayer for their conversion. He had no sooner gone than the good woman of the house, who was a great admirer of him, said, "I will go up to his room: I like to look at the very place where the man of God has been." She went up and noticed on the windowpane those words, "One thing thou lackest." It struck her with conviction in a moment. "Ah!" said she, "I thought he did not care much about us, for I knew he always pleaded with those with whom he stopped, and when I found that he did not do so with us, I thought we had vexed him, but I see how it was; he was too tender in mind to speak to us." She called her daughters up. "Look there, girls," said she, "see what Mr. Whitefield has written on the window, 'One thing thou lackest.' Call up your father." And the father came up and read that too, "One thing thou lackest!" and around the bed whereon the man of God had slept they all knelt down and sought that God would give them the one thing they lacked, and before they left that chamber they had found that one thing, and the whole household rejoiced in Jesus.

It is not long ago since I met with a friend, one of whose church members preserves that very pane of glass in her family as an heirloom. Now, if you cannot admonish and warn in one way, do it in another; but take care to clear your soul of the blood of your relatives and friends, so that it may never crimson your skirts and accuse you before God's bar. So live and so speak and teach, by some means or other, that you shall have been faithful to God and faithful to the souls of men.

III. I must now take you to a third point. We have had the missionary disciple and his great object; we have now, third, *his wise methods.*

I have trenched upon this subject already, but I could not help it. Andrew being zealous was wise. Earnestness often gives prudence, and puts a man in the possession of tact, if not of talent. *Andrew used what ability he had.* If he had been as some young men are of my acquaintance, he would have said, "I should like to serve God. How I should like to preach! And I should require a large congregation." Well, there is a pulpit in every street in London; there is a most wide and effectual door for preaching in this great city of ours beneath God's blue sky. But this young zealot would rather prefer an easier berth than the open air; and, because he is not invited to the largest pulpits, does nothing. How much better it would be if, like Andrew, he began to use the ability he had among those who are accessible to him, and from that stepped to something else, and from that to something else, advancing year by year! Sirs, if Andrew had not been the means of converting his brother, the probabilities are that he never would have been an apostle. Christ had some reason in the choice of his apostles to their office, and perhaps the ground of his choice of Andrew as an apostle was this: "He is an earnest man," said he, "he brought me Simon Peter; he is always speaking privately to individuals; I will make an apostle of him." Now, you young men, if you become diligent in tract distribution, diligent in the Sunday school, you are likely men to be made into ministers; but if you stop and do nothing until you can do everything, you will remain useless—an impediment to the church instead of being a help to her. Dear sisters in Jesus Christ, you must none of you dream that you are in a position in which you can do nothing at all. That were such a mistake in providence as God cannot commit. You must have some talent entrusted to you, and something given you to do which no one else can do. Out of this whole structure of the human body, every little muscle, every single cell, has its own secretion and its own work; and though some physicians have said this and that organ might be spared, I believe that there is not a single thread in the whole embroidery of human nature that could well be spared—the whole of the fabric is required. So in the mystical body, the church, the least member is necessary, the most uncomely member of the Christian church is needful for its growth. Find out, then, what your sphere is and occupy it. Ask God to tell you what is your niche, and stand in it, occupying the place till Jesus Christ shall come and give you your reward. Use what ability you have, and use it at once.

Andrew proved his wisdom in that *he set great store by a single soul.* He bent all his efforts at first upon one man. Afterward, Andrew, through the Holy Spirit, was made useful to scores, but he began with one. What a task for the arithmetician, to value one soul! One soul sets all heaven's bells ringing by its repentance. One sinner that repents makes angels rejoice. What if you spend a whole life pleading and laboring for the conversion of that one child? If you win that pearl, it shall pay you your life worth. Be not therefore dull and discouraged because your class declines in numbers, or because the mass of those with whom you labor reject your testimony. If a man could earn but one in a day, he might be satisfied. "One what?" says one. I meant not one penny, but £1000. "Ah," say you, "that would be an immense reward." So if you earn but one soul you must reckon what that one is; it is one for numeration, but for value it exceeds all that earth could show. What would it profit a man if he gained the whole world and lost his soul? And what loss would it be to you, dear brother, if you did lose all the world and gained your soul, and God made you useful in the gaining of the souls of others? Be content and labor in your sphere, even if it be small, and you will be wise.

You may imitate Andrew in *not going far afield to do good*. Many Christians do all the good they can five miles off from their own house, when the time they take to go there and back might be well spent in the vineyard at home. I do not think it would be a wise regulation of the parochial authorities if they required the inhabitants of St. Mary, Newington, to remove the snow from the pavement of St. Pancras, and the inhabitants of St. Pancras to keep clean the pavement of St. Mary, Newington. It is best and most convenient that each householder should sweep before his own door; so it is our duty to do, as believers, all the good we can in the place where God has been pleased to locate us, and especially in our own households. If every man has a claim upon me, much more my own offspring. If every woman has some demand upon me as to her soul, so far as my ability goes, much more such as are of my own flesh and blood. Piety must begin at home as well as charity. Conversion should begin with those who are nearest to us in ties of relationship. Brethren and sisters, during this month I stir you up, not to be attempting missionary labors for India, not to be casting eyes of pity across to Africa, not to be occupied so much with tears for popish and heathen lands, as for your own children, your own flesh and blood, your own neighbors, your own acquaintance. Lift up your cry to heaven for them, and then afterward you shall preach among the nations. Andrew goes to Cappadocia in his afterlife, but he begins with his brother; and you shall labor where you please in years to come, but first of all your own household, first of all those who are under your own shadow must receive your guardian care. Be wise in this thing; use the ability you have, and use it among those who are near at hand.

Perhaps somebody will be saying, "How did Andrew persuade Simon Peter to come to Christ?" Two or three minutes may be spent in answering that inquiry. He did so, first, by narrating his own personal experience; he said, "We have found the Messiah." What you have experienced of Christ tell to others. He did so next by intelligently explaining to him what it was he had found. He did not say he had found someone who had impressed him, but he knew not who he was; he told him he had found Messiah, that is, Christ. Be clear in your knowledge of the gospel and your experience of it, and then tell the good news to those whose soul you seek. Andrew had power over Peter because of his own decided conviction. He did not say, "I hope I have found

Christ," but, "I have found him." He was sure of that. Get full assurance of your own salvation. There is no weapon like it. He that speaks doubtingly of what he would convince another, asks that other to doubt his testimony. Be positive in your experience and your assurance, for this will help you.

Andrew had power over Peter because he put the good news before him in an earnest fashion. He did not say to him, as though it were a commonplace fact, "The Messiah has come," but no, he communicated it to him as the most weighty of all messages with becoming tones and gestures, I doubt not, "We have found the Messiah, which is called Christ." Now then, brethren and sisters, to your own kinsfolk tell your belief, your enjoyments, and your assurance, tell all judiciously, with assurance of the truth of it, and who can tell whether God may not bless your work?

IV. My time is past, or I meant to have spoken of *the sweet reward* Andrew had.

His reward being that he won a soul, won his brother's soul, won such a treasure! He won no other than that Simon, who at the first cast of the gospel net, when Christ had made him a soul-fisherman, caught three thousand souls at a single haul! Peter, a very prince in the Christian church, one of the mightiest of the servants of the Lord in all his after usefulness, would be a comfort to Andrew. I should not wonder but what Andrew would say in days of doubt and fear, "Blessed be God that he has made Peter so useful! Blessed be God that ever I spoke to Peter! What I cannot do, Peter will help to do; and while I sit down in my helplessness, I can feel thankful that my dear brother Peter is honored in bringing souls to Christ." In this house today there may sit an unconverted Whitefield; in your class this afternoon there may be an unsaved John Wesley, a Calvin, and a Luther, mute and inglorious, yet who is to be called by grace through you. Your fingers are yet to wake to ecstasy the living lyre of a heart that up till now has not been tuned to the praise of Christ; you are to kindle the fire which shall light up a sacred sacrifice of a consecrated life to Christ. Only be up and doing for the Lord Jesus, be importunate and prayerful, be zealous and self-sacrificing. Unite with us, during this month, in your daily prayers; constantly, while in business, let your hearts go up for the blessing, and I make no doubt of it, that, when we have proved our God by prayer, he will pour us down such a blessing that we shall not have room to receive it. The Lord make it so, for his name's sake. Amen.

Nathanael: Under the Fig Tree

Delivered on Lord's Day morning, March 20, 1870, at the Metropolitan Tabernacle, Newington. No. 921.

> *Philip findeth Nathanael, and saith unto him, "We have found him, of whom Moses in the law, and the prophets, did write, Jesus of Nazareth, the son of Joseph." And Nathanael said unto him, "Can there any good thing come out of Nazareth?" Philip saith unto him, "Come and see." Jesus saw Nathanael coming to him, and saith of him, "Behold an Israelite, indeed, in whom is no guile!" Nathanael saith unto him, "Whence knowest thou me?" Jesus answered and said unto him, "Before that Philip called thee, when thou wast under the fig tree, I saw thee." Nathanael answered and saith unto him, "Rabbi, thou art the Son of God; thou art the King of Israel." Jesus answered and said unto him, "Because I said unto thee, I saw thee under the fig tree, believest thou? thou shalt see greater things than these." And he saith unto him, "Verily, verily, I say unto you, Hereafter ye shall see heaven open, and the angels of God ascending and descending upon the Son of man."*
> —JOHN 1:45–51

Very often we address the gospel to the chief of sinners. We believe it to be our duty to do this with the greatest frequency; for did not our Lord, when bidding his disciples to preach the good news in every place, use the words, "beginning at Jerusalem"? Where the chief of sinners lived, there was the gospel first to be preached. But at the same time it would show great lack of observation if we regarded all mankind as being equally gross, open offenders against God. It would not only show a want of wisdom, but it would involve a want of truthfulness; for though all have sinned, and deserve the wrath of God, yet all unconverted men are not precisely in the same condition of mind in reference to the gospel. In the parable of the sower, we are taught that before the good seed fell upon the field at all, there was a difference in the various soils; some of it was stony ground, another part was thorny, a third was trodden hard like a highway, while another plot is described by our Lord as "honest and good ground." Although in every case the carnal mind is enmity against God, yet are there influences at work which in many cases have mitigated, if not subdued, that enmity.

While many took up stones to kill our Lord, there were others who heard him gladly. While to this day thousands reject the gospel, there are others who receive the word with joy. These differences we ascribe to God's prevenient grace; we believe, however, that the subject of these differences is not aware that grace is at work upon him; neither is it precisely grace in the same form as saving grace, for the soul under its power has not yet learned its own need of Christ, or the excellency of his salvation. There is such a thing as a preparatory work of mercy on the soul, making it ready for the yet higher work of grace, even as the plowing comes before the sowing. We read in the narrative of the creation that before the divine voice said, "Let there be light," darkness was upon the face of the deep, yet it is added, "The Spirit of God moved upon the face of the waters"; even so in the darkness of human nature, whereas yet no ray of living light has shone, the Spirit of God may be moving with secret energy, making the soul ready for the hour when the true light shall shine. I believe that in our congregations there are many persons who have been mercifully restrained from the grosser vices, and exhibit everything that is pure and excellent in moral character, persons who are not maliciously opposed to the gospel, who are ready enough to receive it if they did but understand it, who are even anxious to be saved by Jesus Christ, and have a reverence for his name, though as yet it is an ignorant reverence. They know so little of the Redeemer that they are not able to find rest in him; but this slenderness of knowledge is the only thing that holds them back from faith in him. They are willing enough to obey if they understood the command. If they had but a clear apprehension of our Lord's person and work, they would cheerfully accept him as their Lord and God.

I have great hopes that the Lord of love may guide the word which is now to be spoken, so that it may find out such persons, and may make manifest the Lord's secretly chosen ones, those prisoners of hope who pine for liberty, but know not that the Son can make them free. O captive soul, abhorring the chains of sin, your day of liberty is come! The Lord, the liberator, who looseth the prisoners, is come at this very hour to snap thy bonds.

I. In dwelling on this narrative, I shall first say a few words concerning *Nathanael himself.*

We are told that he was a *guileless man,* "an Israelite, indeed, in whom is no guile," that is to say, like Jacob, "he was a plain man," and not like Esau, "a cunning hunter." Some minds are naturally serpentine, tortuous, slippery; they cannot think except in curves; their motives are involved and intricate, and they are of a double heart. These are the men who look one way and row the other; they worship the god Janus with two faces, and are of the same practice, if not of the same persuasion, as the Jesuits. They cannot speak a thing out plainly or look you in the face while they talk, for they are full of mental reservations and prudential cautions. They guard their speech; they dare not send abroad their own thoughts till they have mailed them up to the throat with double meanings.

Nathanael was just the very opposite of all this; he was no hypocrite and no crafty deceiver. He wore his heart upon his sleeve; if he spoke, you might know that he said what he meant and that he meant what he said. He was a childlike, simple-hearted man, transparent as glass. He was not one of those fools who believe everything, but on the other hand, he was not of that other sort of fools so much admired in these days, who will believe nothing, but who find it necessary to doubt the most self-evident truth in order to maintain their credit for profound philosophy. These "thinkers" of this enlightened age are great at quibbles, mighty in feigning or feeling mistrust concerning matters which common sense has no doubts about. They will profess to doubt whether there is a God, though that be as plain as the sun at noonday. No, Nathanael was neither credulous nor mistrustful; he was honestly ready to yield to the force of truth; he was willing to receive testimony and to be swayed by evidence. He was not suspicious, because he was not a man who himself would be suspected; he was truehearted and straightforward; a plain dealer and plain speaker. Cana had not within her gates a more thoroughly honest man. This Philip seems to have known, for he went to him directly, as to a man who was likely to be convinced and worth winning to the good cause.

In addition to being thus a simple-hearted man, Nathanael was *an earnest seeker*. Philip found him out because he felt that the good news would interest him. "We have found the Messiah," would be no gladsome news to anyone who had not looked for the Messiah; but Nathanael had been expecting the Christ, and perhaps had so well understood Moses and the prophets, that he had been led to look for his speedy coming. The time when Messiah would suddenly come in his temple had certainly arrived, and he was day and night with prayer, like all the faithful of the ten tribes, watching and waiting for the appearing of their salvation. He had not as yet heard that the glory of Israel had indeed come, but he was on the tiptoe of expectation. What a hopeful state of heart is yours, my dear hearer, if you are now honestly desirous to know the truth, and intensely anxious to be saved by it! It is well indeed for you if your soul is ready, like the photographer's sensitive plate, to receive the impression of the divine light, if you are anxiously desiring to be informed if there be indeed a Savior, if there be a gospel, if there be hope for you, if there be such a thing as purity and a way to reach it; it is well, I say, if you are anxiously, earnestly desiring to know how and when and where, and determinately resolved, by God's grace, that no exertion shall be spared on your part to run in the way that shall be marked out, and to submit yourself unto the will of God. This was the state of Nathanael, an honest-hearted lover of plain truth, seeking to find the Christ.

It is also true that he was *ignorant* up to a certain point. He was not ignorant of Moses and the prophets; these he had well considered, but he knew not that Christ as yet had come. There was some little distance between Nazareth and Cana, and the news of the Messiah's coming had not traveled thither; if it had been bad news, it would have flown on eagles' wings, but being good news, its flight was slower, for few persons are so anxious to tell out the good as the evil. He had not therefore heard of Jesus of Nazareth till Philip came to him. And how many there are even in this country who do not know yet what the gospel means, but are anxious to know it, and if they did but know it would receive it! "What," say you, "where there are so many places of worship and so many ministers?" Yes, just that. Yes, and in the very heart of our congregations and in the midst of our godly families, ignorance has its strongholds. These uninstructed ones may be Bible readers, they may be gospel hearers, but as yet they may not have been able to grasp the great truth that God was in Christ reconciling the world unto himself. They may never have seen what it is for Christ to stand in the sinner's place, and for that sinner by an act of trust to obtain the blessings which spring out of a substitutionary sacrifice. Yes, and here in this house where I have tried and labored to put the gospel in short Saxon words and sentences that cannot be misunderstood, there may be some who are still saying, "What is this all about? I hear much of believing, but what is it? Who is this Christ, the Son of God, and what is it to be saved from sin, to be regenerated, to be sanctified? What are all these things?" Well, dear friend, I am sorry you should be in the dark, yet am I glad at heart, that though you do not know what I would have you know, yet you are simple hearted, truth loving, and sincere in your seeking. I am persuaded that light will not be denied you, you shall yet know Jesus and be known of him.

In addition to this, however, Nathanael was prejudiced—we must modify that expression—he was somewhat *prejudiced*. As soon as Philip told him that he had found Jesus of Nazareth, the son of Joseph, Nathanael said, "Can any good thing come out of Nazareth?" Here let us remark that his prejudice is exceedingly excusable, for it arose out of the faulty testimony of Philip. Philip was a young convert; he had only found Jesus the day before, and the natural instinct of every truly gracious soul is to try and tell out the blessed things of Christ. So away went Philip to tell his friend Nathanael, but what a many blunders he made in the telling out the gospel! I bless God, blundering as it was, it was enough to bring Nathanael to Christ; but it was full of mistakes. Dear souls, if you know only a little about Christ, and if you would make a great many mistakes in telling out that little, yet do not hold it in, God will overlook the errors and bless the truth. Now observe what Philip said. He said, "We have found Jesus of Nazareth, the son of Joseph," which was our Lord's popular name, but was in no way correct. He was not Jesus of *Nazareth* at all; he was not a native of Nazareth, our Lord was of Bethlehem. He had dwelled at Nazareth certainly, but he was no more entitled to be called of Nazareth than of Jerusalem. Then Philip said, "son of Joseph," but he was only the reputed son of Joseph, he was in truth, the Son of the Highest. Philip gave to our Lord the common and erroneous titles which the unthinking many passed from hand to hand. He did not say, "We have found the Son of God," or, "the Son of David," but yet he uttered all he knew, and that is all God expects of you or me.

Oh, what a mercy it is that the imperfections of our ministry do not prevent God's saving souls by us! If it were not so, how little good would be done in the world! Mr. John Wesley preached most earnestly one view of the gospel, and William Huntingdon preached quite another view of it. The two men would have had a holy horror of each other, and censured each other most conscientiously; yet no rational man dare say that souls were not saved under John Wesley, or under William Huntingdon either, for God blessed them both. Both ministers were faulty, but both were sincere, and both made useful. So is it with all our testimonies. They are all imperfect, full of exaggerations of one truth, and misapprehensions of another; but as long as we witness to the true Christ foretold by Moses and the prophets, our mistakes shall be forgiven, and God will bless our ministry, despite every flaw.

So he did with Nathanael; but Nathanael's prejudice rose out of Philip's blundering way of talking. If Philip had not said, "of Nazareth," then Nathanael would not have said, "Can any good thing come out of Nazareth?" If Philip had said that Jesus was of Bethlehem, and of the tribe of Judah, and that God was his Father, then this prejudice would never have beclouded the mind of Nathanael, and it would have been easier for him to have acknowledged Jesus as the Messiah. We must, therefore, try to avoid mistakes, lest we cause needless prejudice. We should so state the gospel that if men be offended by it, it shall be the gospel which offends them, and not our way of putting it. It may be that you, my friend, are a little prejudiced against Christ's holy gospel, because of the imperfect character of a religious acquaintance, or the rough manners of a certain minister; but I trust you will not allow such things to bias you. I hope that, being candid and honest, you will come and see Jesus for yourself. Revise the report of the disciple by a personal inspection of the Master. Philip made up for his faults when he added, "Come and see." And I would try to prevent mine from injuring you by using the same exhortation,

Come and see Jesus and his gospel for yourself.

One other mark of Nathanael I would mention, he was in all respects a godly, sincere man, up to the measure of his light. He was not yet a believer in Jesus, but still he was an Israelite indeed. He was a man of secret prayer, he did not mock God as the Pharisees did by mere outward worship. He was a worshiper of God in his heart, his soul had private dealings with the God of heaven when no eye saw him. So it is, I trust, with you, dear hearer, you may not yet have found peace, but you do pray, you are desirous of being saved; you do not wish to be a hypocrite; you dread, above all things, falling into formality; you pray that if ever you become a Christian you may be a Christian indeed. Such is the character I am endeavoring to find out, and if it is your character, may you get the blessing that Nathanael did.

II. Now second, we have seen Nathanael, let us for a moment consider *Nathanael's sight of Jesus.*

"Philip saith unto him, Come and see"; and so Nathanael came to see the Savior, which implies, that although he was somewhat prejudiced against this new Messiah, yet he was candid enough to investigate his claims. Beloved friend, to whom I have already spoken, if you have any prejudice against the true gospel of Jesus Christ, whether it be occasioned by your birth and education, or previous profession of some other faith, be honest enough to give the gospel of Jesus Christ a fair hearing. You may hear it in this house; you may read it in these pages. Do not dismiss it until you have thoroughly examined it. All that we would ask of you is now, knowing you to be honest, knowing you to be earnest, seriously to sit down and weigh the doctrines of grace as you shall find them in the Scripture, and especially the life of Christ, and the blessings which he brings to those who believe in him. Look these things over carefully. They will commend themselves to your conscience, for God has already prepared your conscience to judge, righteously; and as you judge, you will perceive a peculiar beauty and a charm about the truths of the gospel which will surely win your heart. Latimer had preached a sermon against the doctrines of the gospel, and among his hearers there was a holy man who

afterward became a martyr, who thought as he listened to Latimer that he perceived something in his tone which showed him to be an honest opponent,
and, therefore, he hoped that if light were brought to him he would be willing to see by it. He sought him out, obtained an interview with him, and his
explanations entirely won honest Hugh to the Reformed opinions, and you
know what a valiant and popular minister of the new covenant he became. So,
my honest friend, give to the gospel of salvation by faith in the precious blood
of Jesus, a fair hearing, and we are not afraid of the result.

Nathanael came to Christ, again, with *great activity* of heart. As soon as he
was told to "come and see," he did come and see. He did not sit still and say,
"Well, if there is any light in this new doctrine, it will come to me," but he
went to it. Do not believe in any teaching which bids men sit down and find
peace in the idea that they need not strive to enter in at the strait gate of truth.
No, brethren, if grace has ever come to you, it will arouse you from lethargy,
and lead you to go to Christ, and you will be most earnest, with all the activity of your spirit, to search for him as for hid treasure. It is a delightful thing
to see a soul on the wing. The mass of our population are, as regards religion,
down on the ground, and unwilling to rise. They are indifferent to spiritual
truth; you cannot get them to give earnest heed to eternal matters; but once
get a mind on the wing with a holy earnestness and solemn thoughtfulness,
and we do believe, with God's grace, that it will before long be brought to a
saving faith in Christ. "Come and see," said Philip, and come and see
Nathanael did. He does not appear to have expected to be converted to Christ
by what he saw with his natural eyes; his judgment was formed from a mental view of him. It is true he saw the person of the Messiah, but he did not
expect to see in the human form any lineaments that might guide his judgment. He waited until the lips of the Messiah had spoken, and then, when he
had seen the omniscience of that mysterious person, and how he could read
his thoughts and spy out his secret actions, then he believed. Now, I fear some
of you live in darkness because you are expecting some kind of physical manifestation. You hope for a vivid dream, or some strange feeling in your flesh,
or some very remarkable occurrence in your family; except you see signs and
wonders you will not believe. No, but a saving sight of Christ is another matter; truth must impress your mental faculties, enlighten your understanding,
and win your affections. The presence of Christ on earth is a spiritual one, and
you will come to see him not with these mortal optics just now, but with the
eyes of your soul. You will perceive the beauty of his character, the majesty of
his person, the all-sufficiency of his atonement; and as you see these things,
the Holy Spirit will lead you to believe in him and live. I pray God that such a

sight as this may be granted to every honest seeker who may hear or read these words.

III. A far greater matter now demands our attention—*Christ's sight of Nathanael.*

As soon as Jesus saw the man, he said, "Behold an Israelite indeed," which shows us that Christ Jesus read Nathanael's heart. I do not suppose that our Lord had ever seen Nathanael with his own human eyes, but yet he understood Nathanael's character, not because he was a great judge of physiognomy and could perceive at once that he had a simple-hearted man before him, but because being Nathanael's Creator, being the searcher of hearts and the trier of the reins, he could read Nathanael as readily as a man reads a book which is open before his eyes. He saw at once all that was within the inquirer, and pronounced a verdict upon him that he was free from falsehood. And then to prove to Nathanael still further how clearly he knew all about him, he mentioned a little incident which I cannot explain, nor can you, nor do I suppose anybody could have explained it except Nathanael and Jesus—a special secret known only to them both. He said to him, "Before that Philip called thee, when thou wast under the fig tree, I saw thee." What he was doing under the fig tree we may guess, but we cannot know to a certainty. Perhaps it would be truest of all to believe that the fig tree was to Nathanael what the Hermonites and the hill Mizar had been to David. David says, "I will remember thee from the land of Jordan, and of the Hermonites, from the hill Mizar." What were those sacred recollections he does not tell us, and although we can form a shrewd guess, David and his God alone knew the full mystery. So between Christ and Nathanael there was a common knowledge connected with that fig tree which we cannot hope to discover, and the moment our Lord mentioned that hallowed spot, its remembrances were to Nathanael so secret and so sacred, that he felt that the omniscient One was before him. Here was evidence which he could not doubt for an instant, for one of the most private and special secrets of his life, which he had never whispered into any human ear, had been brought up as by a talismanic sign. A red-letter day in his private diary had been revived by the mention of the fig tree, and he who could touch so hidden a spring in his soul must be the Son of God.

But what was Nathanael doing under the fig tree, according to our best surmise? Well, as devout [Middle] Easterners are accustomed to have a special place for prayer, this may have been a shadowy fig tree under which Nathanael was accustomed to offer his devotions, and perhaps just before Philip came to him, he may have been engaged in personal and solitary *confession of sin.* He had looked around the garden, and fastened the gate that none might come in, and he had poured into the ear of his God some very tender confession, under the fig tree shade. When Christ said to him, "when thou wast under the fig tree," it brought to his recollection how he poured out his broken and his contrite spirit, and confessed sins unknown to all but God. That confession, it may be, the very look of Christ brought back to his remembrance, and the words and look together seemed to say, "I know your secret burden, and the peace you found in rolling it upon the Lord." He felt therefore that Jesus must be Israel's God.

It is very possible that in addition to his confession, he had under the fig tree made *a deliberate investigation of his own heart*. Good men generally mingle with their confessions self-examination. There it may be, that this man who was free from guile had looked into the tendencies of his nature, and had been enabled with holy surprise to see the fountains of the great deep of his natural depravity; he may have been taken like Ezekiel from chamber to chamber to see the idols in his heart, beholding greater abominations than he suspected to be there, and there humbled before the Lord; beneath that fig tree he may have cried with Job, "I abhor myself in dust and ashes." This also Jesus had seen.

Or under the fig tree he had been engaged in *very earnest prayer*. Was that fig tree to Nathanael what Peniel was to Jacob, a spot wherein he had wrestled till the break of day, pleading with God to fulfill his ancient promise, to send the promised One who should be a light to lighten the gentiles, and the glory of his people Israel? Was it so? We think it probable. That fig tree had been to him a Bethel, no other than the house of God and the very gate of heaven.

And what if we should suggest that, perhaps in addition to his prayer, Nathanael had vowed some solemn vow under the fig tree—if the Lord would but appear and give to him some sign and token for good, then he would be the Lord's, and spend and be spent for him; if the Lord would but send the Messiah, he would be among his first followers; if he would but speak to him by an angel or otherwise, he would obey the voice. Jesus now tells him that he shall see angels ascending and descending; and reveals himself as the Messiah to whom he had solemnly pledged himself. It may be so.

Once more, it may be that under that fig tree he had enjoyed the sweetest *communion* with his God. Beloved friends, do you not remember well certain hallowed spots? I have one or two in my own life too sacred to mention. If my memory should forget all the world besides, yet those spots will evermore be green in my memory, the truly holy place where Jesus my Lord has met with me and showed me his loves. One time it was "the king hath brought me into his chambers"; another time I got me to "the mountain of myrrh and to the hill of frankincense." Once he said, "Come, my beloved, let us go forth into the field; let us lodge in the villages," and anon he changed the scene and said, "Come with me from Lebanon, my spouse, with me from Lebanon: look from the top of Amana, from the top of Shenir and Hermon, from the lions' dens, from the mountains of the leopards." Have we not sometimes had special festivals when he has broached the spiced wine of his pomegranate? When our joy has been almost too much for the frail body to endure, for our joyous spirit like a sharp sword has well-nigh cut through its scabbard? Ah, it is sweetly true, he has baptized us in the fire of his love, and we shall forever remember those secret spots, those dear occasions. This then was a token, a secret token between Christ and Nathanael, by which the disciple recognized his divine Friend and future Master and Lord. He had met the Messiah in spirit before, and now he meets him in very flesh and blood, and by this token doth he know him. In spirit the Lord set his seal upon Nathanael's heart, and now by the sacred signet the Israelite indeed discerns his King.

Thus we see the Lord had seen Nathanael in his previous engagements, before he became actually a believer in Jesus. This fact suggests that each of you who have been sincerely seeking to be set right, and to know the truth, have been fully perceived in all your seekings and desirings by the God of grace. When you let fall a tear because you could not understand the Word, Jesus saw that tear; when you groaned because you could not get satisfaction of heart, he heard that groan. Never true heart seeks Christ without Christ's being well aware of it. Well may he know of it, for every motion of a trembling heart toward himself is caused by his own love. He is drawing you, though you perceive not the hands of a man which encircle you. He is the hidden lodestone by which your heart is moved. I know it is night with you, and you grope like a blind man for the wall; but if your heart says, "Oh, that I could but embrace him! Oh, that he were mine! If I could but find rest in him, I would give all that I have," then be assured that Jesus is close to you: your prayers are in his ear, your tears fall upon his heart; he knows all about your difficulties, all about your doubts and fears, and he sympathizes in the whole, and in due time he will break your snares, and you shall yet with joy draw water out of the wells of salvation. This truth is full of consolation to all who seek with sincerity, though as yet in the dark. Before the minister's voice spoke to you, when you were under the fig tree, when you were by the bedside, when you were in that inner chamber, when you were down in that saw-pit, when you were in the hayloft, when you were walking behind the hedge in the field, Jesus saw you; he knew your desires, he read your longings, he saw you through and through. Even from of old he has known you.

IV. So we have seen Nathanael's sight of Christ, and then Christ's sight of Nathanael; now the fourth thing is *Nathanael's faith*.

I must go over much the same ground again under this head. Nathanael's faith. Note *what it was grounded on*. He cheerfully accepted Jesus as the Messiah, and the ground of his acceptance lay in this, Jesus had mentioned to him a peculiar incident in his life which he was persuaded no one could have known but the omniscient God; thereon he concluded Jesus to be the omniscient God, and accepted him at once as his King. This was very frequently the way in which persons were brought to confidence in Christ. The same thing is recorded in this very gospel a few chapters further on. The Lord sat down on the well and talked to the Samaritan woman, and there was no kind of impression produced upon her until he said, "Thou hast had five husbands, and he whom thou now hast is not thine husband." Then it flashed upon her, "This stranger knows my private history! Then he is something more than he appears to be; he is the great Prophet"; and away she ran with this on her tongue, because it was in her heart, "Come, see a man which told me all things that ever I did: is not this the Christ?" The same was the case with Zacchaeus. You may perhaps think, however, that this mode of conversion was confined to the days of our Lord's flesh, and the age of miracles, but it is not so. The fact is, that at this very day, the discovery of the thoughts of men's hearts by the gospel is still a very potent means in the hands of the Holy Ghost of convincing them of the truth of the gospel. How often have I heard inquirers say, "It seemed to me, sir, as if that sermon was meant for me, there were points in it which were so exactly like myself, that I felt sure someone had told the preacher about me, and there were words and sentences so peculiarly descriptive of my private thought, that I was sure no one but God knew of them. I perceived that God was in the gospel speaking to my soul." Yes, and it always will be so. The gospel is the great revealer of secrets; it is a discerner of the thoughts and intents of the heart. Jesus Christ in the gospel knows all about your sin, all about your seeking, all about the difficulties which you are meeting with. This ought to convince you that the gospel is divine, since its teachings lay bare the heart, and its remedies touch every spiritual disease. The knowledge of human nature displayed in the simplest passage of the gospel is more profound than the productions of Plato or Socrates. The gospel, like a silken clue, runs through all the windings and twistings of human nature in its fallen state. Oh, that its voice may come home personally so to you; may it by the Spirit convince you of sin, of righteousness, and of judgment, and bring you to lay hold on eternal life.

Nathanael's faith, it must be mentioned, was peculiar not only in its ground, but *in its clear and comprehensive character.* He accepted Jesus at once as the Son of God; he was divine to him, and he adored him. He also accepted him as the King of Israel; he was a royal personage to him, and he tendered him his homage. May you and I receive Jesus Christ in this way, as a real man, but yet certainly God, a man who was despised and rejected, but yet the man anointed above his brethren, who is King of kings, and Lord of lords.

I admire Nathanael's faith again, because it was *so quick, unreserved, and decisive.* "Thou *art* the Son of God; thou *art* the King of Israel." Christ was glorified by the decision, the quickness of this faith. Delay in believing him dishonors him. O honest heart, O sincere mind, pray thou that you may as quickly come into the light and liberty of true belief. May the Holy Ghost work in you a ready satisfaction in the atoning sacrifice and divine person of the ever blessed Emmanuel.

V. This brings us to the last point of consideration. We have shown you Nathanael and his sight of Christ, and Christ's sight of him, and then the faith that Nathanael received; now notice *Nathanael's after sight*.

Some persons want to see all that there is in Christianity before they can believe in Jesus, that is to say, before they will go to the dame school [kindergarten] they must needs clamor for a degree at the university. Many want to know the ninth of Romans before they have read the third of John. They are all for understanding great mysteries before they understand that primary simplicity, "Believe and live." But those who are wiser and, like Nathanael, are content to believe at first what they are able to perceive, namely, that Christ is the Son of God and the King of Israel, shall go on to learn more. Let us read our Lord's words, "Thou shalt see greater things than these. Verily, verily, I say unto you, Hereafter ye shall see heaven opened, and the angels of God ascending and descending upon the Son of man." To full-grown disciples Jesus promises, "Greater things than these shall ye do"; to young converts he says, "Greater things than these shall ye see." He gives promises in proportion to our ability to receive them. The promise given to Nathanael was a most fitting one. He was all Israelite indeed—then he shall have Israel's vision. What was the great sight that Israel or Jacob saw? He saw the ladder whereon angels ascended and descended. Precisely this shall Nathanael see. He shall see Jesus Christ as the communication between an opened heaven and a blessed earth, and he shall see the angels ascending and descending upon the Son of man. If you bear the character of Israel, you shall enjoy the privileges of Israel. If you are an Israelite indeed, you shall have the blessing that made Israel glad. Nathanael had owned Jesus as the Son of God: here he is told that he shall see him in his glory as the Son of man. Note that last word of the chapter. It is not so much that Christ humbly called himself the Son of man—though that is true—as this, that to see the glory of Christ as God is a simple thing, but to see and understand the glory of Christ as man, this is a sight for faith, and probably a sight which, so far as our senses are concerned, is reserved for the day of his coming. When he shall appear, the very Man that suffered upon Calvary, upon the great white throne to judge the quick and the dead, if you believe in Jesus as the Son of God, you shall yet see him in his glory as man swaying the universal scepter, and enthroned as King of all the earth. He had called Jesus the King of Israel, if you remember, now he is to see his Lord as the King of the angels, to see the angels of God ascending and descending upon him. Believe, my dear brother in Christ, as far as you know him, and you shall know more of him. Open your eyes but to the candlelight of the law, and you shall soon behold the sunlight of the gospel.

The Lord is very gracious to fulfill the gospel rule, "To him that hath shall be given, and he shall have abundance." If you acknowledge the King of Israel, you shall see him as the Lord of hosts before whom archangels veil their faces, and to whom seraphim are servitors. The great sight, I suppose, Nathanael did see as the result of his faith was not the transfiguration, nor the ascension as some suppose, but a spiritual view of Christ in his mediatorial capacity as the great link between earth and heaven. This is indeed a sight transcending all others. We are not divided from the invisible, we are not separated from the infinite, the mortal has communion with immortal, the sinner speaks with the Holy One, prayers climb up to heaven, and benisons descend by way of the great Substitute. Can you see this, O soul? If so, the sight will make you glad. You are not exiled now, you are only at the foot of the stairs which lead to the upper chamber of your Father's house. Your God is above, and bright spirits traverse constantly the open gangway of the Mediator's person. Here is joy for all the saints, for this ladder can never be broken, our communion is abiding. No doubt, to Nathanael's view, the promise would be fulfilled as he perceived the providence of God as ruled by Christ Jesus, who orders all things for the good of the church. Was not this intended in the figure of angels ascending and descending upon the Son of man, that is, all agencies whether living or material, all subject to the law and the dominion of Christ; so that all things work together for good to them that love God?

Do not go fretting to your homes, and say, "Here are new doctrines springing up, and new gods that our fathers knew not, and ministers are slipping aside from the faith, and bad days have fallen upon the church, and Romanism is coming up, and infidelity with it." All this may be true, but it does not matter one fig for the great end that God has in view. He has a bit for the mouth of leviathan; he can do as he wills with his most powerful enemies; he rides upon the wings of cherubs and rules the storm; the clouds are but the dust of his feet. Never believe that Providence is out of joint; the wheels of this great engine may revolve some this way and some that, but the sure result will be produced, for the great Artist sees the final result to be secure. God's glory shall arise from it all. Angels descend, but they as much do the will of God as those which ascend. Some events seem disastrous, and even calamitous; but they shall all, in the end, prove to be for the best; for he—

> From seeming evil still educeth good,
> And better still, and better still, in infinite progression.

Until the crown shall come upon the head of him who was separated from his brethren, and all the glory shall roll in waves of mighty song at the foot of his throne, may you and I continue to see this great sight more and more clearly. Until the Lord shall descend from heaven with a shout, with the trump of the archangel, and the voice of God, and once for all shall we see heaven and earth blended, may we continue to see angels ascending and descending upon the Son of man. All this matchless glory will come to us through that little window by which we first saw the Savior. If we will not see him as our Lord until we can see all the future, we shall perish in darkness. If you will not believe, neither shall you be established, but if, with simple and true hearts, you have been seeking Jesus, and now come and accept him as the Lord, the King of Israel, then greater things than these shall be in store for you; your eyes shall see the King in his beauty and the land that is very far off, and the day of his pompous appearing, when heaven and earth shall hang out their streamers for overflowing joy, because the King hath come unto his own, and the crown is put upon the head of the Son of David; then shall you see it and see it all, for you shall be with him where he is, that you may behold his glory, the glory which the Father gave him before the foundation of the world.

Thomas: "My Lord and My God"

<figure>ornamental divider</figure>

Delivered on Lord's Day morning, April 13, 1884, at the Metropolitan Tabernacle, Newington. No. 1775.

And Thomas answered and said unto him, "My Lord and my God."
—JOHN 20:28

When the apostles met on the first Lord's Day after Jesus had risen, Thomas was the only disciple absent out of the eleven; on the second Lord's Day, Thomas was there, and he was the only disciple doubting out of the eleven. How much the fact of his doubting was occasioned and helped by the fact of his former absence I cannot say; but still it looks highly probable that had he been there at the first, he would have enjoyed the same experience as the other ten, and would have been able to say as they did, "We have seen the Lord." Let us not forsake the assembling of ourselves together as the manner of some is, for we cannot tell what loss we may sustain thereby. Though our Lord may reveal himself to single individuals in solitude as he did to Mary Magdalene, yet he more usually shows himself to two or three, and he delights most of all to come into the assembly of his servants. The Lord seems most at home when, standing in the midst of his people, he says, "Peace be unto you." Let us not fail to meet with our fellow believers. For my part, the assemblies of God's people shall ever be dear to me. Where Jesus pays his frequent visits, there would I be found.

> My soul shall pray for Zion still,
> While life or breath remains;
> There my best friends, my kindred dwell,
> There God my Savior reigns.

I know that full many of you can most heartily say the same. Oh, that we may behold the Lord Jesus in the present assembly!

On the second occasion Thomas is present, and he is the only one out of the eleven who is vexed with doubts. He cannot think it possible that the Lord Jesus, who was nailed to the cross, and whose side was pierced, could have really risen from the dead. Observe joyfully the Lord's patience with him. All the others had been doubtful too, and the Lord had gently upbraided them for their unbelief and the hardness of their hearts; but Thomas is not convinced by the tenfold testimony of his brethren, who each one well deserved his implicit confidence. After the plain way in which the Lord had told his disciples that he should be crucified and would rise again from the dead, they ought to have expected the resurrection; and inasmuch as they did not they were to be blamed: what shall we say of him who in addition to all this had heard the witness of his ten comrades who had actually seen the Lord? Yet there he is, the one doubter, the one sturdy questioner who has laid down most stringent requirements as to the only way in which he will be brought to believe. Will not his Lord be provoked by his obstinacy? See how patient Jesus is! If we had been in that case, and had died for those people, and had passed through the grave, and risen again for them, we should have felt very greatly grieved and somewhat angered if they had refused to believe in what we had done, but our Lord shows no such sign. He is tender among them as a nursing father. He rebukes their unbelief: for that was needful for their sakes; but he manifests no vexation of spirit. Especially on this occasion he shows his tenderness toward Thomas, and addresses his first words to him. If Thomas will not be convinced except by what I must call the most gross and materialistic evidence, he will give him such evidence: if he must put his finger into the print of the nails, he shall put his finger there, if he must thrust his hand into his side, he shall be permitted to take that liberty. Oh, see how Jesus condescends to the weaknesses and even to the follies of his people! If we are unbelieving it is not his fault; for he goes out of his way to teach us faith, and sometimes he even gives what we have no right to ask, what we have no reason to expect, what it was even sin in us to have desired. We are so weak, so ignorant, so prone to unbelief that he will do anything to create, sustain, and strengthen our faith in him. He condescends to men of low estate. If through our own folly we are such babes that we cannot eat the meat which is fit food for men, our Lord will not grow weary of giving us milk, but he will even break the bread into morsels, and take away the hard crusts, that we may be able to feed thereon. It is not his will that one of his little ones should perish; and therefore he chases away unbelief, which is their deadliest foe.

Our Lord had special reasons for turning as he did to Thomas that day, and for taking so much trouble to bring Thomas out of his unbelieving condition. The reason must have been, surely, first, that he desired to make of Thomas a most convincing witness to the reality of his resurrection. Here is a man who is determined not to be deceived; let him come and use the tests of his own choice. If you tell me that the resurrection of our Lord from the dead was witnessed by men who were prepared to believe it, I reply that the statement is totally false. Not one among that company even knew the meaning of the Lord's prophecy that he would rise again from the dead. It was hard to make any of them catch the idea; it was so foreign to their thought, so far above their expectation. In Thomas we have a man who was specially hard to be convinced, a man who was so obstinate as to give the lie to ten of his friends with whom he had been associated for years. Now, if I had a statement to make which I wished to have well attested, I should like to place in the witness box a person who was known to be exceedingly cautious and wary. I should be glad if it were known that at the first he had been suspicious and critical, but had at length been overwhelmed by evidence so as to be compelled to believe. I am sure that such a man would give his evidence with the accent of conviction as indeed Thomas did when he cried, "My Lord and my God." We cannot have a better witness to the fact that the Lord is risen indeed than that this cool, examining, prudent, critical Thomas arrived at an absolute certainty.

Further, I conceive that our Lord thus personally dealt with Thomas, because he would have us see that he will not lose even one of those whom the Father has given him. The good Shepherd will leave the ninety and nine to seek the one wanderer. If Thomas is the most unbelieving, Thomas shall have the most care. He is only one, but yet he is one, and the Lord Jesus will not lose one whom he has ordained to save. You and I might have said, "Well, if he will not be convinced, we must let him alone; he is only one—we can do without his testimony; we cannot be forever seeking a solitary individual, let him go." Thus might we have done; but thus Jesus will not do. Our good Shepherd looks after the units; he is tenderly observant of each separate individual, and this is a ground of comfort to us all. If one sheep be lost, why not the whole flock? If one be thus cared for, all will be cared for.

This note is also to be heard in reference to this matter: after all, it is to be feared that the dull, the slow, the questioning, the anxious, the weak in faith, make up a very considerable part of the church: I do not know that they are in the majority, but they are certainly far too numerous. If all Christians were arranged and classified, I fear we could not many of us place ourselves in the front rank; but a large portion would have to go among the Little Faiths. Our Lord here shows us that he has a condescending care for those who lag behind. Thomas is a week behind everybody else, yet his Lord has not lost patience, but waits to be gracious. The other ten apostles have all seen the Lord, and been well assured of his resurrection for the last seven days; but that is no reason why the latecomer should be left out in the cold. Our Lord does not leave the rear rank to perish. We know that in the wilderness the

Amalekites slew the hindmost of the children of Israel; but when King Jesus heads the army, no Amalekites shall smite even the hindmost of his people, for the glory of the Lord shall bring up the rear. The walls of Zion enclose babes as well as veterans; the ark of our salvation preserves mice as well as bullocks; our Solomon speaks of the hyssop on the wall as well as of the cedar in Lebanon; and the glory of the Lord may be seen in the preservation of the glowworm's lamp as truly as in the sustenance of the furnace of the sun.

Now if there should be any in this assembly who honestly have to put themselves down in the sick list, I beg them to take comfort while I try and set forth the experience of Thomas and what came of it. First, I shall call your attention to the *exclamation of Thomas*, "My Lord and my God": second, we will consider, *how he came to it*; and third, *how we come to it*; for I trust many of us have also cried, "My Lord and my God."

I. Let us consider *the exclamation of Thomas*, "My Lord and my God."

This is a most plain and hearty confession of the true and proper deity of our Lord Jesus Christ.

It is much as a man could say if he wished to assert indisputably and dogmatically that Jesus is indeed God and Lord. We find David saying, "O LORD of hosts, my King, and my God," and in another place (Ps. 35:23) he says, "my God and my LORD," terms only applicable to Jehovah. Such expressions were known to Thomas, and he as an Israelite would never have applied them to any person whom he did not believe to be God. We are sure therefore that it was the belief of Thomas that the risen Savior was Lord and God. If this had been a mistake, the Lord Jesus would have rebuked him, for he would not have allowed him to be guilty of worshiping a mere man. No good man among us would permit a person to call him God and Lord; we should feel like Paul and Barnabas when they rent their clothes because the men of Lystra were ready to do sacrifice to them; how much more would the holy Jesus have felt a revolting of spirit against the idea of being worshiped and called "my Lord and my God," if he had not been of such a nature that he "thought it not robbery to be equal with God"! The perfect Jesus accepted divine homage, and therefore we are assured that it was rightly and properly given, and we do here at this moment offer him the like adoration.

To escape from the force of this confession, some who denied our Lord's deity in olden times had the effrontery to charge Thomas with breaking the Third Commandment by uttering such a cry of surprise as is common among profane talkers. Just as thoughtless persons take the Lord's name in vain and say, "Good God!" or, "O Lord!" when they are much astonished, so certain ancient heretics dared to interpret these words, "My Lord and my God." It is clear to any thoughtful person that this could not have been the case. For, in the first place, it was not the habit of a Jew to use any such exclamation when surprised or amazed. An irreligious gentile might have done so, but it was the last thing that would occur to a devout Israelite. If there is one thing about which the Jews in our Lord's times were particular beyond everything, it was about using the name of God. Why, even in their sacred books they have omitted the word *Jehovah,* and have only written *Adonai,* because of a superstitious reverence for the very letters of the divine name. How can we, then, believe that Thomas would have done what no Jew at that time would have dreamed of? Israel after the Babylonian captivity had many faults, but not that of idolatry or irreverence to the divine name. I do not know what an Israelite might have said under the influence of a great surprise, but I am absolutely certain that he would not have said, "My Lord and my God."

In the next place, it could not have been a mere *exclamation of surprise,* or an irreverent utterance, because it was not rebuked by our Lord, and we may be sure he would not have suffered such an unhallowed cry to have gone without a reprimand. Observe, too, that it was addressed to the Lord Jesus— "Thomas answered and said unto him, 'My Lord and my God.'" It was not a mere outburst of surprise addressed to no one, but it was an answer directed to the Lord who had spoken to him. It was also such a reply that our Lord Jesus Christ accepted it as an evidence of faith, for in the twenty-ninth verse he says, "Thou hast believed," and that confession was the only evidence of his believing which our Lord had received from Thomas. A mere outcry of confused astonishment in irreverent words would never have been received as a satisfactory proof of faith. Sin is no due evidence of faith. The slander proposed by the Arian must, therefore, be rejected with derision. I am almost ashamed to have mentioned it, but in these days, when every kind of error is rife, it is needful to bring to light and break in pieces many idols which we had rather have left with the moles and bats.

I regard this cry of Thomas, first, *as a devout expression of that holy wonder* which came upon him when his heart made the great discovery that Jesus was assuredly his Lord and God. It had flashed upon the mind of Thomas that this august person whom he had regarded as the Messiah was also God. He saw that the man at whose feet he had sat was more than man, and was assuredly God, and this amazed him so that he used broken speech. He does not say, "Thou art my Lord and my God," as a man would say who is making a doctrinal statement, but he brings it out in fragments, he makes adoration of it, he cries in ecstasy, "My Lord and my God." He is amazed at the discovery which he has made, and probably also at the fact that he has not seen it long before. Why, he might have known it, and ought to have perceived it years before! Had he not been present when Jesus trod the sea? When he hushed the winds, and bade the waters sleep? Had he not seen him open the blind eyes, and unstop the deaf ears? Why did he not cry, "My Lord and my God," then? Thomas had been slow to learn, and the Lord might have said to him, as he did to Philip, "Have I been so long time with you, and yet hast thou not known me?" Now on a sudden he does know his Lord—knows him to such a surprising extent that such knowledge is too wonderful for him. He had come to the meeting to prove whether he who appeared to his brethren was the same man who had died on Calvary, but now he seems to have forgotten that original question; it is more than answered, it has ceased to be a question; he is carried far further by the flood of evidence, he is landed in a full belief of the Godhead of Jesus. He spies out within that wounded body the indwelling Godhead, and at a leap he springs beyond the conviction that it is the same man to the firm assurance that Jesus is God, and consequently in broken accents, but with double assurance, he cries, "My Lord and my God." My brethren, how I wish you would all follow Thomas this morning! I will stop a minute that you may do so. Let us wonder and admire! He that had nowhere to lay his head, he that suffered scourging and spitting, and died on Calvary, is nevertheless God over all, blessed forever. He who was laid in the tomb lives and reigns, King of kings and Lord of lords. Hallelujah! Behold, he comes in the glory of the Father to judge the quick and the dead. Let your spirits drink in that truth and be amazed at it. If the fact that Jesus, the Son of God, suffered and bled, and died for you, never astonishes you, I fear that you do not believe it, or have no intelligent apprehension of the full meaning of it. Angels wonder, should not you? Oh, let us feel a holy surprise today, as we realize the truth that he who has redeemed us from our sins by his blood is the Son of the Highest!

Next, I believe that this was an expression of *immeasurable delight*; for you observe he does not say, "Lord and God," but, "My Lord and my God." He seems to take hold of the Lord Jesus with both hands, by those two blessed "my's"—"My Lord and my God." Oh, the joy that flashed from the eyes of Thomas at that moment! How quickly his heart beat! He had never known such joy as at that instant, and though he must have felt deeply humbled, yet in that humiliation there was an excessive sweetness of intense satisfaction as he looked at his divine Lord and gazed on him, from the pierced feet up to the brow so marred with the crown of thorns, and said, "My Lord and my God." There is in these few words a music akin to the sonnet of the spouse in the

Canticles when she sang, "My beloved is mine, and I am his." The enraptured
disciple saw the friend of his heart standing before him, shining upon him in
love, and knitting his heart to him. I pray you follow Thomas in this joy in
Christ. I pause a minute that you may do so. Before you Jesus now stands,
visible to your faith. Delight yourselves in him. Be always ravished with his
love. He is altogether lovely and altogether yours. He loves you with all the
infinity of his nature. The tenderness of his humanity and the majesty of his
deity blend in his love to you. Oh, love the Lord, his saints, for he deserves
your hearts! Therefore at this moment say, "My Lord and my God."

More than this, I believe that the words of Thomas indicate *a complete
change of mind*—in other words, a most hearty repentance. He has not asked
of the Lord Jesus to be permitted to put his finger into the print of the nails.
No, all that has gone without debate. If you look at the chapter you will find
no statement that he ever did handle the Lord as he had at first proposed.
Whether he did put his finger into the print of the nails and his hand into the
side, must forever be unknown to us until we see Thomas in heaven and ask
him the question. If you read the Savior's words as commanding him to do so,
then we may conclude that he did so; but if you read them as only permitting
him to do it, then I think he did not do it. I put the question to a dear companion of mine; I read the passage, and then I asked, "What think you, did
Thomas put his hand into Christ's side?" and the answer from a thoughtful
mind and a gentle heart was this: "I do not think he could; after the Master
had so spoken to him he would shrink from doing so, and would think it willful unbelief to attempt it." This reply coincided exactly with my own convictions. I feel sure that had it been my case, I should have felt so ashamed at ever
having proposed such a test, and so overwhelmed to find the Lord yielding to
it, that I could not have gone an inch further in the way of seeking tokens and
proofs unless I had been absolutely commanded to do so. So, judging Thomas
to be like ourselves, and indeed much better than any of us, notwithstanding
his imperfection, I gather that he completely turned round, and instead of
putting his finger into the print of the nails, he cried, "My Lord and my God."
The Savior said to him, "Because thou hast seen me, thou hast believed." Now
I lay no stress upon it; but it would seem probable that the Savior might have
said, "Because thou hast touched me, thou hast believed," if Thomas had
indeed touched him; but inasmuch as he only speaks of sight, it may be that
sight was enough for Thomas. I do not insist upon it, but I think it right to suggest it; I feel it is not unreasonable to conclude that all Thomas did was to look
at his Lord. He could do no more; the delicacy of his spirit would not permit
him to accept the offered test; his reverence checked him; he saw and believed.

In him we see a complete change of feeling; from being the most unbelieving of the eleven, he came to believe more than any of them, and to confess Jesus to be God.

This exclamation is also *a brief confession of faith*, "My Lord and my God." Whosoever will be saved, before all things it is necessary that he be able to unite with Thomas heartily in this creed, "My Lord and my God." I do not go in for all the minute distinctions of the Athanasian Creed, but I have no doubt that it was absolutely needful at the time it was written, and that it materially helped to check the evasions and tricks of the Arians. This short creed of Thomas I like much better, for it is brief, pithy, full, sententious, and it avoids those matters of detail which are the quicksands of faith. Such a belief is needful; but no man can truly hold it unless he be taught by the Holy Ghost. He can say the words, but he cannot receive the spiritual truth. No man can call Jesus "Lord" but by the Holy Ghost. It is therefore a most needful and saving creed that we should cry to the Lord Jesus, "My Lord and my God." I ask you to do this now in your hearts. Renew your faith, and confess that he who died for you is your Lord and God. Socinians may call Jesus what they please; to me he is God over all, blessed forever. I know that you say, "Amen."

Further than this, do you not think that these words of Thomas were *an enthusiastic profession of his allegiance* to Christ? "My Lord and my God." It was as though he paid him lowliest homage and dedicated himself there and then in the entirety of his nature to his service. To him whom he had once doubted he now submits himself, for in him he fully believes. He does as good as say, "Henceforth, O Christ, you are my Lord, and I will serve you; you are my God, and I will worship you."

Finally, I regard it as a *distinct and direct act of adoration*. At the feet of the manifested Savior, Thomas cries, "My Lord and my God." It sounds like a rehearsal of the eternal song which ascends before that throne where cherubim and seraphim continually do cry, "Holy, holy, holy, Lord God of Sabaoth." It sounds like a stray note from those choral symphonies which day without night circle the throne of the Eternal. Let us in solemn silence now present our souls before the throne, bowing in reverent adoration unto him that was, and is, and is to come, even the Lamb that was slain, who is risen, and who liveth forever. "My Lord and my God." O Son of Mary, you are also Son of the Highest, and unto my heart and spirit you are my Lord and my God, and I worship you this day!

We have not time or else I would sit down and invite you to spend a few minutes in private, personal worship, following the example of Thomas in adoring our Lord and God.

II. Our next division is to be headed with the question: How *did he come to that exclamation?*

Have you ever thought what Thomas's feelings were when he went to the meeting that evening? His going needed a complicated explanation. Why did he mingle with men whose assertions he doubted? Could he have fellowship with them, and yet give them the lie? Suppose Jesus Christ to be dead and not risen, why does Thomas go? Is he going to worship a dead man? Is he about to renounce the faith of the last two years? How can he hold it if Jesus is not alive? Yet how can he give it up? Was Jesus Christ Lord and God to Thomas when he first entered that meeting? I suppose not. He did not, when he entered the room, believe him to be the same person who had died. The other disciples did believe, and Thomas was now the lone doubter, peculiar, positive, obstinate. Has it never happened to other disciples to drift into much the same condition? Thomas was a lot out of catalogue that evening: he was the odd person in the little gathering, and yet before service was over the Lord had completely altered him. "Behold, there are last which shall be first, and there are first which shall be last."

The first thing, I think, that led Thomas to this confession of his belief in Christ's deity was that *he had his thoughts revealed.* The Savior came into the room, the doors being shut; without opening the doors he suddenly appeared before them by his own divine power. There and then pointing to Thomas he repeated to him the very words which Thomas had said to his brethren. They had not been reported to the Savior, but the Savior had read Thomas's thoughts at a distance, and he was therefore able to bring before him his exact words. Notice that the Savior did not say, "Stoop down and put thy finger into the nail prints in my feet." Why not? Why, because Thomas had not said anything about his feet, and therefore the Savior did not mention them. Everything was exact. We in looking at it can see the exactness; but Thomas must have felt it much more. He was overwhelmed. To have his thoughts put in plain words and to hear his own words repeated by him whom they concerned, this was truly wonderful. "Oh," he said, "he who now speaks to me is none other than God, and he shall be my Lord and my God." This helped him to his assured conviction that one who had read his thoughts must be God.

He was aided still further, for as soon as he perceived that this was the same Jesus with whom he had conversed before, *all the past must have risen before his mind,* and he must have remembered the many occasions in which the Lord Jesus had exercised the attributes of Deity. That past intercourse thus revived before him must all have gone to support the conviction that Jesus was none other than Lord and God.

And then, I think, *the very air, and manner, and presence of the Savior* convinced the trembling disciple. They say there is a divinity that does hedge a king; that I am not prepared to believe; but I am sure there was a majesty about the look of our Lord, a more than human dignity in his manner and tone, and speech and bearing. Our Lord's personal presence convinced Thomas: so that he saw and believed.

But perhaps the most convincing arguments of all were *our Lord's wounds.* It seems a long way around to infer the deity of Christ from his wounds: yet it is good and clear argument. I shall not set it out in order before you, but leave you to think it out for yourselves, yet one little hint I would give you: here is a wound in his side more than sufficient to have caused death; it has gone right to the heart; the soldier with a spear pierced his side, and forthwith flowed there out blood and water, proving that the heart was pierced. The opening was still there, for the Lord invited Thomas to thrust his hand into his side, and yet Jesus lived. Heard you ever such a story as this—a man with a death wound gaping wide inviting another to thrust his hand therein. Had our Lord been living after the way in which we live, by the circulation of the blood, one can hardly see how this could have been possible. *Flesh and blood,* being subject to corruption, cannot inherit the kingdom of God; but the Savior's risen body came not under that description, as indeed his buried body did not, for he saw no corruption. I invite you to note well the distinction which may be seen in our Lord's words concerning his own body. He does not speak of his body as flesh and blood, but he says, "Handle me, and see; for a spirit has not flesh and bones as you see me have." It was a real body and a material body: for he took a piece of a broiled fish and of a honeycomb, and did eat before them; but still his resurrection body, living with an open wound in his side, reaching to the heart, was not after the manner of men. So even in the wounds of Christ, we read that he is man, but not mere man: his wounds in various ways were evidence to Thomas of his deity. Anyhow, the glorious fact rushed upon Thomas's astonished mind in a single moment, and therefore he cried out, "My Lord and my God."

III. Finally, let us see how *we may come to it.*

That is our final point, and the most practical of all. I doubt not that the Spirit of God was at work with Thomas at that time very mightily, and that the true cause of his enlightenment was heavenly illumination. If ever anyone of us shall cry in spirit and in truth, "My Lord and my God!" the Holy Spirit must teach us. Blessed are you who can call Jesus "Lord and God," for flesh and blood has not revealed this unto you, but the Father from heaven. But I will tell you when believers do cry, "My Lord and my God." I remember the first time it filled my heart. Burdened with guilt, and full of fears, I was as wretched as a man could be outside of hell-gate, when I heard the voice of the Lord saying, "Look unto me, and be ye saved, all the ends of the earth: for I am God, and there is none else." I did look there and then; I gave a faith-glance to him who suffered in my stead, and in an instant my peace was like a river. My heart leaped from despair to gladness, and I knew my Lord to be divine. If anyone had said to me then, "Jesus Christ is not God," I would have laughed him to scorn. He was beyond all question my Lord and my God, for he had worked a divine work in me.

It may not be an argument to anybody else, but forgiveness consciously known in the soul is a conclusive argument to the man who has ever felt it. If the Lord Jesus turns your mourning into dancing, brings you up out of the horrible pit and out of the miry clay, and sets your feet upon a rock and establishes your goings, he is sure to be your Lord and God henceforth and forever. In the teeth of all that deny it, in the teeth of all the devils in hell, the redeemed heart will assert the Godhead of its Savior. He that hath saved me is indeed God, and beside him there is none else.

This first avowal has proved to be only the beginning of these confessions. We remember many other acknowledgments of the same fact. We were severely tempted, and yet we did not slip, nor stain our garments, a wonder that we escaped! He that kept us from falling must be God. I know some moments in my life when I could stand and look back in the morning light upon the valley through which I had passed in the dark; and when I saw how narrow the pathway was, how a little step to the left or to the right must have been my total destruction, and yet I had never tripped, but had come straight through in perfect safety, I was astounded, and bowing my head, I worshiped, saying, "The Lord has been my refuge and my defense. He has kept my soul in life and preserved me from the destroyer, therefore will I sing songs unto him as long as I live." Oh, yes, dear children of God, when your heads have been covered in the day of battle, you have magnified the Keeper of Israel, saying, "My Lord and my God." We have felt that we could not doubt again and have joyfully committed ourselves to his keeping as to the guardian care of a faithful Creator.

Such, also, has been the case in time of trouble, when you have been comforted and upheld. A very heavy affliction has fallen upon you, and yet to your surprise it has not crushed you as you feared it would have done. Years before you had looked forward to the stroke with agonizing apprehension, and said, "I shall never bear it"; but you did bear it, and at this moment you are thankful that you had it to bear. The thing which you feared came upon you, and when it came it seemed like a featherweight compared with what you expected it to be, you were able to sit down and say, "The Lord gave, and the Lord hath taken away; blessed be the name of the Lord." Your friends were surprised at you: you had been a poor, wretchedly nervous creature before, but in the time of trial you displayed a singular strength such as surprised everybody. Most of all you surprised yourself, for you were full of amazement that in weakness you were made so strong. You said, "I was brought low, and he helped me." You could not doubt his deity then: anything which would rob him of glory you detested, for your heart said, "Lord, there is none that could have solaced my soul in this fashion save only the Lord God Almighty." Personally I have had to cry out, "It is the Lord's" when I have seen his wonders in the deep. "O my soul, thou hast trodden down strength." My soul shall magnify my Lord and my God, for "he sent from above, he took me; he drew me out of many waters. He brought me forth also into a large place: he delivered me, because he delighted in me."

There have been other occasions less trying. Bear with me if I mention one or two more. When we have been musing, the fire has burned. While studying the story of our Lord, our faith in his deity has been intensified. When the Spirit of God has revealed the Lord Jesus to us and in us, then we have cried, "My Lord and my God." Though not after the flesh, yet in very deed and truth we have seen the Lord. On a day which I had given lip to prayer, I sat before the Lord in holy peacefulness, wrapped in solemn contemplation, and though I did not see a vision, nor wish to see one, yet I so realized my Master's presence that I was borne away from all earthly things, and knew of no man save Jesus only. Then a sense of his Godhead filled me till I would fain have stood up where I was and have proclaimed aloud, as with the voice of a trumpet, that he was my Lord and my God. Such times you also have known.

Jesus is often known of us in the breaking of bread. At the communion table many a time we have seen and adored. It was very precious; we were ready to weep and laugh for joy. Our heart kept beating to the tune of "my Lord and my God." Perhaps it was not in any outward ordinance that your soul thus adored; but quite away in the country, or by the seaside, as you walked along and communed with your own heart, you were suddenly overpowered with a sense of Jesus' glorious majesty, so that you could only whisper to yourself as in a still, small voice, "My Lord and my God." Or perhaps it was when you were laid aside with illness that he made all your bed, and then you knew his power divine. It was a long and weary night to those who watched you, but to you it was all too short, and brimmed with sweetness, for the Lord was there, and he gave you songs in the night. When you awoke you were still with him and felt ready to faint with overwhelming delight because of the brightness of the manifestation. At such a time you could have sung,

> My Christ, he is the Lord of lords,
> He is the King of kings;
> He is the Sun of Righteousness,
> With healing in his wings.
>
> My Christ, he is the heaven of heavens,
> My Christ, what shall I call?
> My Christ is first, my Christ is last,
> My Christ is All in all.

I will tell you yet again when Jesus has been Lord and God both to me and to you, and that is in times when he has blessed our labors, and laid his arm bare in the salvation of men. When our report has been believed by those who rejected it before, and the Lord has sent us a happy season of revival, we have given to him the glory, and rejoiced in his omnipotent love. We prayed for our children, and when to our surprise—it is a shame to say to our surprise, for it ought not to have surprised us—the Lord heard our prayer, and first one and then another came to us and said, "Father, I have found the Lord," then we knew that the Lord he is God, and our God too. We looked up from our prayers with tears in our eyes to think the Lord Jesus could have heard such weak petitions, and we said in the depths of our hearts, "My Lord and my God." We went out and tried to teach a dozen or two in a cottage; poor, broken words were all that we could utter; but the Lord blessed it, and we heard a poor woman crying for mercy as we came out, and we said inwardly, "My Lord and my God." If you have been in the inquiry room after some brother whom God greatly honors has been proclaiming the word with power, and if you have seen the people falling right and left under the shafts of the divine Word, you must have cried, "This is no cunningly devised fable, no fiction, and no fancy," and your heart must have throbbed with all its life, "My Lord and my God." Have you not felt as if you would dare to go through the very streets of hell, and tell the grinning fiends that Christ is King and Lord forever and ever?

The time is very soon coming with some of us when we shall have our last opportunities in this life to find this true. How comforted and refreshed have I often been when visiting dying saints. Truly the Lord has prepared a table for them in the presence of the last enemy. I can truly say that no scenes that these eyes have ever beheld have so gladdened me as the sight of my dear brethren and sisters when they have been departing out of the world unto the Father. The saddest scene has been the happiest. I have known some of them in life as self-distrusting, trembling, lowly minded believers; and when they have come into the valley of death-shade they have displayed no fear, no doubt, but all has been full assurance. Placid, calm, beautiful, joyful, and even triumphant have been the last hours of timid believers. As I have heard their charming words I have been certain of the Godhead of him who gives us victory while we die. It is faith in his name that makes men strong in death. When heart and flesh fail us, only the living God can be the strength of our life, and our portion forever. How sweet to know Jesus as our living God in our dying moments! In him we rejoice with joy unspeakable and full of glory, as we say unto him in death, "My Lord and my God." Come, brothers and sisters, be of good cheer! A little further on we shall come to the narrow stream. This we shall cross in an instant, and then! It will be but a short, short time; twenty years is soon gone, a hundred years even fly as on eagles' wings, and then we shall be forever with the Lord in the glory land. How sweetly will we sing to his eternal praise, "My Lord and my God"! There shall be no doubters in heaven; no skeptics shall worry us there; but this shall be the unanimous voice of all the redeemed: "Jesus is our Lord and God." The united church, freed from every spot and wrinkle, and gloriously arrayed as the bride of Christ, shall be conducted to his throne, and acknowledged as the Lord's beloved, and then shall she with full heart exclaim, "My Lord and my God."

Zacchaeus: Must He?

᷎᷎᷎

Intended for reading on Lord's Day, December 1, 1901; delivered on Lord's Day evening, July 27, 1879, at the Metropolitan Tabernacle, Newington. No. 2755.

And when Jesus came to the place, he looked up, and saw him, and said unto him, "Zacchaeus, make haste, and come down; for today I must abide at thy house."—LUKE 19:5

I think this is the only instance in which our Lord invited himself to anybody's house. He often went when he was bidden; but this time, if I may use the expression, he did the bidding himself. Usually, we must seek the Lord if we want to find him. To the eye, at any rate, the apparent work of grace goes on in this way: a man begins to cry for mercy, as the blind man, who heard that Jesus of Nazareth was passing by, cried to him, "Thou Son of David, have mercy on me." But God is so rich in grace that he does not restrict himself to this usual method. Generally, he is found of them that seek him; but, sometimes, he is found of them that seek him not. Yes, if I tell the whole *truth,* if you go down to the bedrock of actual fact, it is always God who seeks sinners. He always calls them a people who are not a people; and the first movement, between God and the sinner, is never on the sinner's part, but on God's part. Still, apparently, men begin to pray to God, and begin to seek the Lord; and this is the usual order in which salvation comes to them. The prodigal said, "'I will arise and go to my father.' . . . And he arose, and came to his father." The blind man cried, "Jesus, thou Son of David, have mercy on me."

Our text, however, describes a case which shows the freeness of divine mercy; for, although Zacchaeus did not invite Christ to his house, Christ invited himself. Though there was no asking him to be a guest, much less any pressing entreaty on the part of Zacchaeus, Christ pressed himself upon him, and said to him, "Make haste, and come down; for today I must abide at thy house." I reckon that there are some here who are on an errand something like that of Zacchaeus. They want, perhaps, to see the preacher, which is not nearly so good a thing as wanting to see the preacher's Master. Still, that curiosity has brought them into the place where Jesus of Nazareth is wont to come; and I do pray that he may find many to whom he will say, "Make haste, and come and receive me; for I must abide, this very night, with you, and dwell in your house and heart at this time and forever."

I. The first thing I am going to talk about is *the divine necessity which pressed upon the Savior.* He says, "I must." "Today I must abide at thy house."

I do not think of this so much as a necessity upon Zacchaeus as upon Christ. You know that he felt this "must" at other times. In John 4:4, we read, "He must needs go through Samaria." There was a sacred necessity that he should go that way. The most notable instance of all was when "Jesus began to show unto his disciples, how that he must go unto Jerusalem, and suffer many things of the elders and chief priests and scribes, and be killed, and be raised again the third day." In this case, the "must" was of another kind; he must abide in the house of Zacchaeus. What necessity was this which pressed so urgently upon our blessed Master? There were many other houses in Jericho besides that of the tax gatherer. I daresay there were other persons who would, apparently, have been more suitable hosts for the Lord Jesus Christ; yet it was not really so. There was a mighty pressure upon him, who is the omnipotent Lord of all. Necessity was laid upon him who is the blessed and only Potentate, the King of kings, and Lord of lords. He was his own Master, yet he must do something to which he was constrained by an urgent necessity; he must go and lodge that night nowhere else but at the house of Zacchaeus. What did this "must" mean?

I answer, first, it was *a necessity of love.* Our Lord Jesus wanted to bless somebody; he had seen Zacchaeus, and he knew what his occupation was, and what his sin was, and he felt that he must bless him. As he looked at him, he felt as a mother does concerning her child when it is ill, and she must nurse it; or as you might feel concerning a starving man, whom you saw to be ready to expire with hunger, and you felt that you must feed him; or as some men have felt when they have seen a fellow creature drowning, and they have plunged in to save him. They did not stop to think; they dared to do the brave deed without a thought, for they felt that they "must" do it. The compulsions of charity, the necessities of benevolence—these urgent things laid violent hands upon them, so they must do it. Thus Jesus felt—only in a much higher sense— that he must bless Zacchaeus. He must go to his house, that he might enter his heart, to abide there, and to make Zacchaeus holy and happy henceforth and forever. And he is the same Christ now that he was then; he is not less loving, he is the same gracious Savior, and he feels the same necessity, the same hunger after souls, the same thirst of love to bless the sons of men; and I, therefore, hopefully expect that there will be, even in this place and I hope in many other parts of the world, some of whom it will be true that the Lord Jesus Christ must come to their house and heart. So this was a necessity arising out of our Savior's divine benevolence and love.

Next, I think it *was a necessity of his sovereignty*: "I must abide at thy house." Here were scribes and Pharisees and all sorts of people round about him, who were saying, "He is a prophet; he has opened a blind man's eyes; and he must, therefore, as a prophet, be entertained by some notable Pharisee. Some very respectable person must find him a lodging tonight." But our Lord Jesus Christ seems to say, "I cannot be bound; I will not be fettered; I must exert my own will; I must display my sovereignty; and though these people will all murmur, I cannot help that. Zacchaeus, I will come and stay with you, just to show them that I will have mercy on whom I will have mercy, and I will have compassion on whom I will have compassion."

You see, this man was in bad odor. We are not very fond of tax gatherers here; but in the East they like them still less than we do; and among the Jews a tax gatherer, if he was himself a Jew who came to collect an obnoxious impost by a foreign power upon a people who thought that they were the people of God and ought to be free, was a man who was intensely hated for having stooped to become one of the farmers of taxes; and if he was the head farmer, the chief contractor of customs, as Zacchaeus was, he had a very bad name indeed. People did not cultivate his acquaintance; they seldom dropped in to tea at his house; and as a general rule they fought very shy of him. When they mentioned sinners, they always reckoned that Zacchaeus, who had made a fine thing out of the business they specially loathed and was reputed to be very rich, was one of the very worst; nobody thought much of him. I think, too, that he had been excommunicated by a law of the Sanhedrin, for the publicans were generally regarded as excommunicated persons—shut out, certainly, from the society of more respectable people.

Besides, to my mind, Zacchaeus was an eccentric sort of body. That running of his was a very strange action for such a man; wealthy men, even though they happen to be short of stature, do not generally take to running through the streets and climbing trees. I should think Zacchaeus was the sort of man who kept himself to himself; and who, when he meant to do a thing, would do it; and if it was to climb a tree, as a boy might, he did not mind that, for he had got beyond caring for public opinion. He was an oddity; he may have been a very good sort of fellow, in some respects; but it is quite clear that he was an odd sort of person. So our Lord Jesus Christ seemed to say, "I will show these people that, when I save men, it is not because they stand well in society, or because they enjoy an excellent repute, or because there are some beautiful points in their character. I will save this odd man, this Zacchaeus, this despised tax gatherer. I must have him; he is just the sort of man in whom I can best display the sovereignty of my grace." To this day, men cannot bear that doctrine. Free will suits them very well, but free grace does not. They would not let Christ choose his own wife; I say it with the utmost reverence. I mean, they would not let him have the choice of his own bride, his church; but say that must be left to the will of men. But Christ will have his way, whatever they may say. He has a sacred determination, in his blessed heart, that he will do as he pleases; and so, for that reason, he says to Zacchaeus, "I *must* abide at thy house."

Our Lord Jesus was also under another necessity: *he wanted someone in whom he could display the great power of his grace.* He needed a sinner, to begin with; that was to be the raw material out of which he was going to make a saint, and a saint of a very special character. Is there a Christian in this place who comes up to the standard of Zacchaeus after he was converted? I do not wish to be censorious, but I doubt if there is one. Is there anybody here who gives away half his income to the poor? I think that was going a long way in grace in the matter of almsgiving; and then remember that he was but a babe in grace when he did that; so what he did when he grew older, I do not know. But the first day he was born to Christ, he was a saint of that kind; so what kind of a saint he grew to be by and by, I can scarcely imagine. Lord, out of what material did you make such a generous soul as this? Why, out of a grasping, grinding tax gatherer, who sought to grab all he could lay his hands on! The mighty grace of God, better than a magic wand, opened his closed heart, and made it gush forth like a fountain flowing in a thousand generous streams. Jesus seems to say, "I must have Zacchaeus, so that the men of the world may see what I can make out of the most unlikely material; how I can take coarse pebbles from the brook and transmute them into diamonds; how I can bedeck my crown with jewels of the first water [highest quality], which were originally but as the common stones of the street." I wonder whether there is anybody here who feels that he has not anything at all in him that is any good whatever. If so, the Lord could say, "I will make something of that man that will cause all who know him to marvel. I will make his wife wonder what has changed him; I will make all his children say, 'What has come over father?' I will make the whole parish say, 'What a miracle! What a miracle!'" This was the kind of "must" that was laid upon our Savior, and I hope such a *"must"* is laid upon him now.

There was one more *"must"* upon him, namely, he must abide in the house of Zacchaeus *because Zacchaeus was to be his host at Jericho.* Even the Savior must be lodged somewhere; and, in most places, his Father had appointed some gracious spirit to entertain him, and Zacchaeus was to be his host that day; and if he ever came that way again, I feel certain that he would go to his old quarters. Blessed be my Master's dear name, he still has some hosts left where the guest chamber is always ready for him! In every town and village and hamlet, there is some house where there is a prophet's chamber; and if you were to ask, "Is there anybody here who will entertain the Lord Jesus Christ?" you would soon find people who would be glad to have his company. Perhaps there is a large upper room, furnished and prepared, where they might break bread together; or a little room, where two or three might meet with Jesus, a place that never seems so bright as when there are a few praying people met together in it. The Lord must be entertained in this world, and Zacchaeus was to be the man to entertain him in Jericho.

Who is the one here now who will take Jesus in? A stranger from the country, perhaps; there is no preaching place in your village, the gospel is not often proclaimed within miles of the place where you live, and few people go to hear it when it is preached. That is all the more reason why Jesus must come to your house, for he means to have your best room, or that old shed of yours, or that big barn, that the gospel may be preached there. There is a divine necessity laid upon him to have your heart for himself, so that he may come and dwell with you, and make your house his headquarters, whence his disciples may go forth to attack the enemy where you live; and that all in your region may know that the true salvation army has come there, and that the Captain of our salvation has himself come to make his abode in your house and your heart.

There is plenty of room for enlargement upon this point, but we must go on to the next one.

II. If so, second, *let us inquire whether there is such a necessity in reference to ourselves.*

Has the Lord Jesus Christ any necessity to come and stay at your house, to come and abide in your heart? I can answer that question best by putting to you a few inquiries.

First, *are you willing to receive Christ at once?* Then there is a necessity laid upon him to come to you, for he never sent the will into a man without also sending his grace with the will; indeed, the willingness be receive him is the proof of the working of his grace. Do you long and sigh that Christ might be yours? Then, you shall surely have him. Are you earnestly anxious to be reconciled to God by Jesus Christ? Then you may have that great blessing at once. Are you thirsting after righteousness? Then you shall be filled; for what says the Scripture? "Let him that is athirst come"; and lest anybody should say, "Oh! but there is some preparation implied in that word *thirst,* and I am afraid that I do not thirst enough," what does the Scripture further say? "And whosoever will—whosoever will—let him take the water of life freely."

Next, *will you heartily receive Jesus?* Zacchaeus "received him joyfully," and if you will do the same, then he must abide at your house. I think I hear somebody say, "Receive him joyfully? Ah! that I would if he would but come to me. I would give all I have to have Christ as my Savior, to have the new life implanted within me, and to have Jesus dwelling in my heart. I would be willing to live, or be willing to die, if I might but have him as mine." So you will receive him joyfully, will you? Ah, then he is bound to come to you. When the door of your heart is opened, Jesus will not be long before he enters. He will stand and knock even at a closed door; therefore I am sure that he will enter an open one. It is written of Lydia, "whose heart the Lord opened"; and her heart was not long open before the Lord entered it; and if yours is open to Christ, that is a proof that you are one of those in whom he must abide at this time.

Let me ask you another question. *Will you receive Christ, whatever the murmurers may say?* Suppose he comes to you, they will begin to murmur, as they did when he went to be the guest of Zacchaeus. I do not know where you live, but those around you will be sure to find fault both with you and with your Lord too. "They all murmured, saying, That he was gone to be guest with a man that is a sinner." So, you see, they were murmuring at Zacchaeus as well as at Christ, and you will have the same sort of treatment when you receive Christ. Those who used to say, "You are a fine fellow," when they find that you have become a Christian, will call you a mean-spirited wretch. As long as you give them something to drink, they will say what a jolly dog you are; but as soon as ever you have done with their ways, you will be literally like a dog to them, and they will have nothing for you but kicks and curses. In more respectable society, you know how they give a Christian the cold shoulder. Nothing is actually said, but there is a very clear intimation that your room is preferred to your company when you once become a Christian. Can you bear that? Can you dare that? Because, if Christ comes to your house and heart, you must expect that he will bring his cross with him. Are you willing to have Christ, cross and all, and say, "Let the murmurers say what they will, and do what they will, my mind is made up, Christ for me, Christ for me; I cannot give him up"?

Further, will you receive Jesus Christ as your Lord? Zacchaeus did so, for he said, "Behold, Lord." Now are you willing to give up all to Christ, and to let him be Lord over you? Are you willing to do what he bids you, as he bids you, when he bids you, and simply because he bids you? For, verily, I say unto you, you cannot have Christ for your Savior unless you also have him as your Lord. He must rule over us as well as forgive us; as one of our poets says—

> Yet know, nor of the terms complain,
> Where Jesus comes, he comes to reign;
> To reign, and with no partial sway;
> Thoughts must be slain that disobey.

Sins must be given up, evil practices must be forsaken, you must renew after holiness, and endeavor in all things to imitate your Savior, who has left you an example that you should follow his steps. Are you ready for that? Because, if you are, then Christ is ready to abide at your house, and to dwell in your heart.

Once more, *will you be prepared to defend him?* If Jesus comes to a house, it becomes the duty of the host to defend him. So Zacchaeus, not in boasting, but as a kind of answer to the sneers of the murmurers, when they said that Christ had gone to dwell with a sinner, seemed to say, "But I am no longer a sinner as I used to be. If I have wronged anybody, I will restore it fourfold; and, henceforth, the half of my income shall be given in alms to the poor." That was the best defense he could give, and Christ must be defended by the changed lives of his disciples. You must so live that, when men attempt to attack the Savior, they may be compelled to say, "Well, after all, that man is the better for being a Christian." Your children may rail at religion, but they will be compelled to say, "We could speak against Christ and Christians generally, but when we think of how our mother lived, and how she died, our tongues are silenced. Then, there is our old nurse, who feared the Lord; many a joke did we crack about her religion, but ah! there was something about her that was so heavenly that we were obliged to believe in the reality of it whether we would or not." Yes, dear friends, if the Lord Jesus Christ should come to your house, you must say, "It shall be my heart's ambition, as long as I live, to defend his cause by the holiness of the character which I trust his Holy Spirit will work in me." If this is the case with any of you, then he must abide at your house tonight. God grant that he may do so!

III. Now I must close by reminding you of *what will happen if Christ comes to abide in your house.*

First, *you must be ready to meet objections at home.* You who say that you are willing to receive my Master, are you quite sure that you know what that reception involves? Christ says that he wishes to abide at your house, and that he must do so; and you say, "Yes, my Lord, I gladly welcome you to my heart and my home." But stay a moment, my friend; have you asked your wife about that matter? You know that you must not bring home strangers; she will be down upon you if you do; have you counted the cost of your decision? And, my good woman, you say, "I want to bring Christ home with me." Have you asked your husband about it? Sometimes a dear child says, "Jesus Christ shall abide with me," but what will father say? For alas! often the father is at enmity against God. If that is the case in your home, are you prepared to endure hardness for Christ's sake? Our Lord himself said, "A man's foes shall be they of his own household," and it is often so. David said to Jonathan, "What if thy father answer thee roughly?" Suppose that is your experience, can you keep true to Christ under such circumstances? Can you say, "I love my wife; I love my child; I love my father; but I love Jesus more than all of them; and I must have Christ in my heart, and in my house, even if it brings war there"? Ah! then he will come to your house if that be your resolve; but if not, he will not come to take the second place. He will not come there if you turn coward at the first jest that is made against you, or the first hard thing that is spoken against your Lord; but he will come to your house if, despite all rebuffs and rebukes, you are determined that he shall make his abode with you.

But, next, *is your house fit for him to enter and abide there*? I know some houses where my Lord could not lodge for a single night, the table, the talk, the whole surroundings would be so uncongenial to him. Are you prepared, then, to put away everything that would displease him, and to have your house cleansed of all that is evil? You cannot expect the Lord Jesus to come into your house if you invite the devil to come too. Christ would not remain in the same heaven with the devil; as soon as ever Satan sinned, he hurled him out of the holy place; he could not endure to have a sinful spirit, the spirit of evil, there, and he will not come and live in your house if you make provision for the lusts of the flesh, the lust of the eyes, and the pride of life, and all those evil things that he abhors. Are you prepared, by his grace, to make a clean sweep of these things? He will not come to you on any other terms.

Further, *we must admit none who would grieve our Guest*. It is hard to lodge with some people because their children are so badly behaved. My Lord loves not to dwell in families where Eli is at the head of the household, and where the children and young people live as they like; but if he comes to your house, he will want you to be like Abraham, of whom he said, "I know him, that he will command his children and his household after him, and they shall keep the way of the Lord." If he comes to your house, you must ask him to come in the same way that he came to the house of the jailer at Philippi. How was that? I have often heard half of that passage quoted without the context: "'Sirs, what must I do to be saved?' And they said, 'Believe on the Lord Jesus Christ, and thou shalt be saved, *and thy house.*'" Many leave out those last three words, "and thy house," but what a mercy it is when all in the house, as well as the head of the family, have faith in the Lord Jesus Christ! Do you not wish that it may be so in your house? Do you not ardently desire it? I trust that you do.

Once more, *when the Lord Jesus Christ comes into your house, you must entertain him*. He wants no riches at your hands, yet he wants the best that you have. What is the best that you have? Why, your heart, your soul! Give him your heart, give him your life, give him your very self. If you had to entertain the queen—if she had promised to come and spend an evening with you—I will warrant that you would be fidgeting and worrying for weeks about what you should get for such an occasion; and if you have but little means, you would try to get the very best that you could.

I frequently used to go and preach in a country place, where I stayed at a farm; and the dear old man who lived there, used to have about a hundred pounds of beef, at the very least, on his table; and when, year after year, I noticed such enormous joints, I said to him one day, You must have a very curious idea of my appetite; it is not possible that I should ever get through these masses of meat that you put on your table." "Oh!" he replied, "we get through it all very easily after you are gone, for there are plenty of poor people, and plenty of farm laborers round about, and they soon clear it up." "But," I inquired, "why do you have so much when I come?" "Bless you, sir," he answered, "I would give you a piece as big as a house if I could get it—I would, indeed—just to show you how welcome you are to my home." I understood what he meant, and appreciated his kindness; and, in a far higher sense, let us all do as much as ever we possibly can to show the Lord Jesus how welcome he is to our heart and our home. How welcome he ought always to be when he comes, as our blessed Savior, to put away our sin and change our nature and honor us with his royal company, and keep and preserve us even to the end, that he may take us up, and our children too, to dwell at his right hand forever! Oh, there ought to be grand entertainment for such a Guest as he is! Where is the man who is going to ask him home tonight? Here stands my Master, and in his name I ask, Who will take him home tonight? With whom shall Jesus lodge tonight? "Oh!" says one, "if he would but come to me, I would he glad enough to welcome him." He is glad enough to come, for he delights to be entertained in human hearts. O you soldiers, over there, with the red coats on—I am always glad to see you here—shall Jesus Christ abide with you tonight? And you others, in black coats, or in colored dresses, shall Jesus Christ abide with you tonight? You good friends who are up from the country, if you have not taken Christ into your hearts, will you not take him in now? I cannot hear what you say, but he can; and if this be the reply, "God be merciful to me a sinner, and come and lodge with me tonight," it shall be done, and his shall be the praise.

Now the time has gone, but I must say just these few words more. I recollect that, when I was crying to God for mercy, and I could get no answer to my supplication, so that I feared I must really give up prayer as hopeless, the thought which kept me praying was this, "Well, if I do not get salvation, I shall perish." I seemed to fancy that the Lord had kept me waiting—that was only my foolish way of thinking, and it was not true—but I said to myself, "If the Lord keeps me waiting, I also kept him waiting a long while. Was I not for many years resisting him, and refusing him? So that, if he makes me wait for salvation, I must not complain." Then I thought, "Well, now, if I were to keep on praying, and I did not find Christ for twenty years, yet, if I found him at last, the blessing would be well worth having and worth waiting for, so I will never leave off praying for it." And then I thought, "Why should I expect that I must be heard the moment I choose to come to the mercy seat, when I would not hear God's call when he so often spoke to me?" So I still persevered in prayer, yet with this thought, "What can I do else?"—like a whip ever upon my back. I felt that this must be my resolve—

> I can but perish if I go;
> I am resolved to try;
> For if I stay away, I know
> I must forever die.

I like that plan which I have known to be followed by some who have gone to their room and shut the door, determined not to go out till they had found the Savior. They have read the Word, especially such passages as these, "Believe on the Lord Jesus Christ, and thou shalt be saved"; "He that believeth on the Son hath everlasting life"; and they have gone down on their knees and have said, "Lord, this is thy promise. Help me now to believe in Jesus, and give me salvation, for his sake, for I will not leave this place without thy blessing!" Such vehemence, such importunity, is sure to prevail. How dare any one of you continue to live unsaved?

How dare you, sir, again close your eyes in sleep while you are unreconciled to God? What if, instead of waking up in that bedroom of yours, you should lift up your eyes and say, "Where am I? What is this dreadful place? Where are the things I once loved? Where are the things I lived for? Where am I? Where is Christ? Where is the gospel? Where are Sabbath days? Where are the warning words I used to despise? Where is the power to pray? Is all this gone forever? And where am I? In dark, dark, dire despair; an enemy to thee, O God, and an enemy to you forever! Horror and dismay have taken hold upon me."

The very attempt to depict that awful scene makes me feel as though dread would stop my tongue. Oh, I pray you, go not there! There are some who deny the eternity of future punishment; but, for my part, I would not risk such suffering for an hour even if it should end then. What woe it would be to be only an hour in hell! Oh, how you would wish then that you had sought the Savior and had found him. But alas! there is no such thing as an hour in hell; once lost, you are lost forever! Therefore, seek the Lord now; cry, with Jeremiah, "O LORD our God, we will wait upon thee." You cannot brazen it out; you cannot escape from everlasting wrath unless you trust in Jesus, so let this be your cry—

> Thou, O Christ, art all I want;
> More than all in thee I find!
> Other refuge have I none,
> Hangs my helpless soul on thee!

So, Christ of God, we cast ourselves into your arms! Save us, save us, save us, for your sweet mercy's sake! Amen.

Joseph of Arimathaea

꧁꧂

Preached on Lord's Day morning, July 6, 1884, at the Metropolitan Tabernacle, Newington. No. 1789.

> *Joseph of Arimathaea, an honorable counselor, which also waited for the kingdom of God, came, and went in boldly unto Pilate, and craved the body of Jesus. And Pilate marveled if he were already dead: and calling unto him the centurion, he asked him whether he had been any while dead. And when he knew it of the centurion, he gave the body to Joseph. And he bought fine linen, and took him down, and wrapped him in the linen, and laid him in a sepulcher which was hewn out of a rock, and rolled a stone unto the door of the sepulcher.*—MARK 15:43–46

It was a very dark day with the church of God and with the cause of Christ, for the Lord Jesus was dead, and so the sun of their souls had set. "All the disciples forsook him, and fled." "Ye shall be scattered, every man to his own, and shall leave me alone," were the sad words of Jesus, and they had come true. He was dead upon the cross, and his enemies hoped that there was an end of him, while his friends feared that it was even so. A few women who had remained about the cross, true to the very last, were found faithful unto death, but what could they do to obtain his sacred body and give it honorable burial? That priceless flesh seemed to be in danger of the fate which usually awaited the bodies of malefactors: at any rate, the fear was that it might be hurled into the first grave that could be found to shelter it. At that perilous moment, Joseph of Arimathaea, a city of the Jews, of whom we never heard before, and of whom we never hear again, suddenly made his appearance. He was the very man needed for the occasion, a man of influence, a man possessing that kind of influence which was most potent with Pilate—a rich man, a counselor, a member of the Sanhedrin, a person of weight and character. Every Evangelist mentions him and tells us something about him, and from these we learn that he was a disciple, "a good man and a just; who also himself waited for the kingdom of God." Joseph had been retiring and probably cowardly before; but now he came to the cross and saw how matters stood, and then went in boldly unto Pilate, craved the body of Jesus, and obtained it. Let us learn from this that God will always have his witnesses. It matters not though the ministry should forsake the truth, though they that should be leaders should become recreant, the truth of God will not fail for lack of friends. It may be with the church as when a standard-bearer faints and the host is ready to melt with dismay; but there shall be found other standard-bearers, and the banner of the Lord shall wave over all. As the Lord lives, so shall his truth live: as God reigns, so shall the gospel reign, even though it be from the cross. "Tell it out among the heathen that the Lord reigneth from the tree." Such is a singular version of a verse in the Psalms, and it contains a glorious truth. Even while Jesus hangs on the cross in death, he is still keeping possession of the throne, and he shall reign forever and ever.

Let this be remembered for your encouragement in the cloudy and dark day. If you live in any place where the faithful fail from among men, do not wring your hands in grief and sit down in despair, as though it was all over with the cause you love. The Lord lives, and he will yet keep a faithful seed alive in the earth. Another Joseph of Arimathaea will come forward at the desperate moment: just when we cannot do without him, the man will be found. There was a Joseph for Israel in Egypt, and there was a Joseph for Jesus on the cross. A Joseph acted to him a father's part at his birth, and another Joseph arranged for his burial. The Lord shall not be left without friends. There was a dark day in the Old Testament history when the eyes of Eli, the servant of God, had failed him; and worse still, he was almost as blind mentally as physically; for his sons made themselves vile, and he restrained them not. It seemed as if God must forsake his Israel. But who is this little boy who is brought in by his mother? This tiny child who is to be left in the sanctuary to serve his God as long as he lives? This pretty little man who wears the little coat which his mother's hands have lovingly made for him? Look, you that have eyes of faith; for the prophet Samuel is before you, the servant of the Lord, by whose holy example Israel shall be led to better things, and delivered from the oppression which chastised the iniquities of Eli's sons.

God hath today somewhere, I know not where, in yon obscure cottage of an English village, or in a log hut far away in the backwoods of America, or in the slums of our backstreets, or in our palaces, a man who in maturer life shall deliver Israel, fighting the battles of the Lord. The Lord has his servant making ready, and when the time shall come, when the hour shall want the man, the man shall be found for the hour. The Lord's will shall be done, let infidels and doubters think what they please. I see in this advent of Joseph of Arimathaea exactly at the needed time, a well of consolation for all who have the cause of God laid upon their hearts. We need not worry our heads about who is to succeed the pastors and evangelists of today: the apostolic succession we may safely leave with our God.

Concerning this Joseph of Arimathaea, the honorable counselor, I want to speak this morning, praying that I may speak to your souls all along. As I have already said, we hear no more of Joseph than what is recorded here. He shines out when he is wanted, and anon he disappears: his record is on high. We need not mention the traditions about him, for I think that even the quotation of legends has an evil tendency, and may turn us aside from the pure, unadulterated Word of God. What have you and I to do with tradition? Is not the Scripture enough? There is probably no truth in the silly tales about Joseph and Glastonbury; and if there were, it could be of no consequence to us; if any fact had been worthy of the pen of inspiration, it would have been written, and because it is not written, we need not desire to know. Let us be satisfied to pause where the Holy Spirit stays his pen.

I shall use Joseph of Arimathaea this morning in four ways: first, as *our warning*—he was a disciple of Jesus, "but secretly for fear of the Jews"; second, for *our instruction*—he was at last brought out by the cross concerning which holy Simeon had declared that by the death of the Lord Jesus the thoughts of many hearts should be revealed; third, for *our arousing*—there was an occasion for Joseph to come forward, and there is occasion now for all the timid to grow brave; and last, for *our guidance*—that we may, if we have been at all bashful and fearful, come forward in the hour of need and behave ourselves as bravely as Joseph of Arimathaea did on the eve before the Paschal Sabbath.

I. First, then, I desire to look at Joseph of Arimathaea as *our warning*.

He was a disciple of Christ, but secretly, for fear of the Jews: we do not advise any one of you to imitate Joseph in that. Fear which leads us to conceal our faith is an evil thing. Be a disciple by all means, but not secretly; you miss a great part of your life's purpose if you are. Above all, do not be a disciple secretly because of the fear of man, for the fear of man brings a snare. If you are the slave of such fear it demeans you, belittles you, and prevents your giving due glory to God.

> *Fear him, ye saints, and you will then*
> *Have nothing else to fear.*

Be careful to give honor to Christ, and he will take care of your honor. Why was it that Joseph of Arimathaea was so backward? Perhaps it was owing to his natural disposition. Many men are by nature very bold; some are a little too much so, for they become intrusive, self-assertive, not to say impudent. I have heard of a certain class of persons who "rush in where angels fear to tread." They are fearless because they are brainless. Let us avoid fault in that direction. Many, on the other hand, are too retiring: they have to screw their courage up even to say a good word for the Savior whom they love. If they can do so they fall into the rear rank; they hope to be found among the victors when they divide the spoil, but they are not overambitious to be among the warriors while they are braving the foe. Some of these are truehearted notwithstanding their timidity. It was found in the martyr days that certain of those who endured most bravely at the stake were naturally of a fearful mind. It is noted by Foxe that some who boasted of how well they could bear pain and death for Christ turned tail and recanted; while others who in prison trembled at the thought of the fire played the man in death, to the admiration of all that were round about them. Still, dear friends, it is not a desirable thing if you are troubled with timidity to foster it at all. Fear of man is a plant to be rooted up, and not to be nurtured. I should set that plant, if I could, where it would get but little water, and no sunshine, and meanwhile I would beg a cutting from a better tree. Would it not be well often to brace ourselves with such a hymn as this—

> Am I a soldier of the cross,
> A follower of the Lamb?
> And shall I fear to own his cause,
> Or blush to speak his name?
>
> Must I be carried to the skies
> On flowery beds of ease,
> While others fought to win the prize,
> And sailed through bloody seas?

If you know that your temptation lies in the direction of fear, watch and strive against it, and school yourselves evermore to dauntless courage by the help of the Holy Spirit.

I am afraid, too, that what helped to intimidate Joseph of Arimathaea was the fact that he was a *rich man*. A sad truth lies within our Lord's solemn exclamation, "How hardly shall they that have riches enter into the kingdom of God." Riches do not strengthen the heart or make men daring for the good cause. Albeit wealth is a great talent which may be well used by the man who has entered into the kingdom of heaven, yet it brings with it snares and temptations, and when a man has not yet entered into the kingdom it is, in many ways, a terrible hindrance to his entrance. "It is easier for a camel to go through the eye of a needle, than for a rich man to enter into the kingdom." The fishermen of the Galilean lake readily left their bits of boats, and their fishing tackle; but Joseph of Arimathaea was a rich man, and was therefore slow to leave all for Christ's sake. The tendency of great possessions is seen in the case of the young man who turned away in sorrow from the Lord Jesus, when put to the unusual test of selling all he had. Strong swimmers have saved their lives when the ship has struck upon a rock, by casting aside every weight; while others have gone straight down to the bottom because they have bound their gold around their waists. Gold sinks men as surely as lead. Take care, any of you that are well-to-do in this world, that you do not permit the liberality of God to be a cause of disloyalty to him. Beware of the pride of life, the lust for rank, the desire to hoard, for any of these may prevent your service of your Lord. Riches puff men up, and prevent their stooping to find the pearl of great price. A poor man enters a humble village sanctuary where Christ is preached, and he finds eternal life; another man under concern of soul in the same village does not like to go down to the poor conventicle, and remains unblessed. He keeps away because he puts to himself the question, "What will the people say if the squire goes to hear the gospel? What a stir there will be if the son of a lord is converted!" Joseph of Arimathaea's wealth made him unduly cautious; and possibly, without his knowing it, prevented his casting in his lot with the common sort of people who followed the Lord Jesus. His heart was for the prize, but the heavy weight of his substance hindered him in his race; it was an instance of abounding grace that he was helped to run well at the last.

Possibly, too, he may have been checked by the fact that *he was in office, and that he was honorable in it*. It needs great grace to carry human honor; and, truth to tell, it is not particularly much worth carrying when you have it. For what is fame but the breath of men's nostrils? Poor stuff to feed a soul upon! If a man could so live as to gain universal plaudits, if he could write his name across the sky in letters of gold, what of it all? What is there in the applause of a thoughtless multitude? The approbation of good men, if it be gained by persevering virtue, is better to be desired than great riches; but even then it may become a temptation; for the man may begin to question rather, "What will people say?" than, "What will God say?" and the moment he falls into that mood he has introduced a weakening element into his life. The "well done, good and faithful servant" of the Master's own lip is worth ten thousand thunders of applause from senators and princes. Honor among men is, at best, a peril to the best. Joseph was honored in council, and this is apt to make a man prudently slow. The tendency of office is toward caution rather than enthusiasm. I would have those placed in high positions remember this, and candidly judge themselves as to whether their shrinking from the public avow-al of Christ may not be a cowardice unworthy of the position in which the Lord has placed them.

It seems clear that all the earthly things which men covet may not be so desirable as they appear to be; and that which men would give their eyes to procure, they might, if their eyes were opened, think far less of.

I would lovingly inquire of you at this time (for the sermon is meant to be personal all the way through) if any of you who love my Lord and Master are doing so secretly because of the fear of men. You have never openly confessed your faith, and why not? What hinders your taking up a decided position on the Lord's side? Are you wealthy? Are you honorable? Do you occupy an envi-able position in society? And are you such a mean-spirited creature that you have become proud of these glittering surroundings, like a child that is vain of its new frock? Are you so craven that you will not cast in your lot with the fol-lowers of truth and righteousness, because they are persons of low degree? Are you really so base? Is there no holy chivalry in you? Can it be so, that, because God has dealt so well with you, and trusted you so generously, you will repay him by denying his Son, violating your conscience, and turning your back on truth; and all for the sake of being in the fashion? I know it may seem hard to receive the cold shoulder in society, or to have the finger of scorn pointed at you; but to bow before this selfish dread is scarcely worthy of a man, and utterly disgraceful to a Christian man. "Oh, but I am so retiring in disposition." Yes, but do not indulge it, I pray you; for if all were of such a mind, where were the noble advances of truth, her reformations, her revivals? Where would have been our Luther or our Calvin or our Zwingli? Where would have been our Whitefield or our Wesley, if they had thought it to be the main object of desire to walk at ease along the cool sequestered vale of life? Come forth, my brother, for the truth and for the Lord. Recollect that what is right for you would be right for the rest of us: if you do not join the Christian church, for instance, every one of us might also neglect that duty, and where would be the visible church of Christ, and how would the ordi-nances of our holy faith be kept up as a witness among the sons of men? I charge all concealed believers to think over the inconsistency of their con-cealment and to quit that cowardly condition.

I feel sure that Joseph of Arimathaea was a great loser by his secrecy; for you see, he did not live with Jesus, as many other disciples did. During that brief but golden period in which men walked and talked, and ate and drank, with Jesus, Joseph was not with him. He was not among the twelve: as possibly he might have been if he had possessed more courage and decision. He lost many of those familiar talks with which the Lord indulged his own after the multitudes had been sent away. He missed that sacred training and strengthening which fitted men for the noble lives of primitive saints. How many opportunities he must have missed, too, of working for the Master and with the Master! Perhaps we hear no more of him because he had done no more. Possibly that one grand action which has redeemed his name from forgetfulness is all that is recorded because it really was all that was worth recording. Joseph must have been a weaker, a sadder, a less useful man for having followed Christ afar off. I would to God that such reflections as these would fetch out our beloved, truly faithful and honorable Christian men, who hitherto have hidden away among the stuff, and have not come to the front to stand up for Jesus.

II. Second, having viewed Joseph of Arimathaea as a warning, I shall go on to speak of him as a lesson for *our instruction.*

Joseph did come out after all; and so will you, my friends. If you are honest and sincere, you will have to avow your Lord sooner or later. Do you not think it would be better to make it sooner rather than later? The day will come when that shame which you are now dreading will be yours. As surely as you are a sincere believer, you will have to encounter that reproach and derision which now alarm you: why not face them at once and get it over? You will have to confess Christ before many witnesses; why not begin to do so at once? What is the hardship of it? It will come easier to you, and it will bring you a larger blessing, and it will be sweeter in the recollection afterward than if you keep on postponing it. What was it that fetched Joseph of Arimathaea out? *It was the power of the cross!* Is it not a remarkable thing that all the life of Christ did not draw out an open avowal from this man? Our Lord's miracles, his marvelous discourses, his poverty, and self-renunciation, his glorious life of holiness and benevolence, all may have helped to build up Joseph in his secret faith, but it did not suffice to develop in him a bold avowal of faith. The shameful death of the cross had greater power over Joseph than all the beauty of Christ's life.

Now let us see, you timid, backward ones, whether the cross will not have the same influence over you today. I believe it will, if you carefully study it. I am sure it will, if the Holy Spirit lays it home to your heart. I suppose that to Joseph of Arimathaea Christ's death on the cross seemed such *a wicked thing* that he must come out on behalf of one so evil-entreated. He had not consented to the deed of the men of the Sanhedrin when they condemned Jesus to death; probably he and Nicodemus withdrew themselves from the assembly altogether; but when he saw that the crime was actually committed, and that the innocent man had been put to death, then he said, "I cannot be a silent witness of such a murder. I must now side with the holy and the just." Therefore he came out and was found the willing servant of his crucified Master. Come what may of it, he felt that he must own himself to be on the right side, now that they had maliciously taken away the life of the Lord Jesus. It was late, it was sadly late, but it was not too late.

O secret disciple, will you not quit your hiding place? Will you not hasten to do so? You who are quiet and retiring, when you hear the name of Jesus blasphemed, as it is in these evil days, will you not stand up for him? When you hear his deity denied, when his headship in the church is given to another, when his very person is by lewd fellows of the baser sort set up as the target of their criticism, will you not speak up for him? Will you not be shocked by such evil conduct into an open avowal? His cause is that of truth and righteousness, and mercy and hope for the sons of men; therefore he must not be abused while you sit by in silence. Had others favored him you might, perhaps, have been somewhat excused for holding back; but you cannot keep back without grievous sin now that so many deride him. Jesus is worthy of all honor, and yet they heap scorn upon him: will you not defend him? He is your Savior and Lord; oh, be not slow to own that you are his. The cross laid bare the heart of Joseph; he loathed the wickedness which slew the holy and the just, and therefore he girded himself to become the guardian of his sacred body.

But, next, it may have been in part *the wonderful patience of the Master's death* which made Joseph feel he could not hide any longer. Did he hear him say, "Father, forgive them; for they know not what they do"? Did he mark him when those blessed lips said, "I thirst"? Do you think he observed the ribaldry and scorn which surrounded the dying Lord? And did he feel that the stones would cry out if he did not show kindness to his best friend? Since Jesus spoke not for himself, but was dumb as a sheep before her shearers, Joseph is bound to open his mouth for him. If Jesus answered not, but only breathed out prayers for his murderers, the honorable counselor must acknowledge him. The sun has owned him, and veiled his face in sackcloth! The earth has owned him, and trembled to her very heart at his sufferings! Death has owned him, and yielded up the bodies which the sepulcher had hitherto detained! The temple has owned him, and in its horror has rent its veil, like a woman that is utterly broken in heart by the horrors she has seen! Therefore Joseph must own him, he cannot resist the impulse. O brethren, if you have been backward, let some such motive lead you unto the vanguard of the host.

Then there were all *the wonders of that death* which he saw, and to which I have already alluded. They sufficed to convince the centurion that this was a righteous man. They convinced others that he was the Son of God; and he who was already a disciple of Christ must have been greatly confirmed in that conviction by what he saw around the cross. The time was come when he must boldly act as Christ's disciple. Have there been no wonders of conversion around you? No answers to prayer? No providential deliverances? Should not these lead the secret ones to declare themselves?

I do not suppose he fully understood the design of our Lord's death; he had some knowledge of it, but not such a knowledge as we have now that the Spirit of God has appeared in all his fullness and taught us the meaning of the cross. Oh, listen, sirs, you that are not upon his side openly, you that have never worn his livery, nor manifestly entered on his service. He died for you! Those wounds were all for you; that bloody sweat, of which you still may see the marks upon the countenance of the crucified, was all for you. For you the thirst and fever, for you the bowing of the head, and the giving up of the ghost, and can you be ashamed to own him? Will you not endure rebuke and scorn for his dear sake who bore all this for you? Now speak from your soul and say, "He loved me, and gave himself for me." If you cannot say that, you cannot be happy; but if you can, then what follows? Must you not love him and give yourself for him? The cross is a wondrous magnet, drawing to Jesus every man of the true metal. It is as a banner lifted on high, to which all who are loyal must rally. This fiery cross, carried through all lands, will rouse the valiant and speed them to the field. Can you see your Lord suffering to the death for you, and then turn your backs? I pray you may no longer hesitate, but may at once cry, "Set down my name among his followers; for I will fight it out even to the end, till I hear him say—

> Come in, come in;
> Eternal glory thou shalt win.

Thus much by way of instruction taken from the life of Joseph of Arimathaea. If the cross does not bring a man out, what will? If the spectacle of dying love does not quicken us into courageous affection for him, what can?

III. So I have to mention, in the third place, something for *our arousing*.

Perhaps you are saying in your heart that the season in which Joseph lived was one which imperatively demanded that he should leave his hiding place and should go in to Pilate, but that you are under no such constraint. Hearken, friends, many people are not true to their occasions, whatever they may be; they do not consider that they have come to the kingdom for such a time as this. The Lord Jesus is not hanging on a cross today needing to be buried; but other stern necessities exist and call for your exertions. This hour's necessities imperiously demand that every man who is right at heart should acknowledge his Lord and do him service. Every man that loves Christ should at this hour prove it by his actions. A buoy off the Mumbles in South Wales bears a bell which is meant to warn mariners of a dangerous rock. This bell is quiet enough in ordinary weather; but when the winds are out, and the great waves rush in toward the shore, its solemn tones are heard for miles around as it swings to and fro in the hands of the sea. I believe there are true men who are silent when everything is calm, who will be forced to speak when the wild winds are out. Permit me to assure you that a storm is raging now, and it is growing worse and worse. If I rightly read the signs of the times, it is meet that every bell should ring out its warning note lest souls be lost upon the rocks of error. You that have fallen behind, because the fighting did not seem to require you, must quit your positions of ease. I summon you in the Master's name to the war. The Lord hath need of you. If you come not to his help against the mighty, a curse will light upon you. You must either be written across the back as *craven cowards*, or else you will today solemnly espouse the cause of Jesus. Shall I tell you why?

I will tell you why Joseph was wanted, and that was, just because *Christ's enemies had at last gone too far*. When they hunted him about and took up stones to stone him, they went a very long way; when they said he had a devil and was mad, they went much too far; when they asserted that he cast out devils by Beelzebub, the prince of the devils, that was a piece of blasphemy; but now, now they have overstepped the line most fatally; they have actually taken the King of Israel and nailed him up to a cross, and he is dead; and therefore Joseph cannot stand it any longer. He quits their company and joins himself to the Lord Jesus. See how far men are going in these days. In the outside world we have infidelity of so gross, so brutish, a character, that it is unworthy of the civilization, much less of the Christianity, of our age.

Now, you fearful ones, come out, and refuse to be numbered with the unbelieving world. Besides, in the outward Christian church we see men who, having already taken away every doctrine that we hold dear, are now assailing the inspiration of God's own Word. They tell us plainly that they do not believe what the Scriptures say further than they choose to do. The Bible to them is a fine book, but rather out of date. Now if you can be quiet, I cannot. The citadel of Christendom is now attacked. Let no brave man shrink from its defense. If you can hold your tongues and see the faith rent to pieces, I cannot. Why, it is enough to make every man gird on his weapon and rush to the fight.

Years ago, when they talked of the French invading England, an old lady grew very indignant and threatened deadly resistance. When she was asked what the women of England could do, she said they would rise to a man. I have no doubt whatever that they would do their best in any such emergency. Every iron in the fireplace, whether it be poker or shovel, would be grasped to defend our hearths and homes, and just so now, when error knows no bounds, we must stand up for the defense of the truth. Since they push error to extremes, it becomes us to hold by every particle of the faith. I will not, for my own part, give up a corner of my creed for any man. Even if we might have been prepared to modify expressions had the age been different, we are not in that mood now. A generation of vipers shall have a naked [iron] file to bite at. We will modify nothing. If truth bears a stern aspect, we will not veil it. If there be an offense in the cross, we will not conceal it. This shall be my answer to those who would have us attune ourselves to the spirit of the age: I know no Spirit but one, and he is unchanging in every age. Your extravagance of doubt shall have no influence over us except to make us bind the gospel more closely to our hearts. If we gave you an inch, you would take a mile, and so no inch shall be given you. Our resolve is to live for the Book as we read it, for the gospel as we rest in it, for the Lord as he made atonement, for the kingdom as it rules over all. I beg every trembling Christian to take heart, put on his Lord's livery, and advance to the fray. Come out now, if you never did before! Come out, if there is any manliness in you, in these days of blasphemy and rebuke.

> Ye that are men, now serve him,
> Against unnumbered foes;
> Your courage rise with danger,
> And strength to strength oppose.

When Joseph of Arimathaea revealed himself as our Lord's disciple, *our Lord's friends had mostly fled*—we might almost say they had all departed. Then Joseph said, "I will go in and beg for the body." When everybody else runs away, then the timid man grows brave; and often have I noticed it, that when there has been a wide desertion from the faith, then the feeble have become strong. Those poor souls who had said, "You hardly know whether we are the people of God at all, we are so unworthy," have crept out of their dens and have waxed valiant in fight, putting to flight the armies of the aliens. A sister was asked to tell her experience before the church, and she could not do it; but as she went away, she turned around and said, "I cannot speak for Christ, but I could die for him." "Come back," said the minister, "you are welcome here!" They do gloriously, those hidden ones, in days whereof we are apt to fear that no witness for the truth will remain alive. O that you who live where religion is declining may be all the more resolved to serve the Lord Jesus faithfully!

And then, you know, in Joseph's time *the people that were true to the Lord Jesus were such a feeble company.* Those that were not absolutely poor—the women that could minister to him of their substance—were nevertheless unable to go in unto Pilate and beg for the Lord's body. He would not have received them, and if he would they were too timid to have sought an interview; but Joseph is rich, and a counselor, and therefore he seemed to say, "These dear good women need a friend; they cannot get that precious body down from the cross alone. I will go to the Roman governor. Together with Nicodemus, I will provide the linen and the spices, and the women shall help us take Jesus down from the tree and lay him in my new tomb, and swathe his limbs in linen and spices, so as to embalm him honorably." Some of you live in country towns where those who are faithful to God are very poor, and have not much ability among them. If anything should move you to be the more decided, it should be that fact. It is a brave thing to help a feeble company; any common people will follow at the heels of success, but the true man is not ashamed of a despised cause when it is the cause of truth. You who have talent and substance should say, "I will go and help them now. I cannot leave the Master's cause to this feeble folk. I know they do their best, and as that is little, I will join them and lay myself out to aid them for my great Master's sake."

Can you not see my drift? My only desire this morning is to induce any of you who have for a moment faltered to "stand up, stand up for Jesus," and everywhere, in every place as wisdom may suggest, avow his dear and sacred name. Perhaps you are flowers that cannot bloom till the light is darkened, like the night-blooming cereus or the evening primrose. Now is your hour. The evening is already come; bloom, my dear friends, and fill the air with the delightful fragrance of your love. When other flowers are closed, take care to open to the dew. In these dark hours shine out, you stars! The sun has gone, else you might lie hid; but now let us see you! Joseph and Nicodemus had never been seen in the daylight when Jesus was alive; but when the sun was set through his death, then their radiance beamed at its full. O my hesitating brother, now is your time and your hour: boldly avail yourself of it, for our great Master's sake!

IV. Last, there is something in this subject for *our guidance*.

Somebody says, "Well, what do you mean by my coming out? I can see what Joseph did. What am I to do? I do not live at Arimathaea, and there is no Pilate in these days."

Joseph in owning his Lord *put himself under personal risk*. A Christian slave, whose master was executed for being a Christian, went to the judge and begged the body of his master that he might bury it. The judge replied, "Wherefore do you wish for your master's body?" "Because he was a Christian, and I am one." Upon this confession he was himself condemned to die. It might have been so with Pilate; for the Jewish rulers must have hated Joseph and longed for his death. He had been backward a long time, but now he put his life in his hand, and went in boldly to Pilate. We read, "He craved the body of Jesus"; but, as a commentator well says, he was not a craven, though he craved the body. He simply asked for it, begged for it, implored to have it, and the procurator yielded to his wish. Now do you think that if it were needful for you to jeopardize your best earthly interests for Christ, you could do it? Could you lose your character for culture and courage by avowing the old faith in these apostate days? Can you leave all for Jesus? Should it rend the fondest connection, should it break up the brightest prospects, could you take up the cross and follow your Lord? It is due to him who died for you that you should count the cost, and reckon it little enough for his dear sake, if you may but do him honor.

Remember, again, that this good man, Joseph of Arimathaea, when he took the body of Jesus, brought upon himself *ceremonial pollution*. It may seem little enough to you, but to a Jew it was a great deal, especially during the Passover week. He handled that blessed body and defiled himself in the judgment of the Jews. But, oh, I warrant you he did not think it any defilement to touch the blessed person of his Lord, even when the life was gone out of that matchless frame. Nor was it any pollution. It was an honor to touch that holy thing, that body prepared of God. Yet they will say to you, if you come out for Christ and unite with his people, that you lower yourself. They will point at you, give you some opprobrious name, and charge you with fanaticism. Take upon yourself this blessed shame, and say, as David did, "I will be yet more vile." Dishonor for Christ is honor, and shame for him is the very top of all glory. You will not stand back, I trust, but you will come forward and avow your faith, though you thus become as the offscouring of all things.

And then, this man having risked his life, and given up his honor was content to be *at great cost for the burial of Christ*. He went and bought the fine linen, and that rock-hewn sepulcher which it was the ambition of every Israelite to possess, he cheerfully resigned, that the Lord might lie there. Now, whenever you do own Christ, own him practically. Do not keep back your purse from him, or think that you are to say, "I am his," and do nothing for him. I was reading the story of a good old deacon in Maine, in America, who came into a meeting after there had been a missionary collection. The minister there and then asked "our good brother Sewell" to pray. Sewell did not pray, but thrust his hand in his pocket and stood fumbling about. "Bring the box," he said; and when the box came, and he had put his money into it, the minister said, "Brother Sewell? I did not ask you to give anything. I only wished you to pray." "Oh," said he, "I could not pray till I had first given something." He felt obliged first to do something for the great mission work, and having done that he could pray for it. Oh, that all Christ's people felt the justice of that course of conduct! Is it not most natural and proper? Joseph could not, when the Savior wanted burying, have been true to him without burying him. And now that the Savior does not want burying, but wants in all his living power to be preached among the sons of men, if we love him we must do all that lies in us to spread the knowledge of his name. Come out then, come out then, you that are hidden among the stud! Some of you strangers from the country, who have lived in the village and attended the services but never joined the church, do not let another Sunday dawn till you have sent in your name to be classed with the people of God. And any of you that have come often to the tabernacle, and say that nobody has spoken to you, just you speak to somebody and own what the Lord has done for you. Joseph of Arimathaea, where are you? Come forward, man! Come forth; your time has come! Come forth now! If you have followed Christ secretly, throw secrecy to the winds! Henceforth be bravest of the brave, among the bodyguard of Christ, who follow him whithersoever he goeth. Have no fear nor thought of fear, but count it all joy if you fall into manifold trials for his name's sake, who is King of kings and Lord of lords, to whom be glory forever and ever. Amen.

Simon of Cyrene: Up from the Country, and Pressed into the Service

❧⟨⟩❧

Delivered on Lord's Day morning, August 2, 1885, at the Metropolitan Tabernacle, Newington. No. 1853.

*And they compel one Simon a Cyrenian, who passed by, coming out of the country, the father of Alexander and Rufus, to bear his cross.—*MARK 15:21

John tells us that our Savior went forth bearing his cross (John 19:17). We are much indebted to John for inserting that fact. The other Evangelists mention Simon the Cyrenian as bearing the cross of Christ; but John, who often fills up gaps which are left by the other three, tells us that Jesus set out to Calvary carrying his own cross. Our Lord Jesus came out from Pilate's palace laden with his cross, but he was so extremely emaciated and so greatly worn by the night of the bloody sweat, that the procession moved too slowly for the rough soldiers, and therefore they took the cross from their prisoner and laid it upon Simon; or possibly they laid the long end upon the shoulder of the strong countryman, while the Savior still continued to bear in part his cross till he came to the place of doom.

It is well that we should be told that the Savior bore his cross; for if it had not been so, objectors would have had grounds for disputation. I hear them say, "You admit that one of the most prominent types, in the Old Testament, of the sacrifice of the Son of God, was Abraham's offering up his son Isaac; now Abraham laid the wood upon Isaac his son, and not upon a servant. Should not therefore the Son of God bear the cross himself?" Had not our Lord carried his cross, there would have been a flaw in his fulfillment of the type; therefore the Savior must bear the wood when he goes forth to be offered up as a sacrifice. One of the greatest of English preachers has well reminded us that the fulfillment of this type appeared to have been in eminent jeopardy, since, at the very first, our Lord's weakness must have been apparent, and the reason which led to the laying of the cross upon the Cyrenian might have prevented our Lord's carrying the cross at all. If the soldiers had a little earlier put the cross upon Simon, which they might very naturally have done, then the prophecy had not been fulfilled; but God has the minds of men so entirely at his control, that even in the minutest circumstance he can order all things so as to complete the merest jots and tittles of the prophecy. Our Lord was made to be, in all points, an Isaac, and therefore we see him going forth bearing the wood of the burnt offering. Thus you see that it was important that Jesus should for a while bear his own cross.

But it was equally instructive that someone else should be made a partaker of the burden; for it has always been part of the divine counsel that for the salvation of men from sin the Lord should be associated with his church. So far as atonement is concerned, the Lord has trodden the winepress alone, and of the people there was none with him; but as far as the conversion of the world is concerned, and its rescue from the power of error and wickedness, Christ is not alone. We are workers together with God. We are ourselves to be in the hands of God part-bearers of the sorrow and travail by which men are to be delivered from the bondage of sin and Satan, and brought into the liberty of truth and righteousness. Hence it became important that in the bearing of the cross, though not in the death upon it, there should be yoked with the Christ one who should follow close behind him. To bear the cross after Jesus is the office of the faithful. Simon the Cyrenian is the representative of the whole church of God, and of each believer in particular. Often had Jesus said, "Except a man take up his cross daily and follow me, he cannot be my disciple"; and now at last he embodies that sermon in an actual person. The disciple must be as his Master: he that would follow the Crucified must himself bear the cross: this we see visibly set forth in Simon of Cyrene with the cross of Jesus laid upon his shoulder.

> Shall Simon bear the cross alone,
> And all the rest go free?
> No, there's a cross for every one,
> And there's a cross for me.

The lesson to each one of us is to take up our Lord's cross without delay, and go with him—without the camp, bearing his reproach. That many among this vast and mixed congregation may imitate Simon is the anxious desire of my heart. With holy expectancy I gaze upon this throng collected from all parts of the earth, and I long to find in it some who will take my Lord's yoke upon them this day.

I. I will begin with this first remark, that *unexpected persons are often called to cross bearing*.

Like Simon, they are impressed into the service of Christ. Our text says: "They compel one Simon a Cyrenian, who passed by, coming out of the country, the father of Alexander and Rufus, to bear his cross." Simon did not volunteer, but was forced into this work of cross bearing. It would seem from another Evangelist that he speedily yielded to the impressment, and lifted the burden heartily; but at first he was compelled. A rude authority was exercised by the guard, who being upon the governor's business acted with high-handed rigor and forced whomsoever they pleased to do their bidding. By the exercise of such irresponsible power, they compelled a passing stranger to carry Christ's cross. It was specially singular that the man to have this honor was not Peter nor James nor John nor any one of the many who had for years listened to the Redeemer's speech; but it was a stranger from Northern Africa, who had been in no way connected with the life or teachings of Jesus of Nazareth.

Notice, first, that *he was an unknown man*. He was spoken of "as one Simon." Simon was a very common name among the Jews, almost as common as John in our own country. This man was just "one Simon"—an individual who need not be further described. But the providence of God had determined that this obscure individual, this certain man, or I might better say, this uncertain man, should be selected to the high office of cross bearer to the Son of God. I have an impression upon my mind that there is "one Simon" here this morning, who has to bear Christ's cross from this time forward. I feel persuaded that I am right. That person is so far unknown that most probably he does not recognize a single individual in all this throng, neither does anybody in this assembly know anything of him: certainly the preacher does not. He is one John, one Thomas, or one William; or perhaps, in the feminine, she is one Mary, one Jane, one Maggie. Friend, nobody knows you save our Father who is in heaven, and he has appointed you to have fellowship with his Son. I shall roughly describe you as "one Simon," and leave the Holy Spirit to bring you into your place and service. But this "one Simon" was a very particular "one Simon." I lay the emphasis where there might seem to be no need of any: he was one whom God knew and chose and loved and set apart for this special service. In a congregation like the present, there may be somebody whom our God intends to use for his glory during the rest of his life. That person sits in the pew and listens to what I am saying, and perhaps as yet he does not begin to inquire whether he is that "one Simon," that one person; and yet it is so, and before this sermon is ended, he shall know that the call to bear the cross is for him. Many more unlikely things than this have happened in this house of prayer. I pray that many a man may go out from this house a different man from the man he was when he entered it an hour ago.

That man Saul, that great persecutor of the church, afterward became such a mighty preacher of the gospel that people exclaimed with wonder, "There is a strange alteration in this man." "Why," said one, "when I knew him he was a Pharisee of the Pharisees. He was as bigoted a man as ever wore a phylactery, and he hated Christ and Christians so intensely that he could never persecute the church sufficiently." "Yes," replied another, "it was so; but he has had a strange twist. They say that he was going down to Damascus to hunt out the disciples, and something happened; we do not know exactly what it was, but evidently it gave him such a turn that he has never been himself since. In fact, he seems turned altogether upside down, and the current of his life is evidently reversed: he lives enthusiastically for that faith which once he destroyed." This speedy change happened to "one Saul of Tarsus." There were plenty of Sauls in Israel, but upon this one Saul electing love had looked in the counsels of eternity; for that Saul redeeming love had shed its heart's blood, and in that Saul effectual grace worked mightily. Is there another Saul here today? The Lord grant that he may now cease to kick against the pricks, and may we soon hear of him, "Behold, he prayeth." I feel convinced the counterpart of that "one Simon" is in this house at this moment, and my prayer goes up to God, and I hope it is attended with the prayers of many thousands besides, that he may at once submit to the Lord Jesus.

It did not seem likely that Simon should bear the cross of Christ, for he was a stranger who had newly come up from the country. He probably knew little or nothing of what had been taking place in Jerusalem; for he had come from another continent. He was "one Simon a Cyrenian"; and I suppose that Cyrene could not have been less than eight hundred miles from Jerusalem. It was situated in what is now called Tripoli, in Northern Africa, in which place a colony of Jews had been formed long before. Very likely he had come in a Roman galley from Alexandria to Joppa, and there had been rowed through the surf, and landed in time to reach Jerusalem for the Passover. He had long wanted to come to Jerusalem; he had heard the fame of the temple and of the city of his fathers; and he had longed to see the great assembly of the tribes, and the solemn Paschal feast. He had traveled all those miles, he had hardly yet got the motion of the ship out of his brain, and it had never entered into his head that he should be impressed by the Roman guard, and made to assist at an execution. It was a singular providence that he should come into the city at the moment of the turmoil about Jesus, and should have crossed the street just as the sad procession started on its way to Golgotha. He passed by neither too soon nor too late; he was on the spot as punctually as if he had made an appointment to be there; and yet, as men speak, it was all by mere chance. I cannot tell how many providences had worked together to bring him there at the nick of time, but so the Lord would have it, and so it came about. He, a man there in Cyrene, in Northern Africa, must at a certain date, at the tick of the clock, be at Jerusalem, in order that he might help to carry the cross up to Mount Calvary; and he was there. Ah! my dear friend, I do not know what providences have been at work to bring you here today; perhaps very strange ones. If a little something had occurred, you had not taken this journey; it only needed a small dust to turn the scale, and you would have been hundreds of miles from this spot, in quite another scene from this. Why you are here you do not yet know, except that you have come to listen to the preacher, and join the throng. But God knows why he has brought you here. I trust it will be read in the annals of the future:

> Thus the eternal mandate ran,
> Almighty grace arrest that man.

God has brought you here, that on this spot, by the preaching of the gospel, you may be compelled to bear the cross of Jesus. I pray it may be so. "One Simon a Cyrenian . . . coming out of the country," is here after a long journey, and this day he will begin to live a higher and a better life.

Further, notice, *Simon had come for another purpose.* He had journeyed to Jerusalem with no thought of bearing the cross of Jesus. Probably Simon was a Jew far removed from the land of his fathers, and he had made a pilgrimage to the Holy City to keep the Passover. Every Jew loved to be present at Jerusalem at the Paschal feast. So, to put it roughly, it was holiday time; it was a time for making an excursion to the capital; it was a season for making a journey and going up to the great city which was "beautiful for situation, the joy of the whole earth." Simon from far-off Cyrene must by all means keep the feast at Jerusalem. Maybe he had saved his money for months, that he might pay his fare to Joppa; and he had counted down the gold freely for the joy which he had in going to the city of David, and the temple of his God.

He was come for the Passover, and for that only; and he would be perfectly satisfied to go home when once the feast was over, and once he had partaken of the lamb with the tribes of Israel. Then he could say throughout the rest of his life, "I, too, was once at the great feast of our people, when we commemorated the coming up out of Egypt." Brethren, we propose one way, but

God has other propositions. We say, "I will step in and hear the preacher," but God means that the arrows of his grace shall stick fast in our hearts. Many and many a time with no desire for grace, men have listened to the gospel, and the Lord has been found of them that sought him not. I heard of one who cared little for the sermon till the preacher chanced to use that word eternity, and the hearer was taken prisoner by holy thoughts, and led to the Savior's feet. Men have stepped into places of worship even with evil designs, and yet the purpose of grace has been accomplished; they came to scoff, but they remained to pray. Some have been cast by the providence of God into positions where they have met with Christian men, and a word of admonition has been blessed to them. A lady was one day at an evening party, and there met with Caesar Malan, the famous divine of Geneva, who, in his usual manner, inquired of her whether she was a Christian. She was startled, surprised, and vexed, and made a short reply to the effect that it was not a question she cared to discuss; whereupon, Mr. Malan replied with great sweetness, that he would not persist in speaking of it, but he would pray that she might be led to give her heart to Christ, and become a useful worker for him. Within a fortnight she met the minister again, and asked him how she must come to Jesus. Mr. Malan's reply was, "Come to him just as you are." That lady gave herself up to Jesus: it was Charlotte Elliott, to whom we owe that precious hymn—

> *Just as I am—without one plea*
> *But that thy blood was shed for me*
> *And that thou bidd'st me come to thee—*
> *O Lamb of God, I come.*

It was a blessed thing for her that she was at that party, and that the servant of God from Geneva should have been there, and should have spoken to her so faithfully. Oh, for many a repetition of the story "of one Simon a Cyrenian," coming, not with the intent to bear the cross, but with quite another mind, and yet being enlisted in the cross-bearing army of the Lord Jesus!

I would have you notice, once more, that this man was at this particular time not thinking upon the subject at all, for *he was at that time merely passing by.* He had come up to Jerusalem, and whatever occupied his mind he does not appear to have taken any notice of the trial of Jesus, or of the sad end of it. It is expressly said that he "passed by." He was not even sufficiently interested in the matter to stand in the crowd and look at the mournful procession. Women were weeping there right bitterly—the daughters of Jerusalem to whom the Master said, "Weep not for me, but weep for yourselves, and for your children"; but this man passed by. He was anxious to hurry away from so unpleasant a sight, and to get up to the temple. He was quietly making his way through the crowd, eager to go about his business, and he must have been greatly surprised and distressed when a rough hand was laid upon him, and a stern voice said, "Shoulder that cross." There was no resisting a Roman centurion when he gave command, and so the countryman meekly submitted, wishing, no doubt, that he were back in Cyrene tilling the ground. He must needs stoop his shoulder and take up a new burden, and tread in the footsteps of the mysterious personage to whom the cross belonged. He was only passing by, and yet he was enlisted and impressed by the Romans, and, as I take it, impressed by the grace of God for life; for whereas Mark says he was the father of Alexander and Rufus, it would seem that his sons were well known to the Christian people to whom Mark was writing. If his son was the same Rufus that Paul mentions, then he calls her [his mother] "his mother and mine"; and it would seem that Simon's wife and his sons became believers and partakers of the sufferings of Christ. His contact with the Lord in that strange compulsory way probably worked out for him another and more spiritual contact which made him a true cross bearer. O you that pass by this day, draw nigh to Jesus! I have no wish to call your attention to myself, far from it; but I do ask your attention to my Lord. Though you only intended to slip into this tabernacle and slip out again, I pray that you may be arrested by a call from my Lord. I speak as my Lord's servant, and I would constrain you to come to him. Stand where you are a while, and let me beg you to yield to his love, which even now would cast the bands of a man around you. I would compel you, by my Lord's authority, to take up his cross and bear it after him. It would be strange, say you. Yes, so it might be, but it would be a glorious event. I remember Mr. Knill, speaking of his own conversion, used an expression which I should like to use concerning one of you. Here it is: "It was just a quarter past twelve, August 2, when twang went every harp in paradise; for a sinner had repented." May it be so with you. Oh, that every harp in paradise may now ring out the high praises of sovereign grace, as you now yield yourself to the great Shepherd and Bishop of souls! May that divine impressment which is imaged in the text by the compulsion of the Roman soldier take place in your case at this very moment; and may it be seen in your instance that unexpected persons are often called to be cross bearers!

II. My second observation is—*cross bearing can still be practiced.* Very briefly let me tell you in what ways the cross can still be carried.

First, and chiefly, *by your becoming a Christian.* If the cross shall take you up, you will take up the cross. Christ will be your hope, his death your trust, himself the object of your love. You never become a cross bearer truly till you lay your burdens down at his feet who bore the cross and curse for you.

Next, you become a cross bearer *when you make an open avowal of the Lord Jesus Christ.* Do not deceive yourselves; this is expected of each one of you if you are to be saved. The promise as I read it in the New Testament is not to the believer alone, but to the believer who confesses his faith. "He that with his heart believeth and with his mouth maketh confession of him shall be saved." He says, "He that confesseth me before men, him will I confess before my Father; but he that denieth me"—and from the connection it should seem to mean, *he that does not confess me*—"him will I deny before my Father which is in heaven." To quote the inspired Scripture, "He that believeth and is baptized shall be saved." There should be, there must be, the open avowal in Christ's own way of the secret faith which you have in him. Now this is often a cross. Many people would like to go to heaven by an underground railway— secrecy suits them. They do not want to cross the channel; the sea is too rough; but when there is a tunnel made they will go to the fair country. My good people, you are cowardly, and I must quote to you a text which ought to sting your cowardice out of you: "But the fearful and unbelieving shall have their part in the lake which burneth with fire and brimstone." I say no more, and make no personal applications; but, I beseech you, run no risks. Be afraid to be afraid. Be ashamed of being ashamed of Christ. Shame on that man who counts it any shame to say before assembled angels, and men, and devils, "I am a follower of Christ." May you who have been secret followers of the crucified Lord become manifest cross bearers! Do you not even now cry out, "Set down my name, sir"?

Further, some have to take up their cross by *commencing Christian work.* You live in a village where there is no gospel preaching: preach yourself. You are in a backwoods town where the preaching is very far from being such as God approves of: begin to preach the truth yourself. "Alas!" say you, "I should make a fool of myself." Are you ashamed to be a fool for Christ? "Oh, but I should break down." Break down: it will do you good, and perhaps you may break somebody else down. There is no better preaching in the world than that of a man who breaks down under a sense of unworthiness: if that break-down communicates itself to other people, it may begin a revival. If you are choked by your earnestness, others may become earnest too. Do you still murmur, "But I should get the ill will of everybody"? For Christ's sake could you not bear that? When the good monk said to Martin Luther, "Go home to your cell and keep quiet," why did not Martin take the advice? Why, indeed?

"It is very bad for young people to be so forward; you will do a great deal of mischief, therefore be quiet, you Martin. Who are you to interfere with the great authorities? Be holy for yourself, and don't trouble others. If you stir up a reformation thousands of good people will be burned through you. Do be quiet." Bless God, Martin did not go home, and was not quiet, but went about his Master's business, and raised heaven and earth by his brave witness bearing. Where are you, Martin, this morning? I pray God to call you out, and as you have confessed his name and are his servant, I pray that he may make you bear public testimony for him, and tell out the saving power of the Savior's precious blood. Come, Simon, I see you shrink; but the cross has to be carried; therefore bow your back. It is only a wooden cross, after all, and not an iron one. You can bear it: you must bear it. God help you.

Perhaps, too, some brother may have to take up his cross by *bearing witness against the rampant sin which surrounds him.* "Leave all those dirty matters alone; do not say a word about them. Let the people go to the devil, or else you will soil your white kid gloves." Sirs, we will spoil our hands as well as our gloves, and we will risk our characters, if need be; but we will put down the devilry which now defiles London. Truly the flesh does shrink, and the purest part of our manhood shrinks with it, when we are compelled to bear open protest against sins which are done of men in secret. But Simon, the Master may yet compel you to bear his cross in this respect, and if so, he will give you both courage and wisdom, and your labor shall not be in vain in the Lord.

Sometimes, however, the cross bearing is of another and more quiet kind, and may be described as *submission to providence.* A young friend is saying, "For me to live at home I know to be my duty; but father is unkind, and the family generally imposes upon me. I wish I could get away." Ah! dear sister, you must bear Christ's cross, and it may be the Lord would have you remain at home. Therefore bear the cross. A servant is saying, "I should like to be in a Christian family. I do not think I can stop where I am." Perhaps, good sister, the Lord has put you where you are to be a light in a dark place. All the lamps should not be in one street, or what will become of the courts and alleys? It is often the duty of a Christian man to say, "I shall stop where I am and fight this matter through. I mean by character and example, with kindness and courtesy and love, to win this place for Jesus." Of course the easy way is to turn monk and live quietly in a cloister, and serve God by doing nothing; or to turn nun and dwell in a convent, and expect to win the battle of life by running out of it. Is not this absurd? If you shut yourself away from this poor world, what is to become of it? You men and women that are Christians must stand up and stand out for Jesus where the providence of God has cast you: if your calling is not a sinful one, and if the temptations around you are not too great for you, you must "hold the fort" and never dream of surrender. If your lot is hard, look upon it as Christ's cross, and bow your back to the load. Your shoulder may be raw at first, but you will grow stronger before long, for as your day, your strength shall be. "It is good for a man that he bear the yoke in his youth"; but it is good for a man to bear the cross in his old age as well as in his youth; in fact, we ought never to be quit of so blessed a burden. What wings are to a bird, and sails to a ship, that the cross becomes to a man's spirit when he fully consents to accept it as his life's beloved load. Truly did Jesus say, "My yoke is easy, and my burden is light." Now, Simon, where are you? Shoulder the cross, man, in the name of God!

III. Third, *to cross bearing there are noble compulsions.*

Simon's compulsion was the rough hand of the Roman legionary, and the gruff voice in the Latin tongue, "Shoulder that cross"; but we hear gentler voices which compel us this day to take up Christ's cross.

The first compulsion is this: *"the love of Christ constraineth us."* He has done all this for you; therefore by sweet but irresistible compulsion you are made to render him some return of love. Does not Jesus appear to you in a vision as you sit in this house? Do you not see that thorn-crowned head, that visage crimsoned with the bloody sweat, those hands and feet pierced with the nails? Does he not say to you pointedly, "I did all this for thee; what hast thou done for me"? Startled in your seat, you cover your face, and inwardly reply, "I will answer that question by the rest of my life. I will be first and foremost a servant of Jesus: not a trader first and a Christian next, but a Christian first and a businessman afterward." You, my sister, must say, "I will live for Christ as a daughter, a wife, or a mother. I will live for my Lord; for he has given himself for me, and I am not my own, but bought with a price."

The true heart will feel a compulsion arising from a second reflection, namely, *the glory of a life spent for God and for his Christ.* What is the life of a man who toils in business, makes money, becomes rich, and dies? It winds up with a paragraph in the *Illustrated London News*, declaring that he died worth so much: the wretch was not worth anything himself; his estate had value, he had none. Had he been worth anything he would have sent his money about the world doing good; but as a worthless steward he laid his Master's stores in heaps to rot. The life of multitudes of men is self-seeking. It is ill for a man to live the life of swine. What a poor creature is the usual ordinary man! But a life spent for Jesus, though it involve cross bearing, is noble, heroic, sublime.

The mere earthworm leads a dunghill life. A life of what is called pleasure is a mean, beggarly business. A life of keeping up respectability is utter slavery— as well be a horse in a pug mill. A life wholly consecrated to Christ and his cross is life indeed; it is akin to the life of angels; yes, higher still, it is the life of God within the soul of man. O you that have a spark of true nobility, seek to live lives worth living, worth remembering, worthy to be the commence- ment of eternal life before the throne of God.

Some of you ought to feel the cross coming upon your shoulders this morning when you think of *the needs of those among whom you live.* They are dying, perishing for lack of knowledge, rich and poor alike ignorant of Christ; multitudes of them wrapped up in self-righteousness. They are perishing, and those who ought to warn them are often dumb dogs that cannot bark. Do you not feel that you ought to deliver the sheep from the wolf? Have you no bow- els of compassion? Are your hearts turned to steel? I am sure you cannot deny that the times demand of you earnest and forceful lives. No Christian man can now sit still without incurring awful guilt. Whether you live in London or in any other great town amid reeking sin, or dwell in the country amid the dense darkness which broods over many rural districts, you are under bonds to be up and doing. It may be a cross to you, but for Jesus' sake you must uplift it, and never lay it down till the Lord calls you home.

Some of you should bear the cross of Christ *because the cause of Christ is at a discount where you dwell.* I delight in a man in whom the lordlier chivalry has found a congenial home. He loves to espouse the cause of truth in the cloudy and dark day. He never counts heads, but weighs arguments. When he settles down in a town, he never inquires, "Where is the most respectable congrega- tion? Where shall I meet with those who will advantage me in business?" No, he studies his conscience rather than his convenience. He hears one say, "There is a Nonconformist chapel, but it is down a back street. There is a Bap- tist church, but the members are nearly all poor, and no gentlefolk are among them. Even the evangelical church is down at the heel: the best families attend the high church." I say he hears this, and his heart is sick of such talk. He will go where the gospel is preached, and nowhere else. Fine architecture has scant charms for him, and grand music is no part of his religion: if these are substi- tutes for the gospel, he abhors them. It is meanness itself for a man to forsake the truth for the sake of respectability. Multitudes who ought to be found maintaining the good old cause are recreant to their convictions, if indeed they ever had any. For this cause the true man resolves to stick to truth through thick and thin, and not to forsake her because her adherents are poor and despised. If ever we might temporize, that time is past and gone. I arrest yonder man this morning, who has long been a Christian, but has concealed half his Christianity in order to be thought respectable, or to escape the penalties of faithfulness. Come out from those with whom you are numbered, but with whom you are not united in heart. Be brave enough to defend good cause against all comers; for the day shall come when he shall have honor for his guerdon [reward] who accepted dishonor that he might be true to his God, his Bible, and his conscience. Blessed be he that can be loyal to his Lord, cost him what it may—loyal even in those matters which traitors call little things. We would compel that Simon the Cyrenian this day to bear the cross, because there are so few to bear it in these degenerate days.

Besides, I may say to some of you, you ought to bear the cross because you know you are not satisfied; *your hearts are not at rest.* You have prospered in worldly things, but you are not happy; you have good health, but you are not happy; you have loving friends, but you are not happy. There is but one way of getting rest to the heart and that is, to come to Jesus. That is his word: "Come unto me, all ye that labor and are heavy laden, and I will give you rest." If after this you need a further rest for other and higher longings, then you must come again to the same Savior, and hearken to his next word: "Take my yoke upon you, and learn of me; for I am meek and lowly in heart: and ye shall find rest unto your souls. For my yoke is easy, and my burden is light." Some of you professors have not yet found perfect rest, and the reason is because you have looked to the cross for pardon, but you have never taken to cross bearing as an occupation. You are hoping in Christ but not living for Christ. The finding of rest unto your soul will come to you in having something to do or to bear for Jesus. "Take my yoke upon you: and ye shall find rest unto your souls."

There are many ways, then, of bearing the cross for Christ, and there are many reasons why some here present should begin at once to carry the load.

IV. To close: bear with me a minute or two while I say that *cross bearing is a blessed occupation.*

I feel sure that Simon found it so. Let me mention certain blessings which must have attended the special service of Simon. First, *it brought him into Christ's company.* When they compelled him to bear his cross, he was brought close to Jesus. If it had not been for that compulsion, he might have gone his way, or might have been lost in the crowd; but now he is in the inner circle, near to Jesus. For the first time in his life he saw that blessed form, and as he saw it I believe his heart was enamored with it. As they lifted the cross on his shoulders, he looked at that sacred Person, and saw a crown of thorns about his brow; and as he looked at his fellow sufferer, he saw all down his cheeks the marks of bloody sweat, and black and blue bruises from cruel hands. As for those eyes, they looked him through and through! That face, that matchless face, he had never seen its like. Majesty was therein blended with misery, innocence with agony, and love with sorrow. He had never seen that countenance so well, nor marked the whole form of the Son of man so clearly if he had not been called to bear that cross. It is wonderful how much we see of Jesus when we suffer or labor for him. Believing souls, I pray that this day you may be so impressed into my Lord's service, that you may have nearer and dearer fellowship with him than in the past. If any man will do his will he shall know of the doctrine. They see Jesus best who carry his cross most.

Besides, *the cross held Simon in Christ's steps*. Do you catch it? If Jesus carried the front part of the cross and Simon followed behind, he was sure to put his feet down just where the Master's feet had been before. The cross is a wonderful implement for keeping us in the way of our Lord. As I was turning this subject over, I was thinking how of often I had felt a conscious contact between myself and my Lord when I have had to bear reproach for his sake; and how at the same time I have been led to watch my steps more carefully because of that very reproach. Brethren, we do not want to slip from under the cross. If we did so, we might slip away from our Lord and from holy walking. If we can keep our shoulder beneath that sacred load, and see our Lord a little on before, we shall be making the surest progress. This being near to Jesus is a blessed privilege, which is cheaply purchased at the price of cross bearing. If you would see Jesus, bestir yourselves to work for him. Boldly avow him, cheerfully suffer for him, and then you shall see him, and then you shall learn to follow him step by step. A blessed cross, which holds us to Jesus and to his ways!

Then Simon had this honor, that *he was linked with Christ's work*. He could not put away sin, but he could assist weakness. Simon did not die on the cross to make expiation, but he did live under the cross to aid in the accomplishment of the divine purpose. You and I cannot interfere with Jesus in his passion, but we can share with him in his commission; we cannot purchase liberty for the enslaved, but we can tell them of their emancipation. To have a finger in Christ's work is glory. I invite the man that seeks honor and immortality, to seek it thus. To have a share in the Redeemer's work is a more attractive thing than all the pomp and glitter of this world and the kingdoms thereof. Where are the men of heavenly mind who will covet to be joined unto the Lord in this ministry? Let them step out and say, "Jesus, I my cross have taken. Henceforth I will follow thee. Come life or death, I will carry thy cross till thou shalt give me the crown."

While Simon was carrying the cross through the crowd, I doubt not that the rough soldiery would deal him many a kick or buffet—but I feel equally sure that the dear Master sometimes stole a glance at him. *Simon enjoyed Christ's smile.* I know the Lord so well, that I feel sure he must have done so: he would not forget the man who was his partner for the while. And oh, that look! How Simon must have treasured up the remembrance of it. "I never carried a load that was so light," says he, "as that which I carried that morning; for when the blessed One smiled at me amid his woes, I felt myself to be strong as Hercules." Alexander, his firstborn, and that red-headed lad Rufus, when they grew up both felt it to be the honor of the family that their father carried the cross after Jesus. Rufus and Alexander had a patent of nobility in being the sons of such a man. Mark recorded the fact that Simon carried the cross, and that such and such persons were his sons. I think when the old man came to lie upon his deathbed, he said: "My hope is in him whose cross I carried. Blessed burden! Lay me down in my grave. This body of mine cannot perish, for it bore the cross which Jesus carried, and which carried *him*. I shall rise again to see him in his glory, for his cross has pressed me, and his love will surely raise me." Happy are we if we can while yet we live be coworkers together with him, that when he cometh in his kingdom we may be partakers of his glory. "Blessed is the man that endureth temptation: for when he is tried, he shall receive the crown of life, which the Lord hath promised to them that love him." God bless you, and especially you who have come out of the country. God bless you. Amen and amen.

Dismas: The Dying Thief in a New Light

Intended for reading on Lord's Day, January 31, 1886, delivered on Lord's Day evening, August 23, 1885, at the Metropolitan Tabernacle, Newington. No. 1881.

> *But the other answering rebuked him, saying, "Dost not thou fear God, seeing thou art in the same condemnation? And we indeed justly; for we receive the due reward of our deeds: but this man hath done nothing amiss." And he said unto Jesus, "Lord, remember me when thou comest into thy kingdom."*
> —LUKE 23:40–42

A great many persons, whenever they hear of the conversion of the dying thief, remember that he was saved in the very article of death, and they dwell upon that fact, and that alone. He has always been quoted as a case of salvation at the eleventh hour; and so, indeed, he is. In his case it is proven that as long as a man can repent, he can obtain forgiveness. The cross of Christ avails even for a man hanging on a gibbet, and drawing near to his last hour. He who is mighty to save was mighty, even during his own death, to pluck others from the grasp of the destroyer, though they were in the act of expiring.

But that is not everything which the story teaches us; and it is always a pity to look exclusively upon one point, and thus to miss everything else—perhaps miss that which is more important. So often has this been the case that it has produced a sort of revulsion of feeling in certain minds, so that they have been driven in a wrong direction by their wish to protest against what they think to be a common error. I read the other day that this story of the dying thief ought not to be taken as an encouragement to deathbed repentance. Brethren, if the author meant—and I do not think he did mean—that this ought never to be so used as to lead people to postpone repentance to a dying bed, he spoke correctly. No Christian man could or would use it so injuriously: he must be hopelessly bad who would draw from God's longsuffering an argument for continuing in sin. I trust, however, that the narrative is not often so used, even by the worst of men, and I feel sure that it will not be so used by any one of you. It cannot be properly turned to such a purpose: it might be used as an encouragement to thieving just as much as to the delay of repentance. I might say, "I may be a thief because this thief was saved," just as rationally as I might say, "I may put off repentance because this thief was saved when he was about to die." The fact is, there is nothing so good but men can pervert it into evil, if they have evil hearts: the justice of God is made a motive for despair, and his mercy an argument for sin. Wicked men will drown themselves in the rivers of truth as readily as in the pools of error. He that has a mind to destroy himself can choke his soul with the Bread of life, or dash himself in pieces against the Rock of ages. There is no doctrine of the grace of God so gracious that graceless men may not turn it into licentiousness.

I venture, however, to say that if I stood by the bedside of a dying man tonight, and I found him anxious about his soul, but fearful that Christ could not save him because repentance had been put off so late, I should certainly quote the dying thief to him, and I should do it with good conscience, and without hesitation. I should tell him that, though he was as near to dying as the thief upon the cross was, yet, if he repented of his sin, and turned his face to Christ believingly, he would find eternal life. I should do this with all my heart, rejoicing that I had such a story to tell to one at the gates of eternity. I do not think that I should be censured by the Holy Spirit for thus using a narrative which he has himself recorded, recorded with the foresight that it would be so used. I should feel, at any rate, in my own heart, a sweet conviction that I had treated the subject as I ought to have treated it, and as it was intended to be used for men *in extremis* whose hearts are turning toward the living God. Oh, yes, poor soul, whatever your age, or whatever the period of life to which you have come, you may now find eternal life by faith in Christ!

> *The dying thief rejoiced to see*
> *That fountain in his day;*
> *And there may you, though vile as he,*
> *Wash all your sins away.*

Many good people think that they ought to guard the gospel; but it is never so safe as when it stands out in its own naked majesty. It wants no covering from us. When we protect it with provisos, and guard it with exceptions, and qualify it with observations, it is like David in Saul's armor: it is hampered and hindered, and you may even hear it cry, "I cannot go with these." Let the gospel alone, and it will save; qualify it, and the salt has lost its savor. I will venture to put it thus to you. I have heard it said that few are ever converted in old age; and this is thought to be a statement which will prove exceedingly arousing and impressive for the young. It certainly wears that appearance; but, on the other hand, it is a statement very discouraging to the old. I demur to the frequent repetition of such statements, for I do not find their counterpart in the teaching of our Lord and his apostles. Assuredly our Lord spoke of some who entered the vineyard at the eleventh hour of the day; and among his miracles he not only saved those who were dying, but even raised the dead. Nothing can be concluded from the words of the Lord Jesus against the salvation of men at any hour or age. I tell you that, in the business of your acceptance with God, through faith in Christ Jesus, it does not matter what age you now are at. The same promise is to every one of you, "Today if ye will hear his voice, harden not your hearts"; and whether you are in the earliest stage of life, or are within a few hours of eternity, if now you fly for refuge to the hope set before you in the gospel, you shall be saved. The gospel that I preach excludes none on the ground either of age or character. Whoever you may be, "Believe on the Lord Jesus Christ, and thou shalt be saved" is the message we have to deliver to you. If we address to you the longer form of the gospel, "He that believeth and is baptized shall be saved," this is true of every living man, be his age whatever it may. I am not afraid that this story of the dying and repenting thief, who went straight from the cross to the crown, will be used by you amiss; but if you are wicked enough so to use it, I cannot help it. It will only fulfill that solemn Scripture which says that the gospel is a savor of death unto death to some, even that very gospel which is a savor of life unto life to others.

But I do not think, dear friends, that the only specialty about the thief is the lateness of his repentance. So far from being the only point of interest, it is not even the chief point. To some minds, at any rate, other points will be even more remarkable. I want to show you very briefly that there was a specialty in his case as to the means of his conversion; second, a specialty in his faith; third, a specialty in the result of his faith which he was here below; and, fourth, a specialty in the promise won by his faith—the promise fulfilled to him in paradise.

I. First, then, I think you ought to notice very carefully *the singularity and specialty of the means by which the thief was converted.*

How do you think it was? Well, we do not know. We cannot tell. It seems to me that the man was an unconverted, impenitent thief when they nailed him to the cross, because one of the Evangelists says, *"The thieves also, which were crucified with him, cast the same in his teeth."* I know that this may have been a general statement, and that it is reconcilable with its having been done by one thief only, according to the methods commonly used by critics; but I am not enamored of critics even when they are friendly. I have such respect for revelation that I never in my own mind permit the idea of discrepancies and mistakes, and when the Evangelist says "they" I believe he meant "they," and that both these thieves did at their first crucifixion rail at the Christ with whom they were crucified. It would appear that by some means or other this thief must have been converted while he was on the cross. Assuredly nobody preached a sermon to him, no evangelistic address was delivered at the foot of his cross, and no meeting was held for special prayer on his account. He does not even seem to have had an instruction, or an invitation, or an expostulation addressed to him; and yet this man became a sincere and accepted believer in the Lord Jesus Christ.

Dwell upon this fact, if you please, and note its practical bearing upon the cases of many around us. There are many among my hearers who have been instructed from their childhood, who have been admonished and warned and entreated and invited, and yet they have not come to Christ; while this man, without any of these advantages, nevertheless believed in the Lord Jesus Christ and found eternal life. O you that have lived under the sound of the gospel from your childhood, the thief does not comfort you, but he accuses you! What are you doing to abide so long in unbelief? Will you never believe the testimony of divine love? What more shall I say to you? What more can anyone say to you?

What do you think must have converted this poor thief? It strikes me that it may have been—it must have been—*the sight of our great Lord and Savior.* There was, to begin with, our Savior's wonderful behavior on the road to the cross. Perhaps the robber had mixed up with all sorts of society, but he had never seen a man like this. Never had cross been carried by a cross bearer of his look and fashion. The robber wondered who this meek and majestic personage could be. He heard the women weep, and he wondered in himself whether anybody would ever weep for him. He thought that this must be some very singular person that the people should stand about him with tears in their eyes. When he heard that mysterious sufferer say so solemnly, "Daughters of Jerusalem, weep not for me, but for your children," he must have been struck with wonder. When he came to think, in his death pangs, of the singular look of pity which Jesus cast on the women, and of the self-forgetfulness which gleamed from his eyes, he was smitten with a strange relenting: it was as if an angel had crossed his path and opened his eyes to a new world, and to a new form of manhood, the like of which he had never seen before. He and his companion were coarse, rough fellows: this was a delicately formed and fashioned Being, of superior order to himself; yes, and of superior order to any other of the sons of men. Who could he be? What must he be? Though he could see that he suffered and fainted as he went along, he marked that there was no word of complaining, no note of execration, in return for the revilings cast upon him. His eyes looked love on those who glared on him with hate. Surely that march along the Via Dolorosa was the first part of the sermon which God preached to that bad man's heart. It was preached to many others who did not regard its teaching; but upon this man, by God's special grace, it had a softening effect when he came to think over it, and consider it. Was it not a likely and convincing means of grace?

When he saw the Savior surrounded by the Roman soldiery—saw the executioners bring forth the hammers and the nails, and lay him down upon his back, and drive the nails into his hands and feet, this crucified criminal was startled and astonished as he heard him say, "Father, forgive them; for they know not what they do." He himself, probably, had met his executioners with a curse; but he heard this man breathe a prayer to the great Father; and, as a Jew, as he probably was, he understood what was meant by such a prayer. But it did astound him to hear Jesus pray for his murderers. That was a petition the like of which he had never heard, nor even dreamed of. From whose lips could it come but from the lips of a divine Being? Such a loving, forgiving, Godlike prayer proved him to be the Messiah. Who else had ever prayed so? Certainly not David and the kings of Israel, who, on the contrary, in all honesty and heartiness imprecated the wrath of God upon their enemies. Elijah himself would not have prayed in that fashion, rather would he have called fire from heaven on the centurion and his company. It was a new, strange sound to him. I do not suppose that he appreciated it to the full; but I can well believe that it deeply impressed him, and made him feel that his fellow sufferer was a being about whom there was an exceeding mystery of goodness.

And when the cross was lifted up, that thief hanging up on his own cross looked around, and I suppose he could see that inscription written in three languages: "Jesus of Nazareth, the King of the Jews." If so, that writing was his little Bible, his New Testament, and he interpreted it by what he knew of the Old Testament. Putting this and that together—that strange person, incarnate loveliness, all patience and all majesty, that strange prayer, and now this singular inscription, surely he who knew the Old Testament, as I have no doubt he did, would say to himself, "Is this he? Is this truly the King of the Jews? This is he who worked miracles, and raised the dead, and said that he was the Son of God; is it all true, and is he really our Messiah?" Then he would remember the words of the prophet Isaiah, "He was despised and rejected of men, a man of sorrows, and acquainted with grief. Surely, he hath borne our griefs, and carried our sorrows." "Why," he would say to himself, "I never understood that passage in the prophet Isaiah before, but it must point to him. The chastisement of our peace is upon him. Can this be he who cried in the Psalms, 'they pierced my hands and my feet'?" As he looked at him again, he felt in his soul, "It must be he. Could there be another so like to him?" He felt conviction creeping over his spirit. Then he looked again, and he marked how all men down below rejected and despised and hissed at him and hooted him, and all this would make the case the more clear. "All they that see me laugh me to scorn: they shoot out the lip, they shake the head, saying, 'He trusted on the Lord that he would deliver him: let him deliver him, seeing he delighted in him.'"

Peradventure, *this dying thief read the gospel out of the lips of Christ's enemies.* They said, "He saved others." "Ah!" thought he, "did he save others? Why should he not save me?" What a grand bit of gospel that was for the dying thief, "He saved others!" I think I could swim to heaven on that plank, "He saved others"; because, if he saved others, he can of a surety save me.

Thus the very things that the enemies disdainfully threw at Christ would be gospel to this poor dying man. When it has been my misery to read any of the wretched prints that are sent us out of scorn, in which our Lord is held up to ridicule, I have thought, "Why, perhaps those who read these loathsome blasphemies may, nevertheless, learn the gospel from them!" You may pick a jewel from a dunghill and find its radiance undiminished; and you may gather the gospel from a blasphemous mouth, and it shall be nonetheless the gospel of salvation. Peradventure this man learned the gospel from those who jested at our dying Lord; and so the servants of the devil were unconsciously made to be the servants of Christ.

But, after all, surely that which won him most must have been *to look at Jesus again,* as he was hanging upon the cruel tree. Possibly nothing about the physical person of Christ would be attractive to him, for his visage was more marred than that of any man, and his form more than the sons of men; but yet there must have been in that blessed face a singular charm. Was it not the very image of perfection? As I conceive the face of Christ, it was very different from anything that any painter has yet been able to place upon his canvas. It was all goodness and kindness and unselfishness; and yet it was a royal face. It was a face of superlative justice and unrivaled tenderness. Righteousness and uprightness sat upon his brow; but infinite pity and goodwill to men had also there taken up their abode. It was a face that would have struck you at once as one by itself, never to be forgotten, never to be fully understood. It was all sorrow, yet all love; all meekness, yet all resolution; all wisdom, yet all simplicity; the face of a child, or an angel, and yet peculiarly the face of a man. Majesty and misery, suffering and sacredness, were therein strangely combined; he was evidently the Lamb of God, and the Son of man. As the robber looked, he believed. Is it not singular, the very sight of the Master won him? The sight of the Lord in agony and shame and death! Scarcely a word; certainly no sermon, no attending worship on the Sabbath; no reading of gracious books; no appeal from mother or teacher or friend; but the sight of Jesus won him. I put it down as a very singular thing, a thing for you and for me to recollect, and dwell upon, with quite as much vividness as we do upon the lateness of this robber's conversion.

Oh, that God of his mercy might convert everybody in this tabernacle! Oh, that I could have a share in it by the preaching of the word! But I will be equally happy if you get to heaven anyhow; yes, if the Lord should take you there without outward ministries, leading you to Jesus by some simple method such as he adopted with this thief. If you do but get there, he shall have the glory of it, and his poor servant will be overjoyed! Oh, that you would now look to Jesus and live! Before your eyes he is set forth, evidently crucified among you. Look to him and be saved, even at this hour.

II. But now I want you to think with me a little upon *the specialty of this man's faith,* for I think it was a very singular faith that this man exerted toward our Lord Jesus Christ.

I greatly question whether the equal and the parallel of the dying thief's faith will be readily found outside the Scriptures, or even in the Scriptures.

Observe, that this man believed in Christ *when he literally saw him dying the death of a felon,* under circumstances of the greatest personal shame. You have never realized what it was to be crucified. None of you could do that, for the sight has never been seen in our day in England. There is not a man or woman here who has ever realized in their own mind the actual death of Christ. It stands beyond us. This man saw it with his own eyes, and for him to call *him* "Lord" who was hanging on a gibbet, was no small triumph of faith. For him to ask Jesus to remember him when he came into his kingdom, though he saw that Jesus bleeding his life away and hounded to the death, was a splendid act of reliance. For him to commit his everlasting destiny into the hands of One who was, to all appearance, unable even to preserve his own life, was a noble achievement of faith. I say that this dying thief leads the vanguard in the matter of faith, for what he saw of the circumstances of the Savior was calculated to contradict rather than help his confidence. What he saw was to his hindrance rather than to his help, for he saw our Lord in the very extremity of agony and death, and yet he believed in him as the King shortly to come into his kingdom.

Recollect, too, that at that moment when the thief believed in Christ, *all the disciples had forsaken him and fled.* John might be lingering at a little distance, and holy women may have stood farther off, but no one was present bravely to champion the dying Christ. Judas had sold him, Peter had denied him, and the rest had forsaken him; and it was then that the dying thief called him "Lord," and said, "Remember me when thou comest into thy kingdom." I call that splendid faith. Why, some of you do not believe, though you are surrounded with Christian friends, though you are urged on by the testimony of those whom you regard with love; but this man, all alone, comes out, and calls Jesus his Lord! No one else was confessing Christ at that moment: no revival was around him with enthusiastic crowds: he was all by himself as a confessor of his Lord. After our Lord was nailed to the tree, the first to bear witness for him was this thief. The centurion bore witness afterward, when our Lord expired; but this thief was a lone confessor, holding onto Christ when nobody would say "Amen" to what he said. Even his fellow thief was mocking at the crucified Savior, so that this man shone as a lone star in the midnight darkness. O sirs, dare you be Daniels? Dare you stand alone? Would you dare to stand out amidst a ribald crew, and say, "Jesus is my King. I only ask him to remember me when he comes into his kingdom"? Would you be likely to avow such a faith when priests and scribes, princes and people, were all mocking at the Christ, and deriding him? Brethren, the dying robber exhibited marvelous faith, and I beg you to think of this next time you speak of him.

And it seems to me that another point adds splendor to that faith, namely, that *he himself was in extreme torture.* Remember, he was crucified. It was a crucified man trusting in a crucified Christ. Oh, when our frame is racked with torture, when the tenderest nerves are pained, when our body is hung up to die by we know not what great length of torment, then to forget the present and live in the future is a grand achievement of faith! While dying, to turn one's eye to another dying at your side, and trust your soul with him, is very marvelous faith. Blessed thief, because they put you down at the bottom, as one of the least of saints, I think that I must bid you come up higher and take one of the uppermost seats among those who by faith have glorified the Christ of God!

Why, see, dear friends, once more, the specialty of this man's faith was that *he saw so much,* though his eyes had been opened for so short a time! He saw the future world. He was not a believer in annihilation or in the possibility of a man's not being immortal. He evidently expected to be in another world and to be in existence when the dying Lord should come into his kingdom. He believed all that, and it is more than some do nowadays. He also believed that Jesus would have a kingdom, a kingdom after he was dead, a kingdom though he was crucified. He believed that he was winning for himself a kingdom by those nailed hands and pierced feet. This was intelligent faith, was it not? He believed that Jesus would have a kingdom in which others would share, and therefore he aspired to have his portion in it. But yet he had fit views of himself, and therefore he did not say, "Lord, let me sit at thy right hand"; or, "Let me share of the dainties of thy palace"; but he said only, "Remember me. Think of me. Cast an eye my way. Think of your poor dying comrade on the cross at your right hand. Lord, remember me. Remember me." I see deep humility in the prayer and yet a sweet, joyous, confident exaltation of the Christ at the time when the Christ was in his deepest humiliation.

O dear sirs, if any of you have thought of this dying thief only as one who put off repentance, I want you now to think of him as one that did greatly and grandly believe in Christ; and, oh, that you would do the same! Oh, that you would put a great confidence in my great Lord! Never did a poor sinner trust Christ too much. There was never a case of a guilty one, who believed that Jesus could forgive him, and afterward found that he could not—who believed that Jesus could save him on the spot, and then woke up to find that it was a delusion. No, plunge into this river of confidence in Christ. The waters are waters to swim in, not to drown in. Never did a soul perish that glorified Christ by a living, loving faith in him. Come, then, with all your sin, whatever it may be, with all your deep depression of spirit, with all your agony of conscience. Come along with you, and grasp my Lord and Master with both the hands of your faith, and he shall be yours, and you shall be his.

> Turn to Christ your longing eyes,
> View his bloody sacrifice:
> See in him your sins forgiven;
> Pardon, holiness, and heaven;
> Glorify the King of kings,
> Take the peace the gospel brings.

I think that I have shown you something special in the means of the thief's conversion, and in his faith in our dying Lord.

III. But now, third, as God shall help me, I wish to show you another specialty, namely, in *the result of his faith*.

"Oh," I have heard people say, "well, you see, the dying thief was converted; but then he was not baptized. He never went to communion and never joined the church!" He could not do either; and that which God himself renders impossible to us he does not demand of us. He was nailed to the cross; how could he be baptized? But he did a great deal more than that; for if he could not carry out the outward signs, he most manifestly exhibited the things which they signified, which, in his condition, was better still.

This dying thief first of all confessed the Lord Jesus Christ; and that is the very essence of baptism. He confessed Christ. Did he not acknowledge him to his fellow thief? It was as open a confession as he could make it. Did he not acknowledge Christ before all that were gathered around the cross who were within hearing? It was as public a confession as he could possibly cause it to be. Yet certain cowardly fellows claim to be Christians, though they have never confessed Christ to a single person, and then they quote this poor thief as an excuse. Are they nailed to a cross? Are they dying in agony? Oh no; and yet they talk as if they could claim the exemption which these circumstances would give them. What a dishonest piece of business!

The fact is, that our Lord requires an open confession as well as a secret faith; and if you will not render it, there is no promise of salvation for you, but a threat of being denied at the last. The apostle puts it, "If thou shalt confess with thy mouth the Lord Jesus, and shalt believe in thine heart that God hath raised him from the dead, thou shalt be saved." It is stated in another place upon this wise: "He that believeth and is baptized shall be saved"; that is Christ's way of making the confession of him. If there be a true faith, there must be a declaration of it. If you are candles, and God has lit you, "Let your light so shine before men, that they may see your good works, and glorify your Father which is in heaven." Soldiers of Christ must, like Her Majesty's soldiers, wear their regimentals; and if they are ashamed of their regimentals, they ought to be drummed out of the regiment. They are not honest soldiers who refuse to march in rank with their comrades. The very least thing that the Lord Jesus Christ can expect of us is that we do confess him to the best of our power. If you are nailed up to a cross, I will not invite you to be baptized. If you are fastened up to a tree to die, I will not ask you to come into this pulpit and declare your faith, for you cannot. But you are required to do what you can do, namely, to make as distinct and open an avowal of the Lord Jesus Christ as may be suitable in your present condition.

I believe that many Christian people get into a deal of trouble through not being honest in their convictions. For instance, if a man goes into a workshop, or a soldier into a barrack room, and if he does not fly his flag from the first, it will be very difficult for him to run it up afterward. But if he immediately and boldly lets them know, "I am a Christian man, and there are certain things that I cannot do to please you, and certain other things that I cannot help doing, though they displease you"—when that is clearly understood, after a while the singularity of the thing will be gone, and the man will be let alone; but if he is a little sneaky, and thinks that he is going to please the world and please Christ too, he is in for a rough time, let him depend upon it. His life will be that of a toad under a harrow, or a fox in a dog kennel, if he tries the way of compromise. That will never do. Come out. Show your colors. Let it be known who you are, and what you are; and although your course will not be smooth, it will certainly be not half so rough as if you tried to run with the hare and hunt with the hounds, a very difficult piece of business that.

This man came out, then and there, and made as open an avowal of his faith in Christ as was possible.

The next thing he did was to rebuke his fellow sinner. He spoke to him in answer to the ribaldry with which he had assailed our Lord. I do not know what the unconverted convict had been blasphemously saying, but his converted comrade spoke very honestly to him. "Dost not thou fear God, seeing thou art in the same condemnation? And we indeed justly; for we receive the due reward of our deeds: but this man hath done nothing amiss." It is more than ever needful in these days that believers in Christ should not allow sin to go unrebuked; and yet a great many of them do so. Do you not know that a person who is silent when a wrong thing is said or done may become a participator in the sin? If you do not rebuke sin—I mean, of course, on all fit occasions, and in a proper spirit—your silence will give consent to the sin, and you will be an aider and abettor in it. A man who saw a robbery and who did not cry, "Stop thief!" would be thought to be in league with the thief; and the man who can hear swearing or see impurity, and never utter a word of protest may well question whether he is right himself. Our "other men's sins" make up a great item in our personal guilt unless we in anywise rebuke them. This our Lord expects us to do. The dying thief did it, and did it with all his heart; and therein far exceeded large numbers of those who hold their heads high in the church.

Next, *the dying thief made a full confession of his guilt.* He said to him who was hanged with him, "Dost not thou fear God, seeing thou art in the same condemnation? *And we indeed justly.*" Not many words, but what a world of meaning was in them: "we indeed justly." "You and I are dying for our crimes," said he, "and we deserve to die." When a man is willing to confess that he deserves the wrath of God—that he deserves the suffering which his sin has brought upon him—there is evidence of sincerity in him. In this man's case, his repentance glittered like a holy tear in the eye of his faith, so that his faith was bejeweled with the drops of his penitence. As I have often told you, I suspect the faith which is not born as a twin with repentance; but there is no room for suspicion in the case of this penitent confessor. I pray God that you and I may have such a thorough work as this in our own hearts as the result of our faith.

Then, see, *this dying thief defends his Lord right manfully.* He says, "We indeed justly, but this man hath done nothing amiss." Was not that beautifully said? He did not say, "this man does not deserve to die," but, "this man hath done nothing amiss." He means that he is perfectly innocent. He does not even say, "he has done nothing wicked," but he even asserts that he has not acted unwisely or indiscreetly: "this man hath done nothing amiss." This is a glorious testimony of a dying man to one who was numbered with the transgressors, and was being put to death because his enemies falsely accused him. Beloved, I only pray that you and I may bear as good witness to our Lord as this thief did. He outruns us all. We need not think much of the coming of his conversion late in life; we may far rather consider how blessed was the testimony which he bore for his Lord when it was most needed. When all other voices were silent, one suffering penitent spoke out, and said, "this man hath done nothing amiss."

See, again, another mark of this man's faith. He prays, and *his prayer is directed to Jesus.* "Lord, remember me when thou comest into thy kingdom." True faith is always praying faith. "Behold, he prayeth" is one of the surest tests of the new birth. O friends, may we abound in prayer, for thus we shall prove that our faith in Jesus Christ is what it ought to be! This converted robber opened his mouth wide in prayer; he prayed with great confidence as to the coming kingdom, and he sought that kingdom first, even to the exclusion of all else. He might have asked for life or for ease from pain; but he prefers the kingdom, and this is a high mark of grace.

In addition to thus praying, you will see that *he adores and worships Jesus,* for he says, "Lord, remember me when thou comest into thy kingdom." The petition is worded as if he felt, "Only let Christ think of me, and it is enough. Let him but remember me, and the thought of his mind will be effectual for everything that I shall need in the world to come." This is to impute Godhead to Christ. If a man can cast his all upon the mere memory of a person, he must have a very high esteem of that person. If to be remembered by the Lord Jesus is all that this man asks or desires, he pays to the Lord great honor. I think that there was about his prayer a worship equal to the eternal hallelujahs of cherubim and seraphim. There was in it a glorification of his Lord which is not excelled even by the endless symphonies of angelic spirits who surround the throne. Thief, you have well done!

Oh, that some penitent spirit here might be helped thus to believe, thus to confess, thus to defend his Master, thus to adore, thus to worship; and then the age of the convert would be a matter of the smallest imaginable consequence.

IV. Now the last remark is this: There was something very special about the dying thief as to *our Lord's word to him about the world to come.*

He said to him, "Today shalt thou be with me in paradise." He only asked the Lord to remember him, but he obtained this surprising answer, "Today shalt thou be with me in paradise."

In some respects I envy this dying thief; for this reason: that when the Lord pardoned me, and pardoned the most of you, who are present, he did not give us a place in paradise that same day. We are not yet come to the rest which is promised to us. No, you are waiting here. Some of you have been waiting very long. It is thirty years with many of us. It is forty years, it is fifty years, with many others since the Lord blotted out your sins, and yet you are not with him in paradise. There is a dear member of this church who, I suppose, has known the Lord for seventy-five years, and she is still with us, having long passed the ninetieth year of her age. The Lord did not admit her to paradise on the day of her conversion. He did not take any one of us from nature to grace, and from grace to glory, in a day. We have had to wait a good while. There is something for us to do in the wilderness, and so we are kept out of the heavenly garden. I remember that Mr. Baxter said that he was not in a hurry to be gone to heaven; and a friend called upon Dr. John Owen, who had been writing about the glory of Christ, and asked him what he thought of going to heaven. That great divine replied, "I am longing to be there." "Why," said the other, "I have just spoken to holy Mr. Baxter, and he says that he would prefer to be here, since he thinks that he can be more useful on earth." "Oh!" said Dr. Owen, "my brother Baxter is always full of practical godliness, but for all that I cannot say that I am at all desirous to linger in this mortal state. I would rather be gone." Each of these men seems to me to have been the half of Paul. Paul was made up of the two, for he was desirous to depart, but he was willing to remain because it was needful for the people. We would put both together, and, like Paul, have a strong desire to depart and to be with Christ, and yet be willing to wait if we can do service to our Lord and to his church. Still, I think he has the best of it who is converted and enters heaven the same night. This robber breakfasted with the devil, but he dined with Christ on earth, and supped with him in paradise. This was short work, but blessed work. What a host of troubles he escaped! What a world of temptation he missed! What an evil world he quitted! He was just born, like a lamb dropped in the field, and then he was lifted into the Shepherd's bosom straight away. I do not remember the Lord ever saying this to anybody else. I daresay it may have happened that souls have been converted and have gone home at once; but I never heard of anybody that had such an assurance from Christ as this man had: "Verily, I say unto thee"; such a personal assurance: "Verily I say unto thee, Today shalt thou be with me in paradise." Dying thief, you were favored above many, "to be with Christ, which is far better," and to be with him so soon!

Why is it that our Lord does not thus imparadise all of us at once? It is because there is something for us to do on earth. My brethren, are you doing it? *Are you doing it?* Some good people are still on earth: but why? But why? What is the use of them? I cannot make it out. If they are indeed the Lord's people, what are they here for? They get up in the morning and eat their breakfast, and in due course eat their dinner, and their supper, and go to bed and sleep; at a proper hour they get up the next morning, and do the same as on the previous day. Is this living for Jesus? Is this life? It does not come to much. Can this be the life of God in man? O Christian people, do justify your Lord in keeping you waiting here! How can you justify him but by serving him to the utmost of your power? The Lord help you to do so! Why, you owe as much to him as the dying thief! I know I owe a great deal more. What a mercy it is to have been converted while you were yet a boy, to be brought to the Savior while you were yet a girl! What a debt of obligation young Christians owe to the Lord! And if this poor thief crammed a life full of testimony into a few minutes, ought not you and I, who are spared, for years after conversion, to perform good service for our Lord? Come, let us wake up if we have been asleep! Let us begin to live if we have been half dead. May the Spirit of God make something of us yet: so that we may go as industrious servants from the labors of the vineyard to the pleasures of the paradise! To our once crucified Lord be glory forever and ever! Amen.

Stephen: Stephen's Death

❧

Delivered on Lord's Day morning, May 24, 1874, at the Metropolitan Tabernacle, Newington. No. 1175.

And they stoned Stephen, calling upon God, and saying, "Lord Jesus, receive my spirit." And he kneeled down, and cried with a loud voice, "Lord, lay not this sin to their charge." And when he had said this, he fell asleep.
—ACTS 7:59–60

It is of the greatest service to us all to be reminded that our life is but a vapor, which appears for a little while and then vanishes away. Through forgetfulness of this, worldlings live at ease, and Christians walk carelessly. Unless we watch for the Lord's coming, worldliness soon eats into our spirit as does a canker. If you have this world's riches, believer, remember that this is not your rest, and set not too great a store by its comforts. If, on the other hand, you dwell in straitness, and are burdened with poverty, be not too much depressed thereby, for these light afflictions are but for a moment, and are not worthy to be compared with the glory which shall be revealed in us. Look upon the things that are as though they were not. Remember you are a part of a great procession which is always moving by; others come and go before your own eyes, you see them, and they disappear, and you yourself are moving onward to another and more real world. "'Tis greatly wise to talk with our last hours," to give a rehearsal of our departure, and to be prepared to stand before the great tribunal of the judgment. Our duty is to trim our lamps against the time when the Bridegroom comes; we are called upon to stand always ready, waiting for the appearing of our Lord and Savior Jesus Christ, or else for the summons which shall tell us that the pitcher is broken at the fountain, and the wheel broken at the cistern, that the body must return to the earth as it was, and the spirit unto God who gave it.

This death scene of Stephen's may aid our meditations while, by the help of the Holy Spirit, we cast our minds forward to the time when we also must fall asleep. This is the only martyrdom which is recorded in the New Testament in detail, the Holy Ghost foreseeing that there would be martyrdoms enough before the church's history would end, and that we should never lack memorials such as those with which Foxe's martyrology and works of the like order supply us. It is equally remarkable that this is the only death scene in the New Testament which has been described at length, with the exception of our Lord's. Of course we are told of the deaths of other saints, and facts relating thereto are mentioned, but what they said when they died, and how they felt in passing out of the world, are left unrecorded, probably because the Holy Spirit knew that we should never lack for holy deathbeds and triumphant departures. These he well knew would be everyday facts to the people of God. Perhaps, moreover, the Holy Spirit would have us gather from his silence that he would not have us attach so much importance to the manner of men's deaths as to the character of their lives. To live like Jesus most nearly concerns us; a triumphant death may be the crown, but a holy life is the head that must wear it. To obey our Lord's commands during our life is our most pressing business; we may leave the testimony of death to be given us in the selfsame hour. We shall have dying grace in dying moments, and at this present our chief business is to obtain the grace which will enable us to adorn the doctrine of God our Savior in all things. However, as we have this one case of Stephen given us at full length, we should prize it the more highly, and study it the more carefully, because it is the only one. Let us do so this morning.

There are three things upon which I shall speak: *The general character of Stephen's death*; second, *its most notable peculiarity*; and third, *things desirable in reference to death suggested to us by Stephen's departure*.

I. Let us look at Stephen's death, and notice *its general character.*

It strikes us at once that it happened in the very midst of his service. He had been appointed an officer of the church at Jerusalem, to see that the alms were distributed properly among the poor, especially among the Grecian widows. He discharged his duty to the satisfaction of the whole church, and thereby he did most useful service, for it gave the apostles opportunity to give themselves wholly to their true work, namely, that of preaching and prayer, and it is no small matter to be able to bear a burden for another if he is thereby set free for more eminent service than we could ourselves perform. If it be so that I cannot preach myself, yet if I can take away from one who does preach certain cares which burden him, if I thus enable him to preach the more and the better, I am virtually preaching myself. The care which Stephen exercised over the poor tended also to prevent heart burning and division, and this was a result of no mean order. But, not content with being a deacon, Stephen began to minister in holy things as a speaker of the word, and that with great power, for he was full of faith and of the Holy Ghost. He stands forth on the page of the church's history, for the time being, as quite a leading spirit; so much so, indeed, that the enemies of the gospel recognized his prominent usefulness and made him the object of their fiercest opposition, for they generally rage most against those who are doing most good. Stephen stood in the front rank of the Lord's host, and yet he was taken away! "A mystery," say some. "A great privilege," say I. My brethren, who desires to be removed at any other time? Is it not well to die in harness while yet you are useful? Who wants to linger till he becomes a burden rather than a help? If we are called to depart in the middle of service, we must submit to it thankfully, and may even wish to have it said of us, he did—

> His body with his charge lay down,
> And ceased at once to work and live.

He was removed in the very prime of his usefulness, just when many were being converted by his ministry, when, through his faith, miracles were being worked on all sides, when he seemed, indeed, to be necessary to the church. And is not this well? Well, first, that God should teach his people how much he can do by a man whom he chooses; well, next, that he should show them that he is not dependent upon any man, but can do his work even without the choicest laborer in his vineyard. If our life can teach one lesson, and when that is taught, if our death can teach another, it is well to live and well to die, and far more desirable than to tarry long and take one's flight in the dreary winter of declining influence. Let me be reaped, if I may venture on a choice, when my ministry shall be like the wheat in Pharaoh's dream, with seven ears rank and good, and not in a time when the east wind has shriveled me into barrenness. If God be glorified by our removal, is it not well? And may he not be more than ordinarily glorified when he lays us aside in order to show his church that he can do without his servants, or can raise up others in their stead? Happy is that messenger whose absence as well as his presence fulfills his Master's will.

But *Stephen's death was painful, and attended with much that flesh and blood would dread.* He died not surrounded by weeping friends, but by enemies who gnashed their teeth; no holy hymn made glad his death chamber, but the shouts and outcries of a maddened throng rang in his ears. For him no downy pillow, but the hard and cruel rocks; battered and bruised by a whirlwind of stones he laid him down to sleep, and woke up in the bosom of his Lord. Now brethren, this is all the more for our comfort, because if he died in perfect peace, no, in joy and triumph, how much more may we hope to depart in peace! Since we shall not have these grim attendants upon our departing hours, may we not hope that we shall be sustained and buoyed up by the presence of our Lord and Master even as he was, and grace will be made perfect in our weakness? Every circumstance tells on our side by way of comfort. If he slept amid a storm of stones, how may we hope to fall asleep right peacefully, in the same faith in Jesus, when the saints are gathered around our bed to bid us farewell!

More particularly, however, I want to call your attention to the fact that *Stephen's departing moments were calm, peaceful, confident, joyous.* He never flinched while he was addressing that infuriated audience. He told them the plain truth, with as much quiet deliberation as if he had been gratifying them with a pleasing discourse. When they grew angry he was not afraid; his lip did not quiver; he did not retract or soften down a single expression, but cut them to the heart with even more fidelity. With the courage of a man of God, his face was set as a flint. Knowing that he was now preaching his last sermon, he used the sharp two-edged sword of the Word, piercing into their very souls. Little cared he how they frowned; nothing was he abashed when they gnashed their teeth. He was as calm as the opened heaven above him, and continued so though they hurried him out of the city. When they had dragged him outside the gate, and stripped off their clothes to carry out his execution, he did not let fall a single timorous word or trembling cry; he stood up and committed his soul to God with calmness, and when the first murderous stones felled him to the earth he rose to his knees, still not to ask for pity, nor to utter a craven cry, but to plead with his Lord for mercy upon his assailants; then, closing his eyes like a child tired out with the sport of a long summer's day, and drops asleep upon its mother's lap, "he fell asleep."

Believe, then, O Christian, that if you abide in Christ, the like will be the case with you. You shall be undisturbed at the premonitions of decay; when the physician shakes his head your heart shall not fail; when friends look sad you will not share their sorrow. We wept when we were born though all around us smiled; so shall we smile when we die while all around us weep. The dying Christian is often the only calm and composed person in all the group which fills the chamber from which he ascends to heaven. Talking of what he enjoys and expects, he glides gently into glory. Why should we expect it to be otherwise? Stephen's God is our God; Stephen's faith we already possess in its germ, and we may have it in the same degree; the Holy Spirit dwells in us even as he did in Stephen, and if he puts not forth the same energy, what hinders him but our unbelief? Getting more faith we shall enjoy the same tranquil repose of spirit when our appointed hour shall come. Brethren, let us not fear death, but descend Jordan's shelving bank without the slightest dismay.

Some other points about Stephen's departure I beg you to notice, points relating to the state of his mind. *His mind was in a very elevated condition.* Here let us first remark *his intense sympathy with God.* All through that long speech of his you see that his soul is taken up with his God, and the treatment which he had received from Israel. He does not speak against his countrymen from any ill will, but he seems to take them very little into consideration. His God absorbs all his thoughts; and he tells how his God had sent Joseph, but his brethren persecuted him; his God had sent Moses, but they rebelled against him; his God had now sent Jesus, and they had been his betrayers and murderers. He had pity upon them in his heart, that is clearly seen in his dying prayer for them, but still his main feeling is sympathy with God in the rebellions which he had endured from the ungodly. Surely this is the mind which possesses the saints in heaven. I see, as I read Stephen's speech, that he regarded impenitent sinners from the standpoint of the saints above, who will be so taken up in sympathy with God, and the righteousness of his government, that the doom of the finally rebellious will cause them no pain. The triumph of right over willful wrong, of holiness over the foulest and most wanton sin, of justice over the ingratitude which made light of redeeming love, will clear the soul of all emotion but that which rejoices in every act of the most High, because it is and must be right. I know how easily this remark may be misrepresented; still it is true, and let it stand.

Notice, too, how *Stephen's mind clung only to that which is purely spiritual.* All ritualism was clean gone from him. I daresay at one time Stephen felt a great reverence for the temple; the first Jewish Christians still continued to feel a measure of that awe of the temple which, as Jews, they had formerly indulged; but Stephen says, "Howbeit the most High dwelleth not in temples made with hands; as saith the prophet, 'heaven is my throne and earth is my footstool: what house will ye build me? saith the Lord; or what is the place of my rest?'" It is noteworthy how the saints, when they are near to die, make very little of what others make a great deal of. What is ritual to a dying man— a man with his eyes opened, looking into the future, and about to meet his God? Sacraments are poor supports in the dying hour. Priestcraft, where is it? The reed has snapped beneath the weight of a burdened conscience, and the tremendous realities of death and judgment. The peculiar form of worship which a man contended for in health, and the little specialties of doctrines which he made much of aforetime, will seem little in comparison with the great spiritual essentials, when the soul is approaching the presence chamber of the Eternal. The saint in death is growingly spiritual, for he is nearing the land of spirits, and that city of which John said, "I saw no temple therein."

Brethren, it is a grand thing to grow in spiritual religion till you break the eggshell of form, and shake it off, for the outward fashion of ceremonies, and even of simplicities, is too often to men what the eggshell is to the living bird; and when the soul awakens into the highest forms of life, we chip and break that shell and leave our former bondage. Stephen came right away from those superstitious reverences, which still cast their blight over many Christians, and worshiped God, who is a Spirit, in spirit and in truth.

It is most clear *that he rose beyond all fear of men.* They grin at him, they howl at him, but what matters that to him? He will be put to a blasphemer's death outside the city by the hands of cruel men; but that daunts him not. His face glows with joy unspeakable; he looks not like a man hurried to his execution, but as one on the way to a wedding. He looks like an immortal angel rather than a man condemned to die. Ah, brethren, and so will it be with all the faithful! Today we fear man, who is but a worm; today we are so weak as to be swayed by the estimation of our fellows, and we listen to kindly voices, which counsel us to speak with bated breath upon certain points, lest we grieve this one or that; but the fitter we are for heaven, the more we scorn all compromise, and feel that for truth, for God, for Christ, we must speak out, even if we die, for who are we that we should be afraid of a man that shall die, and the son of man that is but a worm? It is a blessed thing if this shall be growingly our condition.

At the same time *Stephen was free from all cares.* He was a deacon, but he does not say, "What will those poor people do? How will the widows fare? Who will care for the orphans?" He does not even say, "What will the apostles do now that I can no longer take the labor from off their shoulders?" Not a word of it. He sees heaven opened, and thinks little of the church below, love it though he does with all his heart. He trusts the church militant with her Captain: he is called to the church triumphant. He hears the trumpet sound, "Up and away," and lo, he answers to the summons. Happy men who can thus cast off their cares and enter into rest. Why should it not be thus with us? Why, like Martha, do we allow our much serving to cumber us? Our Lord managed his church well enough before we were born; he will not be at a loss because he has called us home, and therefore we need not trouble ourselves as though we were all-important, and the church would pine for lack of us.

At the same time, *Stephen had no resentments.* That was a sweet prayer of his, "Lay not this sin to their charge." Just as Daniel before Belshazzar saw the scale and saw Belshazzar weighed in it and found wanting, so Stephen saw the balances of justice, and this murder of his, like a great weight, about to be placed in the scale against the raging Jews, and he cried, "Lord, cast not this sin into the balance." He could not say, as the Savior did, "They know not what they do," for they did know it and had been troubled by his speech, so that they stopped their ears, to hear no more; but he pleads for them as far as truth would permit him, while breathing out his soul. Every child of God ought to lay aside all resentments at once, or rather he should never have any. We are to carry in our hearts no remembrance of ills, but to live every day freely forgiving, as we are every day freely forgiven; but as we get nearer to heaven there must be growing love to those who hate us, for so shall we prove that we have been made ready for the skies.

To close up this description of his death, *Stephen died like a conqueror*. His name was *Stephanos*, or crown, and truly that day he not only received a crown, but he became the crown of the church as her first martyr. *He* was the conqueror, not his enemies. They stoned his body, but his soul had vanquished them. It was not in their power to move him; his quiet look defied their fury. He went home to his God to hear it said, "Servant of God, well done," and in nothing had his foes despoiled him on the way there. He was more than a conqueror through him that loved him. These are some of the characteristics of Stephen's departure, and I trust that in our measure they may be ours. God grant them to us, and we will give him all the glory.

II. Now I call your attention to a very interesting point—*the most notable peculiarity of Stephen's death.*

It was notable for this one point, that it was full of Jesus, and full of Jesus in four ways: Jesus was *seen*, *invoked*, *trusted*, and *imitated*.

First, *the Lord Jesus was seen*. The martyr looked up steadfastly into heaven and saw the glory of God, and Jesus standing on the right hand of God. At first he was probably in the council hall of the Sanhedrin, but the vision seemed to divide the roof, to roll away the firmament, and set open the gates of heaven, so that into its innermost chambers the anointed eye was able to gaze. It is said he saw *the Son of man*. Now this is the only place in Scripture where Jesus is called the Son of man by anyone but himself. He frequently called himself the Son of man, that was indeed a common name for himself, but his disciples did not call him so. Perhaps the glory of the rejected Messiah as man was the peculiar thought which was to be conveyed to Stephen's mind, to assure him that as the despised Lord had at length triumphed, so also should his persecuted servant. At all times it is a gladsome sight to see the representative man exalted to the throne of God, but it was peculiarly suitable for this occasion, for the Lord himself had warned his enemies, "Hereafter shall ye see the Son of man sitting on the right hand of power."

He had spoken those words to the very men who now heard Stephen bear witness that it was even so.

Stephen saw his Lord *standing*; now our Lord is generally described as sitting, but it was as if the sympathizing Lord had risen up to draw near to his suffering servant, eager both to sustain him and to receive him when the conflict was over. Jesus rose from the throne to gaze upon himself suffering again in the person of one of his beloved members. The place occupied by the Lord was "at the right hand of God." Stephen distinctly saw the ineffable brightness of eternal glory, which no human eye can see until strengthened by superior grace, and amid that glory he saw the Son of man in the place of love, power, and honor, worshiped and adored.

Now when we come to die, dear friends, we may not, perhaps, expect with these eyes to see what Stephen saw, but faith has a grand realizing power. The fact that Jesus is enthroned is always the same, and so long as we are sure that he is at the right hand of God, it little matters whether we see him with our natural eyes, for faith is the substance of things hoped for, and the evidence of things not seen. Brethren, if your faith shall be strong when you come to die, as doubtless it will be, you will have a sight and sense of Jesus in his manhood at the right hand of God, and this will effectually take away from you all fear of death; for you will feel, "If the man Christ is there, I, being already represented by him, shall also be there; I shall rise from the dead; I shall sit at the right hand of the Father; his eternal power and Godhead will raise me up to be where he is, for has he not said, "I will that they also whom thou hast given me be with me where I am"? I will, however, venture further. I am convinced, from my own observation, that not to a few but to many dying saints, something more is given than the realizations of faith. Much more frequently than we suppose, supernatural glimpses of the divine splendor are vouchsafed to the saints in the hour of their departure. I have heard persons comparatively uninstructed and certainly unimaginative speak of what they have seen in their last hour, in such a way that I am certain they never borrowed the expressions from books, but must have seen what they described. There has been a freshness about their descriptions which has convinced me they did see what they assured me they beheld; and, moreover, the joy which has resulted from it, the acquiescence in the divine will, the patience with which they have borne suffering, have gone far to prove that they were not under the influence of an idle imagination, but were really enabled to look within the veil. The flesh in its weakness becomes, if I may so say, a rarefied medium; the mists are blown away, the obscuring veil grows thinner, disease makes rents in it, and through the thin places and the rents the heavenly glory shines. Oh, how little will a man fear death, or care about pain, if he expects to breathe out his soul on a better Pisgah than Moses ever climbed! Well did we sing just now—I am sure I sang it with all my heart—

> *Oh, if my Lord would come and meet,*
> *My soul would stretch her wings in haste,*
> *Fly fearless through death's iron gate,*
> *Nor fear the terror as she passed.*

Now this model departure, which is given in Scripture as a type of Christian deaths, has this for its ensign, that Christ was visible; and such shall be the character of our departure, if through faith we are one with Jesus; therefore, let us not fear.

Next, notice that *Jesus was invoked*, for that is the meaning of the text. "They stoned Stephen, calling upon," or invoking, "and saying, 'Lord Jesus, receive my spirit.'" Dying Christians are not troubled with questions as to the deity of Christ. Dear friends, Unitarianism may do to live with, but it will not do to die with, at least for us. At such a time we need an almighty and divine Savior; we want "God over all, blessed forever" to come to our rescue in the solemn article. So Stephen called upon Jesus, and worshiped him. He makes no mention of any other intercessor. O martyr of Christ, why did you not cry, "Ave Maria! Blessed virgin, succor me"? Why did you not pray to St. Michael and all angels? Ah no! The abomination of saint and angel worship had not been invented in his day, and if it had been he would have scorned it as one of the foul devices of hell. There is "one mediator between God and men, the man Christ Jesus." He invoked Christ, and no one else.

Neither do we find him saying a word as to his good works and alms-deeds and sermons and miracles. No, he invoked the Lord Jesus and leaned on him wholly. Ah, brethren, it is well to live and to die resting wholly upon Jesus. If you lie down tonight and quietly think of your departure, and inquire whether you are ready to die, you will not feel at your ease till your heart stands at the foot of the cross, looking up and viewing the flowing of the Savior's precious blood, believing humbly that he made your peace with God. There is no right living, or joyful dying, except in invoking Christ.

What next did Stephen do? *He trusted Jesus* and confided in him only; for we find him saying, "Lord Jesus, receive my spirit." He felt that his spirit was about to leave the body to fly into the unknown world. Perhaps a shiver came over him of natural awe at the great mystery, even as it comes over us when we think of being disrobed of the familiar garment of our body; but he placed his unclothed spirit in the hands of Jesus, and his fear and care were over. See, he has quite done with it now! He prays no more for himself, but intercedes for his enemies; and then closes his eyes and falls asleep. This is the simple and sublime art of dying. Once more we take our guilty soul and place it in the dear pierced hand of him who is able to keep it; and then we feel assured that all is safe. The day's work is done, the doors are fastened, the watchman guards the streets; come, let us fall asleep. With Jesus seen, invoked, and trusted, it is sweet to die.

Notice, once again, that in Stephen we see *Jesus imitated*, the death of Stephen is a reproduction of the death of Jesus; let us hope that ours will be the same. It was so, even in little circumstances. Jesus died without [outside] the gate, so did Stephen; Jesus died praying, so did Stephen; Jesus died saying, "Father, into thy hands I commit my spirit"; Stephen cannot approach God absolutely, but he approaches him through the Mediator, and he says, "Lord Jesus, receive my spirit." Christ dies pleading for his murderers, so does Stephen: "Lord, lay not this sin to their charge." Now, if our death shall be a reproduction of the death of Jesus, why need we fear? It has hitherto been sweet to be made like him, and it will still be sweet: even to suffer with him has been delightful; surely it will be joyful to die with him. We are willing to sleep in Jesus' bed and lie as he did in the bosom of the earth, to arise in his likeness at the resurrection.

Thus you see, dear brethren, that Stephen's death was radiant with the glow of his Lord's brightness. Christ was glorified and reflected in him. None could question whose image and superscription he bore. If our lives shall be of that order, our deaths also shall be of the like character. Let your life be looking unto Jesus, pleading with Jesus, trusting in Jesus, copying Jesus, and then your departing moments will be attended by visions of Jesus and reproductions of his dying behavior. As you have been with him in the trials of life, he will be with you in the closing scenes of death. Happy they whose deathbed Jesus makes, and who sleep in Jesus, to be brought with him when he returns to take the kingdom.

III. From Stephen's departure we gather something as to *the kind of death which we may wisely desire.*

First, it is very desirable that *our death should be of a piece with our life.* Stephen was full of faith and of the Holy Ghost in life, and so was he full of the Holy Ghost in death. Stephen was bold, brave, calm, and composed in life; he is the same amid the falling stones. It is very sad when the reported account of a man's death does not fit in with his life. I am afraid that many funeral sermons have done great mischief by their flattery, for persons have very naturally said, "This is very strange, I never knew that the departed person was a saint until I heard this account of his end. Really, when I hear these wonderful things about him—well, I should not have thought it." No, it will not do to have no character for piety but that which is hurriedly run up in a few days of sickness and death. It is ill to die with a jerk, getting as it were upon another line of rails all on a sudden. It is better to glide from one degree of grace to another, and so to glory. We ought to die daily, die every morning before we go down to breakfast, that is to say, we should rehearse it all, so that when we come to die it will be no new thing to us. Death may be the fringe or border of life, but it should be made out of the same piece. A life of clay is not to be joined to a death of gold. We cannot hope to dine with the world and sup with God. We ought to dwell in the house of the Lord every day.

Again, it is most desirable that *death should be the perfecting of our whole career*, the putting of the cornerstone upon the edifice, so that when nothing else is wanted to complete the man's labors he falls asleep. Dear brethren, is it so with you? Suppose you were to die this morning in the pew; would your life be a complete life, or would it be like a broken column snapped off in the center? Why, there are some who even in their business lives have left many needful things undone; for instance, they have not made their wills yet and will cause much sorrow to wife and children through their neglect. Some Christian people do not keep their worldly affairs in proper order, but are lax, disorderly, and slovenly, so that if they were to die, there would be many things because of which they would feel loathe to die. Mr. Whitefield used to say when he went to bed at night, "I have not left even a pair of gloves out of their place: if I die tonight, all my affairs, for time and eternity, are in order." That is the best way to live; so that, let death come when it may, at midnight, cock-crowing, or midday, it will be a desirable *finis* to a book of which we have written the last line; we have finished our course, and served our generation, and our falling asleep is the fit conclusion of the matter.

May our death not be one of a kind which needs flurry and hot haste to make the man ready. There are people in the world who, if they were going off by train and knew of it a month beforehand, would be all in a fever an hour before they started; though they know the time the train starts, they cannot arrive a few minutes before by any means, but rush in just as the bell rings, and leap into a carriage only in time to save the train. Some die in that fashion, as if they had so much to do and were in such a hurry; and besides, had so little grace that they could be only saved so as by fire. When worldly Christians die, there is a deal to be done to pack up and get ready for departing; but a true Christian stands with his loins girded, he knows he has to travel; he does not know exactly when, but he stands with his staff in his hand. He knows the Bridegroom is soon coming, and he therefore keeps his lamp well trimmed. That is the way to live and the way to die. May the Holy Spirit put us in such a condition, that the angel of death may not summon us unawares, or catch us by surprise; then will going home be nothing out of the common way, but a simple matter. Bengel, the famous commentator, did not wish to die in spiritual parade, with a sensational scene, but to pass away like a person called out to the street door from the midst of business. His prayer was granted. He was revising the proof sheets of his works almost to the moment when he felt the death stroke. Is not this well? Equally desirable was the end of the Venerable Bede, who died as he completed his translation of the gospel of John. "Write quickly," said he, "for it is time for me to return to him who made me." "Dear master," said the pupil, "one sentence is still wanting." "Write quickly," said the venerable man. The young man soon added, "It is finished"; and Bede replied, "Thou hast well said, all is now finished," and he fell asleep. So would I desire to depart, so might every Christian desire; we would make no stir from our daily holiness, we would change our place but not our service; having waited on our Lord at this end of the room, we are called up higher, and we go.

It must be a dreadful thing for a professing Christian to die full of regrets for work neglected and opportunities wasted. It is sad to have to say, "I must leave my Sunday school class before I have earnestly warned those dear children to flee from the wrath to come." It would be wretched for me to go home today and say, "I have preached my last sermon, but it was not earnest nor calculated either to glorify God or benefit my fellowmen." Can the end of a wasted life be other than unhappy? Will it not be sorrowful to be called away with work undone and purposes unfulfilled? O my brethren, do not live so as to make it hard to die.

It must also be a sad thing to be taken away unwillingly, plucked like an unripe fruit from the tree. The unripe apple holds fast to its place, and so do many hold hard to their riches and cleave so fondly to worldly things that it needs a sharp pull to separate them from the world. The ripe fruit adheres but lightly, and when a gentle hand comes to take it, it yields itself freely, as if willing to be gathered, like an apple of gold into a basket of silver. God make you unworldly, and forbid that you should cleave so resolutely to things below as to make death a violence and departure a terror.

Brethren, we would not wish to die so that it should be a matter of question, especially to ourselves, to which place we are going, and yet you will die in that way if you live in that way. If you have no assurance of salvation, do you expect it to come to you on your dying bed? Why, my dear friend, when the pain increases and the brain becomes weary, you are very likely to suffer depression, and therefore you need strong faith to begin with for your own comfort then. Would you like friends to go out of your death chamber saying, "We hope he is saved, but we stand in doubt concerning him"? Your life should prevent that. Holy Mr. Whitefield, when someone observed, "I should like to hear your dying testimony," said, "No, I shall, in all probability bear no dying testimony." "Why not?" said the other. "Because I am bearing testimony every day while I live, and there will be the less need of it when I die." That seraphic apostle preached up to the last afternoon, and then went upstairs to bed and died. There was no need for anyone to ask, "What did he say when he was dying?" Ah no; they knew what he said when he was living, and that was a great deal better. Let your testimony in life be such that, whether you speak or not in your last moments, there shall be no question about whose you were nor whom you served.

In conclusion, one would desire to die so that *even our death should be useful*. I feel persuaded that Stephen's death had a great deal to do with Saul's conversion. Have you ever observed the evident influence of Stephen upon Paul? Augustine says, "If Stephen had never prayed, Saul had never preached." I do not say that the death of Stephen converted Saul; far from it; that change was worked by a divine interposition when Saul was on the road to Damascus; but what he saw in Stephen's martyrdom had made the soil ready to receive the good seed. Saul, in after life, seems to me to be always taking his text from Stephen's sermon. Read that sermon through at home, and see if it is not so. Stephen spoke about the covenant of circumcision, and that was a very favorite topic with Paul. When Paul stood at Athens on Mars' Hill and addressed the Areopagites he said to them, "God that made heaven and earth dwelleth not in temples made with hands," almost the identical words which Stephen had quoted, and surely the remembrance of Stephen before the Sanhedrin must have rushed over the apostle's mind at the time. There is yet another passage—and indeed I might carry on the parallel a very long way—where Stephen used the expression, "They received the law by the disposition of angels," an idea peculiar to Paul. Paul is the child of Stephen; Stephen dying is the seed out of which Paul springs up. What a privilege so to die that a phoenix may rise out of our ashes! If we have been useful ourselves up to the measure of a moderate ability, we may, as we die, call forth greater workers than ourselves; our expiring spark may kindle the divine light in some flaming beacon, which far across the seas shall scatter the beams of gospel light. And why not? God grant that we may, both in life and in death, serve him well. I would that even in our ashes might live our former lives, that being dead we yet may speak.

It was a happy thought of an earnest divine, who asked that when he was dead he might be placed in his coffin where all his congregation might come and see him, and that on his bosom should be placed a paper bearing this exhortation, "Remember the words which I have spoken to you, being yet present with you." Yes, we will go on telling of Jesus and winning souls in life and death, if God so helps us. Beloved believers, love the souls of men, and pray God to save them. As for you who are not saved yourselves, I implore you think of what your condition will be when you come to die; or, if a seared conscience should cause you to die in peace, think what you will do at the judgment, when that conscience will become tender. What will you do when the lips of the dear Redeemer shall say, "Depart, ye cursed, into everlasting fire in hell"?

> Ye sinners, seek his grace,
> Whose wrath ye cannot bear;
> Look to the dying Savior's face,
> And find salvation there.

Paul: As Pattern Convert

Published on Thursday, August 14, 1913; delivered at the Metropolitan Tabernacle, Newington. No. 3367.

> *Howbeit for this cause I obtained mercy, that in me first Jesus Christ might show forth all longsuffering, for a pattern to them which should hereafter believe on him to life everlasting.*—1 TIMOTHY 1:16

It is a vulgar error that the conversion of the apostle Paul was an uncommon and exceptional event, and that we cannot expect men to be saved nowadays after the same fashion. It is said that the incident was an exception to all rules, a wonder altogether by itself. Now my text is a flat contradiction to that notion, for it assures us that, instead of the apostle as a receiver of the longsuffering and mercy of God being at all an exception to the rule, he was a model convert, and is to be regarded as a type and pattern of God's grace in other believers. The apostle's language in the text, "for a pattern," may mean that he was what printers call a first proof, an early impression from the engraving, a specimen of those to follow. He was the typical instance of divine longsuffering, the model after which others are fashioned. To use a metaphor from the artist's studio, Paul was the ideal sketch of a convert, an outline of the work of Jesus on mankind, a cartoon of divine longsuffering. Just as artists make sketches in charcoal as the basis of their work, which outlines they paint out as the picture proceeds, so did the Lord in the apostle's case make, as it were, a cartoon or outline sketch of his usual work of grace. That outline in the case of each future believer he works out with infinite variety of skill, and produces the individual Christian, but the guiding lines are really there. All conversions are in a high degree similar to this pattern conversion. The transformation of persecuting Saul of Tarsus into the apostle Paul is a typical instance of the work of grace in the heart.

We will have no other preface, but proceed at once to two or three considerations. The first is that—

I. *In the conversion of Paul, the Lord had an eye to others, and in this Paul is a pattern.*

In every case the individual is saved, not for himself alone, but with a view to the good of others. Those who think the doctrine of election to be harsh should not deny it, for it is scriptural; but they may to their own minds soften some of its hardness by remembering that elect men bear a marked connection with the race. The Jews, as an elect people, were chosen in order to preserve the oracles of God for all nations and for all times. Men personally elected unto eternal life by divine grace are also elected that they may become chosen vessels to bear the name of Jesus unto others. While our Lord is said to be the Savior specially of them that believe, he is also called the Savior of all men; and while he has a special eye to the good of the one person whom he has chosen, yet through that person he has designs of love to others, perhaps even to thousands yet unborn.

The apostle Paul says, "I obtained mercy, that in me foremost Jesus Christ might show forth all longsuffering, for a pattern to them which should hereafter believe." Now, I think I see very clearly that *Paul's conversion had an immediate relation to the conversion of many others*. It had a tendency, had it not, to excite an interest in the minds of his brother Pharisee? Men of his class, men of culture, who were equally at home with the Greek philosophers and with the Jewish rabbis, men of influence, men of rank, would be sure to inquire, "What is this new religion which has fascinated Saul of Tarsus? That zealot for Judaism has now become a zealot for Christianity; what can there be in it?" I say that the natural tendency of his conversion was to awaken inquiry and thought, and so to lead others of his rank to become believers. And, my dear friend, if you have been saved, you ought to regard it as a token of God's mercy to your class. If you are a workingman, let your salvation be a blessing to the men with whom you labor. If you are a person of rank and station, consider that God intends to bless you to some with whom you are on familiar terms. If you are young, hope that God will bless the youth around you, and if you have come to older years, hope that your conversion, even at the eleventh hour, may be the means of encouraging other aged pilgrims to seek and find rest unto their souls. The Lord, by calling one out of any society of men, finds for himself a recruiting officer, who will enlist his fellows beneath the banner of the cross. May not this fact encourage some seeking soul to hope that the Lord may save him, though he be the only thoughtful person in all his family, and then make him to be the means of salvation to all his kindred.

We notice that *Paul often used the narrative of his conversion as an encouragement to others*. He was not ashamed to tell his own life story. Eminent soul winners, such as Whitefield and Bunyan, frequently pleaded God's mercy to themselves as an argument with their fellowmen. Though great preachers of another school, such as Robert Hall and Chalmers, do not mention themselves at all, and I can admire their abstinence, yet I am persuaded that if some of us were to follow their example, we should be throwing away one of the most powerful weapons of our warfare. What can be more affecting, more convincing, more overwhelming than the story of divine grace told by the very man who has experienced it? It is better than a score of tales of converted Africans, and infinitely more likely to win men's hearts than the most elaborate essays upon moral excellence. Again and again, Paul gave a long narrative of his conversion, for he felt it to be one of the most telling things that he could relate.

Whether he stood before Felix or Agrippa, this was his plea for the gospel. All through his epistles there are continual mentions of the grace of God toward himself, and we may be sure that the apostle did right thus to argue from his own case: it is fair and forcible reasoning, and ought by no means to be left unused because of a selfish dread of being called egotistical. God intends that we should use our conversion as an encouragement to others, and say to them, "Come and hear, all you that fear God, and I will tell you what he has done for my soul." We point to our own forgiveness and say, "Do but trust in the living Redeemer, and you shall find, as we have done, that Jesus blots out the transgressions of believers."

Paul's conversion was an encouragement to him all his life long to have hope for others. Have you ever read the first chapter of the epistle to the Romans? Well, the man who penned those terrible verses might very naturally have written at the end of them, "Can these monsters be reclaimed? It can be of no avail whatever to preach the gospel to people so sunken in vice." That one chapter gives as daring an outline as delicacy would permit of the nameless, shameful vices into which the heathen world had plunged, and yet, after all, Paul went forth to declare the gospel to that filthy and corrupt generation, believing that God meant to save a people out of it. Surely one element of his hope for humanity must have been found in the fact of his own salvation; he considered himself to be in some respects as bad as the heathen, and in other respects even worse: he calls himself the *foremost* of sinners (that is the word); and he speaks of God having saved him foremost, that in him he might show forth all longsuffering. Paul never doubted the possibility of the conversion of a person however infamous, after he had himself been converted. This strengthened him in battling with the fiercest opponents—he who overcame such a wild beast as I was, can also tame others and bring them into willing captivity to his love.

There was yet another relation between Paul's conversion and the salvation of others, and it was this: *It served as an impulse,* driving him forward in his life-work of bringing sinners to Christ.

"I obtained mercy," said he, "and that same voice which spoke peace to me said, 'I have made thee a chosen vessel unto me to bear my name among the gentiles.'" And he did bear it, my brethren. Going into regions beyond that, he might not build on another man's foundation, he became a master builder for the church of God. How indefatigably did he labor! With what vehemence did he pray! With what energy did he preach! Slander and contempt he bore with the utmost patience. Scourging or stoning had no terrors for him. Imprisonment, yes, death itself, he defied; nothing could daunt him. Because the Lord had saved him, he felt that he must by all means save some. He could not be quiet. Divine love was in him like a fire, and if he had been silent, he would ere long have had to cry with the prophet of old, "I am weary with restraining." He is the man who said, "Necessity is laid upon me; yea, woe is unto me, if I preach not the gospel." Paul, the extraordinary sinner, was saved that he might be full of extraordinary zeal and bring multitudes to eternal life. Well could he say—

> The love of Christ doth me constrain
> To seek the wandering souls of men;
> With cries, entreaties, tears to save,
> To snatch them from the fiery wave.
>
> My life, my blood, I here present,
> If for thy truth they may be spent;
> Fulfill thy sovereign counsel, Lord!
> Thy will be done, thy name adored!

Now, I will pause here a minute to put a question. You profess to be converted, my dear friend. What relation has your conversion already had to other people? It ought to have a very apparent one. Has it had such? Mr. Whitefield said that when his heart was renewed, his first desire was that his companions with whom he had previously wasted his time might be brought to Christ. It was natural and commendable that he should begin with them. Remember how one of the apostles, when he discovered the Savior, went immediately to tell his brother. It is most fitting that young people should spend their first religious enthusiasm upon their brothers and sisters. As to converted parents, their first responsibility is in reference to their sons and daughters. Upon each renewed man, his natural affinities, or the bonds of friendship, or the looser ties of neighborhood should begin to operate at once, and each one should feel, "No man liveth unto himself."

If divine grace has kindled a fire in you, it is that your fellowmen may burn with the same flame. If the eternal fount has filled you with living water, it is that out of the midst of you should flow rivers of living water. You are blessed that you may bless; whom have you blessed yet? Let the question go around. Do not avoid it. This is the best return that you can make to God, that when he saves you, you should seek to be the instruments in his hands of saving others. What have you done yet? Did you ever speak with the friend who shares your pew? He's been sitting there for a long time, and may, perhaps, be an unconverted person; have you pointed him to the Lamb of God? Have you ever spoken to your servants about their souls? Have you yet broken the ice sufficiently to speak to your own sister or your own brother? Do begin, dear friend.

You cannot tell what mysterious threads connect you with your fellowmen and their destiny. There was a cobbler once, as you know, in Northamptonshire. Who could see any connection between him and the millions of India? But the love of God was in his bosom, and Carey could not rest till, at Serampore, he had commenced to translate the Word of God and preach to his fellowmen. We must not confine our thoughts to the few whom Carey brought to Christ, though to save one soul is worthy of a life of sacrifice, but Carey became the forerunner and leader of a missionary band which will never cease to labor till India bows before Emmanuel. That man mysteriously drew, is drawing, and will draw India to the Lord Jesus Christ. Brother, you do not know what your power is. Awake and try it.

Did you never read this passage: "Thou hast given him power over all flesh, that he should give eternal life to as many as thou hast given him"? Now the Lord has given to his Son power over all flesh, and with a part of that power Jesus clothes his servants. Through you, he will give eternal life to certain of his chosen; by you, and by no other means, will they be brought to himself. Look about you, regenerate man. Your life may be made sublime. Rouse yourself! Begin to think of what God may do by you! Calculate the possibilities which be before you with the eternal God as your helper. Shake yourself from the dust and put on the beautiful garments of disinterested love to others, and it shall yet be seen how grandly gracious God has been to hundreds of men by having converted you. So far, then, Paul's salvation, because it had so clear a reference to others, was a pattern of all conversions.

II. Now, second, *Paul's foremost position as a sinner did not prevent his becoming foremost in grace, and herein again he is a pattern to us.*

Foremost in sin, he became also foremost in service. Saul of Tarsus was a *blasphemer,* and he is to be commended because he has not recorded any of those blasphemies. We can never object to converted burglars and chimney sweepers, of whom we hear so much, telling the story of their conversion; but when they go into dirty details, they had better hold their tongues. Paul tells us that he was a blasphemer, but he never repeats one of the blasphemies. We invent enough evil in our own hearts without being told of other men's stale profanities. If, however, any of you are so curious as to want to know what kind of blasphemies Paul could utter, you have only to converse with a converted Jew, and he will tell you what horrible words some of his nation will speak against our Lord. I have no doubt that Paul in his evil state thought as wickedly of Christ as he could—considered him to be an imposter, called him so, and added many an opprobrious epithet. He does not say of himself that he was an unbeliever and an objector, but he says that he was a blasphemer, which is a very strong word, but not too strong, for the apostle never went beyond the truth. He was a downright, thoroughgoing blasphemer, who also caused others to blaspheme. Will these lines meet the eye of a profane person who feels the greatness of his sin? May God grant that he may be encouraged to seek mercy as Saul of Tarsus did, for "all manner of sin and blasphemy" does he forgive unto men.

From blasphemy, which was the sin of the lips, Saul proceeded *to persecution,* which is a sin of the hands. Hating Christ, he hated his people too. He was delighted to give his vote for the death of Stephen, and he took care of the clothes of those who stoned that martyr. He hauled men and women to prison, and compelled them to blaspheme. When he had hunted all Judea as closely as he could, he obtained letters to go to Damascus, that he might do the same in that place. His prey had been compelled to quit Jerusalem and fly to more remote places, but "being exceeding mad against them, he persecuted them unto strange cities." He was foremost in blasphemy and persecution. Will a persecutor read or hear these words? If so, may he be led to see that even for him pardon is possible. Jesus, who said, "Father, forgive them; for they know not what they do," is still an Intercessor for the most violent of his enemies.

He adds, next, that he was *injurious,* which, I think, Bengel considers to mean that he was a despiser: that eminent critic says—blasphemy was his sin toward God, persecution was his sin toward the church, and despising was his sin in his own heart. He was injurious—that is, he did all he could to damage the cause of Christ, and he thereby injured himself. He kicked against the pricks and injured his own conscience. He was so determined against Christ that he counted no cost too great by which he might hinder the spread of the faith, and he did hinder it terribly; he was a ringleader in resisting the Spirit of God which was then working with the church of Christ. He was foremost in opposition to the cross of Christ.

Now notice that he was saved as a pattern, which is to show you that if you also have been foremost in sin, you also may obtain mercy, as Paul did: and to show you yet again that if you have not been foremost, the grace of God, which is able to save the chief of sinners, can assuredly save those who are of less degree. If the bridge of grace will carry the elephant, it will certainly carry the mouse. If the mercy of God could bear with the hugest sinners, it can have patience with you. If a gate is wide enough for a giant to pass through, any ordinary-sized mortal will find space enough. Despair's head is cut off and stuck on a pole by the salvation of "the chief of sinners." No man can now say that he is too great a sinner to be saved, because the chief of sinners was saved eighteen hundred years ago. If the ringleader, the chief of the gang, has been washed in the precious blood, and is now in heaven, why not I? Why not *you*?

After Paul was saved, he became a foremost saint. The Lord did not allot him a second-class place in the church. He had been the leading sinner, but his Lord did not, therefore, say, "I save you, but I shall always remember your wickedness to your disadvantage." Not so: he counted him faithful, putting him into the ministry and into the apostleship, so that he was not a whit behind the very chief of the apostles. Brother, there is no reason why, if you have gone very far in sin, you should not go equally far in usefulness. On the contrary, there is a reason why you should do so, for it is a rule of grace that to whom much is forgiven, the same loves much, and much love leads to much service.

What man was more clear in his knowledge of doctrine than Paul? What man more earnest in the defense of truth? What man more self-sacrificing? What man more heroic? The name of Paul in the Christian church stands in some respects the very next to the Lord Jesus. Turn to the New Testament and see how large a space is occupied by the Holy Spirit speaking through his servant Paul; and then look over Christendom and see how greatly the man's influence is still felt, and must be felt till his Master shall come. O great sinner, if you are even now ready to scoff at Christ, my prayer is that he may strike you down at this very moment, and turn you into one of his children, and make you to be just as ardent for the truth as you are now earnest against it, as desperately set on good as now you are on evil. None make such mighty Christians and such fervent preachers as those who are lifted up from the lowest depths of sin and washed and purified through the blood of Jesus Christ. May grace do this with you, my dear friend, whoever you may be.

Thus we gather from our text that the Lord showed mercy to Paul, that in him foremost it might be seen that prominence in sin is no barrier to eminence in grace, but the very reverse. Now I come to where the stress of the text lies.

III. *Paul's case was a pattern of other conversions as an instance of longsuffering.*

"That in me foremost Jesus Christ might show forth all longsuffering, for a cartoon or pattern to them which should hereafter believe." Thoughtfully observe the great longsuffering of God to Paul: he says, "He showed forth all longsuffering." Not only all the longsuffering of God that ever was shown to anybody else, but all that could be supposed to exist—all longsuffering.

> *All thy mercy's height I prove,*
> *All its depth is found in me,*

as if he had gone to the utmost stretch of his tether in sin, and the Lord also had strained his longsuffering to its utmost.

That longsuffering was seen first *in sparing his life* when he was rushing headlong in sin, breathing out threatenings, foaming at the mouth with denunciations of the Nazarene and his people. If the Lord had but lifted his finger, Saul would have been crushed like a moth, but almighty wrath forbore, and the rebel lived on. Nor was this all; after all his sin, the Lord allowed mercy to be possible to him. He blasphemed and persecuted, at a red-hot rate; and is it not a marvel that the Lord did not say, "Now, at last, you have gone beyond all bearing, and you shall die like Herod, eaten of worms"? It would not have been at all wonderful if God had so sentenced him; but he allowed him to live within the reach of mercy, and, better still, he in due time actually sent the gospel to him, and laid it home to his heart. In the very midst of his rebellion the Lord saved him. He had not prayed to be converted, far from it; no doubt he had that very day along the road to Damascus profaned the Savior's name, and yet mighty mercy burst in and saved him purely by its own spontaneous native energy. Oh, mighty grace, free grace, victorious grace! This was longsuffering indeed!

When divine mercy had called Paul, *it swept all his sin away*, every particle of it, his bloodshedding and his blasphemy, all at once, so that never man was more assured of his own perfect cleansing than was the apostle. "There is therefore now," says he, "no condemnation to them which are in Christ Jesus." "Therefore, being justified by faith, we have peace with God." "Who shall lay anything to the charge of God's elect?" You know how clear he was about that; and he spoke out of his own experience. Longsuffering had washed all his sins away. Then that longsuffering reaching from the depths of sin lifted him right up to the apostleship, so that he began to prove God's longsuffering in its heights of favor. What a privilege it must have been to him to be permitted to preach the gospel. I should think sometimes when he was preaching most earnestly, he would half stop himself and say, "Paul, is this you?" When he went down to Tarsus especially he must have been surprised at himself and at the mighty mercy of God. He preached the faith which once he had destroyed. He must have said many a time after a sermon, when he went home to his bedchamber, "Marvel of marvels! Wonder of wonders, that I who once could curse have now been made to preach—that I, who was full of threatening and even breathed out slaughter, should now be so inspired by the Spirit of God that I weep at the very sound of Jesus' name, and count all things but loss for the excellency of the knowledge of Christ Jesus my Lord."

O brothers and sisters, you do not measure longsuffering except you take it in all its length from one end to the other, and see God in mercy not remembering his servant's sin, but lifting him into eminent service in his church. Now this was for a pattern, to show you that he will show forth the same longsuffering to those who believe. If you have been a swearer, he will cleanse your blackened mouth, and put his praises into it. Have you had a black, cruel heart, full of enmity to Jesus? He will remove it and give you a new heart and a right spirit. Have you dived into all sorts of sins? Are they so shameful that you dare not think of them? Think of the precious blood which removes every stain. Are your sins so many that you could not count them? Do you feel as if you were almost damned already in the very memory of your life? I do not wonder at it, but he is able to save to the uttermost them that come unto God by him. You have not gone further than Saul had gone, and therefore all longsuffering can come to you, and there are great possibilities of future holiness and usefulness before you. Even though you may have been a streetwalker or a thief, yet if the grace of God cleanses you, it can make something wonderful out of you: full many a lustrous jewel of Emmanuel's crown has been taken from the dunghill. You are a rough block of stone, but Jesus can fashion and polish you, and set you as a pillar in his temple.

Brother, do not despair. See what Saul was and what Paul became, and learn what you may be. Though you deserve the depths of hell, yet up to the heights of heaven grace can lift you. Though now you feel as if the fiends of the pit would be fit companions for such a lost spirit as yourself, yet believe in the Lord Jesus, and you shall one day walk among the angels as pure and white as they. Paul's experience of longsuffering grace was meant to be a pattern of what God will do for you.

> Scripture says, "Where sin abounded,
> There did grace much more abound";
> Thus has Satan been confounded,
> And his own discomfit found.
> Christ has triumphed!
> Spread the glorious news around.
>
> Sin is strong, but grace is stronger;
> Christ than Satan more supreme;
> Yield, oh, yield to sin no longer,
> Turn to Jesus, yield to him—
> He has triumphed!
> Sinners, henceforth him esteem.

IV. *The mode of Paul's conversion was also meant to be a pattern,* **and with this I shall finish.**

I do not say that we may expect to receive the miraculous revelation which was given to Paul, but yet it is a sketch upon which any conversion can be painted. The filling up is not the same in any two cases, but the outline sketch. Paul's conversion would serve for an outline sketch of the conversion of any one of us. How was that conversion worked? Well, it is clear that there was nothing at all in Paul to contribute to his salvation. You might have sifted him in a sieve, without finding anything upon which you could rest a hope that he would be converted to the faith of Jesus. His natural bent, his early training, his whole surroundings, and his life's pursuits, all lettered him to Judaism, and made it most unlikely that he would ever become a Christian. The first elder of the church that ever talked to him about divine things could hardly believe in his conversion. "Lord," said he, "I have heard by many of this man, how much evil he hath done to thy saints at Jerusalem." He could hardly think it possible that the ravening wolf should have changed into a lamb. Nothing favorable to faith in Jesus could have been found in Saul; the soil of his heart was very rocky, the plowshare could not touch it, and the good seed found no roothold. Yet the Lord converted Saul, and he can do the like by other sinner, but it must be a work of pure grace and of divine power, for there is not in any man's fallen nature a holy spot of the size of a pin's point on which grace can light. Transforming grace can find no natural lodgment in our hearts, it must create its own soil; and, blessed be God, it can do it, for with God all things are possible. Nature contributes nothing to grace, and yet grace wins the day. Humbled soul, let this cheer you. Though there is nothing good in you, yet grace can work wonders, and save you by its own might.

Paul's conversion was an instance of divine power, and of that alone, and so is every true conversion. If your conversion is an instance of the preacher's power, you need to be converted again; if your salvation is the result of your own power, it is a miserable deception, from which may you be delivered. Every man who is saved must be operated upon by the might of God the Holy Spirit: every jot and tittle of true regeneration is the Spirit's work. As for our strength, it wars against salvation rather than for it. Blessed is that promise, "Thy people shall be willing in the day of thy power." Conversion is as much a work of God's omnipotence as the resurrection; and as the dead do not raise themselves, so neither do men convert themselves.

But Saul was changed immediately. His conversion was once done, and done at once. There was a little interval before he found peace, but even during those three days he was a changed man, though he was in sadness. He was under the power of Satan at one moment, and in the next he was under the reign of grace. This is also true in every conversion. However gradual the breaking of the day, there is a time when the sun is below the horizon, and a moment when he is no longer so. You may not know the exact time in which you passed from death to life, But there was such a time, if you are indeed a believer. A man may not know how old he is, but there was a moment in which he was born. In every conversion there is a distinct change from darkness to light, from death to life, just as certainly as there was in Paul's. And what a delightful hope does the rapidity of regeneration present to us! It is by no long and laborious process that we escape from sin. We are not compelled to remain in sin for a single moment.

Grace brings instantaneous liberty to those who sit in bondage. He who trusts Jesus is saved on the spot. Why, then, abide in death? Why not lift up your eyes to immediate life and light?

Paul proved his regeneration by his faith. He believed unto eternal life. He tells us over and over again in his epistles that he was saved by faith, and not by works. So is it with every man; if saved at all, it is by simply believing in the Lord Jesus. Paul esteemed his own works to be less than nothing, and called them dross and dung, that he might win Christ, and so every converted man renounces his own works that he may be saved by grace alone. Whether he has been moral or immoral, whether he has lived an amiable and excellent life, or whether he has raked in the kennels of sin, every regenerate man has one only hope, and that is centered and fixed in Jesus alone. Faith in Jesus Christ is the mark of salvation, even as the heaving of the lungs or the coming of breath from the nostrils is the test of life. Faith is the grace which saves the soul, and its absence is a fatal sign. How does this fact affect you, dear friend? Have you faith or no?

Paul was very positively and evidently saved. You did not need to ask the question, Is that man a Christian or not? For the transformation was most apparent. If Saul of Tarsus had appeared as he used to be, and Paul the apostle could also have come in, and you could have seen the one man as two men, you would have thought them no relation to one another. Paul the apostle would have said that he was dead to Saul of Tarsus, and Saul of Tarsus would have gnashed his teeth at Paul the apostle. The change was evident to all who knew him, whether they sympathized in it or not. They could not mistake the remarkable difference which grace had made, for it was as great as when midnight brightens into noon. So it is when a man is truly saved: there is a change which those around him must perceive. Do not tell me that you can be a child at home and become a Christian, and yet your father and mother will not perceive a difference in you. They will be sure to see it. Would a leopard in a menagerie lose his spots and no one notice it? Would an Ethiopian be turned white and no one hear of it? You, masters and mistresses, will not go in and out among your servants and children without their perceiving a change in you if you are born again. At least, dear brother or sister, strive with all your might to let the change be very apparent in your language, in your actions, and in your whole conduct. Let your conversation be such as becomes the gospel of Christ, that men may see that you, as well as the apostle, are decidedly changed by the renewal of your minds.

May all of us be the subjects of divine grace as Paul was: stopped in our mad career, blinded by the glory of the heavenly light, called by a mysterious voice, conscious of natural blindness, relieved of blinding scales, and made to see Jesus as one all in all. May we prove in our own persons how speedily conviction may melt into conversion, conversion into confession, and confession into consecration.

I have done when I have inquired how far we are conformed to the pattern which God has set before us. I know we are like Paul as to our sin, for if we have neither blasphemed nor persecuted, yet have we sinned as far as we have had opportunity. We are also conformed to Paul's pattern in the great longsuffering of God which we have experienced, and I am not sure that we cannot carry the parallel further: we have had much the same revelation that Paul received on the way to Damascus, for we, too, have learned that Jesus is the Christ. If any of us sin against Christ, it will not be because we do not know him to be the Son of God, for we all believe in his deity, because our Bibles tell us so. The pattern goes so far: I would that the grace of God would operate upon you, unconverted friend, and complete the picture, by giving you like faith with Paul. Then will you be saved, as Paul was. Then also you will love Christ above all things, as Paul did, and you will say, "But what things were gain to me, those I counted loss for Christ. Yea, doubtless, and I count all things but loss for the excellency of the knowledge of Christ Jesus my Lord." He rested upon what Christ had done in his death and resurrection, and he found pardon and eternal life at once, and became, therefore, a devoted Christian.

What say you, dear friend? Are you moved to follow Paul's example? Does the Spirit of God prompt you to trust Paul's Savior, and give up every other ground of trust and rely upon him? Then do so and live. Does there seem to be a hand holding you back, and do you hear an evil whisper saying, "You are too great a sinner"? Turn around and bid the fiend depart, for the text gives him the lie. "In me *foremost* hath Jesus Christ showed forth all longsuffering, for a pattern to them which should hereafter believe on his name." God has saved Paul. Back, then, O devil! The Lord can save any man, and he can save me. Jesus Christ of Nazareth is mighty to save, and I will rely on him. If any poor heart shall reason thus, its logic will be sound and unanswerable. Mercy to one is an argument for mercy to another, for there is no difference, but the same Lord over all is rich unto all that call upon him.

Now I have set the case before you, and I cannot do more; it remains with each individual to accept or refuse. One man can bring a horse to the trough, but a hundred cannot make him drink. There is the gospel; if you want it, take it, but if you will not have it, then I must discharge my soul by reminding you that even the gentle gospel—the gospel of love and mercy has nothing to say to you but this, "He that believeth not shall be damned."

> How they deserve the deepest hell,
> That slight the joys above;
> What chains of vengeance must they feel,
> Who break the bonds of love.

God grant that you may yield to mighty love, and find peace in Christ Jesus.

Onesimus: The Story of a Runaway Slave

Published in 1875; delivered at the Metropolitan Tabernacle, Newington. No. 1268.

Perhaps he therefore departed for a season, that thou shouldest receive him forever.—PHILEMON 15

Nature is selfish, but grace is loving. He who boasts that he cares for nobody, and nobody cares for him, is the reverse of a Christian, for Jesus Christ enlarges the heart when he cleanses it. None so tender and sympathetic as our Master, and if we be truly his disciples, the same mind will be in us which was also in Christ Jesus. The apostle Paul was eminently large-hearted and sympathetic. Surely he had enough to do at Rome to bear his own troubles and to preach the gospel. If, like the priest in the parable of the good Samaritan, he had "passed by on the other side," he might have been excused, for he was on the urgent business of that Master who once said to his seventy messengers, "Salute no man by the way." We might not have wondered if he had said, "I cannot find time to attend to the wants of a runaway slave." But Paul was not of that mind. He had been preaching, and Onesimus had been converted, and henceforth he regarded him as his own son. I do not know why Onesimus came to Paul. Perhaps he went to him as a great many scapegraces have come to me—because their fathers knew me; and so, as Onesimus' master had known Paul, the servant applied to his master's friend, perhaps to beg some little help in his extremity. Anyhow, Paul seized the opportunity and preached to him Jesus, and the runaway slave became a believer in the Lord Jesus Christ.

Paul watched him, admired the character of his convert, and was glad to be served by him, and when he thought it right that he should return to his master, Philemon, he took a deal of trouble to compose a letter of apology for him, a letter which shows long thinking, since every word is well selected: albeit that the Holy Spirit dictated it, inspiration does not prevent a man's exercising thought and care on what he writes. Every word is chosen for a purpose. If he had been pleading for himself, he could not have pleaded more earnestly or wisely. Paul, as you know, was not accustomed to write letters with his own hand, but dictated to an amanuensis. It is supposed that he had an affliction of the eyes, and therefore when he did write he used large capital letters, as he says in one of the epistles, "Ye see how large a letter I have written unto you with my own hand." The epistle was not a large one, but he probably alluded to the largeness of the characters which he was obliged to use whenever he himself wrote. This letter to Philemon, at least part of it, was not dictated, but was written by his own hand. See verse 19: "I Paul have written it with mine own hand. I will repay it." It is the only note of hand which I recollect in Scripture, but there it is—an IOU for whatever amount Onesimus may have stolen.

Let us cultivate a large-hearted spirit, and sympathize with the people of God, especially with new converts, if we find them in trouble through past wrongdoing. If anything needs setting right, do not let us condemn them offhand, and say, "You have been stealing from your master, have you? You profess to be converted, but we do not believe it." Such suspicious and severe treatment may be deserved, but it is not such as the love of Christ would suggest. Try and set the fallen ones right, and give them again, as we say, "a fair start in the world." If God has forgiven them, surely we may, and if Jesus Christ has received them, they cannot be too bad for us to receive. Let us do for them what Jesus would have done had he been here, so shall we truly be the disciples of Jesus.

Thus I introduce to you the text, and I notice concerning it, first that it contains *a singular instance of divine grace.* Second, it brings before us *a case of sin overruled.* And, third, it may be regarded as *an example of relationship improved by grace,* for now he that was a servant for a season will abide with Philemon all his lifetime, and be no more a servant but a brother beloved.

I. But, first, let us look at Onesimus as *an instance of divine grace.*

We see the grace of God in his *election.* He was a slave. In those days slaves were very ignorant, untaught, and degraded. Being barbarously used, they were for the most part themselves sunk in the lowest barbarism, neither did their masters attempt to raise them out of it; it is possible that Philemon's attempt to do good to Onesimus may have been irksome to the man, and he may therefore have fled from his house. His master's prayers, warnings, and Christian regulations may have been disagreeable to him, and therefore he ran away. He wronged his master, which he could scarcely have done if he had not been treated as a confidential servant to some extent. Possibly the unusual kindness of Philemon, and the trust reposed in him may have been too much for his untrained nature. We know not what he stole, but evidently he had taken something, for the apostle says, "If he hath wronged thee, or oweth thee ought, put that on mine account." He ran away from Colosse, therefore, and thinking that he would be less likely to be discovered by the ministers of justice, he sought the city of Rome, which was then as large as the city of London now is, and perhaps larger. There in those back slums, such as the Jews' quarter in Rome now is, Onesimus would go and hide; or among those gangs of thieves which infested the imperial city, he would not be known or heard of any more, so he thought; and he could live the free and easy life of a thief. Yet, mark you, the Lord looked out of heaven with an eye of love, and set that eye on Onesimus.

Were there no free men, that God must elect a slave? Were there no faithful servants, that he must choose one who had embezzled his master's money? Were there none of the educated and polite, that he must needs look upon a barbarian? Were there none among the moral and the excellent, that infinite love should fix itself upon this degraded being, who was now mixed up with the very scum of society? And what the scum of society was in old Rome I should not like to think, for the upper classes were about as brutalized in their general habits as we can very well conceive; and what the lowest scum of all must have been, none of us can tell. Onesimus was part and parcel of the dregs of a sink of sin. Read Paul's first chapter of the epistle to the Romans, if you can, and you will see in what a horrible state the heathen world was at that time, and Onesimus was among the worst of the worst; and yet eternal love, which passed by kings and princes, and left Pharisees and Sadducees, philosophers and magi, to stumble in the dark as they chose, fixed its eye upon this poor benighted creature that he might be made a vessel to honor, fit for the Master's use.

> When the Eternal bows the skies
> To visit earthly things,
> With scorn divine he turns his eyes
> From towers of haughty kings.
>
> He bids his awful chariot roll
> Far downward from the skies,
> To visit every humble soul,
> With pleasure in his eyes.
>
> Why should the Lord that reigns above
> Disdain so lofty kings?
> Say, Lord, and why such looks of love
> Upon such worthless things?

Mortals, be dumb; what creature dares
Dispute his awful will?
Ask no account of his affairs,
But tremble and be still.

Just like his nature is his grace,
All sovereign, and all free;
Great God, how searchless are thy ways,
How deep thy judgments be!

"I will have mercy on whom I will have mercy, and I will have compassion on whom I will have compassion" rolls like thunder alike from the cross of Calvary and from the mount of Sinai. The Lord is a sovereign, and does as he pleases. Let us admire that marvelous electing love which selected such a one as Onesimus!

Grace also is to be observed, in the next place, in the *conversion* of this runaway slave.

Look at him! How unlikely he appears to become a convert. He is an Asiatic slave of about the same class as an ordinary lascar, or heathen.. He was, however, worse than the ordinary lascar who is certainly free, and probably an honest man, if he is nothing else. This man had been dishonest, and he was daring withal, for after taking his master's property he was bold enough to make a long journey from Colosse to reach Rome. But everlasting love means to convert the man, and converted he shall be. He may have heard Paul preach at Colosse and Athens, but yet he had not been impressed. In Rome, Paul was not preaching in St. Peter's; it was in no such noble building. Paul was not preaching in a place like the tabernacle, where Onesimus could have a comfortable seat—no such place as that—but it was probably down there at the back of the Palatine hill, where the praetorian guard have their lodgings, and where there was a prison called the Praetorium. In a bare room in the barrack prison, Paul sat with a soldier chained to his hand, preaching to all who were admitted to hear him, and there it was that the grace of God reached the heart of this wild young man, and, oh, what a change it made in him immediately! Now you see him repenting of his sin, grieved to think he has wronged a good man, vexed to see the depravity of his heart as well as the error of his life. He weeps; Paul preaches to him Christ crucified, and the glance of joy is in his eye: and from that heavy heart a load is taken. New thoughts light up that dark mind; the very face is changed, and the entire man renewed, for the grace of God can turn the lion to a lamb, the raven to a dove.

Some of us, I have no doubt, are quite as wonderful instances of divine election and effectual calling as Onesimus was. Let us, therefore, record the lovingkindness of the Lord, and let us say to ourselves, "Christ shall have the glory of it. The Lord has done it; and unto the Lord be honor; world without end."

The grace of God was conspicuous in *the character which it worked in Onesimus* upon his conversion, for he appears to have been helpful, useful, and profitable. So Paul says. Paul was willing to have had him as an associate, and it is not every man that is converted that we should altogether choose as a companion. There are odd people to be met with who will go to heaven, we have no doubt, for they are pilgrims on the right way, but we would like to keep on the other side of the road, for they are cross-grained, and there is a something about them that one's nature can no more delight in than the palate can take pleasure in nauseous physic. They are a sort of spiritual hedgehogs; they are alive and useful, and no doubt they illustrate the wisdom and patience of God, but they are not good companions: one would not like to carry them in his bosom. But Onesimus was evidently of a kind, tender, loving spirit. Paul at once called him brother, and would have liked to retain him. When he sent him back, was it not a clear proof of change of heart in Onesimus that he would go back?

Away as he was in Rome, he might have passed on from one town to another and have remained perfectly free, but feeling that he was under some kind of bond to his master—especially since he had injured him—he takes Paul's advice to return to his old position. He will go back, and take a letter of apology or introduction to his master; for he tells that it is his duty to make reparation for the wrong that he has done. I always like to see a resolve to make restitution of former wrongs in people who profess to be converted. If they have taken any money wrongfully they ought to repay it; it were well if they returned sevenfold. If we have in any way robbed or wronged another, I think the first instincts of grace in the heart will suggest compensation in all ways within our power. Do not think it is to be got over by saying, "God has forgiven me, and therefore I may leave it." No, dear friend, but inasmuch as God has forgiven you, try to undo all the wrong, and prove the sincerity of your repentance by so doing. So Onesimus will go back to Philemon, and work out his term of years with him, or otherwise do Philemon's wishes, for though he might have preferred to wait upon Paul, his first duty was due to the man whom he had injured. That showed a gentle, humble, honest, upright spirit; and let Onesimus be commended for it; no, let the grace of God be extolled for it. Look at the difference between the man who robbed, and the man who now comes back to be profitable to his master.

What wonders the grace of God has done! Brethren, let me add: What wonders the grace of God can do! Many plans are employed in the world for the reformation of the wicked and the reclaiming of the fallen, and to every one of these, as far as they are rightly bottomed, we wish good success; for whatever things are lovely and pure, and of good report, we wish them God-speed. But mark this word: the true reforming of the drunkard lies in giving him a new heart; the true reclaiming of the harlot is to be found in a renewed nature. Purity will never come to fallen women by those hideous Contagious Diseases Acts, which, to my mind, wear, like Cain, a curse upon their forehead. Womanhood will but sink the lower under such laws. The harlot must be washed in the Savior's blood, or she will never be clean. The lowest strata of society will never be brought into the light of virtue, sobriety, and purity, except by Jesus Christ and his gospel; and we must stick to that. Let all others do what they like, but God forbid that I should glory save in the cross of our Lord Jesus Christ. I see certain of my brethren fiddling away at the branches of the tree of vice with their wooden saws, but, as for the gospel, it lays the ax at the roots of the whole forest of evil, and if it be fairly received into the heart it fells all the upas trees at once, and instead of them there spring up the fir tree, the pine tree, and the box tree together, to beautify the house of our Master's glory. Let us, when we see what the Spirit of God can do for men, publish the grace of God, and extol it with all our might.

II. And now, second, we have in our text, and its connections, a very interesting *instance of sin overruled.*

Onesimus had no right to rob his master and run away; but God was pleased to make use of that crime for his conversion. It brought him to Rome, and so brought him where Paul was preaching, and thus it brought him to Christ, and to his right mind. Now, when we speak of this, we must be cautious. When Paul says, "Perhaps he departed for a season, that thou shouldest receive him forever," he does not excuse his departure. He does not make it out that Onesimus did right—not for a moment. Sin is sin, and, whatever sin may be overruled to do, yet sin is still sin. The crucifixion of our Savior has brought the greatest conceivable blessings upon mankind, yet nonetheless it was "with wicked hands" that they took Jesus and crucified him. The selling of Joseph into Egypt was the means in the hand of God of the preservation of Jacob, and his sons, in the time of famine; but his brethren had nothing to do with that, and they were nonetheless guilty for having sold their brother for a slave.

Let it always be remembered that the faultiness or virtue of an act is not contingent upon the result of that act. If, for instance, a man who has been set on a railway to turn the switch forgets to do it, you call it a very great crime if the train comes to mischief and a dozen people are killed. Yes, but the crime is the same if nobody is killed. It is not the result of the carelessness, but the carelessness itself which deserves punishment. If it were the man's duty to turn the switch in such-and-such a way, and his not doing so should even by some strange accident turn to the saving of life, the man would be equally blameworthy. There would be no credit due to him, for if his duty lies in a certain line, his fault also lies in a certain line, namely, the neglecting of that duty. So if God overrules sin for good, as he sometimes does, it is nonetheless sin. It is sin just as much as ever, only there is so much the more glory to the wonderful wisdom and grace of God who, out of evil, brings forth good, and so does what only omnipotent wisdom can perform. Onesimus is not excused, then, for having embezzled his master's goods nor for having left him without right; he still is a transgressor, but God's grace is glorified.

Remember, too, that this must be noticed—that when Onesimus left his master he was performing an action the results of which, in all probability, would have been ruinous to him. He was living as a trusted dependent beneath the roof of a kind master, who had a church in his house. If I read the epistle rightly, he had a godly mistress and a godly master, and he had an opportunity of learning the gospel continually; but this reckless young blade, very likely, could not bear it, and could have lived more contentedly with a heathen master, who would have beaten him one day and made him drunk another. The Christian master he could not bear, so away he went. He threw away the opportunities of salvation, and he went to Rome, and he must have gone into the lowest part of the city, and associated, as I have already told you, with the very grossest company. Now, had it come to pass that he had joined in the insurrections of the slaves which took place frequently about that time, as he in all probability would have done had not grace prevented, he would have been put to death as others had been. He would have had short shrift in Rome: half suspect a man and off with his head was the rule toward slaves and vagabonds. Onesimus was just the very man that would have been likely to be hurried to death and to eternal destruction. He had put his head, as it were, between the lion's jaws by what he had done. When a young man suddenly leaves home and goes to London, we know what it means. When his friends do not know where he is, and he does not want them to know, we are aware, within a little, where he is and what he is at. What Onesimus was doing I do not know, but he was certainly doing his best to ruin himself. His course, therefore, is to be judged, as far as he is concerned, by what it was likely to bring him to; and though it did not bring him to it, that was no credit to him, but all the honor of it is due to the overruling power of God.

See, dear brethren, how God overruled all. Thus had the Lord purposed. Nobody shall be able to touch the heart of Onesimus but Paul. Onesimus is living at Colosse; Paul cannot come there, he is in prison. It is needful, then, that Onesimus should be got to Paul. Suppose the kindness of Philemon's heart had prompted him to say to Onesimus, "I want you to go to Rome, and find Paul out and hear him." This naughty servant would have said, "I am not going to risk my life to hear a sermon. If I go with the money you are sending to Paul, or with the letter, I shall deliver it, but I want none of his preaching." Sometimes, you know, when people are brought to hear a preacher with the view of their being converted, if they have any idea of it, it is about the very last thing likely to happen, because they go there resolved to be fireproof, and so the preaching does not come home to them: and it would probably have been just so with Onesimus. No, no, he was not to be won in that way, he must be got to Rome another way. How shall it be done? Well, the devil shall do it, not knowing that he will be losing a willing servant thereby. The devil tempts Onesimus to steal. Onesimus does it, and when he has stolen he is afraid of being discovered, and so he makes tracks for Rome as quickly as he can, and gets down among the back slums, and there he feels what the prodigal felt—a hungry belly, and that is one of the best preachers in the world to some people: their conscience is reached in that way. Being very hungry, not knowing what to do, and no man giving anything to him, he thinks whether there is anybody in Rome that would take pity on him. He does not know anybody in Rome at all, and is likely to starve. Perhaps one morning there was a Christian woman—I should not wonder—who was going to hear Paul, and she saw this poor man sitting crouched up on the steps of a temple, and she went to him and spoke about his soul. "Soul," said he, "I care nothing about that, but my body would thank you for something to eat. I am starving." She replied, "Come with me, then," and she gave him bread, and then she said, "I do this for Jesus Christ's sake." "Jesus Christ!" he said, "I have heard of him. I used to hear of him over at Colosse." "Whom did you hear speak about him?" the woman would ask. "Why, a short man with weak eyes, a great preacher, named Paul, who used to come to my master's house." "Why, I am going to hear him preach," the woman would say, "will you come and hear him with me?" "Well, I think I should like to hear him again. He always had a kind word to say to the poor." So he goes in and pushes his way among the soldiers, and Paul's Master incites Paul to speak the right word.

It may have been so, or it may have been the other way—that not knowing anybody else at all, he thought, "Well, there is Paul, I know. He is here a prisoner, and I will go down and see what prison he is in." He goes down to the Praetorium and finds him there, tells him of his extreme poverty, and Paul talks to him, and then he confesses the wrong he has done, and Paul, after teaching him a little while, says, "Now, you must go back and make amends to your master for the wrong you have done."

It may have been either of these ways; at any rate, the Lord must have Onesimus in Rome to hear Paul, and the sin of Onesimus, though perfectly voluntary on his part, so that God had no hand in it, is yet overruled by a mysterious providence to bring him where the gospel shall be blessed to his soul.

Now, I want to speak to some of you Christian people about this matter. Have you a son who has left home? Is he a willful, wayward young man, who has gone away because he could not bear the restraints of a Christian family? It is a sad thing it should be so—a very sad thing, but do not despond or even have a thought of despair about him. You do not know where he is, but God does; and you cannot follow him, but the Spirit of God can. He is going a voyage to Shanghai. Ah, there may be a Paul at Shanghai who is to be the means of his salvation, and as that Paul is not in England, your son must go there. Is it to Australia that he is going? There may be a word spoken there by the blessing of God to your son which is the only word which ever will reach him. I cannot speak it; nobody in London can speak it; but the man there will; and God, therefore, is letting him go away in all his willfulness and folly that he may be brought under the means of grace, which will prove effectual to his salvation. Many a sailor boy has been wild, reckless, godless, Christless, and at last has got into a foreign hospital. Ah, if his mother knew that he was down with the yellow fever, how sad her mind would be, for she would conclude that her dear son will die away at Havana or somewhere, and never come home again. But it is just in that hospital that God means to meet with him. A sailor writes to me something like that. He says, "My mother asked me to read a chapter every day, but I never did. I got into the hospital at Havana, and, when I lay there, there was a man near to me who was dying, and he died one night; but before he died he said to me, 'Mate, could you come here? I want to speak to you. I have got something that is very precious to me here. I was a wild fellow, but reading this packet of sermons has brought me to the Savior, and I am dying with a good hope through grace. Now, when I am dead and gone, will you take these sermons and read them, and may God bless them to you. And will you write a letter to the man that preached and printed those sermons, to tell him that God blessed them to my conversion, and that I hope he will bless them to yourself'?" It was a packet of my sermons, and God did bless them to that young man who, I have no doubt whatever, went to that hospital because there a man who had been brought to Christ would hand to him the words which God had blessed to himself and would bless to his friend.

You do not know, dear mother, you do not know. The worst thing that can happen to a young man is sometimes the best thing that can happen to him. I have sometimes thought when I have seen young men of position and wealth taking to racing and all sorts of dissipation, "Well, it is a dreadfully bad thing, but they may as well get through their money as quickly as ever they can, and then when they have got down to beggary they will be like the young gentleman in the parable who left his father." When he had spent all, there arose a mighty famine in that land, and he began to be in want, and he said, "I will arise and go to my father." Perhaps the disease that follows vice—perhaps the poverty that comes like an armed man after extravagance and debauch—is but love in another form, sent to compel the sinner to come to himself and consider his ways and seek an ever-merciful God. You Christian people often see the little gutter children—the poor little guttersnipes in the street—and you feel much pity for them, as well you may. There is a dear sister here, Miss Annie Macpherson, who lives only for them. God bless her and her work! When you see them you cannot be glad to see them as they are, but I have often thought that the poverty and hunger of one of these poor little children has a louder voice to most hearts than their vice and ignorance; and God knew that we were not ready and able to hear the cry of the child's sin, and so he added the child's hunger to that cry, that it might pierce our hearts. People could live in sin, and yet be happy, if they were well-to-do and rich; and if sin did not make parents poor and wretched, and their children miserable, we should not see it, and therefore we should not arouse ourselves to grapple with it. It is a blessing, you know, in some diseases when the patient can throw the complaint out upon the skin. It is a horrible thing to see it on the skin, but still it is better than its being hidden inside; and oftentimes the outward sin and the outward misery are a sort of throwing out of the disease, so that the eye of those who know where the healing medicine is to be had is thereby drawn to the disease, and so the soul's secret malady is dealt with. Onesimus might have stopped at home, and he might never have been a thief, but he might have been lost through self-righteousness. But now his sin is visible. The scapegrace has displayed the depravity of his heart, and now it is that he comes under Paul's eye and Paul's prayer and becomes converted.

Do not, I pray you, ever despair of man or woman or child because you see their sin upon the surface of their character. On the contrary, say to yourself, "This is placed where I can see it, that I may pray about it. It is thrown out under my eye that I may now concern myself to bring this poor soul to Jesus Christ, the mighty Savior, who can save the most forlorn sinner." Look at it in the light of earnest, active benevolence, and rouse yourselves to conquer it. Our duty is to hope on and to pray on. It may be, perhaps, that "he therefore departed for a season, that thou shouldest receive him forever." Perhaps the boy has been so wayward that his sin may come to a crisis, and a new heart may be given him. Perhaps your daughter's evil has been developed that now the Lord may convince her of sin and bring her to the Savior's feet. At any rate, if the case be ever so bad, hope in God, and pray on.

III. Once more: our text may be viewed as *an example of relations improved*, **"He therefore departed for a season, that thou shouldest receive him forever; not now as a servant, but a brother beloved, specially to one, but how much more unto thee?"**

You know we are a long while learning great truths. Perhaps Philemon had not quite found out that it was wrong for him to have a slave. Some men who were very good in their time did not know it. John Newton did not know that he was flying wrong in the slave trade, and George Whitefield, when he left slaves to the orphanage at Savannah, which had been willed to him, did not think for a moment that he was doing anything more than if he had been dealing with horses, or gold and silver. Public sentiment was not enlightened, although the gospel has always struck at the very root of slavery. The essence of the gospel is that we are to do to others as we would that others should do to us, and nobody would wish to be another man's slave, and therefore he has no right to have another man as his slave. Perhaps, when Onesimus ran away and came back again, this letter of Paul may have opened Philemon's eyes a little as to his own position. To doubt he may have been an excellent master, and have trusted his servant, and not treated him as a slave at all, but perhaps he had not regarded him as a brother; and now Onesimus has come back he will be a better servant, but Philemon will be a better master, and a slaveholder no longer. He will regard his former servant as a brother in Christ.

Now this is what the grace of God does when it comes into a family. It does not alter the relations; it does not give the child a right to be pert, and forget that he is to be obedient to his parents; it does not give the father a right to lord it over his children without wisdom and love, for it tells him that he is not to provoke his children to anger, lest they be discouraged; it does not give the servant the right to be a master, neither does it take away from the master his position, or allow him to exaggerate his authority, but all round it softens and sweetens. Rowland Hill used to say that he would not give a halfpenny for a man's piety if his dog and his cat were not better off after he was converted. There was much weight in that remark. Everything in the house goes better when grace oils the wheels. The mistress is, perhaps, rather sharp, quick, tart; well, she gets a little sugar into her constitution when she receives the grace of God. The servant may be apt to loiter, be late up of a morning, very slovenly, fond of a gossip at the door; but, if she is truly converted, all that kind of thing ends. She is conscientious and attends to her duty as she ought. The master, perhaps—well, he is the master, and you know it. But when he is a truly Christian man, he has a gentleness, a suavity, a considerateness about him. The husband is the head of the wife, but when renewed by grace he is not at all the head of the wife as some husbands are. The wife also keeps her place, and seeks, by all gentleness and wisdom to make the house as happy as she can. I do not believe in your religion, dear friend, if it belongs to the tabernacle, and the prayer meeting, and not to your home. The best religion in the world is that which smiles at the table, works at the sewing machine, and is amiable in the drawing room. Give me the religion which blacks boots, and does them well; cooks the food, and cooks it so that it can be eaten; measures out yards of calico, and does not make them half an inch short; sells a hundred yards of an article, and does not label ninety a hundred, as many tradespeople do. That is the true Christianity which affects the whole of life.

If we are truly Christians we shall be changed in all our relationships to our fellowmen, and hence we shall regard those whom we call our inferiors with quite a different eye. It is wrong in Christian people when they are so sharp upon little faults that they see in servants, especially if they are Christian servants. That is not the way to correct them. They see a little something wrong, and, oh, they are down upon the poor girls, as if they had murdered somebody. If your Master, and mine, were to treat you in that style I wonder how you would get on? How quick some are in discharging their maids for small [mistakes]. No excuse, no trying the persons again: they must go. Many a young man has been turned out of a situation for the veriest [slightest] trifle, by a Christian employer, when he must have known that he would be exposed to all sorts of risks: and many a servant has been sent adrift as if she were a dog, with no sort of thought whether another position could be found, and without anything being done to prevent her going astray. Do let us think of others, especially of those whom Christ loves even as he does us. Philemon might have said, "No, no, I don't take you back, Mr. Onesimus, not I. Once bitten, twice shy, sir. I never ride a broken-kneed horse. You stole my money; I am not going to have you back again." I have heard that style of talk, have not you? Did you ever feel like it? If you have, go home and pray to God to get such a feeling out of you, for it is bad stuff to have in your soul. You cannot take it to heaven. When the Lord Jesus Christ has forgiven you so freely, are you to take your servant by the throat and say, "Pay me what you owe"? God forbid that we should continue in such a temper. Be pitiful, easily entreated, ready to forgive. It is a deal better that you should suffer a wrong than do a wrong: much better that you should overlook a fault which you might have noticed, than notice a fault which you ought to have overlooked.

> *Let love through all your actions run,*
> *And all your words be kind,*

is said in the little hymn which we used to learn when we were children. We should practice it now, and—

> *Live like the blessed virgin's Son*
> *That meek and lowly child.*

God grant we may, of his infinite grace.

I want to say this, and then I have done. If the mysterious providence of God was to be seen in Onesimus getting to Rome, I wonder whether there is any providence of God in some of you being here tonight! It is possible. Such things do happen. People come here that never meant to come. The last thing in the world they would have believed if anybody had said it is that they would be here, yet here they are. With all manner of twists and turns they have gone about, but they have got here somehow. Did you miss a train, and so stepped in to wait? Does not your ship sail quite so soon as you expected, and so are you here tonight? Say, is that it? I do pray you, then, consider this question with your own heart. "Does not God mean to bless me? Has he not brought me here on purpose that this night I may yield my heart to Jesus as Onesimus did?" My dear friend, if you believe on the Lord Jesus Christ, you shall have immediate pardon for all sin, and shall be saved. The Lord has brought you here in his infinite wisdom to hear that, and I hope that he has also brought you here that you may accept it, and so go your way altogether changed.

Some three years ago I was talking with an aged minister, and he began fumbling about in his waistcoat pocket, but he was a long while before he found what he wanted. At last he brought out a letter that was well-nigh worn to pieces, and he said, "God almighty bless you! God almighty bless you!" And I said, "Friend, what is it?" He said, "I had a son. I thought he would be the stay of my old age, but he disgraced himself, and he went away from me, and I could not tell where he went, only he said he was going to America. He took a ticket to sail for America from the London Docks, but he did not go on the particular day that he expected." This aged minister bade me read the letter, and I read it, and it was like this: "Father, I am here in America. I have found a situation, and God has prospered me. I write to ask your forgiveness for the thousand wrongs that I have done you, and the grief I have caused you, for blessed be God, I have found the Savior. I have joined the church of God here, and hope to spend my life in God's service. It happened thus: I did not sail for America the day I expected. I went down to the tabernacle to see what it was like, and God met with me. Mr. Spurgeon said, 'Perhaps there is a runaway son here. The Lord call him by his grace.' And he did." "Now," said he, as he folded up the letter and put it in his pocket, "that son of mine is dead, and he is in heaven, and I love you, and I shall do so as long as I live, because you were the means of bringing him to Christ." Is there a similar character here tonight? I feel persuaded there is—somebody of the same sort; and in the name of God I charge him to take the warning that I give him from this pulpit. I dare you to go out of this place as you came in. O young man, the Lord in mercy gives you another opportunity of turning from the error of your ways, and I pray you now here—as you now are—lift your eye to heaven, and say, "God be merciful to me a sinner," and he will be so. Then go home to your father and tell him what the grace of God has done for you, and wonder at the love which brought you here to bring you to Christ.

Dear friend, if there is nothing mysterious about it, yet here we are. We are where the gospel is preached, and that brings responsibility upon us. If a man is lost, it is better for him to be lost without hearing the gospel than to be lost as some of you will be if you perish under the sound of a clear, earnest enunciation of the gospel of Jesus Christ. How long halt some of you between two opinions? "Have I been so long time with you," says Christ, "and yet hast thou not known me?" All this teaching and preaching and invitation, and yet do you not turn?

O God, do thou the sinner turn,
Convince him of his lost estate.

Let him linger no longer, lest he linger till he rue his fatal choice too late. God bless you, for Christ's sake. Amen.

Sermons on Men in the Bible
Charles H. Spurgeon

The text of this book is set in Dante 11/14 and Delphin IA,
with Poetica® Ornaments.

Typeset in QuarkXPress.

Preface by Patricia Klein.

These sermons by Charles Spurgeon have been
gently edited and updated for the modern reader.

Interior design and typesetting by Rose Yancik, of Y Designs.
www.ydesigns.us